DEVILS ON THE
DEEP BLUE SEA

DEVILS ON THE DEEP BLUE SEA

THE DREAMS, SCHEMES
AND SHOWDOWNS THAT BUILT
AMERICA'S CRUISE-SHIP EMPIRES

KRISTOFFER A. GARIN

VIKING

VIKING
Published by the Penguin Group
Penguin Group (USA) Inc., 375 Hudson Street, New York, New York 10014, U.S.A.
Penguin Group (Canada), 90 Eglinton Avenue East, Suite 700,
Toronto, ON M4P 2Y3 Canada
(a division of Pearson Penguin Canada Inc.)
Penguin Books Ltd., 80 Strand, London WC2R 0RL, England
Penguin Ireland, 25 St. Stephen's Green, Dublin 2, Ireland (a division of Penguin Books Ltd)
Penguin Books Australia Ltd, 250 Camberwell Road, Camberwell, Victoria 3124, Australia
(a division of Pearson Australia Group Pty Ltd)
Penguin Books India Pvt Ltd, 11 Community Centre, Panchsheel Park,
New Delhi – 110 017, India
Penguin Group (NZ), Cnr Airborne and Rosedale Roads, Albany, Auckland 1310,
New Zealand (a division of Pearson New Zealand Ltd)
Penguin Books (South Africa) (Pty) Ltd, 24 Sturdee Avenue, Rosebank,
Johannesburg 2196, South Africa

Penguin Books Ltd, Registered Offices: 80 Strand, London WC2R 0RL, England

First published in 2005 by Viking Penguin, a member of Penguin Group (USA) Inc.

1   3   5   7   9   10   8   6   4   2

Copyright © Kristoffer A. Garin, 2005
All rights reserved

LIBRARY OF CONGRESS CATALOGING-IN-PUBLICATION DATA
Garin, Kristoffer A.
Devils on the deep blue sea : the dreams, schemes, and showdowns that built America's
cruise ship empires / Kristoffer A. Garin.
p.   cm.
Includes index.
ISBN 0-670-03418-5
1. Cruise lines—United States. 2. Cruise ships—United States. 3. Ocean travel. I. Title.
G550.G37 2005
387.5'42''0973—dc22   2005042212

Printed in the United States of America

For my mother, who would have loved this;
For Pop, who helps at every step;
And for Semra, without whom I never would have made it home.

A NOTE ON QUOTATIONS

Much of this book is informed by interviews I conducted between the spring of 2002 and the summer of 2004. Dozens of people connected to the cruise industry gave generously of their time for this project, together contributing hundreds of hours.

With very few exceptions, all of these conversations have been recorded, and I have provided those who wished to have them with copies of the tapes. Those who asked not to be named in the following pages have not been. I've taken great pains to ensure that each quotation is accurate and used in faithful context; however, for readability's sake, I have at times taken the liberty of deleting those stammers, repetitions and minor grammatical errors that, though perfectly natural in speech, translate poorly to the page. Where necessary, I have likewise substituted appropriate pronouns for full names, and vice versa. These changes have been made as sparingly as possible and at no time affect the meaning of the quotations in any way. In every instance where they occur, their sole purpose has been to ensure that the speakers come across as clearly and intelligently in these pages as they have in their conversations with me.

Kris Garin
Kigali, Rwanda
October 2004

It was the Law of the Sea, they said. Civilization ends at the waterline. Beyond that, we all enter the food chain, and not always right at the top.

—Hunter S. Thompson

If you can count your money, you don't have a billion dollars.

—J. Paul Getty

ACKNOWLEDGMENTS

I have had so much help.

This effort would never even have begun had it not been for the generosity and imagination of Andy Tobias, who actually believed the things my father told him about me, and my agent, Joni Evans, who risked squandering an incredible idea on an untested young reporter and continues to make me believe in the impossible. My editor, Rick Kot, graciously eased fears along the way and, once my work was in his hands, improved this book immeasurably. Alessandra Lusardi was kind, helpful and effective throughout, and working with her has been delightful.

I am forever grateful to my dad, Michael Garin, for being so proud of me and so smart about this project, and for being there when things took longer than expected. Unwavering moral support also came from a slew of Garins, Berkowitzes, Abelsons, Kaufmanns, Mesulams and a Weintraub—all of them the kind of people who make you glad to have a family.

John Lester, Adam Rzepka, Aaron Chew and Matt McCleery all read parts of this book and enriched it with their insights. Danny Abelson did the same, and held my hand besides; his influence is all over these pages. I owe Miriam Edelstein many drinks. Without the education I received at the *Journal News*, and earlier from Natalie Gummer, James Russell and others, I'd never have been able to take this on when the opportunity presented itself. Thanks too to Don Welsh, for opening doors once school was out, and Dick Robertson for *Love Boat* archives and a lifetime of unofficial uncle-ing.

If at times in this book I've been hard on the people behind the cruise business, I hope I've also conveyed my sincere respect for their accomplishments. Within this industry, I've had more assistance than I can spell out here. The public relations personnel at Carnival and Royal Caribbean went out of their way to facilitate my work, Tim Gallagher, Jennifer De La Cruz and Jaye Hilton especially so. John Maxtone-Graham and Bård Kolltveit were more than generous with the fruits of their labors. Pete Whelpton, Carmen Lunetta, the indefatigable Jay Lewis of MarketScope, Will Chambers, Ken Dubbin, Greg Miller, Rod McLeod and Giora Israel all need to be singled out for spending time with me again and again assisting a project that they knew would not be treating their life's work with kid gloves. Special thanks are due to Richard Fain, who brought extraordinary candor, intellect and enthusiasm to our conversations.

A certain relative of Stanton and Flossie, who goes unnamed by choice, has my fondest gratitude; getting to know him has been a surprise and a pleasure.

Finally, although I still can't believe all this got started in the first place, I'm even more astonished that it was ever completed—and that would never have happened without Semra. In work and play, she sets an example of pride, joy and curiosity that elevates my work and gives meaning to my life.

CONTENTS

DEVILS ON THE
DEEP BLUE SEA

LONDON, APRIL 2003

Victory.

Who would have thought, back when the late Ted Arison set this wheel in motion all those years ago with a desperate call paid for with borrowed money, that things could possibly end here: with his son cementing the family empire with a stroke of the pen—signing over $5.5 billion, just like that? And with enough to his name to pay that out of pocket, if he'd wanted to.

The newspapers were calling it the deal of the year—an against-the-odds triumph, a cliffhanger, a scrap that kept an industry on tenterhooks and gripped the financial world on both sides of the Atlantic. In a spectacular coup Arison's upstart Carnival Corporation had seized a former bastion of the British Empire, the passenger arm of the 163-year-old Peninsular & Oriental Steamship Company. In the storied world of international shipping, it was as if Sherlock Holmes had turned the keys to 221B Baker Street over to Columbo.

Micky Arison, Carnival's chairman and CEO and very much his father's son, knew that it was much more than that. This victory was the culmination of a forty-year odyssey. Everybody's smiling for the occasion, but Micky is the man today. You can just tell; his smile is the *smile. And that suit—how it makes him look sleek, even as it shows off his bulk; that beefiness that makes such an impression when he leans in toward you across the negotiating table. He looks like a million bucks, which is actually funny, since he's worth that about six thousand times over.*

One would have thought that this deal had been about oil, or arms or phar-

maceuticals, the way everyone had been talking about it—not cruise ships. Still, it was a $13 billion industry where before there had been nothing, and now it was as good as under his thumb. Not bad for a college dropout.

Hilarious, really, to think back. So many moments when it could have failed before it had even begun—that first voyage, with the ship up on the rocks; the creditors' hounding; the endless specter of bankruptcy; the countless times it almost slipped away. Carnival Cruise Lines: Ted had started it and kept it going after taking a beating that would have sent anyone else crawling into a hole, had kept it alive with nothing but spit and string and guile and built it into a beautiful money machine. Then Micky had taken over, and Carnival became something no one could have expected, swallowing the competition one by one, until only a handful of worthy rivals remained. Then Micky took them, too. That was what today was about.

They're calling him the "Emperor of the Waves." Ted would have gotten a kick out of that.

CHAPTER ONE

THE PERFECT BUSINESS

Morning, near America.

It looks like something yanked from a futurist's dream: a space station, a great white mechanical whale nosing its way back to Miami through the ocean dawn, its belly stuffed with the celebrants of American leisure. Three city blocks long, twenty stories from top to bottom, lit up like a Christmas tree, it is the *Voyager of the Seas*, the largest cruise ship in the world—an enormity of sleekness and power.

Out on deck, a smattering of early risers and endurance drinkers meanders comfortably in the gathering breeze. Some, casual in shorts and T-shirts, hold cups of perfectly brewed coffee in their hands, and the steam puffs out like winter breath as they sip. A few are still in evening wear from the night before. They teeter as they stroll, the most elegant among the women carrying their high heels in one hand and leaning happily against their tuxedoed men. To the east, behind the ship, the sun is just beginning to warm the horizon; soon joggers will be making the rounds on the rubberized, brick-colored track set into the deck's teakwood planking. Inside, along the honeycombed corridors that run through the ship, the rest of *Voyager's* thirty-eight hundred or so passengers are still sleeping soundly after yet another night of revelry, each under high-thread-count sheets in ultramodern little cabins ordered just so, their thermostats set to their individual tastes as they enjoy the final hours of their weeklong Caribbean cruise.

They came from Akron to be here, from San Antonio and Boston and

Birmingham and New York and Des Moines, from all over the country to spend their holiday week at sea. They are among the more than ten million Americans—among the twelve million or so people worldwide—drawn to cruise ships each year by the promise of days on tropical shores, nights steaming gently across the open, empty waves. A few passengers are rich, but most are not—at least not by U.S. standards. Cruising has changed immeasurably in the last thirty years; *Voyager*, like most big cruise ships today, hosts a remarkable cross section of America's middle class. At a time when a tank of gas and three meals at McDonald's can cost as much as $65, some passengers have actually gotten their cabins for as little as $150 a night, meals and entertainment included.

It's been a week of sunshine, of gambling, of live music and twenty-four-hour room service all on the clear, exquisite waters of the Caribbean Sea—a week that's taken the *Voyager*'s passengers to five different countries, whisking them through each by bus, van and taxicab like visiting dignitaries; a week that, from the moment they first craned their necks pierside to fit the ship into their field of vision, has seen them systematically enchanted by a small army of workers dedicated solely to their pleasure and comfort. And the food—oh, don't *remind* them of the food. It was just so good; there was just so *much* of it.

And now the week is done. Almost. For those passengers who are awake to experience the dawn, this is a supremely relaxing moment. Real Life is closing in at nearly thirty-five miles per hour, but it still feels very, very far away.

That's by design, that feeling; *Voyager* is a reality unto itself. The ship is entirely self-contained, a shrine to the indomitable drive of twenty-first-century *Homo americanus*, nothing short of a technological marvel. Five Goodyear blimps could fit inside with room to spare; the combined steel in its hull and superstructure could stretch more than five times around the equator. It holds twenty-five hundred toilets. Every day, its engines generate enough electricity to power a typical American home for 180 years or more.

In their days aboard, *Voyager*'s passengers have become a part of this closed system. They have bathed in the ship's three swimming pools, soaked in its seven hot tubs. Rain or shine, they've lounged amid the mosaics and classical-style statuary of the ten-thousand-square-foot solarium—tanning

when the sun is out, at other times enjoying the manufactured humidity beneath the shelter of a retractable glass dome. They've taken their meals in the
three-story dining room, enjoyed cocktails in any one of more than a dozen
bars and performance lounges. There's a library and Internet café on two
floors; many have passed through. Twenty-four hours a day, room service has
been available at no additional cost. Everywhere they've been served drinks,
fresh towels and little snacks by smiling attendants even as their children have
been mercifully . . . elsewhere, entertained by an entire child-care staff dedicated to securing a little peace and quiet for the grown-ups.

When they've been in the mood to get physical, there's been miniature golf, rock climbing, basketball on a full-size outdoor court, a simulated
driving range. Along with the dozens of exercise machines in the fifteen-
thousand-square-foot fitness area, the staff has offered yoga, aerobics and
dance lessons of all kinds; personal training; body fat and nutritional analysis. The ship even has an ice-skating rink, complete with a Zamboni. When
the impulse has been less athletic, there have been mud baths, aromatherapy
massage, facials, manicures and hair stylings; a sports bar, a cigar bar, a
British-style pub, a jazz club, cafés, a poolside bar and grill; art auctions,
in-cabin movies and video games; musical theater in the evenings on a
Broadway-size stage. At the center of it all is the "Royal Promenade," a block-
and-a-half-long, four-story indoor boulevard lined with shops and bars.
There's even a classic car parked along the way for effect; jugglers, magicians
and sketch artists roam the storefronts, cornering passersby—and, to capture
it all, camera crews from the ship's own TV station, broadcasting continu-
ously on its closed-circuit system. Twice weekly, the boulevard is taken over
by a Mardi Gras–style parade, complete with a marching band and staff in
masks and costumes, even on stilts. Above the storefronts cabins with windows face the "street," just like second-floor apartments. It's a bizarre sight,
showcasing the extent to which *Voyager* has been constructed as a world unto
itself.

The size of all this, again, is extraordinary. Stand the ship on its end in
downtown Miami, and it would be the tallest building within 670 miles. It's
too big to pass through the Panama Canal. *Voyager* is to the *Titanic* what a
Humvee is to a Honda Civic. Its size is officially registered as 142,000 tons,
although technically that's a measure of volume, not weight, corresponding
to the amount of water it would take to fill the passenger areas inside the
ship—enough, for the record, to fill about twenty-five hundred swimming

pools. But at just under 54,000 actual tons—empty—*Voyager* is no light-weight. Stretch a chain of elephants up and down the length of Manhattan, or pile Chevrolet Suburbans nine times the height of Mount Everest, and you're in the neighborhood.

And, of course, the ship is nowhere *near* empty. Forget the hardware store–type stuff: the more than half-million gallons of fuel, the medical supplies, the thousands of lightbulbs, the cleaning products, the dry cleaning and photo development chemicals, the medical supplies, the white paint—and unless you paint highways, there's more of *that* than you're likely to see in your entire life. Forget the passengers themselves, who alone weigh nearly three hundred tons, and who'll collectively gain something on the order of fifteen tons during their cruise. And forget their luggage, which weighs closer to six hundred tons. The real wonder is the food. A cruise ship like *Voyager* is the world's biggest lunch box. In a single week, its chefs will serve up more than 160,000 meals. That's upwards of five tons of meat alone—including a ton of bacon, and two and a half times that in beef. Adding to *Voyager*'s weight are a ton of potatoes and more than twice that in flour, some 1.5 tons of chicken parts, forty thousand eggs, three thousand whole lobsters and seven hundred gallons of ice cream—not to mention something like five thousand bottles of wine, one thousand bottles of hard liquor and twenty thousand cans of beer. Without disturbing the nearly eight thousand passengers coming on or off the ship, it all needs to be loaded in the course of a few hours into the ship's eighteen apartment-size freezers and refrigerators, even as the upwards of twenty tons of trash and human and food waste—twenty-five hundred toilets, remember?—generated during the previous voyage is carted off in the opposite direction.

Lesson one: time is money, and empty ships earn none. This ship is a leisure *machine*. Eight hours from the moment *Voyager* ties up at the pier, it will be sailing out to sea again, carrying a fresh load of vacationers. The last day of a cruise may be a slow, lazy one for passengers, but for the crew, it's anything but. Turnaround day, the busiest day of a cruise ship's working week, begins around midnight, and not just out at sea. By the time *Voyager* arrives in Miami, thousands of people—truck drivers, dockworkers, Coast Guard security patrols, customs and immigration officers, liaisons to the airlines—will have been working for hours.

The announcement will have gone though the ship around dinnertime the evening before: *Please pack tonight, ladies and gentlemen; make sure to leave your bags outside your door before nodding off.* And all through the night, the ship's staff will have been trundling the Samsonite, the American Tourister, the neat rolling suitcases, the duffels bulging with duty-free treasure, along the corridors, into freight elevators that passengers never see, and down to the artery the crew calls "I-95"—an entire deck, more or less, below the waterline. At one end it breaks up into the refrigeration complex; at the other, warehousing for cleaning and other stores. Between are dozens of doors, leading to engines the size of single-family homes, to trash compactors and incinerators of a size to rival a small town's, to offices and utility areas of all kinds. The hallway itself is big enough to accommodate an oversize pickup truck. As the shoreline nears, I-95 is so gridlocked with luggage carts that it almost looks like its namesake at rush hour.

And still, it's barely dawn. As soon as the ship docks, the cargo doors on either side will open like curtains on a stage and the real frenzy will begin. The food delivery trucks that have been waiting at the pier now start unloading their giant crates and pallets, their operators using long mechanical arms to pass them up to the bay. There, the ship's small fleet of miniature forklifts twirl and brush past one another like ballerinas, nearly silent except for the soft electrical whine of their engines, then making giant crashes of sound each time they set a load down. It looks chaotic, but every item is earmarked for a specific recipe to be served in a specific part of the ship at a specific hour on a specific day. The chefs must be able to find what they need at a moment's notice; placement must be exact.

By nine A.M., *Voyager's* public areas will be overrun by passengers, who have been forced out of their rooms so that they can be cleaned for the afternoon's new passengers, but not been cleared yet to proceed to immigration. Chairs all taken, many in the bleary crowd will settle for seating on staircases while they wait to be released; they'll flop onto their carry-ons, even onto the floor. Such disorder in what is normally so shipshape a system makes the place feel more like a Red Cross emergency center than a luxury liner. Just the night before, these people were royalty; now they're refugees.

At any given moment, well over two hundred thousand vacationers are out at sea aboard ships like *Voyager.* A type of travel that was once distant and exotic now feels as safe and comprehensible—and nearly as accessible—as the nearest strip mall.

Mention cruise ships to most anyone, and many things may spring to mind, but bare-knuckled capitalism is generally not one of them. Hawaiian shirts, maybe, or rum drinks. Maybe *The Love Boat* reruns. Maybe Grandma, who goes cruising every chance she gets and dragged the whole family along for that miserable week a few years ago. Or maybe the ships themselves. They are massively impressive, but we tend to think of them also as frivolous—hokey or glamorous, depending on your taste, but certainly not *aggressive*. It's difficult to reconcile the decadence of cruising with our image of a modern industrial giant: rapacious, insatiable, feral.

And yet the cruise lines are all that and more.

Tourism is the largest industry in the world, and cruising is not only its fastest-growing sector by far, but one of the few to see a genuine concentration of power. According to industry estimates, approximately one in seven Americans has been on a cruise. That sample includes the impoverished, the incarcerated and the very young, but if you trim the sample to a likelier demographic, the statistic approaches one in three. Of those who have cruised, as many as 90 percent say they intend to do so again. The industry has set new records for both passenger numbers and profits nearly every year since the 1960s, so that today it is a $13 billion business—and growing faster than ever. It's predicted that it will more than double in size before it levels off.

Ten of the sixteen cruise lines operating out of U.S. ports are subsidiaries of two closely held companies, Carnival Corporation and Royal Caribbean Cruise Lines. Incredibly, more than 90 percent of the industry's passenger capacity is controlled by only three families, and nearly half of it is effectively in the hands of just one man: Carnival's chairman and CEO, Micky Arison. Today, the cruise industry is a moneymaking machine with a worldwide reach that is incredible in its relentless efficiency. Behind the gracious veneer of cultural icons like *The Love Boat* and even Hollywood's *Titanic*—and often operating beyond the reach of regulators and law enforcement—it has quietly grown to become one of the most profitable and tightly controlled businesses in existence.

Voyager of the Seas cost Royal Caribbean more than a half-billion dollars when it was built in 1999—about the same as a major metropolitan convention center or a sports stadium with a capacity of seventy thousand. In 2004 Carnival took delivery of seven comparable "megaships" in as many months—each costing hundreds of millions of dollars, the most expensive of them going for more than $800 million. Nobody spends that kind of money unless he's expecting to get a whole lot more in return.

And the cruise lines do. The 2003 profits of the industry's two juggernauts came to $2 billion, which represents more than the combined profits of Southwest Airlines, AT&T Wireless, Staples and Best Buy. In October of 2004 Carnival announced that with another fourteen new cruise ships on order, it was initiating a $1 billion buyback of its shares *and* increasing its dividends by 20 percent.

One has to ask: How, with ships so expensive and with fares as low as $150 per night, is this even possible? What these companies have achieved, they have won through a profound mastery of the emerging global economy. Take away the sequins and the belly-flop competitions, the midnight buffets and the ice sculptures, and what remains is the concept of the twenty-first-century transnational corporation taken to its logical extreme—and perhaps beyond.

Entirely within the bounds of the law, or nearly so, cruise lines like Carnival and Royal Caribbean have managed to create a global enterprise of unparalleled flexibility and freedom. A ship like *Voyager* gets most of its customers in the United States; its workers come from impoverished nations like Indonesia, Honduras or the Philippines; often as not, it's been built in a western European nation whose government was willing to subsidize its construction in order to preserve the jobs it created; the company that owns it lists its shares on the New York Stock Exchange, has its corporate headquarters in Miami and instead of taxes pays nominal fees to countries like Liberia, Panama or the Bahamas, which happily claim them as corporate citizens, no questions asked. Everything a cruise ship produces or consumes is, by definition, an export.

Forty years ago, the cruise business was a decaying backwater of a passenger shipping industry already made obsolete by the dawn of the jet age. Today, through the efforts of a handful of brilliant entrepreneurs, it has spawned staggering personal fortunes—empires, really. Carnival has produced two of the one hundred richest people in the world, siblings with a combined fortune of about $10.5 billion. Royal Caribbean's two biggest investors include the Pritzker clan, the legendary financiers of whose $7.6 billion in holdings the cruise line is a major part. Companies that not long ago literally could not afford to pay vendors in advance for the food they served now negotiate mergers worth billions, command attention on Wall Street whenever they speak and imperiously dictate terms to those who seek the privilege of hosting their ships, whether municipal governments in the U.S. or the troubled sovereign nations of the Caribbean.

That journey between then and now is nothing short of epic—a drama of high-stakes gamesmanship complete with a cast of characters that by turns runs to the inspiring, the cruel, the courageous and the ruthless. The years have seen these players contend with everything from shipwreck to extortion at the hands of organized crime, to feuds, to coups—and even federal felony convictions at nearly every major cruise line. The story of the industry they've built is a testament both to the heights individuals can achieve when they refuse to imagine limits to their potential—and to the depths they can sink to when they're no longer capable of imagining a limit to their power. It's a story, in other words, of what happens when little guys become big guys.

It is also a saga of a culture in profound transformation. This industry could not have become what it is without the emergence of a new American middle class, without the decline of our manufacturing sector and the rise of our service economy, without the rise of mass air travel, without television, the sexual revolution and the suburbanization of the heartland.

We have entered the new century as perhaps the most comprehensively entertained culture in the world. We have more time available for the pursuit of our collective appetites than any people in history—more time to ask ourselves the question "What do we want?" The cruise ship industry, for better or worse, appears to be one of our big new answers.

The previous century's clash of ideologies has come to a celebrated end, and debates continue to rage over what will replace them. It was capitalism that defeated the horrors of communist totalitarianism, and it is to the free markets that we widely believe the future will belong. But in what form? In this new, smaller world, what will the relationship between business, government and society be? The framework of capitalism accommodates a huge spectrum of possibilities, from the near-socialism of today's western Europe to libertarian visions in which even the fire departments are run as private businesses.

The cruise industry as it exists today is one extreme on this spectrum. In nearly every facet of its operations—in the vast disconnect between its capital base, its labor and its markets; in the extreme consolidation of its power and wealth; in its relentless appetite for innovation; in its nearly total freedom from a strong governmental hand—the cruise industry is business at its most unfettered. The same quirks of law and history that have enabled it to grow at such a remarkable rate have also given us a glimpse into a possible future in which government has receded almost entirely into the background and society in nearly every aspect is governed by the markets alone.

Ideologues of whatever persuasion will be disappointed to find cruise shipping ill-suited for propaganda purposes. Where poor or nonexistent oversight has permitted, cruise lines like Carnival and Royal Caribbean have indeed committed excesses, some of them truly outrageous. And there is more than a little in their everyday practices that most reasonable people would recognize as problematic. Yet in other cases the industry has tempered its self-interest in surprising ways—especially given how little outside influence it has had to contend with. The caricature of the evil, soulless corporation is far from a seamless fit here.

"America," John Updike once wrote, "is a vast conspiracy to make you happy." His unlikely, ambivalent formulation captures the soul of this remarkable industry—and of the contradictions of our age that it embodies.

Happy sailing.

CHAPTER TWO

O'ER LAND OR SEA OR FOAM

He not busy being born is busy dying.

—Bob Dylan

By the winter of 1957, the year the freak cold snap Floridians remember as the "big freeze" turned Miami Beach into a ghost town and iced the oranges as they hung on the trees, Frank Fraser's little cruise business was doing well—so well, in fact, that there'd even been talk of a competitor or two coming to town. Not that there wasn't room for another cruise operation at Miami's creaky old port. Fraser's outfit only had a pair of thirty-year-old ships, and the demand for sailings was definitely more than they could handle. But then again, it still wasn't entirely clear that his idea wasn't a fad that would run its course in due time. For a little while longer, at least, Fraser would continue to have the sleepy Port of Miami more or less to himself.

Later generations of cruising insiders would remember F. Leslie Fraser as the grandfather of a $13 billion industry. It wasn't that Fraser had invented the concept of an ocean cruise; he hadn't. As early as the turn of the century, the occasional transatlantic ocean liner might be diverted from its regular run to wend its way through the Greek Isles or the West Indies carrying a complement of the idle rich. And as the decades wore on, it grew more and more common for the management of a New York–based liner to augment a winter season's weak transatlantic bookings with a tropical cruise or two. Such ships would always be back on the New York–Southampton or the New York–Marseille run at the first sign of spring. From the perspective of most shipowners in those days, pleasure cruises tended to be a distraction from the more serious and profitable business of passenger shipping, a necessary evil to mitigate the financial pain of sailing below capacity during a dry spell.

Fraser's innovation was the notion of an industry devoted solely to running cruises—a *Miami* industry. The Port of Miami had certain undeniable geographic advantages, in spite of its cow-town reputation. And Fraser did well, not that anyone took much notice. So far as the shipping world was concerned, Miami's little waterfront might as well have been a million miles from the bustling harbors of the Northeast, where great things happened and the huge ocean liners continued to dominate the transatlantic trade—where the real money was.

This suited Fraser just fine. Even if the big passenger lines had been interested in his business model—and Fraser had never approached them as prospective partners—their ships were poorly suited to making a successful business out of pleasure cruising. Even the most modern ocean liner designs were still based on the economics of the great immigrant trade that had defined passenger shipping during the early part of the century. That business, built on a rigid stratification between an opulent first-class world abovedecks and the cramped spaces below (where the huddled masses had historically been quartered), was about as far from pleasure cruising as you could get.

In fact, the notion that today's cruise industry is the direct descendant of the great ocean liners of the past, however treasured in marketing circles, has little historical basis. Ocean liners did have their share of romance, and thanks to films like Cary Grant's *An Affair to Remember* and the fawning of society-page editors who made first-class passenger lists a staple of their columns, the image of the luxury liner had become firmly anchored in the popular imagination. But it was poor immigrants who drove the "Golden Age" of passenger shipping, not Astors and Fords and Rockefellers sipping manhattans and dancing the foxtrot abovedecks. Even aboard the most grandiose ships, the class stamped on a passenger's ticket determined which dining rooms he could eat in, which lounges and public areas he could visit and even where he was permitted to walk. Most knew they'd never get anywhere near the fifteen-room suites with their sundecks, grand pianos and private dining rooms.

The immigrant trade was immensely profitable—a textbook economy of scale long before the term was ever used. Then as now, passenger shipping was largely a fixed-cost business where expenses like fuel, the captain and the crew—and indeed the ship itself—had to be paid for whether there was one paying passenger on board or one thousand. The real profit, therefore, lay not in the consumers of grandeur above, but in maximizing the cheap passages—packing in the "talking cargo" as tightly as possible and spending as little as possible in the process. The throngs of people streaming out of Europe couldn't afford to pay much for a ticket, but most of them were so desperate for the chance at a new life that they'd put up with almost any conditions, as long as they ended up in America. Many such people can fit into a very small space, and to the delight of many a shipowner, many did.

In 1880 the population of the United States was just over fifty million. At the turn of the century that figure was just under seventy-six million, and by the time World War I effectively ended America's period of mass migration the census estimate was fast approaching the one hundred million mark. Nearly every European immigrant who came to America during this period came by passenger ship; so, for that matter, did every diplomat, businessman, artist and piece of mail to cross between Europe and America.

Throughout the nineteenth century, emigrants had crossed the Atlantic in what was known as "steerage," spaces not unlike a cargo hold and with scarcely more amenities. First aboard sailing ships, then on paddle-wheeled steamers and finally on the early versions of the modern propeller-driven ship, they made the journey by the millions, or died trying. The sailing ships had been the worst, earning the nickname of "coffin ships," for their death rates of 10 percent or higher among steerage passengers. Grim, foul affairs by all accounts, coffin ship crossings ran just under a month with a favorable wind. In storms or bad calms, the trip could take half again as long. The stink of the chamber pots made the tiny quantities of food—rotten already—all but inedible, and there were few opportunities for sunlight and fresh air. The sheer volume of formerly hopeful immigrants arriving as cadavers was staggering, to the point that the era's Ellis Island officials finally began imposing a ten-dollar fine on ship captains for each corpse brought to the New World.

The race to build bigger and faster vessels began in earnest with the arrival of steamship technology in the latter half of the nineteenth century. Great coal-fired iron hulks replaced wooden sailing ships, and their scale and speed brought astonishing profitability, quickly drawing eager investors. These new vessels shrank the world in their day as radically and as suddenly as the Internet has in our own. Instead of a few hundred low-paying passengers, the liners could carry several thousand, still packed into tight, unventilated spaces, but under mildly better circumstances than before and—more important—for far shorter lengths of time. By the turn of the century the crossing from New York to Southampton had been pared down to a matter of days. Profits skyrocketed as bigger, faster ships not only carried more people, but made many journeys in the time previously required for a single trip. Transatlantic business and leisure travel picked up among the well-heeled as schedules became more reliable and crossings on the bigger ships grew safer and more comfortable. Lines touted the sumptuousness of their first-class service to attract the international luminaries of the day, but it was clear where the real money was. Companies like the Holland America Line, Swedish America Line and Hamburg American Line chose their names carefully in order to market their real product—the promise of a new life on the grey Atlantic's western shore.

The lucrative trade soon fostered fierce competition, spawning entire side industries. Passenger lines established sales offices far inland in European countries, the better to secure passengers before a competitor could get their rubles or kopeks or zlotys. Some chartered special trains to carry emigrants from Russia, Poland, Czechoslovakia and elsewhere thousands of miles to the west to the ports of England and France. At the peak of this human torrent, shipping firms were essentially buying passengers, kicking back a portion of profits to the governments of Central Europe in order to ensure that the steady flow of exiles and undesirables was not interrupted.

As World War I approached, ships began to offer ventilation, toilets and running water for their steerage-class passengers. Even on ultra-modern vessels like the doomed *Titanic*, however, conditions were never better than rough. Meals in steerage were still a hurried affair, often as not consumed standing up in claustrophobic dining areas. People washed their own plates in the same basins that were used for bathing, and women who took the semiprivacy of the mealtime rush as a chance to wash or dress quickly without being ogled often paid for their modesty by missing meals altogether. Appetites, in any case, would hardly have been hearty; the recent luxury of toilets notwithstanding, the stink of mass seasickness reached into every belowdecks crook and corner. Laws passed on both sides of the Atlantic attempted to address issues of overcrowding, adequate sustenance and the rampant sexual abuse of female passengers. Ship's officers, however, quickly learned to quell complaints by telling their hapless charges that the officials at

Ellis Island would turn them back if they didn't "look happy" when they disembarked. On their arrival to New York Harbor, emigrants massed at the
rails while the ship's crew tossed overboard the "verminous mattresses" they'd
been sleeping on.

The Great War put an end to the profitable symbiosis of mass migration and
transatlantic luxury travel—temporarily, it was thought at the time. Following
the armistice, a glut of demobilized wartime tonnage flooded the market, driving ship values down sharply and taking ticket prices with them. Low-cost
operators came onto the scene in droves, eager to break into the immigrant
trade.

But an increasingly isolationist government had come to power in Washington, putting an end to the heyday of immigration. In 1921 Congress
passed the Emergency Quota Act, also known as the "3 Percent Act." Ostensibly enacted in response to fears of Bolshevik infiltrators from the Soviet
Union, the act was in fact widely understood to be part of a burgeoning
movement to curtail the entrance into the country of Catholics, Jews,
"worms and riffraff from southern Europe," as one legislator put it on the
floor of Congress, and anyone else who didn't fit the WASP profile of
America's financial and political elites. At its heart, the new policy was a national grandfather clause on immigration, restricting the total number of new
entrants from any given country to 3 percent of the number of their fellow
nationals residing in the U.S. recorded in the 1910 census. There was no mis-
taking the message. The following year, total immigration numbers plummeted from somewhere between 750,000 and one million to 358,000; more
than half of the new citizens came from western and northern Europe. A second law curtailed immigration even more radically in 1924, lowering the
overall annual quota to 164,000 and pushing the percentage down to 2 percent of Americans from the *1890* census, which had been taken before the
great rush from eastern and southern Europe had even begun. Fully half of
those allowed into the U.S. the following year were British.

For the vast industry that had evolved to service the immigrant trade,
the combination of an artificially inflated supply of ships and a passenger
market whittled to less than 20 percent of prewar levels was as good as a
death sentence.

Many smaller transatlantic operators disappeared almost overnight in the inevitable shakeout. Those that could set about trying to salvage their invest-ments by upgrading the suddenly useless steerage accommodations for the newly flush American middle class of the boom-time 1920s. If the west-bound traffic had dried up, the thinking went, perhaps the new prosperity in the U.S. might give rise to a new flow in the other direction. The lines came up with a new designation of "tourist third class" for the upgraded facilities. For the trickle of immigrants still making the crossing, and for those who were willing to abide restrictive rules and cramped quarters in return for a few dollars' savings, plain old "third class" more or less approximated the old steerage.

The innovation staved off destruction for some of the stronger com-panies, thanks in large part to their pitch-perfect marketing efforts to sell America on an innovative vision of international travel. Lines announced eighty-dollar-round-trip tickets in tourist class—far more than a steerage fare, but still a fraction of the going rate for a first-class passage. They sought out a new class of Americans, encouraging them to think of themselves in a different way—humble financially, perhaps, but with high social aspirations. It was an early, brilliant iteration of the "affordable luxury" approach to branding that today has us happily paying five dollars for cappuccinos. In-stead of marketing to the stolid middle class, lines called upon "sub-debs, younger members of the smart set, college professors and students, men and women of the business world" to claim the status that was their destiny. Ad-vertisements stroked the nouveau riche, cautioning with a conspiratorial air that "the initiate takes pains to choose the ship that suits him or her as care-fully as a prima donna chooses a gown." Press agents did a masterful job of seeing to it that the fashion magazines of the day weighed in on what, sud-denly, had become critical questions of seagoing etiquette. *Vogue* observed that on the return voyage from Europe, "many otherwise excellent ladies try to wear each Paris frock at least once, to cheat the customs. To put it frankly, however, it simply isn't considered smart to appear too opulent. It subjects one to the suspicion of having nowhere else to wear one's clothes."

While the 1920s did indeed see a new popularization of the European "Grand Tour" among ordinary Americans, that went only so far. It was grati-fying to think of a democratized American class of international sophisti-cates, but there was of course no such thing. In fact, as one historian points out, "The new category of passenger had few features in common other than a desire to travel cheaply and a willingness to forgo the luxury of first class, which they could not afford in any case." There was no genuine social level-ling here; tourist-class accommodations, moreover, were hardly more than glorified dormitories and had little appeal of their own. As had always been the case, unless you were in first class, the only reason to board an ocean liner was to get from one place to another.

But if Congress had taken from the steamship lines with one hand by curtailing immigration, it also gave lavishly—if unintentionally—when it enacted the national prohibition on alcohol at around the same time. Other than the bootleggers and organized crime syndicates, perhaps no one in the world benefited as much as ship lines did from the unpopular ban. Suddenly, there was a compelling reason to book an international sailing—and the des-tination didn't much matter, so long as the ship carried French champagne, Scotch whiskey and Jamaican rum. In spite of the dry run at home, the liquor cabinets of European ocean liners were as open as ever, and as the pace of the 1920s picked up, the urge to celebrate without fear of arrest helped persuade thousands of Americans to sign on for a European tour. It was a win-win situation for everyone but the teetotalers: shipping firms got new passengers, thirsty citizens found relief from a ridiculous law and the "booze cruise" took its place in the American vernacular.

Some of these early cruises were spectacular affairs in their own right, like the "millionaire's cruise" sponsored by American Express in 1923, where a suite could run you twenty-five thousand dollars—more than a quarter-mil-lion in today's dollars. But such events were the exception. Far more typical were Cunard's fifty-dollar "whoopee cruises" from New York to Nova Scotia, on which, as one crewmember remembers it, "Sugar daddies and their in-evitable blondes were plentiful." You could hardly miss the tantalizing point of the brochures, with their promise that "as you sail away, far beyond the range of amendments and thou-shalt-nots, those dear little iced things begin to appear, sparkling aloft on their slender crystal stems. . . . Utterly French, utterly harmless—and oh so garglingly good!"

Shipping executives may have toasted the health of U.S. Representative Volstead, but that bit of extra help didn't change their fundamental predica-ment: like it or not, they were being forced to shift to a leisure model, and with that came the unfamiliar challenges of running a seasonal business. The same economies of scale that had served the industry so well when aspiring Americans had been lining up across the European continent to book passage on their ships now came back to haunt them. Because the prospect of crossing the North Atlantic in February was enough to make even the most committed lush think twice, cruises to the Caribbean became essential for keeping ships operational during the winter months, though with the class system a continued impediment to extended stays in tourist class, they were more stopgaps than real moneymakers. Even without the class problem, the ships were simply not built for tropical climates; their small windows, their limited deck space, their recreational facilities (such as they were) deep in the ship had all been conceived with the wind and snow and waves of the North Atlantic in mind. They had no air-conditioning, and the dark paint on their hulls was a magnet for the tropical sun. And then there was the question of outlook. Rather than embracing an exciting new direction for their business, shipowners saw these tropical sojourns as a distraction, a necessary evil. The competitive spirit of earlier decades, when national pride hung on which flag flew over the fastest or most impressive ships, cast a long shadow, and many who still saw their ships as thoroughbreds considered cruises to be hardly a step above the glue factory. Though they depended on them, traditional passenger lines looked at the tourist cabins, the Dixieland bands, the egg-rolling competitions and costume balls as gimmicks, in place only to pad their primary function of transporting people from one place to another.

Notwithstanding a gentle decline over the years, most of the strong lines survived in this way through the roaring twenties, the years of the Great Depression and up to the start of World War II, when the era of passenger shipping came to an abrupt end. Japan's surrender at the end of the war ushered in not only the nuclear age, but the jet age as well; with the prospect of fast, safe and affordable air travel on the horizon, traveling by sea soon became a quaint relic of a slower time. A handful of new liners was built during the late 1940s and 1950s, and the work of relocating the displaced millions of Europe sustained some of the older tonnage during the immediate postwar years. But the passenger lines were finally coming to understand that the mainstay of their business was about to literally vanish into thin air.

So by the early 1950s, when Frank Fraser first made his move in Miami, cruises per se were certainly nothing new. The concept of a year-round, cruise-only business operating out of Miami, on the other hand, was revolutionary. It was one of those rare ideas that promises either limitless opportunity or certain destruction, and nothing in between. As long as the industry stayed in New York, its leaders would remain doggedly loyal to three centuries of maritime history, even as they watched their enterprises slowly fade away around them. Few realized it at the time, but operating out of Florida opened up a world of possibilities—especially for a man with Fraser's connections.

Cruising may have been new to him, but the business of running ships was in his blood. No one knew more about operating freighters between Miami and the tiny nations of the Caribbean and Central America than Frank Fraser. He'd been doing it all his life, just like his father and grandfather before him. The family had immigrated to Jamaica from Scotland generations before and eventually took ownership of several plantations on the north side of the island. There they grew citrus and bananas, which they exported to the U.S. using their own ships. Born in 1904, Fraser carried himself like the blustery colonial aristocrat that he was. Heavyset and gruff, full of charm when he wanted to be, he kept a cigarette perpetually dangling from his mouth even when he talked, and people said his looks were reminiscent of those of the actor Sidney Greenstreet. His circle included film stars like Errol Flynn as well as many of the region's most influential power players—the Bosch family, for one, which ran the Bacardi Rum empire in Cuba, and also the long-standing dictator of the Dominican Republic, General Rafael Trujillo. One would not have been surprised to learn, on meeting him, that Fraser's ventures throughout the West Indies had earned him his share of infamy as well as treasure.

The relationship with Trujillo turned out to be one of the most important of Fraser's life. The two men had grown close doing business during World War II, when German submarines sitting off Miami turned the Caribbean shipping lanes into a shooting gallery and threatened to cut off the Dominican Republic's much-needed imports of manufactured goods as well as the agricultural exports Trujillo used to pay for them. Fraser's fleet of banana boats had turned out to be just small enough that the Germans couldn't be bothered "to waste a torpedo" on them, in the words of one of his later captains, and as competitors running larger ships went down one after another at the hands of the wolf pack, Fraser did a lively business maintaining the commercial link between the United States and the Dominican Republic and other parts of the Caribbean, winning the strongman's firm patronage as a result. He could have had no more potent an ally. From the time he came to power in 1930 until his death in 1961, the general held sway over the Dominican Republic through the ruthless and violent deployment of his secret police and through his absolute control of the state-run monopolies that dominated the Dominican economy. It was about him that FDR's secretary of state is said to have made the famous remark "He's a son of a bitch, but he's *our* son of a bitch." The possibly genocidal Trujillo, whose temperament had earned him the unaffectionate nickname of "the Goat," was not a man of casual acquaintances, but he and Fraser seemed to understand each other.

And then again, the banana business makes for strange bedfellows. Fraser had never thought much about getting into the passenger trade, no doubt in part due to a lifelong affliction with seasickness. But he'd always had an eye for a good deal and he could see Miami's potential as a cruise port. A few years after the war, Trujillo offered him favorable charter terms for the *Nuevo Dominicano*, a passenger ship owned by the Dominican government, and just like that, Fraser set about developing a year-round Miami-based cruise operation.

In the 1940s Miami may have been Podunk to the great population centers of the Northeast, but there was no denying its geographical advantages. Taking a winter cruise to Nassau, or Cuba, or Jamaica, or Key West aboard a New York–based ocean liner meant enduring at least three days of nasty weather before reaching the sunshine, while a cruise from Miami wouldn't miss a minute of the beautiful weather. Even if the big lines had wanted to, homeporting in Miami wouldn't have been feasible for them. Most liners couldn't even dock at the city's shallow port as of 1950, for one thing, and in any case they saw little point in expanding outside of New York—especially in what appeared to be the waning days of their industry. But with a smaller ship run as a single-class vessel, Fraser thought, a year-round cruise operation could be just the thing. Why not? With the deal Trujillo had gotten him on the *Nuevo Dominicano*, it hardly seemed like much of a risk.

And then there was the success of the S.S. *Florida*, whose cleverly marketed overnight runs to Havana accounted for nearly half of Miami's passenger-ship traffic in the years after the war. The *Florida*'s owners had hit upon a solution to the problem of Miami's remoteness, coordinating their sailing schedule with express trains from the Northeast. Customers in New York and Washington could begin a complete package right in their hometown, cutting days of the eastern seaboard's harsh winter weather from their trip by riding the rails to Miami secure in the knowledge that their ship would wait for them if the train was held up; the "Havana Special" was a favorite among those in the know.

Fraser's thinking was essentially along the same lines, except instead of selling the prospect of less time at sea, he'd be selling *better* time—more sunshine for the money, in other words. He began running the *Nuevo Dominicano* out of Miami in 1950, and set his two young sons, Frank and Lewis, to work in the Miami office. Fraser quickly realized he had a success on his hands. Three hundred feet long and entirely without air-conditioning, the *Nuevo Dominicano* carried 177 passengers when full. Crews from those days remember it as hot and undersized, but a pleasant enough vessel all the same. Between wartime sinkings and the subsequent decline in the seagoing passenger trade, a surplus of trained crew was available for passenger ships, and Fraser had no trouble hiring a top-notch staff who were all to happy to have the work. Because of his seasickness, Fraser himself declined to sail on the voyages. On turnaround days he'd watch from the pier as the ship geared up for departure, never removing the cigarette from his mouth as he barked and cursed whenever things fell behind schedule. He was quite a sight with his dander up; his subordinates joked at such moments that the long ash teetering on the end of his cigarette "must have been afraid to fall off."

Despite a promising first year, however, the enterprise was destined to be short-lived. Trujillo's friendship may have won Fraser the *Nuevo Dominicano* at a steep discount, but such associations are rarely without consequences. Just as he was settling into his cruise operation, their dealings took a turn that ended up costing Fraser not only his ship but his British citizenship and very nearly his freedom.

Whether it was because he owed Trujillo for the *Nuevo Dominicano* charter or simply because he saw the chance to turn a quick buck for himself, Fraser found himself embroiled in an arms-trading scheme worthy of Ian Fleming. The *Nuevo Dominicano* had sailed under the Canadian flag as the S.S. *New Northland* before it was sold to the Dominican Republic and eventually to Fraser. Keen to build up his navy—already a formidable force by regional standards at the time—but short on international goodwill, Trujillo now dispatched Fraser to acquire several decommissioned Canadian naval vessels, using his shipping background as a cover. Although the Canadians sold Fraser the ships on the condition that they be converted into commercial cargo ships and not put to any military use, he nevertheless immediately turned around and sold them, unconverted, to the Dominican navy. In the ensuing scandal Fraser was forced to renounce his commonwealth citizenship and flee to Santo Domingo, where Trujillo conferred Dominican citizenship upon him and pronounced him immune from extradition. For nearly two years he hid in the Dominican Republic under his patron's protection while the affair was sorted out.

The responsibility for running Fraser's ship during his involuntary exile fell to an ad hoc company run by Trujillo's cronies. Without Fraser's gruff voice and dancing cigarette to keep things in line, basic routines and standards quickly fell by the wayside, and in November of 1953 the *Nuevo Dominicano* was grounded and sank off the coast of Cuba. By way of making the loss up to his friend, Trujillo had his government sell Fraser a twenty-five-thousand-acre banana plantation at a nominal price. To the best of Fraser's knowledge the gift made him the owner of the world's largest private enterprise of this sort.

Fraser's warship troubles were finally resolved in 1954, and he was not long in returning to the Port of Miami. Flush with cash and energy alike after his long rest, he bought a pair of twenty-seven-year-old ships from a struggling Massachusetts firm called Eastern Steamship Lines, along with the rights to the company name. Confident in his investment this time around, he had both refitted and air-conditioned—a lavish expenditure at the time. Identical twins, the *Yarmouth* and the *Evangeline*, each carried as many as 450 cruise passengers. Two years after he'd left Miami as a fugitive, Fraser returned to the cruise business with a combined capacity of more than five times what he'd started with the first time around.

He launched the *Yarmouth* with ten-day cruises to Nassau, Haiti and Jamaica. The *Evangeline* worked longer trips to Central and South America. At $130 for a weeklong voyage, these were no millionaires' cruises, but the ships did depart port to band music, blasts of their whistle and confetti and streamers filling the air, just like any grand liner taking leave of New York. Those who sailed on Fraser's new ships seem to remember the experience fondly. Air-conditioning in those days was still a rare luxury in and of itself—especially on a ship. Brochures trumpeted "well appointed staterooms . . . all with hot and cold running water," and a tiny swimming pool not much bigger than a Jacuzzi sat on the very stern. The shipboard atmosphere was tranquil, clearly geared for the older clientele that made up almost the entire market for cruises in those days. Bouillon was served poolside at eleven, and in the afternoon there was tea. The promenade decks had been reengineered during the refit to allow uninterrupted strolling all the way around the vessel and had been fitted with a canopy so that "you could have your promenade without getting a sunburn." Deck chairs were likewise arranged in the shade, and the long days at sea tended to pass quietly and happily. There was plenty of time between ports, passengers were promised, to "rest up." Because Fraser again had his pick of the general surplus of good crew looking to work on passenger ships, service on the *Evangeline* and *Yarmouth* was excellent and re-laxed, "just like the West Indies afloat."

Port days, if anything, were even nicer. Big as the ships were compared with the *Nuevo Dominicano*, they were still of a size to fit into the rhythm and pace of the dusty, Third World harbors they visited, without overwhelm-ing them. In town, passengers said they felt they were able to be "kind of incognito, or fit in with the crowd" by virtue of their small numbers, despite the fact that they were often among the only white faces in sight. And they were welcomed in most places, although perhaps not to the extent suggested by the brochure explaining how "The natives sing while they work or play . . . a happy lot, carefree and gay." It was a far quieter world in those days, and the notion that much of the region might one day be awash in cruise ships was too remote even to consider. When the *Yarmouth* anchored at Port Antonio, Jamaica, for the first time in June of 1954, it was the first passenger ship the town had seen since before the war.

Fraser also owned a large turn-of-the-century hotel overlooking Port An-tonio, not far from the family plantations. As with his plantations and ba-nana boats, Fraser was quick to find synergies. The Jamaican stays always featured a special night at the hotel, from where the guests could look down and see their ship swinging gently at anchor below. The red carpet was rolled out as the passengers danced to band music or took in a native show. On oc-casion, they might look to the dance floor and see a big man in a well-cut suit, with a smile on his face, a cigarette dangling from his mouth and a large tray of glasses balanced precariously on his head as he danced gracefully around the room—their host, incognito.

This time, Fraser managed to stay out of trouble long enough to reap the fruits of his labor. By 1959 things were going so well that he bought another, bigger ship. Refitted and air-conditioned like the others, the 750-passenger *Bahama Star* just about doubled the Eastern Steamship Lines' capacity all over again; by that time the only problem with demand was meeting it. The *Bahama Star* sailed three- and four-day cruises to Nassau, and the ship ran as full and as profitably as the *Yarmouth* and the *Evangeline* had before it. The following year Fraser invested in a smaller luxury ship with room for three hundred, the *Ariadne*, and started marketing "the only luxury ship for Caribbean cruises from downtown Miami."

That was as far as fate would permit Fraser to take the company he'd built. In 1961 doctors told him he had a serious heart condition, and the treatments of the day offered him little hope of surviving for long. Although his two oldest sons, Lewis and Frank Jr., had worked in the company's offices and on the ships, they were still too young and inexperienced to take over the business. One of South Florida's most successful businessmen, W. R. Lovett of Jacksonville, had been a 49 percent partner in the purchase of the *Ariadne* the year before, and it didn't take much to persuade him to expand his investment. A character himself, Lovett had built the Winn-Dixie and Piggly Wiggly food store chains and was said to have a personal fortune approaching $100 million—real money in those days. He knew a good deal when he saw one. In no time at all, the F that had marked the smokestacks of Fraser's ships since the *Nuevo Dominicano* days was painted over with a big white L. The doctors' predictions, sadly, were accurate and Fraser died the following summer at the age of fifty-seven. As it happened, General Trujillo, who had played such a dramatic role in Fraser's cruise business, ended his thirty-one-year reign within months of Fraser's selling out: a group of conspirators, including high-ranking military officers and several of his own relatives, shot the dictator to death as he sat in his official car.

Eastern Steamship had settled comfortably into its routines by this time, and Lovett, who like his predecessor had a hand in many different enterprises, was content for several years to let things go on much as they had. Shoreside Miami, on the other hand, was in the middle of a revolution that would transform the face of the city and set the stage for the development of a modern cruise ship industry beyond anybody's dreams.

Historical circumstance and new technologies were bringing unprecedented boom times to South Florida. During the war years, more than 4.5 million U.S. servicemen had passed through the area either for training or recuperation, many of them staying at Miami Beach hotels converted into barracks. Discharged, contemplating their prospects in Eisenhower's America, many had found they'd gotten "sand in their shoes," as the saying went, and were eager to return to the balmy climate. The new wave of settlers "chose Miami for her sunshine and the informality of her dress, and for the glam- our associated with the name, perhaps. They also chose it because they could get a piece of land, build their own homes, enjoy outdoor living, swim- ming and tennis and backyard barbeques. They fanned out all over the place."

And for each family that came to stay, many more came to visit, fueling the giddy heyday of America's playground. As one writer who lived through those days described the moment, "A visit to Miami Beach was tied up with the Miami moon, the Atlantic Ocean, swaying palms aglow with indirect lighting, swaying rhumba dancers, gallons of suntan oil, gallons of frozen daiquiries, Bloody Marys and dry martinis. Gallons of Chanel Number Five. Gallons of everything." Superstars like Jackie Gleason and Walter Winchell regularly broadcast their programs from the wonderland Gleason had taken to billing as "the fun and sun capital of the world." The funnyman's catch- phrase, "How sweet it is," became a local motto. Audiences as large as fifty- five million tuned in to Winchell's weekly radio broadcasts from Miami Beach—"heaven," as he called it. A group of travel agents got together at a convention during these years and worked out that Miami Beach had built more hotels since the war than the rest of the world put together.

Then, just as the torrent of young families attracted to the city's oppor- tunities were laying the foundation for growth, a technological advance— no bigger than a television set—began to dot the windowsills of America and vault Miami into the future. The age of affordable air-conditioning had arrived.

The weather had always been a mixed blessing for Miamians. During the delightful winter months the city was every bit the booming tourist mecca, its beaches and hotels having drawn American vacationers since the 1920s. But the summer heat had always been unbearable. The worst of it— stifling, buggy days that stretched out for what seemed like forever, and the nights yet more uncomfortable—sent even the locals scuttling north for some escape, if they could afford it. Florida had seen its share of economic booms in the past, but without any real industrial base to offset its depen- dence on tourism, growth beyond a certain point had always been hampered by the region's unavoidably seasonal appeal. During the 1920s and 1930s lo- cal boosters had gone to great expense to expand the window, pleading with visitors to "Stay through May" and offering discounts of all kinds, but the reality of summertime Miami just wasn't something you could talk your way around. The city's dependence on just four months' worth of income for its year-round sustenance put its affairs on a knife's edge—and, like any tourist economy, made it agonizingly vulnerable to the caprices of national prosperity. Miami had teetered on the brink of insolvency during the depression years—still flush in the winter months, but broke overall. Properties that northern investors had traded back and forth at roaring premiums during the 1920s—oftentimes sight unseen—were in the 1930s auctioned off by the dozen on the steps of city hall in lieu of back taxes. At one point during the crisis, with a raft of municipal bonds coming due, the city was running a deficit so colossal that its budget wasn't sufficient even to cover debt payments.

But with the new widespread availability of "manufactured air," Miami's desperate, long-standing dream of a year-round "season" was poised to become a reality. The technology had been a long time coming. Primitive forms of air-conditioning had existed since the ancient Egyptians hung damp mats in the doorways of their homes, and centuries passed without any significant breakthrough. In the 1880s, some factory complexes used enormous bellows to manually pipe cold air into various storage rooms from a central facility that, in the parlance of the day, had been "mechanically refrigerated"—filled with ice, in other words. Needless to say, only the most urgent storage applications merited this Rube Goldberg approach.

The first versions of modern air-conditioning date back to turn-of-the-century printing and textile plants, where too much heat swelled and warped raw materials until the machines on the assembly line couldn't process them. After years of working on the problem engineers realized that, rather than introducing cold from a heavy, expensive external source like ice, they could affect temperature by controlling humidity and ventilation. At a time when many factories even in the north were still closing for the summer due to the weather, the technology was quickly refined for industrial applications, but it remained far too costly for popular consumption. The very wealthy enjoyed access to home air-conditioning as early as 1914, even before small businesses, but depression scarcity and wartime manufacturing priorities would ensure that it would be decades before the masses had the chance to experience such luxury.

Perhaps unsurprisingly enough to anyone who's walked into a Saturday matinee on a hot day drenched in sweat and left with chattering teeth, most Americans' first encounter with air-conditioning was at the movies. By the 1920s the country's most popular form of entertainment had become something of a public heath crisis, as audiences for whom indoor plumbing was still a status symbol crowded into tight, unventilated theaters for hours-long marathons of newsreels, cartoons and double features. "Heat and odors accumulating over multiple performances became unbearable," as one account recalls, to the point where many cinemas had no choice but to shut their doors on the hottest days of the year. As soon as air-conditioning technology improved enough to make it feasable, just about every movie theater in the country was proudly "conquering the great indoors." Department stores and other high-traffic businesses were likewise quick to invest in what they saw as a new way to entice prospective customers in off the street during the hot months, and by the late 1930s air-conditioned interiors were relatively commonplace.

The affordable window units beloved around the world today first came on the market in 1951, gaily promising a cool home "for the millions, not just for millionaires." In Miami, where beating the heat was something of an unofficial religion with superstitions, myths and rituals all its own, the new appliances changed the face of the expanding city almost overnight—literally. Southern architecture, its aesthetics dominated by the relentless priority of keeping cool, was thrown into sudden, radical upheaval. Just at the outset of the largest construction boom in the city's history, the big front porches and shady overhanging eaves, the high ceilings and attics and cross-ventilated rooms that for generations had seen grandchildren grow into grandparents all fell out of favor. Ranch houses were what the new Miamians wanted; with big windows and sliding glass doors, and a big green yard, where the porch would have been, for mowing. The windows stayed shut, to keep the cold from getting out.

But the influx of new people and businesses during the 1950s put unprecedented strains on the city's infrastructure. As incoming building materials and commercial goods began bottlenecking at the outdated seaport, talk turned to the urgent need for upgrading the facility—or replacing it entirely. "A new seaport is one of the primary needs of the Miami society," one columnist wrote, summing the matter up in the spirit of the day. "To the housewife, it means a cent saved here and there on many of the foods shipped into this area. To the man on the job, or one who runs a small business, it means the possibility of lower taxes." And with the cargo crisis casting such an optimistic spotlight on the future of the waterfront, it wasn't long before some of that radiance was refracted onto Miami's burgeoning cruise ship industry.

For years, the town's promoters had advanced the slogan "Miami: Winter Cruise Capital of the World." But that concept was now rejected as old thinking, limited thinking—the seasonal thinking. As the debate over the seaport gathered momentum, the architects of the waterfront's new master plan saw a chance to set the city's sights a little higher. After several years of municipal bickering, plans were finally announced near the end of the decade for a sparkling new cargo and passenger port, to be erected on a specially built artificial island in Biscayne Bay.

The new facility, to be called Dodge Island, would stand on the doorstep of downtown, a showcase for the new Miami. All offices at the new port, needless to say, were to be air-conditioned. Once it was finished, the existing facilities, a half-mile away, would be turned into a mix of bayside parkland and retail space. The powers that be called the plan "Operation Magic Wand."

With a wave of that wand, Miami had decided to bet heavily on the young cruise industry. The Florida commerce department spoke glowingly of "Miami's changing attitude towards the ship tourist, who up to now had been a negligible factor in the Gold Coast's travel economy." Dodge Island was to be a "clean port," confining the noise and debris of refueling operations and heavy industrial cargoes to the far side of the landfill. From downtown, all that would be visible would be the shimmering waters of Biscayne Bay and a brand-new cruise pier capable of simultaneously handling three five-hundred-passenger ships—bringing visitors to spend money on drinks and souvenirs in town and adding the perfect touch to the postcard cityscape. Designed in consultation with passenger line executives and customs and immigration officials, the pier and its accompanying passenger terminal were intended to reflect the newest, sleekest innovations of the day. "A novel, supermarket-type passenger and baggage processing procedure," for example, was to cut the ninety minutes it took passengers to clear customs at the old seaport almost in half.

Focusing on cruise traffic was a farsighted move on the part of Miami's government, especially considering that it came at a time when commercial jet service was widely believed to be on the brink of delivering a death blow to passenger shipping. "The seaport can be the greatest single economic shot in the arm our economy had ever had," one Dade County commissioner insisted at the time. "We need to break with the past, gamble a little, use a lot of imagination and come up with something unique—the finest ship passenger facility in the world." In fact, the ambitious master plan actually proved to be too conservative; by the time Dodge Island's "efficient modern passenger terminal" was finished in 1966 it was already playing catch-up, so rapidly was the cruise ship market growing. What had seemed a risky investment at the time already looked overcautious; midway through construction, cruise traffic at the old seaport had already surpassed the projections assembled by Dodge Island's optimistic designers.

Engineers scrambled to adjust their designs to fit stunning new growth estimates as tourism boosters who'd been sold on Dodge Island as a shining new Magic City landmark worried that the glamorous, headline-grabbing passenger ships might end up with the short end of the pier. A headline in the *Miami Herald* posed the anxious question "Future Port Outdated Already?"

They were right to worry. Fraser had been more or less on his own with the *Nuevo Dominicano* in 1950. By 1964 five Miami cruise lines were running nine ships on short hops to the Bahamas or on longer Caribbean cruises, accounting for the majority of the 250,000 people passing through the old seaport annually. The congestion at the piers was getting to the point where traffic jams would block the cruise ships in for hours past their scheduled departures as nonplussed passengers lined the deck and scowled for shutterbugs dispatched by the local papers.

That the facility was built at all was a remarkable accomplishment, given the frontier-town tenor of Miami politics in those days. As one editorial put it, the project proceeded "in the classic Dade County fashion of an argument involving political pressures and real estate speculation." In a town notorious for its close ties between business, politics and organized crime, even the dirt being dredged from the seabed was contested, as officials tried to steer it to favored developers working on artificial islands of their own. "One term of office as sheriff of Dade County," the saying went, "and a man can retire." A project as massive, as rich and as headline-grabbing as the new seaport could easily have been ruined by graft and political infighting, but somehow it stayed on the rails. Looking back on those days, one Miamian intimate with county commission back channels reminisced, "We've got more than our share of crooks, but if I ever saw an example of government working for the community, it was the county commission of the sixties, when they were sold on the idea of the port." The remarkable consensus on modern Miami's need for a new port kept things moving forward. The public optimism was palpable; even the press couldn't keep its tough stance for long. "South Florida Gaining as Hub of Hemisphere," the *Herald* crowed in a banner headline anticipating the success of the new port's cargo arm. Reporters waxed positively giddy at the thought of the town's reaping vast new income as a key transshipment point for millions of tons of freight flowing between Latin America and the U.S. "Dodge Port Taking Shape," another headline reported as work approached its end. "Rosy Future Predicted."

Barely a year before the new passenger terminal at Dodge Island was completed, though, disaster struck the young cruise industry. In the autumn of 1965, just as the high season was ramping up, the *Yarmouth Castle*—Frank Fraser's old *Evangeline*—caught fire and sank between Miami and the Bahamas, killing ninety-one people in what remains one of the worst sea disasters in modern U.S. history. As regulators and an appalled public took their first real look at the cruise business in the aftermath of the sinking, many of the people who'd been so enthusiastically focused on the new port, the new cruise market and the new Miami were suddenly forced to confront the fact that most of its ships were in fact very, very old and operating with virtually no oversight.

Ironically enough, the thirty-eight-year-old ship had just come out of an extensive refitting. A new operation, Yarmouth Cruise Lines, had bought both the *Evangeline* and its sister ship, the *Yarmouth*, the previous year, renaming the *Evangeline* the *Yarmouth Castle* and marketing the two ships as "twin sisters." *Yarmouth Castle* was in poor shape, however, and after canceling several cruises due to maintenance issues, the new owner sent it to Tampa for a multimillion-dollar overhaul on the advice of his general manager, an elegant, intense young Korean War vet named Edwin Stephan, who would later found Royal Caribbean Cruise Lines. Supervised by Pete Whelpton, Stephan's operations chief, the shipyard replaced the archaic refrigeration system and refurbished the generators and steam turbines. When the work was finished, the ship sailed for Miami to pick up a load of passengers for the Bahamas run, and Whelpton, eager to get back to his wife after weeks away, went back to his hotel to pack up and catch a flight home.

He was preparing to leave when the call came in from Stephan: there were problems with the wiring involving small flash-fires, and the chief engineer wanted Whelpton aboard to help him evaluate the situation. Stephan told him to get the next plane to Miami and catch the *Yarmouth Castle* before it sailed that afternoon. The taxi from Miami International Airport pulled up to the pier just as the ship was easing its way out into the channel. Whelpton watched it steam into the distance, little knowing that his lateness might well have just saved his life. Several years later, the folk singer Gordon Lightfoot wrote a song about the disaster whose opening lines capture that moment perfectly:

> *Well, it's four o'clock in the afternoon and the anchors have been weighed*
> *From Miami to Nassau, she's bound across the waves.*
> *She'll be headin' south through Biscayne Bay into the open sea.*
> *Yarmouth Castle, she's a-dyin' and don't know it.*

Stephan sent Whelpton home to see his wife, with instructions to catch an early flight to Nassau and sail back to Miami with the chief engineer. It was the middle of the night when the phone on his bed table jarred him from his slumber. "I'll never forget," Whelpton recalls. "Two-thirty A.M., my phone rang. It was the Coast Guard telling me that my ship was in the Florida Straits, on fire."

Officials later estimated that the blaze had broken out sometime around midnight, in a stairwell near the front of the vessel. There it spread, undiscovered, until a quarter to one, but word didn't reach the bridge for another twenty-five minutes. In the words of one historian, "The ensuing minutes—and even hours—were marked by a terrible breakdown of proper marine safety procedures and protocols." The radio room was one of the first spaces to be struck, knocking out the ship's ability to call for help. The Coast Guard first heard about the unfolding emergency from a passing freighter whose lookout had seen the flames on the horizon and began steaming to the aid of the burning vessel. Another of Frank Fraser's old ships, the *Bahama Star*, had left Miami on the Nassau run not long after the *Yarmouth Castle*, and it, too, was soon racing toward the violent orange glow. Approaching the scene, the *Bahama Star*'s crew and passengers gathered at the rails, aghast, and watched the growing flames cast more and more light upon the dark ocean.

By the time Whelpton got the news—more than two hours into the fire—the evacuation of the *Yarmouth Castle*, such as it was, had barely begun. Along with Stephan in their offices at the Port of Miami, he was ultimately able to have a brief conversation with the captain, but learned little about what was really happening out there. "The captain couldn't say anything, because everybody in the whole world now was listening," he remembers. "The ship's on fire, and all the captain would say is, 'My crew did a wonderful job. They're very brave people.' "

The record indicates otherwise. Of the ninety-one people who died that night, only two—a doctor and a nurse—were members of the ship's crew. The *Yarmouth Castle*'s passengers were largely left to their own devices in what was a worst-case scenario, to say the least. Many of the ship's lifeboats had been rendered unworkable, careless deckhands having covered their riggings in so many layers of paint over the years that they might as well have been welded to the davits. Others lacked oarlocks and foundered in drunken circles as their terrified occupants tried desperately to paddle away. Passengers later spoke of fruitless searches for life preservers in their cabins and on deck.

The captain himself, a young Greek named Byron Voutsinas, would face searing criticism during the subsequent investigation for allegedly abandoning the ship in a lifeboat early on in the disaster. He returned after making contact with the freighter, however, and would strenuously insist that his only purpose had been to secure the assistance he'd been unable to request from the engulfed radio room. Other accounts would claim that the freighter's captain, disgusted, turned Voutsinas away. According to one, his second mate had seen him leaving in the empty lifeboat and shouted after him, "Come back and help passengers! Remember the penalty for this!"

Not in dispute is the fact that Carl Brown, captain of the *Bahama Star*, looked over the rails at one point during the chaos to see a *Yarmouth Castle* lifeboat making its way toward him half empty, with only crew members aboard. "Return to your ship and pick up more passengers," he yelled at them through his bullhorn, enraged. Brown himself would later be hailed as a national hero for his conduct. "Listen to me," he shouted to the terrified tourists clamoring at the *Yarmouth Castle*'s rails. "Our boats are coming to you. Go down the ropes hanging over the side or jump in the water. Be careful that you don't land on other people." Brown pulled 367 survivors out of the water, bringing the *Bahama Star* so close to the burning ship that the paint on his smokestack blistered from the heat. The freighter that had first called in the fire rescued another ninety-two.

Those who could hear Brown's instructions were, of course, the lucky ones. Many people, sleeping soundly after an evening in which drinks had flown liberally, were trapped inside the burning ship before they even understood what was happening. The public address system failed utterly, and there was no organized, cabin-by-cabin alert. "I thought it was a couple of drunks," recalled one man who'd been fortunate enough to be notified. "But after the shouts continued I went out into the lobby. I was surrounded by flames." Another passenger opened her cabin door to see a woman running past her in hysterics—totally nude—shrieking, "My baby! My baby!"

The *Yarmouth Castle* could almost have been designed to burn, the blaze tore through the old ship with such speed. "It had a wood-framed deck, with layers of canvas that had all been painted," Whelpton would later recall, shaking his head. "It went up like a tinderbox—*phoom!*" Not even the sprinklers worked, despite the fact that someone had had the presence of mind to pull the fire alarm early on. Whelpton later worked out that they'd been disengaged—a revelation he kept to himself. It was the unofficial practice aboard to divert the sprinkler system's saltwater intakes into the swimming pool to fill it up before reaching Nassau. Later, hearing a friend describe one of the night's weirdest scenes, Whelpton would feel a sick chill of recognition. "He said to me, 'I'm walking along the decks and the water is up to just below the knees. The funniest thing, Pete. The swimming pool was filling, the ship was burning, there was no sprinklers working—and the swimming pool was filling. It was so strange.' And I just looked at him, but I knew why. The minute he said it, I said, 'Oh, my god. I know what happened.' "

The ship sank just after six A.M., settling with its victims on the seabed eighteen hundred feet below. It's virtually impossible that any of them drowned, the heat and flames had been so intense. Later that morning, when Whelpton flew over the site where the *Yarmouth Castle* had vanished, he recalled, "You could see the salt water bubbling where the ship went down— that's how hot it was."

National attention was focused on the Port of Miami in the wake of the tragedy. Labor unions, already edgy in the face of the fast-vanishing jobs in the transatlantic trade, were quick to point out that the *Yarmouth* was Panamanian registered, flying a "flag of convenience" that allowed its owner to escape taxes, labor laws and safety regulation in spite of the fact that it sailed from an American port and catered to a market made up almost exclusively of American passengers. Pitching Congress on his plan for a new cabinet-level transportation department, President Lyndon Johnson used the *Yar-*

mouth Castle disaster to help make his case at his State of the Union speech that year.

Unsurprisingly, Yarmouth Cruise Lines did not survive the incident. Other cruise lines weathered the disaster, but the formerly promising winter season of 1965 turned out to be a lean one all around.

The timing felt particularly unlucky for Frank Jr., and Lew Fraser, who less than a month earlier had signed the papers for the ship they hoped would be their family's triumphant return to the cruise business. "When the *Yarmouth Castle* fire hit," Lew remembers, "the market went kaput. It disintegrated. But we were stuck with the ship, so we brought it in anyway."

In fact, the disaster may have done more to help their fledgling operation than to hurt it. If any ship in Miami was well positioned to survive the subsequent regulatory and public relations scrutiny, it was the one they'd chartered, a near-new car ferry from Israel named the *Nili*. Because it was up to the latest international safety standards, the *Nili*'s youth became its biggest selling point in a market where old tonnage was suddenly deeply suspect. And the Miami establishment, committed to the cruise industry by this point, gave it all the help it could. "At the very moment while you read this through the Miami Beach sun," one local paper breathlessly reported, "a new cruise ship is hurrying to reach Miami in time for the holiday cruise season." The reporter went on to observe that the *Nili* was "not only one of the newest ships operating from this port, but also one of the fastest" and touted "up-to-the-minute safety." Comfort, too, would be assured even in a heavy sea, thanks to twin stabilizers built into the hull. The Frasers marketed their ship aggressively as "The Newest, the Nicest, the *Nili*," and after a difficult few months, they were "packing them in like sardines."

After their father had sold Eastern Steamship, the brothers stayed close to their roots, keeping an office in the old Port of Miami to manage the family's other concerns—the bananas, the freighters, the hotel—just up the stairs from the rooms where Ed Stephan and Pete Whelpton ran their operation. By 1965 much of the estate had been liquidated and distributed to Fraser's heirs and beneficiaries. That the brothers had been able to do this with "zero tax consequences" was a point of pride, but with that work finished, they were casting about for a new venture—and with a good amount of ready capital in hand. "I used to see these ships—they were packing them aboard," Lew remembers. "My brother and I, we said, 'Why the heck don't we get back involved with the cruise business?' "

In the summer of 1965 the pair entered talks with Somerfinn Car Ferries, an Israeli company run by a man named Meyer Halevy. Halevy had taken delivery of the *Nili* that same year with the intention of running a ferry service between Haifa and various European cities. He hadn't met with much success, however, and was facing serious financial pressure—although just how much, the Fraser brothers wouldn't learn until it was too late. They arranged a one-year charter on the 518-passenger ship for about nineteen hundred dollars a day—a "ridiculously low rate," as Lew Fraser put it. Halevy sent the son of one of his cousins, Meshulam Zonis, a bullnecked, improbably short young clerk from Romania, with the ship to act as his representative. Zonis, a ferociously intelligent man whose genius for tightfistedness would become legend on the Miami docks, spoke at least eight languages, all of them with hands gesticulating wildly in every direction, his words wrapped in an accent that many found all but impenetrable. He was Somerfinn's man, as he announced, there "to protect their interests, that something will not get broken, that they will not do conversions that are against the safety and security rules and regulations and all that."

The *Nili* began on the Nassau run in December 1965, with Pete Whelpton as the new line's general manager. Retracing the last steps of the *Yarmouth Castle*, the crew must have felt at first as if they were sailing through a graveyard but the world soon moved on. By summertime the Frasers were already talking about bringing in a second ship. It would have to be modern, they agreed, like the *Nili*. Somerfinn had a similar vessel in its fleet, but it was unclear at the time whether or not the ship would be available for charter. It turned out not to matter. Fate was about to force the Fraser family right back out of the cruise business.

After an unsuccessful three-week trip through Europe hunting for another ship with the same Israeli broker who'd found him the *Nili*, Lew got an unsettling message from his attorney in Miami: there was trouble, and it was coming up fast. As a prelude to renegotiating the *Nili* charter, Lew had directed the lawyer to look into Halevy's business more closely. He'd been hoping to find an edge at the bargaining table, but what he discovered cut both ways. "His whole empire, he had problems all over it," Fraser recalls. "And my lawyer, he says, 'Don't do anything with these ships, because you're going to wind up in a heck of a mess.' His whole empire was crashing down around him." The *Nili*, they discovered, was likely a few weeks away from being seized at the pier in Miami to service Halevy's mountain of bad debts in Israel and elsewhere.

Appalled, Fraser contacted Halevy directly and arranged to see him in Switzerland. The following year's charter rates were the ostensible reason for the meeting, but the crucial point was finding a way to exempt the *Nili* from any claims the creditors on a Somerfinn bankruptcy could advance. Fraser recalls that good-faith negotiations went to numbers as high as thirty-two hundred dollars per day—nearly double what they'd been the year before—before they broke off. Fraser was willing to meet his price, but not without a guarantee that he and his brother would be able to hang on to the ship if Somerfinn failed. The Israeli government held the second mortgage on the *Nili* and had already expressed its concerns that Halevy might try to take the ship to a free port in Central America in the event of bankruptcy rather than surrender it. They were watching, and ready to pounce at the first sign of collapse. Halevy was unable—or unwilling—to offer the security the Frasers demanded, and the negotiation concluded with the termination of their charter.

The brothers searched for another ship as good as the *Nili* but couldn't find anything that met their criteria. At the brink of real success, their business had collapsed as quickly as it had begun, and there wasn't a thing they could do about it.

Back in Israel, however, unexpected events were taking shape. Desperate as Halevy's situation was—Whelpton described him as "hiding out in a basement" toward the end—a last-ditch prospect had come up just as he and the Frasers were parting ways. Halevy had been contacted by a mutual friend: there was a little-known Israeli businessman, the friend explained, recently returned from New York and flush from selling out of an airfreight consolidation company he'd started and taken public. He'd heard about the *Nili* and had expressed an interest. The guy's name was Ted Arison. Would Halevy see him?

CHAPTER THREE

DODGE CITY

All you need in this life is ignorance and confidence;
then success is sure.

—Mark Twain

Decades later, long after Carnival Cruise Lines had made Ted Arison one of the very richest men in the world, people trying to describe his personality would again and again settle on a single word: optimism. The hardball, the penny-pinching, the no-free-lunch contracts that would later give Carnival such power to intimidate and command respect, these would all be associated with other members of the organization—never Ted. That was just the kind of guy he was: always the good cop, the closer, carrying himself with a courtliness and quiet charisma and that masked both the precariously narrow margin of his early days and the hard edge that won him his riches. *Optimism.* Looking at the deal Ted ended up making to take over the *Nili*, it's easy to see why he needed so much of it. It's unclear whether or not he'd grasped just how precarious Meyer Halevy's finances had in fact been, but even if Ted had believed them to be rock solid, the charter would still have been a huge risk for him. What did he know about running a cruise ship, of all things? He was a cargo man—in *airplanes*, no less. But he was an optimist. He had a feeling. And he got into the cruise business, sinking everything he had into chartering a ship from a company all but guaranteed to go belly-up before the year was out. And he never looked back.

For this son of an old-time Israeli shipping family whose star had faded, the move was actually a homecoming of sorts. Before the war, when Ted was a boy, the Arisons had been wealthy shipowners in Palestine and Europe. On the eve of the Nazi invasion of Yugoslavia they made a desperate run to the airport; a family agent had secured the last seats on the last plane to Haifa. "If we hadn't made that last flight," Ted would later remember, "we would have been in the Holocaust." Having narrowly escaped, he turned right around and got as close to the conflict as he could: sixteen years old, he lied about his age to join the British army's Jewish brigade. "I just have to go out there and kill as many Germans as I can," he'd remember thinking. "Period!" When he wasn't fighting, he was working with underground factions to smuggle the displaced Jews of Europe into Palestine under the noses of the British. V-day didn't end Ted's war. He went on to fight in the Israeli independence movement—not only against the armies of Israel's neighbors in 1947, but also as a guerilla fighter with groups known for demolishing bridges and blowing up hotels and barracks in their efforts to chase the British out. Ted's father died not long after the war, leaving him very well off and in control of the family business. As Ted would later recount, however, he wanted to be a self-made man; he disposed of the family's assets, turned most of the income over to his sister and mother, and set out on his own.

His first effort, a cargo shipping line not unlike his late father's business, did well for a time, but Ted put too much faith in a market vastly overinflated by the Korean War. He bought too many ships too quickly, and the business disintegrated not long after the cease-fire. In subsequent years he drifted to New York as a manager for El Al's air cargo operation at Kennedy airport—Idlewild, they called it in those days. Living sometimes in a house on Long Island and sometimes in a three-bedroom apartment on Queens Boulevard, Ted worked long hours, perhaps in part to avoid the pain of the troubled marriage that was just about the only thing he and his first wife had in common. He was getting by, but he was aimless. As a child he'd wanted to be a great concert pianist—a "national treasure"—not a businessman, but his career had always been in the gritty, practical side of commerce and transportation. In later years, when he had all the money in the world at his disposal and every opportunity to pursue deferred dreams, he would lavishly endow a symphony for Miami, but he never took up music again. His homes all had grand pianos, but they were mechanical; they played themselves. Ted's son would later say that although he must have heard his father talk about his childhood fantasy a thousand times, he never once heard him play.

Once Ted had learned the ropes in New York, he and a partner started their own company consolidating airfreight, and were quickly making good money. They took the company public in the early sixties, and then his part-ner bought him out for several million dollars. As part of the deal, Ted had signed a noncompetition agreement that obligated him to spend at least four years away from the airfreight business, and so the plan was to return to Israel and "retire" on his windfall—which is to say, to look around for some new venture to invest it in. With the kids out of school for the summer, the family packed their worldly belongings into forty-foot shipping containers and pre-pared for the trip, only to learn on the eve of departure that Ted wasn't going with them. He'd sunk his money into a pair of cruise ships, he told them; he was going to Miami, instead.

It was a rash decision, but not quite so very rash as it sounds. Purely by co-incidence, Ted had actually been aboard the *Nili* the year before, in the Ba-hamas. He'd flown to Nassau on business to see a refrigerated shipping company he'd considered getting involved with and happened to be traveling with an engineer who'd worked on the *Nili* in Israel. The ship was in Nassau that day, and they stopped by the pier to have a look. Meshulam Zonis, Halevy's representative, was living aboard with his wife at the time and was only too happy to take a fellow countryman on a tour of his domain. The little man, brimming with vitality and competence as he ran through his endless anecdotes and jokes, had made an impression on Arison. So had the ship. When he heard it was coming on the market, he jumped. Had he been privy to the same information as Fraser, Ted almost certainly would have walked away, but he wasn't—and didn't. With a low price on the table and the memory of that hot, blue day gleaming in his mind's eye, Ted quickly arranged to take over not only an immediate charter on the *Nili* but also—sight unseen—on her newly available sister ship, which would be available in the fall.

Before finalizing the charters, he purchased the *Nili's* sold-out winter and spring bookings from a skeptical Lew Fraser for about thirty-five cents on the dollar. He also hired Zonis away from Halevy, gaining not only a manager with firsthand knowledge of the operation but a man who, he would later learn, had an encyclopedic memory for facts and details as well as a unique ability to "make a nickel sweat." The two were a sight walking together along the Dodge Island waterfront: one tall and quiet, with crinkling eyes and slen-der pianist's fingers at his sides, the other a miniature tornado, voice career-ing from whisper to shout and back again as his stubby arms waved, grabbed, poked to make a point. Much of Ted's future success would depend on Zonis's gifts, and Zonis in turn came to look on his boss with an almost fanatical respect. The two would be inseparable for the next thirty-five years.

Lacking the money to set up a freestanding operation, Ted found a spare room in the dockside offices of a longshoring company run by a family of self-described "tough Jews" who liked the fact that he was Israeli. They gave him a break on rent and helped him when it came to dealing with the unions. By the end of September, Ted had several weeks of sold-out sailings under his belt—and it was still the slow season. The second ship would soon be on its way, and winter was sure to bring more passengers than even both vessels together could hope to handle. Any satisfaction he felt was born of blissful ignorance, however, for back in Israel the wolves were closing in. By Thanksgiving Ted had lost his ship, his investment—everything. Halevy's company imploded, just as Lew Fraser had feared, and true to its word, the Israeli government seized the *Nili*, tying it up at the dock until further notice.

Things went even worse with the other ship, which had run into a string of luck so bad it was almost impossible to believe. As often happened in the shipping business in those days, labor troubles had come first. Arison may not have grasped the seriousness of Halevy's predicament when he cut his deal, but the maritime unions in Israel had, and refused to allow the ship to sail from Haifa unless Arison deposited guarantees against the crew's payment—guarantees he had no way of paying. The country was in a severe recession at the time, however, and faced with the prospect of finding work among the hundreds of thousands already jobless in the shoreside economy, the crew defied their union's orders and slipped the ship out of port in the dead of night. Their victory was short-lived; stopping in Naples to prepare for the Atlantic crossing, the ship collided with another in the harbor and was seriously damaged. Days later, Ted found out about Halevy and realized it wouldn't have mattered anyway.

The despondent Ted had experienced career reversals before, but nothing of this magnitude. To fail so quickly in such a large enterprise was nothing short of devastating. He should have known better. From the greatest success of his career, the optimist had gone to his biggest failure in an instant, and now he was facing not only humiliation, but also the strong likelihood of personal bankruptcy. Even Lew Fraser had gotten thirty-five cents on the dollar for his bookings. Ted had nothing; he was so broke that he had to take up a collection to buy turkeys for his crew before laying them off. Ted was in no mood for a graceful exit. "When Arison finally went belly-up with the ship, all the travel agents came to him," one former colleague recalls. "And they said to Ted, 'Yeah, but what about our deposits for tickets, cruises or everything?' He said, 'Go see the government of Israel; ask them for the money.' "

Thanksgiving dinner, held at the home of Ted's attorney, Gene Hyman, predictably started as a depressing affair. Not one to dance around a delicate subject, Hyman began pressing his friend and client on his future plans. "You've still got the business," he said. "Why don't you charter another ship?" Pushing his food around on the plate, Ted admitted that one possibility had surfaced, but quickly added that he didn't see how anything could come of it. He'd had news from a shipbroker in Israel—the same man who'd taken Fraser around Europe the previous summer, in fact—that a vessel much like the *Nili* may have recently come on the market in Norway. Unbeknownst to Ted, Fraser had already expressed interest in the ship and had asked the broker to keep him in mind if it ever became available. But whether through luck or connections, Ted had gotten the word first. He was right about one thing: his ability to buy the vessel was more than a long shot. He was an unknown in the shipping industry by that point—or at least he hoped so, because his two shipping ventures had hardly been the sort on which to build a reputation—and in any case his finances had been reduced to almost nothing. He wasn't sure, he said, if he was even going to bother contacting the Norwegian owner. Hyman's excitement was building but Ted waved his urgings away.

Zonis has lost track of how many times he's told the story of what happened next. "Ted says, 'There is a ship, but who will trust us? Who will believe us?' So he said, 'There is these owners in Norway, and they have a ship; the ship is in Bergen, and doing nothing. But *I* cannot offer them *nothing*!' So he says, 'I have a plan, because I don't sleep nights now, but how would I go? I don't have even the money for the telephone long distance to Norway!' So Hyman says, 'Pick up my phone and call them.' "

In fact, just talking about making a deal had begun to cheer Ted up. The two of them waited and talked at Hyman's place until the wee hours of the morning, when the business day in Europe was beginning, and Ted went ahead and made his fateful call.

The Norwegian's name was Knut Kloster, and Ted could hardly have picked a better time to reach out to him. Even as the call found him in Oslo, the young chief of one of Norway's great shipping families was struggling with a crisis of his own. Kloster was another cargo man who'd made an unhappy foray into the passenger trade—spectacularly unhappy, in fact. Ted's ship had been taken from him because he'd failed to sufficiently vet an unscrupulous business partner—a sad tale, but common enough. Kloster's venture, on the other hand, had run afoul of the caprices of Western Europe's last fascist dictator, General Francisco Franco of Spain.

Like Ted, Kloster had started with a sound enough concept. Flush with cash from a booming tanker market in Norway, Kloster had ordered a passenger ship with an eye toward diversifying his fleet. It was a savvy move; few businesses are more cyclical than oil shipping, and moving a chunk of the profits into something steadier made a lot of sense. Kloster had designed his ship, the *Sunward*, as a car ferry, with the idea of carrying vacationing Britons on weeklong cruises from Southampton, England, to the empire's tiny outpost of Gibraltar on the southern tip of Spain, where they would disembark with their cars and tour southern Europe on a motoring holiday until they were ready to meet the ship and sail home again. It wasn't a cruise ship, exactly; though it catered to holiday travel, the *Sunward*'s primary function was still transportation. Still, it featured bars and a restaurant and overnight cabins, offering plenty of opportunities for people to spend money aboard. Kloster took delivery in late spring of 1966—the same time as Ted was negotiating to take over the *Nili*—and the summer's first voyages were a great success, with the ship sailing full in both directions. But by midseason, the forces of history had intruded.

Franco was by now an old man, in the last decade of his life. Since having come to power in the Spanish civil war, his regime had survived Hitler, the Allies, a postwar expulsion from the United Nations, and the long decades of the Cold War. Franco was now determined to satisfy his lifelong obsession with seeing Gibraltar returned to Spanish hands. In this, he was staking his claim to a long tradition in his country, and it's easy to understand why. Gibraltar overlooks the straits that bear its name, a stretch of water barely eight miles wide at its narrowest point and the only passageway between the Atlantic and the Mediterranean. Control of Gibraltar meant immense military and economic influence in the region. Posturing across the Spanish border, with actions that ranged from diplomatic pouting to military invasion, had been perennial since Britain seized the strategic peninsula in the early eighteenth century and made it a bulwark of its Mediterranean sea power. Each Spanish attempt had been beaten back, however, and 1965 saw British guns and ships still in command with no intention of giving it up. It wasn't exactly an occupation; the following year, in a referendum on whether to rejoin Spain or remain under British control, Gibraltar's citizens would reject Franco by a vote of 12,138 to 44. If he could not impose his will through force or appeal or popular opinion, the generalissimo decided, then he would isolate the territory. The border was closed indefinitely; even the telephone lines were cut.

The plight of flustered British tourists being turned away from checkpoints manned by the aging strongman's army hardly ranks as one of history's most dramatic moments, but in its own way the scenario does a fair job of capturing the absurdity of that dwindling dictatorship in a world that had outgrown it. It must have been quite a sight: lines of family automobiles snaking back from the fortified frontier for hundreds of yards, horns tooting confusion and displeasure, as travelers watched their ship sail slowly away without them.

Kloster didn't see much humor in the situation. For him, it was the second blow to fall on his new business in short order. He'd already been coping—barely—with the UK's having unexpectedly decided to tackle a domestic financial crisis by putting limits on the amount of currency British citizens could take out of the country. The new ship's summer honeymoon was officially over. When the phone rang on Kloster's desk that morning in November, the *Sunward* had already been sitting dockside for weeks with no prospect of making enough to even pay off the interest on its financing.

After introducing himself, Ted launched directly into the pitch that he and Hyman had been refining all night. "You have a ship," he began. "We know she's doing nothing. We might wind up doing something great for each other." Ted could sympathize, he said, better than anyone. His own predicament was a mirror image: Kloster had a ship with no passengers; he had passengers without a ship. They were both victims of unforeseeable circumstances. What had happened with the *Nili*, Ted continued, was no more his fault than the *Sunward*'s situation was Kloster's. "All kind of vendors, they are dying to do business with me. They know what happened; it all happened in front of their eyes," he said. "I have passengers, I have cargo, I have work, I have crew," he said. "I have the organization waiting. I need only the ship." Never mind Gibraltar, Ted wheedled. There was more money to be made in Miami than Kloster could possibly imagine. This was a moment for both of them: "If you can get on a plane—even if today—come here, and I'll put you in touch with all the people. This cannot be explained by telephone. You have to see it with your own eyes."

Two days later, Kloster and his operations chief, Kjell Nielsen, stepped off a plane at Miami International Airport, scanning the crowd in the terminal and trying to identify the stranger who'd called with such an interesting offer.

Kloster's visit was an almost miraculous second chance, but there were still a million ways for it to go wrong. He and Ted were perfect for each other, as far as that went, but Kloster had the stronger negotiating position by far. The *Sunward* was a thing, a great big object of steel that, although it may have been costly to keep out of operation, would nonetheless remain much the same in a week or a year. What Ted had to offer was extremely perishable. His whole side of the negotiating table consisted of little more than a delicately constructed, temporary web of commitments from passengers, suppliers and crew—none of whom would wait around very long for a cruise line without a ship. Kloster was hurting, true, but his main business was still in oil; the success or failure of the *Sunward* wasn't going to bring him down. Even if Ted did succeed in selling Kloster on the idea of Miami cruising, he'd only be halfway home. He needed any deal to take place almost immediately, and there was no way of predicting whether Kloster might take his time in making a decision—or worse. There were other successful cruise operators in Miami, after all; the Frasers were desperate for a ship, and they were hardly alone. If the Norwegian decided he didn't like what he saw in Ted, there was nothing to stop him from simply getting someone else.

The fact that everything was riding on this meeting was almost too much, even for Ted. Meeting Kloster and Nielsen at the airport, some of his anxiety must have revealed itself. From the first handshake, he came off as gloomy and withdrawn, and the conversation in the car was flat as he drove them to their hotel. After making plans to meet first thing in the morning, Ted went back to his little apartment, shoulders slumped. The visitors retired for the night with serious doubts about the man they'd flown halfway around the world to meet.

Things went much better the next day, however. The first order of business was a tour of the tiny Arison Shipping Company offices—quickly accomplished—and discussion of the *Nili*'s performance, which was as impressive as the office was shabby. Early on, Ted wisely introduced his secretary and future wife, Lin, whose good looks and sunny manner went some way toward establishing the rapport that had been missing the night before. From that moment on, everything went right. True to his word, Ted had managed to round up the *Nili*'s food, beverage, entertainment, slot machine and gift shop concessionaires. In the hectic, catch-as-catch-can life of the Miami docks in those days—"mobile communication" was a matter of how much legwork you could coax from whoever answered the pay phone on the pier— getting all those people together at one time for just about anything was like getting cats to march in a parade, but Ted managed it, despite the fact that he hadn't known a single one of them for longer than three months. He'd prepared a powerful presentation. Each concessionaire outlined in some detail the numbers they'd been making on the *Nili* and spoke of his willing- ness to work with a new, Arison-operated partnership. "It was Ted Arison with his salesmanship," Zonis would later recall. "But he also was not by himself. All these concessionaires said they were ready to sign the agreements because they know that this is going to be the answer for a good trade, with a future."

Afterwards, Ted led Kloster and Nielsen across Biscayne Boulevard for a tour of the old seaport. For Kloster, one look at Miami's fleet of aging clunkers—some of them dating back to the 1920s—was at least as com- pelling as any sales pitch Ted could make. Kloster's sleek, modern ship would make them look like old jalopies in the Monaco Grand Prix. This was com- petition so far behind the times that it was better than no competition at all: if people paid good money to sail on those things, he thought, just wait until they got a look at the *Sunward*. As he looked back over his shoulder at the city, Kloster's eye settled on the Dade County courthouse, built forty years earlier as the tallest courthouse in the south and still cresting Miami's skyline. Then he looked back at the ships. This was a town, he marveled, with serious room to grow.

Finally, the three of them crossed the newly built Dodge Island Bridge to meet with Miami's recently appointed port director, a retired navy admiral by the name of Erwin Stevens, and Stevens's right-hand man, a jolly but fiercely ambitious young engineer named Carmen Lunetta. There was nothing on Dodge Island at that time but a little office tower, some scattered cargo sheds, crude outbuildings and one or two gantry cranes. Along with a half-finished passenger terminal, the sparse structures stood against a backdrop of con- struction equipment and piles of asphalt. The very ground they were built on was literally fashioned from sand dredged out of the seabed to deepen the channel for the larger vessels everybody hoped would soon be coming to town. There was little about the place that felt sleek or modern, despite the promises of Operation Magic Wand. It felt rough, like a working port—not a launching pad for a trip to tourist paradise. But each one of them could smell the potential in the air as surely as the tang of hot tar that wafted over them. At the landfill's gravelly edge, they stopped to stare down the channel toward the open sea. Ted stood back and waited to see if the two Norwegians, the old admiral and the fidgety young engineer, would be able to hammer out a plan.

He could hardly have known it at the time, but if there was one way to sell Knut Kloster on something, it was to dress it in visionary robes, to give it the gloss of a progressive future. Kloster was a dreamer, too, although he lacked Ted's hard edge. An unusual free spirit in Norway's reserved professional environment, he'd joined the family business in his twenties after graduating from MIT, a young idealist full of fire and liberal thinking in the heart of the Norwegian establishment. The Kloster fortune had begun with his grandfather, who in the days before refrigeration had made his living shipping loads of ice from northern Norway. Kloster's father had grown that business into an empire of oil tankers to rival that of any of the world's seafaring nations. Kloster was barely thirty when his father's death in 1959 left the reins of the company in his hands, and in many ways he had never lost his student's fervor for new ideas. He believed that he was living in exciting times, that capitalism, done right, could change the world. Speaking for the family's third generation in the public eye, Kloster sought to establish a bold new legacy of his own—to bring in more riches, yes, but more important, to have a hand in shaping the coming era.

However much of this—if any—Ted had intuited on the waterfront that day, the master salesman was smart enough to know when he'd played his part and it was time to let the others do their work. Kloster and the admiral understood each other right away; Stevens was passionate about tying Miami's future to what he saw as a promising new seagoing leisure trade. True, Dodge Island lacked a finished passenger terminal, he explained, but Miami was at a crossroads. Big things were in store. The city had already grown at an astonishing rate since the end of World War II, and with a new, modern port, the sky was the limit. The new Miami was going be a gateway for holiday traffic sailing out from the north and cargo coming up from the south, Stevens promised, and new entrants could rely on his support. Relationships with the county commission were good, and for once Miami's sluggish, can-tankerous and often corrupt politics was lined up firmly behind developing the port. His bold claims made all the more convincing by his military speech and squared, compact stance, Stevens assured Kloster that the right hands were holding the purse strings; with the port's friends in high places smoothing the usual delays in getting out contract bids and issuing revenue bonds, he said, Lunetta could get anything built in record time. The young engineer, talking a mile a minute and sketching blueprints in the air, mod-estly agreed: if Kloster committed the ship, he'd have a terminal. And as for Ted, Stevens assured Kloster that he'd seen his operation at work in the weeks before the *Nili* had been arrested. The man, in his opinion, seemed to know how to run a cruise ship.

It was a moment to remember. Five short years would see the two dream-ers arrayed against each other in a bitter combat of litigation and low blows, but for now they were coming closer and closer to a partnership whose early life would be defined by amity, high-mindedness and financial success be-yond their wildest expectations.

The numbers looked good, and the idea of captaining so new an industry was as irresistible to Kloster as it had been to Ted. Standing there on the rough edge of Dodge Island's fresh concrete apron with men he'd known for all of thirty-six hours, Kloster agreed to start a new chapter for himself and his family—but on one condition. Terminal or no, the *Sunward* was to berth on Dodge Island when it arrived, not at the old port with Miami's other pas-senger ships. Kloster was for the future, not the past. He was going to put Miami on the map.

As Lunetta remembers it, the asphalt outside the terminal was still cooling under his feet when the *Sunward* steamed into Miami three weeks later to be-gin its tenure as the flagship of Norwegian Caribbean Lines (with Arison Shipping Company as managing agent). With the clock ticking on Ted's bookings and Kloster losing money every day his ship stood still, everything about the process had been fast. Only four months had passed since Ted first signed the unlucky charters in Israel. The *Sunward* sailed out again on De-cember 20 for an inaugural Christmas cruise, and it was just as well that the *Nili* wasn't around; the *Sunward* was both newer and nicer.

The arrival of NCL that winter was the tipping point for the cruising business. Old-timers and the ship-obsessed would fondly recall Fraser and some of the other pioneers, but billions of dollars and tens of millions of passengers later, Ted Arison and Knut Kloster would be remembered as the modern cruise industry's founding fathers. For one thing, NCL was soon making a hell of a lot more money than anyone else in Miami ever had. Getting Kloster to fly over on a hunch may have been Ted's miracle, but with the company up and running, it was Christmas all around. Under Ted's management, the ship was earning more on its weeklong runs to Jamaica than Kloster had ever hoped to earn shuttling British retirees to and from southern Europe.

The partners had arrived at something along the lines of a franchise arrangement. Kloster owned the ship and the company name; Ted ran the hotel and entertainment side of the ship day to day, handled the marketing and dealt with the travel agents. He used his own staff and concessions for everything but the maritime personnel, who were Kloster employees working under Kjell Nielsen, who moved to Miami and took up a bristly and suspicious residence in Ted's offices. Ted collected the money and deposited the receipts, minus his cut, in an account linked to Oslo and periodically sent the balance sheets and budgets to Kloster for approval. Zonis's function having been more or less usurped by the Norwegian management, Ted set him up as the head of a new Arison Shipping subsidiary set up to handle the stevedoring, longshore and cargo work for the *Sunward*, with NCL as its only client.

Cruises on the *Sunward* sold as fast as Ted's people could take the orders; passengers rolled into the Port of Miami by the hundreds in their tail-finned Buicks and Chevrolets. Almost immediately, Kloster began funneling his profits into more ships. Rather than chartering or buying older vessels from other shipowners, the typical practice at the time, he put the capital reserves from his tanker business to work building them from scratch and sent them to Miami as quickly as he could. In New York Harbor, the greatest passenger port in the history of the world, passenger shipping executives were somberly inscribing their own tombstones, but Miami was absorbing new tonnage at rates no one had seen since the war. After the *Sunward* came the *Starward* and then the *Skyward*, which an overjoyed Kloster asked Lin Arison to do him the honor of christening.

With success came friendship between the Israeli and the Norwegian, and their families. When Ted's sister married, Kloster was one of the four men holding up the huppah. A bond also developed between Kloster and Ted's young son, Micky, who'd remained in boarding school outside New York when the rest of the family had returned to Israel in 1966. As graduation approached, Micky Arison had begun coming to Miami for his school vacations, and before long, between courses at Miami-Dade Junior College, he was spending his summers running bingo games and shore excursions as a member of the NCL cruise staff. Like his father at his age, Micky found himself the son of a thriving shipping man and deeply ambivalent about his place in the family. He had no aptitude as a student, but he was smart, and Kloster's ideas excited him. As the political climate of the Vietnam era continued to intensify, he sometimes identified more with Kloster's worldview than his father's. "I was very, very antiwar," Micky recalls. "Kloster was right on my wavelength. He used to stay at my father's house, in the days before it got negative. We used to stay up all night talking until all hours in the morning. He was very into philosophy and the peace movement and all this kind of stuff that a young kid who was very idealistic at the time was into."

Sporting love beads and shoulder-length hair, Micky began spending more and more of his time on the ships, living a wild and happy life. He'd always been painfully shy, and the sun and freely flowing rum and the rest of it helped him come out of his shell. To his father's undisguised chagrin, Micky soon dropped out of junior college and took a full-time job on the NCL cruise staff. Ted, who between his work and his marriage had always been a distant father, decided to take a hand. "If it had been totally up to me, I'd probably still be on the ships," Micky recalls, sitting at Ted's old desk years after his death. "I completely loved it, but my father basically threw me off. He said, 'You're getting too attached to it.' There was just too much alcohol, too many women, too much fun. And he was getting very nervous. I got very tight with the cruise director on the ship; we were very close friends, and he had a drinking problem, and I could quickly see that if I had stayed, I probably would have wound up with one, too. So he got me off the ship and got me to go back to school."

These were the years when Kloster was at his best. Between Ted, Nielsen and Zonis, NCL's day-to-day operations were well in hand, and the young industrialist was free to explore his idealistic impulses. For Kloster, the new business wasn't just a company; it was a laboratory of ethics and philosophy—and nowhere more so than on the subject of NCL's corporate citizenship in the Caribbean.

Though he loved the modernism of the new ships, Kloster couldn't shake a certain ambivalence about the cruise business. A committed progressive, he had always held that capitalism had not only the ability to improve society, but the obligation to do so. Here he was, finally part of something new, but at the end of the day he was still ferrying suburbanites on frivolous voyages that ended exactly where they began and left little by way of a meaningful or lasting impression. The islands of the Caribbean, he fervently believed, were home to vibrant, contemporary cultures—not just fun-and-sun playgrounds for fat Americans to visit and photograph. They were real places, he fumed, with real people living there and facing real problems—not the "happy natives" his incurious passengers were expecting. Though he held his tongue in front of the customers, privately Kloster savored the mottos of Jamaica's left-leaning politicians, a favorite being "To Hell with Paradise." It was the era of the civil rights movement, and Kloster wanted to use his cruises to help bridge the gap between the sanitized world of his almost exclusively white, middle-class passengers and those of the black people who populated the so-called paradises where a family's annual income could be far less than the price of a single cruise. His ultimate goal was nothing less than world peace. He discovered a kindred spirit in Herb Hiller, the press agent for Arison Shipping and now NCL's jazzy vice president of public relations. With the help of his new friend, Kloster began cooking up ways to encourage his passengers to interact on a deeper, more challenging level with the people and places they were visiting.

The pair would philosophize endlessly in fertile, zany sessions at Hiller's Coconut Grove home, quoting the Kennedy brothers to each other and returning again and again to RFK's principle, better known today as "doing well by doing good," that "There is no basic inconsistency between idealism and realistic opportunity." Outwardly different in their appearance, the two of them were nevertheless cut from the same cloth. Kloster preferred to dress in the brown suits and skinny ties of the day's European intellectuals, keeping his hair neatly trimmed and letting his words and his intense liquid blue eyes proclaim his radicalism. Hiller, you could peg from a mile away. He'd developed into a full-fledged hippie as the sixties wore on, and corporate VP or no, he wore "a full flowing beard and has the evangelical fervor to go with it," as the *New York Times* put it in a profile.

Nothing was out of bounds as they puzzled out the tensions of their trade. Kloster drew in equal parts from his high-mindedness and the borderline hostility he felt toward his passengers. One brainstorm came as the result of a scene he'd witnessed on a tour of a Jamaican coffee factory where ancient black women sat on the floor sorting beans as the tourists shuffled through, gaping and whispering to each other. To Kloster, it felt like a zoo; worse, it took the dignity of labor and turned it into a spectacle. He wanted to turn the thing on its head. "Of course, our passengers wanted to take pictures," he remembers. "To create some kind of balance between these old ladies sitting there with their coffee beans and these American passengers coming in with their condos, it was suggested we should give all the ladies an Instamatic camera." Why not let his passengers be photographed? he thought. Let them see how they liked it. Needless to say, a number of such crackpot ideas never quite got off the ground.

The biggest success to come out of the Coconut Grove discussions was a program instituted for the *Starward*'s Jamaican itinerary in early 1971, which Kloster innocuously dubbed "New Experiences." It was an intriguing concept and got a lot of positive attention. With the cooperation of the Jamaican tourist board, NCL arranged for a Jamaican "family in residence" to sail gratis aboard each cruise; in return, they were to make themselves available as ambassadors of Jamaican life and culture. "The passengers will be invited to meet the Jamaicans informally, to dine together, drink, dance and play together, to ask questions and pump them for all kinds of information in friendly conversations with no holds barred, including political and racial problems," an editorial in the *New York Times* reported. "They will try to explain Jamaica by displaying Jamaican books, newspapers and magazines, costumes from various sections of the island and some of the genuine native handcrafts—none of this for sale, only for show-and-tell." In addition, arrangements were also made to provide local tours guided by the ship's Jamaican room stewards and waiters, who were given a mandate to show passengers the "real" Jamaica. A crew member might take his charges "to visit his home, to visit the ships, to meet his friends, neighbors and relatives, to walk around downtown and ride up into the lovely hills that rise sharply behind the coast." Perhaps the most interesting—and promising—element of the entire experiment was "Meet the People," where passengers could sign up to spend the day with Jamaicans with whom they had a shared professional affinity—doctors could meet doctors, teachers could meet teachers, and so on, to spend an afternoon in conversation.

Of course, there were problems on both sides of the starry-eyed program. Then as now, the middle-class Jamaican families Kloster had envisioned—

the teachers, small-business owners and public officials deemed "articulate enough to communicate"—were in short supply, thanks to the country's dismal economy, and the legions of unemployed, uneducated shantytown and rural poor who made up most of its population were just a little too, well, *Jamaican*. The tourist board soon ran out of qualified families, putting an end to one aspect of the program. Moreover, as the novelty wore off, a deeper issue emerged: Kloster and Hiller had envisioned the programs as an antidote to the legacy of colonialism and the unequal power dynamics and cultural perceptions it had engendered. But for all the good intentions of New Experiences, the end result was that many of these problems were simply playing themselves out in another way.

For the Jamaicans, there was an inescapable subtext: if you're black and from the Third World, however much you elevate yourself in your own community, the best you can hope is to be a walking public service announcement for curious American eyes. It was one thing to make spectacles out of illiterate coffee workers, and quite another to do so with the society's elites. Despite an outward vocabulary of respect, there was a presumptuousness all its own in the notion that legions of Americans should be allowed into the private spaces of Jamaican homes and businesses week after week simply because they might find the experience fascinating. By the same token, there was hardly a surplus of Jamaican crew excited about the idea of spending the one day they had in their homes each week with the same passengers they'd worn themselves out serving.

Outright contempt among some in the Miami offices didn't help things. The *New York Times* may have praised the program, but Florida was still the Deep South, and Kloster's efforts were unfolding in the middle of the most racially charged period in American history. "Not all our people in Miami appreciated what we did," he remembers. "One of the most influential people in our organization referred to this program as the 'Take a Nigger to Lunch Program.' "

Hiller, certainly, was hardly the man to convert such skeptics. His love-child affectations didn't help him, and as time went by the internal memos he distributed grew stranger and stranger until they eventually featured what has to be some of the weirdest prose produced in the annals of corporate America. NCL's vice-president of public affairs wrote like the Maharishi with an MBA. "We know the cruise package is a saleable format," he began, normally enough, in one 1970 memo to Ted. Then he went off the rails. "We see only what we approach," he went on. "We are the sum of our experience, funneled into the nose cone of our coming. That nose cone has behind it a bomb of incredible magnitude. It is a potential culture obliterator. It comes zooming, buzzing, hovering around in an environment. It bobs about, like some visitor on a strange planet, wondering about all the forms and shapes and impulses around it from the senses of its most advanced state. It is a vast energy package."

What really doomed the program, though, wasn't any of these difficulties, which, really, were to be expected in so ambitious an effort. New Experiences died in 1971 when a rift opened between Kloster and Ted—slowly at first, and then so sudden and severe that it threatened to destroy the company almost overnight. And when it hit, there would be no time to attend to anything else. In a flash, Kloster would see his world at NCL transformed from a utopia of backyard philosophizing with Hiller into a parade of courtroom appearances and desperate scrambles to keep his company alive. It would be years before Kloster would again have the opportunity to indulge his ideals with the attention they deserved.

By then, the world would be a very different place.

But back in the late 1960s all that upheaval was yet to come, and NCL was riding high. Kloster's Miami success hadn't gone unnoticed back home, in the exclusive, old-world confines of the Oslo Shipping Club, where the men who controlled the Norwegian bulk and tanker trades gathered to sip drinks, exchange gossip and contemplate their floating empires. Over lunches on the top floor of an office building in downtown Oslo, the chiefs of the country's shipping elite had watched NCL's operation unfold—with skepticism at first, then with growing interest. The group's smartest members were already wrestling with the double-edged nature of their own success. After World War II, a maritime tradition dating back to the Vikings had helped make Norway into the world's foremost seafaring nation, while thanks to newly discovered oil reserves this land of fishing villages and valley farming towns was fast growing into one of the richest societies in the world. In spite of their new prosperity, however, many old-line Norwegian shipping families felt exposed. In a culture that prized steadiness and self-reliance, dependency on the volatile politics of oil had troubling implications. "In the tanker and bulk market, you have no influence at all," the head of one firm reflected. "It's a cyclical market that depends on factors over which you have no control—whereas in something like the cruise industry, you have an opportunity to create something which is not in the same way dependent on outside factors."

Norway's lead in the shipping industry was not in jeopardy, but even under ideal market conditions, low-cost competitors in Southern Europe were impossible to ignore. The Greeks, especially, were geniuses at running ancient tonnage no one else would touch—and at a steep discount. Rumblings coming out of the Far East were also cause for long-term concern. Diversifying into new businesses, if it could be done right, held real appeal. However, the steady, pragmatic Norwegian temperament was hardly suited to running pleasure ships for Americans, whose tastes ran to excess, nor was it inclined to embrace unnecessary risk. For all its drawbacks, the oil trade was still a known quantity, and in business, especially, the Scandinavian outlook has always tended toward conservatism. Even with ready cash to invest, many of the Shipping Club's members felt there was as much risk in entering what they saw as the highly litigious and unpredictable U.S. business environment as there was opportunity. There was no doubting that Kloster had struck gold in Miami, but he'd done so only by lending his ships to a ready-made operation geared to the American market—a once-in-a-lifetime circumstance. If the idea of getting into cruising tempted the Norwegians, it was also something they had no intention of leaping into blindly.

Across the Atlantic, however, news of the Norwegians' interest—cautious as it was—had reached one Miamian who'd been harboring big ideas of his own ever since the *Yarmouth Castle* had gone down on his watch.

When Pete Whelpton picked up the telephone jangling on his office desk, the voice on the other end carried the same mix of urgency and poise as it had on the day it had ordered Whelpton back to Miami, too late, to help troubleshoot the doomed cruise ship.

"Pete," the voice said in its familiar Midwestern lilt. "I want to show you something." Ed Stephan, Whelpton's old boss, had hatched a plan.

Without any formal parting of the ways, the two had fallen out of steady touch since the fire. A Wisconsinite who'd decided to leave the farmlands and cold weather forever behind him, Stephan had come to Miami after a stint as an army radar technician in the Korean War. When the money ran out, he'd enrolled in hotel school on the G.I. Bill, and had worked his way up through the Miami Beach hotels during their heyday, doing everything from parking cars to overnight accounting work. He'd even dabbled in teaching night school and in spite of a painful shyness turned out to be as competent and effective at that as he was at everything else he tried. During the early 1960s he and a partner had won the lucrative parking concession at the Port of Miami, but after several months of an apparently endless war of attrition with a private garage down the street, he decided the string of scratched paint jobs, bent antennae, broken windows and openhanded, useless cops wasn't worth the hassle, and he advised the port to take the operation in-house, instead. That move had cost him quite a bit of money, but it had won him friends on the waterfront and helped establish his reputation. By the time he started running Yarmouth Cruise Lines, he'd made a name for himself as an honest, if eccentric, manager.

Tall and slim, with arresting blue eyes, Stephen had a country club regular's natty style of dress. No one would have called him outgoing, but he was universally admired by those who had worked with him. Whelpton trusted him implicitly. On entering Stephan's office—he always kept his door closed—it wasn't unusual to see his rangy frame hunched over a yellow pad, scribbling furiously with one hand as he held a pocket calculator in the other, working the buttons faster and faster with his thumb as he gained momentum on whatever problem engaged him. "His mind," remembers Whelpton, "worked like a computer. I told my wife, he's going to burn out one of these days. You're going to smell something, and it's going to be Ed's brains. Because it was so amazing what this guy could do." Something about him inspired loyalty, but charm would not be the word for it. One employee, shortly after his mother's death, received Stephan's awkward condolences through the crack of his office door, while he stood uncomfortably in the hallway outside. But he didn't mind. "Ed deserves to have that kind of idiosyncrasy," the man would later reflect, "because by keeping those kinds of distractions away from him, he's able to do great things." Even a disaster like the *Yarmouth Castle*, which was sufficient to end almost anyone's career, hadn't hurt his reputation—although years later he'd acknowledge that he was haunted by it. Not long after the fire, when a local hotelier started Commodore Cruise Lines, he wanted Stephan as his manager, and got him—for a while, at least.

Whelpton, Stephan's old operations man, had also tried to stay in the business after the accident but hadn't had the same luck. The Fraser brothers made him their general manager when they took over the *Nili*, but he'd barely settled into the rhythms of running the ship when Lew Fraser pulled him aside and told him the line was going under. Whelpton handed out severance checks to the crew, then took one for himself.

Stephan had wanted to tap him for Commodore but Whelpton, at heart a brawler with something of a bullying streak, had fallen afoul of the owner during a stint at one of his Miami Beach hotels, and the hire was declared out of the question. The depth of his boss's anger at Whelpton had stunned Stephan, who'd never been on the receiving end of his old deputy's brass-knuckles style of management. He called Whelpton, asking, "What the hell did you do to this guy?" Stephan, no social butterfly himself, couldn't have cared less; Whelpton may have been rough around the edges, but was a master of the intricacies of running a profitable hotel operation. If anyone had the background to know how things really worked, it was him: one year in the 1950s, before Whelpton had first gotten involved with the cruise business, he'd pulled down more money as a bellhop parking cars than the hotel's general manager had made in salary. After *Yarmouth*, Whelpton hadn't had much trouble finding a comfortable position managing another hotel on Miami Beach. The salary was good, and it came with free housing and swimming pool access for his kids. It was a position his wife didn't want him to leave, but then, she'd never worked for Stephan. When the call came, he made plans to see his old boss right away.

Arriving at Stephan's house, Whelpton found laid out on the floor—all over the floor—pages and pages of blueprints, covered in numbers and drawings and all manner of scribbled notes. "The whole time Ed was on the beach, on his living room floor, he was designing a cruise ship. He lay the drawings out and drew every day, every night," Whelpton would later recall. "His focus was scary in those days. He didn't want to watch TV, he didn't want to go to sports events, he didn't want to go to parties, he didn't want to do anything except focus on that business, on that project. Every waking moment that he wasn't managing Commodore he was drawing, looking for money, looking for people. He was like a man driven."

Stephan explained to Whelpton that he was looking at plans for the cruise ship of the future. He'd designed it especially for Caribbean cruising: light and fast to save fuel while steaming from port to port, and with a draft shallow enough to dock right at the piers in the small island harbors, eliminating the need for costly and unreliable local ferries to take passengers to shore from a deepwater anchorage. Problems with an old ship had almost driven them both out of the industry, Stephan reminded his colleague—had almost killed the industry itself. But look at how well NCL was doing now with their new ships—and even they were still working with tonnage designed to carry cars in the North Atlantic. Someone starting from scratch, he said, eliminating all the old inefficiencies, could make a killing. And that someone was going to be him.

The conventional wisdom among ship designers had always been to make staterooms as large as possible, since that was where the people would be spending most of their time during the rough North Atlantic crossing. Stephan reversed the equation. His ship would have smaller cabins than anyone had thought to build before, which would allow him not only to pack in a greater number of passengers—creating a "volume economy," as he called it—but to maximize revenue-generating public spaces like bars and gift shops and to foster a festive communal atmosphere on board by forcing people to walk around. His past never far from his mind, Stephan had executed his design with safety foremost: firefighting systems, watertight doors—everything was to be top of the line. Even the corridors ran the length of the ship so that in the event of an evacuation panicked and disoriented passengers wouldn't get lost on their way to the lifeboats. The finishing touch was to be a decorative superstructure inspired by Seattle's Space Needle—a sort of crown to ensure that the sleek new ship's profile would be unmistakable, the cornerstone of a powerful new brand. It would be like no ship anyone had ever seen, he said. He wanted to build three of them.

Despite assurances from a Finnish shipyard that such a vessel could be built without undue expense, the search for investors had so far been unsuccessful. Stephen had already been to Norway, drawn by its reputation for safe and diligent seamanship, but had gotten nowhere. The prospect of breaking into the Miami cruise market was tempting enough to get him through the door to see many of the nation's top shipping men, but again and again their innate conservatism sent away from each meeting empty-handed.

Stephan's break finally came thanks to lust and a padded expense account. As the story goes, a Norwegian shipbroker in New York at the time had been looking for a way to visit his girlfriend, a radio operator on one of the cruise ships sailing out of Miami, on his employer's dime. But what was there for a serious shipbroker to do in Florida? Complaining to a friend, the frustrated fellow heard about "a crazy guy in Miami named Ed Stephan, who's got an idea about these tailor-made cruise ships for the Caribbean." Why not fly down to Miami and interview him for your company, the friend suggested, and then take the cruise and visit your girlfriend?

After seeing the drawings—and his radio operator—the broker was sold. He brought Stephan and his concept back to Oslo, and this time, with a local hand to smooth the way, things fell into place. It was late 1967, and the timing couldn't have been better. Israel's Six Day War had sent tanker rates soaring, leaving the Norwegians sitting on even more liquid cash than usual and freshly uneasy about what to do with it. The windfall was great news, but no one knows better than a Norwegian that every summer has a tough winter following on its heels, and world events had once again underscored the industry's dependence on circumstances beyond its control.

Stephan's first few meetings in the second Oslo round went nowhere, as before. Then, unexpectedly, his introduction to one Sigurd Skaugen, a blustery, commanding grand old Shipping Club patriarch well into his seventies, turned into a six-hour marathon. Rich from the fat of the tanker trade, the Skaugens had actually had some experience with passenger ships carrying emigrants from Europe to Australia after World War II. Although that business had soon dried up, they'd liked it and for some time had been looking for a way to profitably return to it. Like his counterparts, Skaugen had been hungrily eyeing the profits Kloster was bringing home from Miami, but he seemed to lack the gene that was keeping so many of them on the sidelines. He was getting to be an old man and had little patience for wasting time. A few hours with Stephan convinced him that he was looking at a unique opportunity to take the lead in a new Norwegian industry. Toward the end of the session, as Stephan was still wondering what to make of this atypical Scandinavian, Skaugen's top technical officer passed in the hallway outside. Speaking for Stephan's sake in his imperfect English, the old sea dog yelled to his deputy then and there that "We shall into cruise!"

But not right away. In order to defray the considerable expense and risk of Stephan's proposal, Skaugen wanted to bring in a partner. After casting around for a while, he cut a deal with a friendly rival, another family firm named for one of Skaugen's contemporaries, Anders Wilhelmsen.

The Skaugens and Wilhelmsen would take equal shares in the new company, which would be named Royal Caribbean Cruise Lines. They agreed to build two of Stephan's new ships, and possibly a third if things went well. Operationally, Royal Caribbean would be organized much like NCL. The Norwegians would own the vessels and the company and supply the marine personnel; Stephan would run the operation out of Miami as president, a Royal Caribbean executive rather than an independent agent—a crucial difference, as it later turned out.

The news spread quickly through Europe, where a real passenger ship hadn't been built for years. Shipyards from around the continent bid for the contracts, and Stephan spent much of 1968 flying between Miami, Italy, Germany, Norway and Finland, frustrating his employers at Commodore Cruise Lines to no end, but somehow hanging on to his job there until the new venture firmed up. By autumn, the bidding was down to the Finns and an Italian yard, neck and neck in terms of both pricing and financing. The Norwegians had a strong preference for their fellow Scandinavians but were running the auction for all it was worth. The day they closed the deal, the Finns were in Skaugen's Oslo offices going over their offer for the umpteenth time. The Norwegians were ready to sign, but so long as the shipyard didn't know that, they planned to continue pressing for concessions, with Skaugen in the next room on the telephone, using the Italians as leverage. The back-and-forth might have gone on for hours more if it hadn't been for one of the Finnish executives' sharp eye. Making a trip to the bathroom, he noticed a Skaugen secretary ascending a stairway carrying a silver tray full of champagne glasses. In an instant it dawned on him—concessions or not, these guys had no intention of going with the Italians! His bladder forgotten, he raced back to the conference room before his team could give away another point.

"No more haggling!" he yelled as he burst through the door. "No more haggling, I've seen the champagne!"

Delivery for the first of Stephan's ships, the *Song of Norway*, was scheduled for October 1970 at a cost of just over $13 million. Returning to Miami after the negotiations, Stephan immediately tendered his resignation to Commodore, put Whelpton back on his payroll and set about assembling his ideal cruise operation. Once again, however, Whelpton's personality got in the way. Gruff, swearing and swaggering, he'd impressed the Norwegians as "a typical American with boots and spurs, coming across and not using knife and fork properly." Word came down from Oslo that the ownership didn't want him in the company; Stephan used their refusal to draw a line in the sand. Nonconfrontational to a fault on most occasions, he turned Whelpton's hire into a major issue, demanding that the Norwegians leave day-to-day operating authority in Miami—and respect his decisions whether they agreed with them or not. It was a brave stance: with the contracts signed, he no longer owned his design, and the Norwegians could easily have disposed of him. But they agreed to his terms, and Whelpton got the job, although the twelve-thousand-dollar salary he was offered meant taking a big pay cut on top of losing his rooms at the hotel. He never thought twice about it. "If I can feed my family," he told Stephan, "I'll go to work for you."

When it came to maritime matters, however, Skaugen made it very clear that the Norwegians would brook no challenge to his authority. Back in Oslo, he'd hired a former liner captain, Aage Lindstad, to command the *Song of Norway* when it arrived. In the meantime, Lindstad was dispached to consult with Whelpton and Stephan in Miami about shipboard protocols for the new venture. The three of them got to work designing uniforms, drawing up schedules, laying down the shipboard routines and in every other way building a brand-new cruise operation from the ground up. Everyone was excited; none of them had ever been given the opportunity to exercise in advance such complete control over everything from the ship's design to the menus to how much cash should be kept on board in the purser's safe. Stephan and Whelpton knew Caribbean cruising as well as anyone in the world, and Lindstad knew ships. Steps from the port, in a cramped two-room office furnished mostly with apple crates, they covered the walls with charts, lists, and diagrams laying out every detail just so, then tearing it all down again until it was perfect.

Turf fights between Lindstad and Whelpton broke out almost immediately. Even with delivery more than a year away, it was obvious that the shipboard chain of command was going to present a fundamental conflict. The emerging organizational structure was all but guaranteed to create a politics that pitted Lindstad's officers against Whelpton's hotel staff, the one group armed with a direct line to the ownership in Norway, the other with control of the new company's revenue generating operations.

Sensing that they were staking the boundaries of their future fiefdoms, Lindstad and Whelpton circled each other like a pair of bull moose. Each privilege or responsibility accorded to their people on board became a signifier of their respective statuses within the company, from big issues like salary, shore leave and cabin allocation to the countless tiny perks and disciplines to be left to the discretion of the ship's captain—Lindstad himself, in this case. They called their list of rules "the Bible," but it was more like a constitution for a self-contained, intensely political society. Whelpton, already on thin ice with the Norwegians, lost many of these fights, and petty though they may seem now, each defeat rankled bitterly. The Norwegian deck and engine crew, for example, would wear gold stripes to mark their rank; the hotel officers would wear silver. "You could be a three-stripe hotel officer," Whelpton would ruefully recall years later, "but you were still a *silver* three-striper." Well into the 1990s, resentments born during these sessions would play a significant—and often destructive—role in the life of the company.

With strong support both from Stephan in Miami and the owners back in Oslo, the issues dealing strictly with maritime personnel were mostly sorted out within a month or so. There was a logic to thinking of them as a different class of employee. From a technical point of view, at least, many of the Norwegian officers would have more or less the same responsibilities as they would have working on a freighter. As far as they were concerned, the cargo just happened to be different. Much to their chagrin, however, their bosses didn't see it quite that way. Back in Norway the seafarers were forced to suffer though seminars designed to polish their less than courtly social skills. These courses covered "every aspect of passenger interface, from conversation, social niceties, stage presence and dancing to American table manners and knowledge of food and wine, as well as insights into American history and society." The charm boot camp's final exam was a dinner dance in Oslo, with delighted female volunteers from the American embassy rating the sailors' performance. All too happy to be done with the training, Lindstad soon afterwards flew to Finland to supervise the completion of the ship.

Stephan and Whelpton, meanwhile, were preparing their side of things in Miami. As the delivery date approached, the staff rapidly outgrew the tiny office they'd rented; Stephan, focused as always on the shipboard product to the exclusion of just about everything else, looked up from his sketches long enough to find a trailer somewhere and have it attached to the back of the building. With a month to go, Whelpton hired his hotel staff—mostly West Indians willing to work for far less than the "exorbitant" salaries Americans demanded. Carpenters built mock-ups in an empty warehouse in Miami, and with stopwatch in hand Whelpton drilled his people for weeks, as relentless as any field marshal. Timed to the second, waiters carried trays around corners again and again at full tilt, developing the instincts that would keep them from colliding in the ship's narrow gangways as they raced to serve hundreds of hot meals. Room stewards practiced loading and unloading simulated baggage under the same scrutiny. Those were long, brutal days, and more than a few didn't make it through. "I got mad a lot," Whelpton remembers. "And when I got mad, guys got fired."

Fireworks lit up the sky when the *Song of Norway* sailed from Dodge Island on its November 7, 1970, maiden voyage. The space needle Stephan had originally envisioned had morphed into a Frisbee-shaped lounge built into the smokestack, where passengers could sip cocktails from the highest point on the ship. It gave the ship an unmistakable profile, and for years Royal Caribbean advertisements showed only a close-up of the stack, sandwiched between the company logo and a single line of copy urging readers to "Sail a skyscraper." Inside, the ship was decorated in the era's bold colors and the glass-and-metal modernism of Scandinavian industrial design. Scooped chairs upholstered in green leather ringed the dining room tables, framed against walls composed of alternating hardwood and mirrored panels. In the lobby, concentric circles exploded in blacks and yellows from the bright red carpeting. At the center of the room, a standing floral arrangement reached up toward its own reflection in a huge mirrored disc set into the wood-paneled ceiling. The cabins were indeed tiny, but neatly so—carefully designed to take advantage of every bit of space. To offset any disappointment at their size, Stephan stocked them with more than sixty complimentary items, from playing cards to Hershey bars to bottles of premium shampoo stamped with the Royal Caribbean logo.

The *Song of Norway* carried ten thousand passengers in its first five months, selling out its cabins on every voyage. By late 1972 Royal Caribbean had all three ships Stephan had hoped for, and the company was sending millions of dollars back to Norway at the end of each year. The results exceeded even Stephan's expectations. Aside from a bare minimum of ads in the trade press and with the local papers in Miami, Royal Caribbean hardly bothered to advertise at all for almost ten years after the *Song of Norway* first came to Miami.

The ships were selling themselves.

~

Meanwhile, NCL was fast coming to the end of its salad days. It wasn't the competition; there was more than enough demand for this new kind of cruise. And it certainly wasn't the money, which was still coming in plentifully. At least, it hadn't started with the money. NCL had been enjoying phenomenal success by any measure, but almost since Kloster had first dispatched the *Sunward* to Miami, tensions had been mounting between the Norwegians—working under Kloster's operations head Kjell Nielsen—and Ted's people. To some extent, the conflicts played out along the same lines as the power struggles between Whelpton and Lindstad at Royal Caribbean, but things soon passed the point of healthy competition. Happy as they were with Ted's results, Kloster and his people had a strong nationalistic streak that revealed itself in everything from the company name to Kloster's barely disguised contempt for his passengers. They chafed at the idea of their business being in American hands, and micromanagement from Oslo was soon chipping away at the company's reserve of goodwill. "The tail was wagging the dog," one executive there at the time remembers. "They really wanted it to be a Norwegian-run company." Ted and Kloster continued to enjoy the same fond relationship they'd built up over the course of their five years together, but somehow the rapport between their subordinates had become toxic.

By 1970 things had degenerated to the point where Kloster and Ted decided to look outside for help. At considerable expense, they arranged for their Norwegian and American executives, along with the captains and chief engineers from the various ships, to attend a seminar led by a self-styled management guru named Jerry Barnum. The group gathered at one of Miami's top hotels for several days of harangues, interrogations and exercises at the feet of the wise man. Barnum's philosophy of "directed energy" was a striking departure for the taciturn Norwegians and the hard-bitten, fast-talking Miami men alike. Colleagues who'd come to dislike and distrust one another spent their afternoons in "walk and talk" sessions where small groups from the various factions would stroll together and discuss the issues hanging in the air between them. In the conference room Barnum reigned supreme, playing the parts of ringmaster, drill sergeant and psychiatrist with equal relish. He reduced a few executives to tears; others simply sat stone-faced, waiting for the indignity to end.

Memorable though they were, the sessions were a Band-Aid on a bullet wound. Things got better for a short time, but resentments proved too deep, especially among the Norwegian faction. The inevitable showdown had merely been deferred.

The endgame began soon after the conference, when Nielsen began raising questions about Ted's handling of company funds. Kloster's representative in Miami had always felt there was something not quite right about the way the Israeli was running things, but he'd never been able to determine what it was. Eventually, Kloster gave him permission to initiate an investigation. What followed would tear the young company apart and leave a black mark on Ted's reputation for decades.

Even today there is widespread disagreement as to whether Ted had actually been cheating Kloster, although no one disputes the fact that he took highly unorthodox liberties with his financiers. Duke Hatfield, the auditor who alleged Ted's handling of the NCL finances made him "the biggest crook in Miami," is certainly exaggerating, but on the other hand even Micky Arison's defense of his father hinges on the very technical assertion that money *owed* to NCL did not yet *belong* to NCL.

The controversy revolved around the advance payments, which in the cruise business are known as the "float." Especially in those days, when information moved at the speed of pens, paper and operator-assisted rotary phones, it was common for passengers to book and pay for a cruise as early as a year before sailing. Under the terms of his contract with Kloster, Ted was responsible for collecting those deposits. Once a given cruise was over, he sent the money to Oslo, but by that time it had been held in a Miami account for a year. As the operation grew, the size of the float grew with it, and soon it was adding up to millions and millions of dollars—just sitting there.

For someone like Ted Arison, the situation was tantamount to blasphemy.

"What Ted said to himself is, 'Well, here I'm sitting with X millions of dollars of permanent money. Rather than just have it sit there and not earning, I'm going to invest it,' " Micky remembers. "And he invested it in cargo ships, he invested it in real estate, he invested in lots of stuff."

In other words Ted was treating the float as his personal venture capital fund. It was a perfect system, so long as his investments stayed profitable enough for him to send the money to Oslo at the end of every cycle, and so long as he—and not Kloster—went on holding the deposits between the time of collection and when the cruises actually took place. The only thing that could go wrong was if something or someone somehow diverted the flow of deposits on the back end. As Nielsen's investigation got under way, however, that was exactly what happened.

New to the cruise industry, the Norwegians hadn't quite grasped the concept of the float at first, and the balance sheets Ted had been sending them didn't make things any clearer. According to Kloster, the advance cash Ted was playing with was masked in a mixed account that blended the money actually in Ted's possession with the money still owed as the balance of cruise payments. Lumped together under the heading "accounts receivable," it was all but impossible to distinguish what was where and who was in control of it.

As more ships were added to the fleet, however—and as more loans were taken back in Oslo to finance them—Ted's bookkeeping came under increased scrutiny. Kloster was the shipowner, after all; any liability for canceled cruises or other problems would fall at his doorstep, not Ted's, and he felt that he needed to be protected. The arrangement depended upon a certain amount of naivete on the part of the Norwegians, and accounts suggest that Ted may have overestimated just how long that innocence would last. It was Nielsen who first became suspicious of the situation, only too happy to have a concrete issue to focus the frustrations that had been simmering for so long. He quickly voiced his concerns to Kloster, but it took time before the seriousness of his allegations penetrated.

Kloster's first response was to confront Ted with the allegations. Ted, stalling, immediately went on the defensive, trying to undermine the credibility of Kloster's deputy rather than addressing the issue itself. "Arison attempted to manipulate Kloster," remembers one Kloster attorney close to the events. "At first Arison told Kloster, 'I think you'd better send this fellow to a psychiatrist or something, because I don't think he's mentally on track.' " "The dancing around continued for a while," one of Nielsen's people remembers. "There was one thing, I would say, that probably was the biggest asset of Ted Arison: his mouth. He was a salesman. He could talk his way into anything, out of anything."

But a swift tongue can go only so far. Undeterred, and with alarm in Oslo growing, Nielsen finally got the authority in 1971 to bring in a team of outside auditors. Even then, Kloster was hoping to find a reasonable explanation for the discrepancies. "I didn't know then if it was theft," recalls the lead accountant on the audit. "All I knew is it was unaccounted-for assets of the

Klosters." But as the details of Ted's arrangement unfolded, it became clear that there was a serious discrepancy between what he had told the Norwegians and what was actually happening with their money in Miami. All told, nearly $7 million was missing—more than two-thirds of the company's annual revenues.

Backed into a corner, Ted insisted that it was all a misunderstanding. As managing agent, he argued, the float was his until the cruises were completed. "As long as he paid it," Micky says, "the reality was, he had all the right in the world." In fact, Ted argued, not only hadn't he tried to *hide* his activities—he'd offered Kloster a share in every one of them, out of a sense of obligation to their partnership, and had been turned down on almost every occasion. Appalled, Kloster countered that he'd had no idea that the risky propositions Ted was forever proposing were being funded with his own money.

Kloster responded by demanding that Ted turn the float over to him. "It had worked fine as long as the agreement was ongoing," Micky remembers. "At the point that Kloster started to threaten to cancel the agreement, and that money would have stopped, Ted was in deep shit." Through intermediaries, the two tried to negotiate a payment plan. Ted agreed to dispose of some of his other assets, but only on the condition that he retain control of the float in order to ease himself out of them. Sudden liquidation was out of the question, he explained—it would put him out on the street again. It became clear that the parties had reached an impasse. Kloster didn't trust Ted to handle his money, and Ted didn't trust Kloster to stick to any compromise once he'd gotten his money back. Each believed the other was acting in bad faith, and the lawyers soon took over. But Ted, who knew he stood little chance of coming out well from a lawsuit, had no intention of waiting around while everything he'd worked for was taken away from him all over again.

Kloster's attorneys swore out a complaint in Miami, and a Florida judge immediately ruled that the audit's findings were sufficiently damaging to have the company placed in receivership, along with the float. The wheels of justice were too slow, however, and by the time the ruling came down, Ted had taken all the cash on hand in NCL's regional sales offices and closed out the company's bank accounts in Miami. Kloster came to Florida looking for his money, but Ted was already in Europe looking for another ship.

Before leaving, Ted had made an impassioned speech in the Miami office, promising that he'd be back with a new ship and pleading with his people to "keep the organization together." Few stayed with him, however, for reasons of self-preservation as much as out of ethical misgivings. Kloster moved to Miami soon afterwards to take over the NCL operation, and most among Ted's staff who were offered positions accepted them. The handful who remained with Ted watched balefully as the defectors filed out of the Arison Shipping Company offices to the space Kloster had rented a few doors down. The emotions of the moment were incandescent—especially for the Arison camp, which felt backed into a corner and had a hard time not taking it personally. "Myself and the ones who stayed, we viewed it as a loyalty thing," Micky said. "Everybody walked out of the office to say good-bye and go down the street to Kloster. I was trying to photograph those people in my mind as they went by; I still have those images. "

Ted wasn't the only one to have a brush with the law during this affair. Thrust into an unfamiliar operational role, Kloster was facing the direst of situations. It was bad enough that, with the deposits god-knows-where and under Ted's control, he'd have to carry his passengers more or less for free during the coming months. But Ted, who'd started from scratch with only the *Nili*'s bookings, had known where to hit for maximum effect. When he left, he also made off with the passenger lists and documentation for every advance booking NCL had. Without that information Kloster had no way of even knowing who his passengers were—or which berths for his upcoming cruises had been sold and which were still available. Running a business under those circumstances was impossible, a death sentence. The cash situation was painful, but Kloster could survive that. As long as Ted held those lists, however, he had NCL in a stranglehold. For the man who only a few months earlier had been quoting the Kennedy brothers and dreaming utopian dreams, it was a moment of truth. "We had to do something really dramatic," Kloster remembers. "This was life or death, and since Ted Arison, our impression was that he was trying to kill us by doing all this, we broke into his office at night and got all the printouts from all the machines."

Dodge Island had turned into Dodge City. All of this was impossibly foreign to the members of the cozy confines of the Oslo Shipping Club, but with the printouts in their possession, the Norwegians at least had a chance. Some of the missing deposits had been insured, but the payout was nowhere near enough to sustain the operation until income from new bookings could begin to replace the "permanent money" Ted had taken. Leverage from

NCL's rapid expansion was already alarmingly high, but survival would mean taking on even more debt. The banks in Norway already had tens of millions of dollars in ship mortgages riding on NCL's survival and quickly agreed to the bridge loan Kloster needed to make it though this period.

NCL survived, but Kloster faced a fearsome struggle in trying to take over the cruise operations while putting together new financing at the same time. During the months after Ted's departure, every day began the same way: with an update from his corporate attorney, who had been out looking for money to pull the company through.

It would be years before the former partners reached a settlement. The courts eventually ordered Ted to give back about 60 percent of what he had "seized," as the official Carnival version of the story describes his actions today. But by that time he was already well on the way to establishing his fortune, having put the NCL float to good use one last time.

Dizzying as the economics of the breakup were, the episode also had its share of personal pain. Notwithstanding the tensions that had strained the organization almost from the beginning, most who'd been there at the time recall a certain sweetness to NCL's early days: the ship, the offices, the wacky ideas—all of it suffused by a contagious pioneering spirit. In the course of the dispute, however, friendships that had grown around the business were damaged irreparably. Kloster, wearing his heart on his sleeve as always, felt utterly betrayed.

Some time later, as the breakup was unfolding in the courts, Kloster spotted Micky walking into an industry function. Agitated, he made a beeline for the young man who not so long before had sat at his feet in Coconut Grove, contentedly listening to predictions about the new world they would all create together. "He started yelling at me in front of everybody," Micky recalls. "He almost made it sound like he was upset that I took my father's side, because he thought we were friends." Micky had always liked Kloster, but this was business and he was his father's son. There was only one possible response: "I was like, 'What are you, crazy?'"

Kloster had also grown very fond of Ted's wife, Lin, during NCL's happy years—so much so that he'd asked her to be the godmother of one of his ships. Now that relationship, too, had to be abandoned. More than thirty-five years later, tears still came into his eyes when he recalled being forced to deal with "Lin, beautiful Lin" as an enemy by association.

And, of course, there was the genuine friendship that Kloster and Ted—

the two great optimists, one as bright as a diamond, the other as hard—had shared. It was gone forever. During the height of the litigation, the two bumped into each other in the men's room of the Dade County courthouse and, as was his wont, Kloster's emotions got the better of him. "Goddamnit," he blurted out. "Why are we doing this to each other? We *liked* each other."

Ted, already on to bigger things, walked out of the room without a word.

CHAPTER FOUR

MARDI GRAS ON THE ROCKS

If only God would give me some clear sign! Like making a large deposit in my name in a Swiss bank.

—Woody Allen

His stint operating the shining new ships of Norwegian Caribbean Lines having come to a screeching halt—and with a battalion of his former partner's lawyers clamoring for his head—Ted returned from Europe with nothing but his dreams and the deed to a dilapidated old tub he'd found in Greece. It wasn't pretty, it wasn't clean, and as subsequent cruises would prove, it wasn't even necessarily safe. You could have called Ted's new flagship an ugly duckling among Miami's modernizing flock of cruise ships, but even that would have been too generous. No one but Ted saw that kind of potential in her chubby, rusted lines.

"He'd told us he'd bought this incredible ship," remembers Micky Arison, still incredulous so many years and billions of dollars later. "It was such a piece of crap. It was dirty, in horrendous shape. I thought my father had lost his mind, basically." As one might expect, those less close to Ted chose their words less tactfully. And it was hard to disagree; the only place the ship wouldn't have stood out was in a junkyard. It looked more like a historical exhibit at an underfunded museum than the foundation for one of the twentieth century's great personal business empires.

But it was all Ted had. He renamed it the *Mardi Gras* and began preparing it to sail under the auspices of his new company, Carnival Cruise Lines. In retrospect, people would say that only a great optimist like Ted could have made a success of a ship like that. At the time, they said that only a fool would have bought it. Ted, undaunted, could hardly have cared less. The ink still wet on the pages of his brochures, he began touting the *Mardi Gras* as "the flagship of the golden fleet," blithely refusing to acknowledge the fact that, as one of his longtime lieutenants is fond of pointing out, "It wasn't golden, and there *was* no fleet."

No one had known what to expect after the NCL breakup. Ted's falling out with Kloster had earned him no small amount of notoriety, and in some circles his return to the Port of Miami had been eagerly anticipated. He'd done well there, after all. But this wasn't a ship—it was a joke. The port's Spanish-speaking workers quickly came up with an ungenerous nickname, *Mierda Grassa*, which translates roughly to "fat piece of shit." The notion that the *Mardi Gras*—though it was bigger than any other Miami cruise ship almost by half—could seriously compete with the gleaming white fleets of NCL and Royal Caribbean seemed laughable. Anyone still harboring doubts on that score joined the skeptical majority a mere twenty minutes after the *Mardi Gras* pulled away from the Dodge Island pier on its maiden voyage.

Ted was on the bridge for the occasion with the ship's captain, but as required by law, the ship was under the command of a local pilot until they reached open water. Clunker or not, a new cruise ship coming to town was still a big deal in those days, and the *Mardi Gras* had rated the Biscayne Pilot Association's senior member. A Carnival seaman was at the helm, taking his direction as Ted and the captain looked on. Micky was out on one of the bridge wings—a sort of observation balcony attached to the bridge—with a girlfriend, watching the little waves at the waterline whip in the stiffening breeze and mildly enjoying his father's folly.

As it approached the opening of the channel and prepared to head out into the open sea, the ship's movement suddenly felt wrong. At the same instant, Micky heard the exclamation from inside the bridge—a sharp, clipped, horrified *"Oh, my god."*

Panicked bodies jolted him from his reverie as they shoved past him to watch the collision. "I looked over my shoulder and I see sand flying out the side of the ship," Micky remembers. "That's when I realized."

Disaster. Ruin. Humiliation.

Within the hour, television and radio networks across the country were carrying the story, which was covered prominently in the *New York Times* and other national papers the next day. With good reason: a stone's throw from downtown Miami, with upwards of three hundred influential travel agents and a full complement of passengers aboard, the *Mardi Gras* had run aground.

Back in the NCL offices, where the Arison name was spoken in hisses or hushed tones if it was mentioned at all, a cheer went up at the news. Everyone ran outside to get a look. Kjell Nielsen, the Norwegian operations chief who'd endured the worst of it during Ted's maneuvering, gazed out at the foundering ship with a sense of deep satisfaction and clapped his boss on the shoulder. "Well, Knut," he gloated. "I give him six months."

For Knut Kloster, the emotions were more complicated. Still wounded and angry, he savored a certain sense of justice watching his former partner—his betrayer—endure so humiliating a debut. But justice doesn't pay the bills, and Kloster was in dire straits. No one knew better than he did that any chance of recovering his money rested on Ted's making some kind of success out of this new venture. Kloster was a sort of involuntary investor in that ridiculous ship, after all, and if Carnival went down, millions of dollars that rightfully belonged to him would go down with it irretrievably.

The lawsuit against Ted was proving to be as complex as Kloster had feared—a dogged slog though a morass of Swiss bank accounts and offshore holding companies. Before the case was over, its paperwork would break Florida records, jamming cabinet after cabinet in the Dade County courthouse's storage rooms. It was no accident that Ted's tracks were tough to follow. As their dispute had grown more and more heated in the weeks leading up to the breakup, the optimist had for once been busily preparing for the worst. Merely getting his hands on the money in the Miami accounts wouldn't be enough, he knew. The assets involved were huge—$6 to $7 million, an amount nearly equal to NCL's entire annual revenue at the time—and two things were certain: Ted was on dicey legal ground, at best, and Kloster would fight for the deposits with everything he had. Once open hostilities broke out, there was little question that the courts would order the funds either returned or placed in receivership pending the outcome of the proceedings. Ted could not simply use the money, even if he moved quickly, for anything he spent it on—a new ship, for example—would likewise fall under the jurisdiction of the Florida courts, and he'd be facing a lien before the paint dried. Having the cash didn't mean he'd be able to keep it, his lawyers advised him, especially if he wanted to continue operating in Miami.

And so the trail would have to be wiped clean. Luckily, Ted knew just the guy.

Movie buffs may remember Meshulam Riklis as "Mr. Pia Zadora," the billionaire accused of rigging the 1981 Golden Globe Awards for his then-wife, the twenty-five-year-old future B-list queen and Hollywood Squares regular. The business community knew him as a brilliant financial architect with a stage magician's gift for staying one step ahead of his audience—his bondholders, in the case of Riklis-juggled companies like Rapid-American, Faberge and the McCrory chain of dime stores. "Riklis Driving," the title of a Forbes profile, pretty much summed up the general feeling about the man's style. Born in Turkey, Riklis had immigrated to the United States from Tel Aviv in the late 1940s, making ends meet as a Hebrew tutor as he studied to become a securities analyst. Even in his hand-to-mouth days, he was always a man who knew how to make an impression. The rabbi who hired Riklis for the tutoring job as a hardship case, for example, remembers him showing up to work, just a few days after starting, in a stretch limousine. Questioned about his conveyance, Riklis explained that he'd met the president of Honeywell at a dinner party a few nights earlier, and he'd loaned him the car and driver. This was not a man who was going to be tutoring bar mitzvahs for the rest of his life. By 1955 Riklis had his first company chairmanship, and by the 1970s he controlled a debt-fueled empire worth $3 billion—on paper, at least. One of the architects of the go-go era of junk debt, he raised $600 million during the 1960s in the bonds he described as "revolutionary funny money," well before people like Michael Milken—a Riklis protégé—put the practice on the front pages.

Every step of his rise to power was steeped in controversy. It was during Riklis's chairmanship that Wall Street wags dubbed the Rapid-American Corporation "Rancid American." *BusinessWeek* made note of his "fecund financial imagination" and accused him of building his company on "a flimsy foundation of debt." Tracing the tendrils of his holdings, the *Los Angeles Times* would later uncover "a web of relationships that appear to benefit Riklis to the detriment of the company." It was, the paper said, "vintage Riklis." Some knew him as the "Nightmare on Wall Street." Ted, who'd known Riklis since their school days in Tel Aviv, just called him "Rik."

The Golden Globes affair came about in the early 1980s as part of Riklis's efforts to jump-start his wife's career. Thirty years his junior, Zadora had been a young star on Broadway when they'd met. Smitten, Riklis had begun his courtship when she was seventeen—as a millionaire "stage-door Johnny," hanging around after her performances. She held out until her early twenties, at which point the two entered into wedded bliss. After headlining for a while at the Riklis-controlled Riviera Hotel in Las Vegas and doing TV commercials for a Riklis subsidiary, Zadora got her big Hollywood break with the starring role in the 1981 box office bomb *Butterfly*, as a "nymphet who tries to seduce her backwoods father," as *People* magazine tartly summed it up. Riklis produced the picture. Up against a now-legendary debut performance from the likes of Kathleen Turner, among others, Zadora came out as the surprise winner of the "best new talent" award. The accomplishment was all the more remarkable given that *Butterfly* hadn't even had its U.S. release as of voting time.

Never let it be said that Riklis didn't love his wife. He adored her, fawned on her, and by all accounts they were great friends—even after she left him. In their palatial Manhattan apartment, the living room and dining room spaces were demarcated by an oversized statue of Zadora that her husband had commissioned. It was an eight-foot-tall nude done in shining gold. As per Riklis's request, according to the sculptor, the piece was "larger than life" in more ways than one. "He asked us to enhance it a little," he explained. "You should see the breasts!" It later came out that, in addition to hosting lavish advance screenings for them at his Beverly Hills mansion, Riklis had flown a large group of Golden Globe voters—mostly underpaid stringers and freelancers—to Las Vegas for an all-expenses-paid junket at the Riviera, ostensibly to "see Zadora perform" several months before the vote. Though the excursion fit—very technically—within the bylaws that governed the awards, the Hollywood press made a scandal of it, and the general feeling was that Riklis had bought the award for his wife. Thanks to this and other scandals, the Golden Globes would be a cynical joke to Hollywood insiders for years to come. Zadora, who quickly became a favorite target of late-night comedians, fervently denied the allegations. "You must know that such an award cannot be bought," she retorted. "That would ruin my husband's career." Notwithstanding his wife's concern, Riklis himself was unperturbed at what he called the "ridiculous" claims of tampering. So what if he had? He was in good company. After all, as he insisted at the time, "Bo Derek would be nowhere without her husband."

For a master numbers-spinner like Riklis, solving Ted's problem was hardly a complicated undertaking. "It wasn't a tough sell," Micky Arison remembers. "We gave him the money; he turned around and bought the *Mardi Gras*. That maneuver was just to keep Kloster from grabbing the money before we could buy the ship."

Capitalized more or less untraceably with the "seized" NCL funds, Carnival Cruise Lines thus came into being in late 1971 as a subsidiary of the Boston-based American International Travel Service, a Riklis company. Of course, "Rik" wasn't just doing charity work for an old pal. AITS had been marketing package tours to Europe as "Italian Carnival," or "French Carnival" vacations for years; a cruise arm seemed like a good fit, and the name was a no-brainer. With Ted's company, he was getting what promised to be a profitable expansion of his holdings, and at almost no risk to himself.

AITS left Ted largely on his own as he assembled his operation in Miami with the few remaining NCL people who hadn't gone with Kloster; it was known that he and Riklis were friends, and in any case no one there knew the cruise business any better than Ted did. Finally, in March, three frantic months after the breakup with Kloster, the *Mardi Gras* tooted its foghorn on a clear tropical afternoon and sailed out of Miami on its maiden voyage.

The AITS people hadn't expected to get their first update on its progress from the evening news. The ship had problems, they knew; no one had believed things would go as smoothly as they had for the custom-designed new vessels Royal Caribbean and NCL had been introducing. But a *grounding*? It was too much. Standing around the radio in Boston listening to coverage of the fiasco, dumbfounded AITS managers wondered just what the hell they had gotten themselves into. Fifteen hundred miles to the south, trapped aboard a foundering ship that had scarcely left the pier, Ted was asking himself the same thing.

In and around Government Cut, the channel leading from Dodge Island out to the sea, all hell had broken loose. As tugboats labored mightily to free the *Mardi Gras* from the sandbar it had settled upon, onlookers crowded the nearby roadways to watch the show. Some took to their fishing boats and pleasure craft for a better view, while the local press, for its part, embraced a story odd and ironic enough to thrill even the most jaded of newsroom hearts. At the other cruise lines, executives chuckled and shook their heads— *poor bastard*—until it dawned on them with a stab that their own ships, already full of new passengers, might be blockaded for the night.

And up on the bridge of the *Mardi Gras*, shattered, Ted Arison was watching the latest in a long string of last chances teeter on the edge of disaster and wondering just what a person had to do to get ahead in this world.

Other than opening the bars, there was little to be done until high tide, still several hours away. The ship was stuck, all right; Ted still couldn't believe it. The day had been particularly windy, which wouldn't have been a problem if the pilot, a Cuban, hadn't tried to get cute. A veteran tugboat captain and by all accounts a professional, he had nonetheless decided to honor the occasion with an unfortunate linguistic flourish. He'd directed the ship's all-Italian crew out of the Dodge Island jetties in the usual way. With the dock cleared, a simple turn where the channel doglegged was all that remained to set the ship on a clear course out to the open sea. "Turn left," he'd commanded proudly in what he believed to be perfect Italian.

The seaman at the helm snapped to, obeying what he'd heard as a clear order to make a right turn. To compensate for the stiff breeze and the vessel's limited steering at low speed, moreover, the pilot had ordered him to cut the rudder more aggressively than usual, and this, too, he did with precision, if not a lot of thought. As the ship began to turn, the captain saw what was happening in an instant and tried to countermand the order, knowing even as he shouted the words that he was too late. Abruptly relieved of his command, the pilot stood helplessly and watched the consequences of his career-ending mistake.

The ship had been moving too slowly for the sort of big impact that tears vessels open; what the people on board experienced was more of a low shudder, a groaning, and then a stop. The wind caught the side of the *Mardi Gras* as if it were a sail, and the ship began to pivot on its stern, finally settling firmly on the sandbar. Looking down the starboard side as it executed its improbable pirouette, confused passengers saw the propeller kicking up foamy waves of sand ten, fifteen feet into the air.

It was all over in a moment, and a quick attempt at reversing the engines eliminated any hope of the ship's getting free under its own power. A cursory check made it clear that it was in no danger of sinking, however, and the decision was made not to evacuate. Instead, Ted opened the bars and waited. Until the tugboats arrived, there was no way of knowing how long it would take to pull the *Mardi Gras* off that sandbar or how badly the bottom of the hull was damaged.

And so unfolded a quintessential Miami crisis—memorialized with free drinks all around. After the initial moment of uncertainty, most of the passengers relaxed and enjoyed the unexpected fruits of an open bar. It's tough, after all, to feel all that imperiled when you're virtually within shouting distance of droves of gawking drivers on the side of the highway. The booze flowed freely, as the notion that a ship could be a destination in itself was put to an unexpectedly literal test. A clever bartender helped things along by whipping up a new rum drink, served on Carnival ships for years thereafter, that he named "Mardi Gras on the Rocks."

Ted was in no shape to deal with his guests; he wouldn't leave the bridge for a moment. His young son and future heir, on the other hand, didn't hesitate. "Ted was devastated. He didn't sleep; he stayed on the bridge the entire time. I was in the bar," Micky remembers with a laugh. "Everybody was having a good time. It was very partylike. I was just engaged, I was with a young girl. We were having a great time. There was nothing I could do—he could find me in the back of the disco."

Desperately short of operating cash, Ted had rushed the ship into service before it was anywhere near to meeting the standards set by competitors like NCL and Royal Caribbean. "The *Mardi Gras*," as Ted's right-hand man Meshulam Zonis would later put it with uncharacteristic brevity, "was no picnic." The port hadn't had a spare gangway for the *Mardi Gras*, and Ted hadn't been able to afford a new one, so passengers boarded and disembarked via a contraption cobbled together under Zonis's direction from discarded shipping containers, their tops sliced off and their ends welded together. The thing looked like a water slide in a junkyard.

On board, many of the cabins lacked electrical outlets, and some didn't even have toilets or showers. At the time of sailing, entire sections of the ship—Ted described them to the *Miami Herald* as "remote"—were cordoned off, still under renovation by squads of laborers. The cavernous space that would later house a do-it-yourself salon for the women passengers was still empty and off-limits, populated only by mice and cockroaches. When the ship returned to Miami at the end of the week, one couple complained that things were so bad they'd had to scrub the floor of their cabin before they could unpack their luggage. This luckless couple was also among the several aboard who discovered on returning to Miami that their car, parked at the direction of Carnival staff, had been either ticketed or towed.

Although he acknowledged that the crew had been slow to clean up the debris from the gala bon voyage party the night before—where open boxes of liquor were pillaged by many of the guests, who in turn walked off at the end of the night stumbling over exposed, wrist-thick electrical cables—Ted insisted that within hours of sailing "The ship was in excellent, spic-and-span condition" and that in spite of its unfortunate beginning and the ship's disrepair, or perhaps even because of it, most of the passengers "had a ball."

The rescue operation on shore was left to Zonis, who'd stayed behind to attend to the logistics for the following week's cruise. Exhausted from a long day of loading passengers and troubleshooting last-minute problems, he and some of the other Carnival staff were driving to a local restaurant to celebrate when they heard the news on the car's FM radio. Zonis raced back to the port and joined the hastily assembled ad hoc working group of thirty or so officials from the Coast Guard, the port and the Biscayne Bay pilots that had already formed on the pier. Their first attempts were not encouraging. Miami tugboats, first on their own and then with reinforcements from nearby Fort Lauderdale, were unable to pull the ship free, an effort the *Miami Herald* uncharitably described as "ants pushing a beetle."

Keenly aware that all eyes were on him, Zonis decided his first move should be to secure a private method of communicating with Ted. Remembering a favorite toy of his son's, the little man left the dock and ran to a nearby Radio Shack, where he bought a pair of children's walkie-talkies. Rudimentary though they were, the devices could handle the short range between the docks and the grounded ship. (And they were cheap; even in a crisis, Zonis never overpaid.) He had one sent out to Ted, and the two strategized together in Hebrew—much to the consternation of the local press. "Somebody told me that they were standing next to two people from the *Miami Herald*," Zonis recalls. "They said, 'I know there is two people speaking in a very unusual language, on a very incredibly unusual frequency. I know they're speaking with the ship, but I cannot understand a word.' "

Night fell, but the darkness didn't deter the rubberneckers lined up around the port and along the roadways bordering the channel. Patrol boats, their blue lights flashing, circled the crippled ship like bodyguards, keeping curious boaters at a safe distance. An hour or two after sundown, Coast Guard officials finally cleared the cruise ships still waiting at the pier to sail through the narrow opening the *Mardi Gras* had left; the usual speed limits were suspended in order to give them maximum maneuverability, and the ships sailed with their entire front ends darkened so as not to ruin their crews' night vision with the glare as they made their way. Passing close enough to

Ted's passengers that they could make out the patterns on their ties, officers on the other ships debated whether their wakes would help to free the *Mardi Gras* or force it farther up on the sandbar. Either way, they all agreed, it wasn't their problem.

High tide came and went, leaving the *Mardi Gras* still stuck and the situation bleaker than ever. Ted and Zonis decided to unload some fuel. If the ship could be lightened, they reasoned, they'd have a better chance of floating it off during the next high tide, twelve hours later. They were supposed to be halfway to Puerto Rico by now, but instead they stood watching the twinkling lights of the Miami skyline while pumping tons of perfectly good diesel out of their fuel tanks onto a special freighter that had pulled up alongside. The cruise ship rose only infinitesimally in the water, but it was enough. Finally, twenty-eight hours after the *Mardi Gras* had first set sail, it made its way down the channel into open waters—dragged, stern first and in an utterly undignified manner, by a small armada of grumpy tugboats. A Coast Guard escort reported that the ship was leaking no fuel, and once it was determined that no water was coming in, Ted made the decision to continue on with the cruise as if nothing had happened. But even here the fates seemed to be conspiring against him; the tanker that had lightened the *Mardi Gras*, it turned out, had no license to *refuel* the ship. If he wanted to complete his itinerary, Ted would have to sail without it and take on what he needed for the return trip when he stopped in Puerto Rico.

On arrival in San Juan, however, Ted learned that his infant company's reputation had preceded it. Kjell Nielsen in his bitterness had estimated Carnival would last six months, but no one in San Juan believed Ted's new company would last anywhere near that long, or much cared. Given his performance so far, the idea of extending credit to him was laughable. If Ted wanted to get his ship back to Miami, they told him, he was going to have to pay in cash.

Riklis had laundered the NCL money willingly enough, but Carnival's powerful new owner had brought no serious influx of new capital with him. Ted was already on a shoestring—and a frayed one at that. And so he and his crew spent the night emptying every slot machine and cash register on the ship; the *Mardi Gras* steamed back to Miami on fuel that had literally been paid for with nickels and dimes.

~~~

There's no better metaphor for Carnival's early days than Ted's paying for that first refueling with thousands of dollars in loose change. For years thereafter the company operated at a loss, every penny a desperate fight. Month after month, Ted would return home to his wife in the evenings, shoulders slumped from the strain of yet another day on the edge of bankruptcy. "Lin," he'd say, "I don't see the light at the end of the tunnel."

It was a toss-up whether things were worse at sea or ashore. The Carnival offices were a gloomy affair, situated on the second floor of a walk-up office building in a blighted swath of downtown Miami. The neighborhood had so declined that Ted had had to install a video camera at the top of the stairs to prevent anyone dangerous from gaining entrance. Spirits at Carnival were low; there was none of the passion and creative spirit of the early days at NCL. Tough and clever as he was, Ted sometimes lacked the discipline necessary to drive a struggling organization, and Carnival was carrying its share of deadwood. "There were a lot of issues at the time that my father either didn't want to see or didn't want to deal with," remembers Micky, who was in and out of college then and often spent his days hanging around his father's office. "Me, just being around, I could see it. And I didn't have enough experience with anything else, but I knew it wasn't right." Carnival's marketing and sales people were "old-school" Miami men. On Saturdays, after the ship sailed, they'd all head for their regular stools at a local dive. "And they'd sit there until they were hammered before going home," Micky recalls. Unfortunately for Ted, the celebration tended to go on throughout the week, beginning each day around lunchtime. As Micky recalls, "Travel agents would even know not to call these guys in the afternoon, because they were hammered." Many of these had come over with Ted from NCL, and what he saw as their loyalty to him only made things harder.

Of course, even a smart, aggressive team wouldn't have had an easy time selling a shoddy product, which is exactly what the *Mardi Gras* was. "We were the runt of the litter," as one early member of the sales team remembers. "We were definitely on the bottom of the food chain." Being on the road for Carnival cruises as a sales rep was a brutal job, demanding the daily ability to weather hours on the receiving end of unsatisfied agents' wrath. "People would come up to me," one veteran remembers, "and say, 'Oh, I've been on Carnival.' You were always holding your breath. Half the people loved it and half the people hated it. You wouldn't say, 'Did you have a good time?' You'd always kind of wait to see what they would say."

The *Mardi Gras* had already been laid up in dry dock for several years when Ted took it over, and it showed. Not that it would have been an ideal cruise ship even in pristine condition, for aside from a major rodent and cockroach infestation, the ship had been designed for the obsolete passenger trade and a major portion of its accommodations, originally intended for third-class passengers, were laid out in a spartan style completely unsuitable for cruises. Ted had neither the time nor the money for a major drydock overhaul, and so he did it on the fly. As the ship sailed, teams of carpenters worked in sealed-off areas, converting unused public areas into cabins and upgrading what had been the emigrant and third-class facilities into something Carnival could sell. There was much work to be done and hardly any capital available to fund it.

Things would have been far worse, perhaps impossible, without Zonis. By applying his mania for cost controls to every aspect of Carnival's shipboard operation, he kept the company alive. He sold confetti to the passengers to toss down to the dock when the *Mardi Gras* sailed, and when the ship was gone, he had his people sweep it up again to sell to the next bunch the following week. He kept his eye on every little detail, "finding pennies in millions of dollars," and stretching every last one of them as far as it could possibly go. "Zonis is aware of everything," one associate remembers. "And he will push you to the limit. Don't bite off more than you could chew, because if you want to volunteer to do more work for him, he'll take it—that doesn't mean he'll pay you for it." He also made sure that every penny that could have been coming into the company was. "A cruise passenger is like a wet towel," he'd say with a smile, making a back-and-forth wringing motion with his hands. "First you squeeze him this way, and then you squeeze him this way."

Zonis was the guy who saw to it that Ted's ideas happened, the enforcer. Neither of them would have made it without the other. "They kind of played good-guy, bad-guy," remembers one longtime Carnival vendor. "Ted was aloof. He stayed above it. . . . He always went out of his way to make sure that he said hello, and maybe a hug. And it was nothing but the best, and 'Is everything okay?' If something had to be said, it was always Zonis that said it." The little Romanian suffered from none of Ted's softness when it came to dealing with people. Outwardly affectionate and irresistibly charming when he wanted to be, he was nonetheless the terror of the Carnival fleet. When word ran through the gangways or walkie-talkies that "Mr. Zonis is on board," backs straightened and pulses quickened. His word was law, and his unpredictability made him that much more intimidating. One moment he could be jovially telling a shaggy dog story or asking after one of his staff's children by name; an instant later, seeing something out of order, he could become enraged, arms waving, his broad face turning beet red as he ordered some poor crewmember off his ship over a minor infraction.

Everything was personal to him—the good and the bad. Operationally, the company ran according to Zonis's simple, direct instinct for power politics; the more information, decisions and relationships that ran through him and him alone, the happier he was. And he remembered everything. Everyone knew that Zonis spoke for Ted. Suppliers made deals based on his handshake. When a shipment of pillowcases or tablecloths was delivered, drivers refused to budge until Zonis came huffing down the gangway to pay— although in truth this was less out of any sense of loyalty than from their refusal to take a check. Carnival, constantly juggling a reservoir of ready cash much smaller than its expenses, quickly gained a reputation as a deadbeat customer; many suppliers insisted on cash on delivery, and Zonis was the only person who handled that kind of money. People were managed in a similar way. For decades, Zonis flew to Italy to "look in the eyes" of every captain and chief engineer before he hired. The details of their pay were guarded like state secrets.

Whenever possible, Zonis established his relationships with Carnival employees as their key interface with senior management, resenting any encroachment from his colleagues and sometimes going to great lengths to maintain his influence. When he realized, for example, how big a role the carpenters were going to play as renovations continued, he remembered something a friend in Spain had once told him about a boys' home in Seville. Apparently the priest who ran the place had prevailed upon local craftsmen to donate tools and vocational training to his wards, and over the years many of the street children who lived there had become skilled woodworkers. The economy in Franco's Spain was so bad at that time that everyone was desperate for work. That was enough for Zonis; he returned from Seville after a short visit with 170 orphans in tow. They worked as Carnival employees for years, reporting only to him, until Spain's economy improved enough for them to return home and labor, in Zonis's words, "for more than peanuts."

Working grueling hours that he never seemed to notice, sleeping little and guarding every shred of information as if it were a wayward lover, Zonis kept things going on board the *Mardi Gras* through the company's leanest years. When the child of a Carnival employee answered the phone during Sunday dinner and said there was a strange man on the phone who he couldn't understand, his parents knew immediately who it was.

Little by little, "by hook or by crook," as Zonis puts it, toilets and showers were installed in more and more of the *Mardi Gras*'s cabins. The job was done hurriedly—in some cases with disastrous results. On one occasion the captain of the *Mardi Gras* was inspecting a passenger gangway when he heard screaming and banging on the walls. A passenger, it turned out, had been trapped inside her tiny bathroom, unable to turn off or redirect the scalding hot water pouring out of the showerhead. The doorknobs and faucets had both been installed backwards, and in her panic she was unable to work either. Smashing his way into the cabin and then the bathroom with the help of one of Zonis's carpenters, the captain found her half dead and laid her out on the floor as they waited for the doctor to arrive. Studying the tiny lavatory, he dropped his gaze to what he thought at first was a pair of panty hose hanging over the edge of the sink. With a start, he realized that he was looking at a great piece of the woman's skin, hanging in a long, gauzy bunch. She died several months later in a Saint Thomas hospital, he remembers, "of an ulcer, because she didn't want to eat anymore."

Full of empty spaces, the ship also continued to have terrible problems with vermin that no one could solve. It was Zonis who found a Scottish exterminator in town who was already under contract to work on Royal Caribbean's ships, where, of course, you could eat off the floor. The next thing the man knew, Zonis had cornered him on the dock one afternoon and sucked him into one of his endless, wheedling conversations. Soon afterwards, the man was aboard the *Mardi Gras*, taking a look around. Better at his job than anyone Carnival could afford to hire, he grasped the problem instantly: the sprays that the local contractors had been using to "fog" the galleys, he explained, were only forcing the vermin to flee for the relative safety of the passenger spaces. Rather than pay the high-priced firm the man worked for, Zonis hired him away.

Over time, the improvements went some way toward making the ship presentable. None of them made up for the food, however, much of which was military surplus—and some stuff even the army wouldn't take. Large quantities of cheese came aboard so rotten that they never made their way to a passenger's plate; more than once, the crew took one look at the stinking pile they had been sent and threw the lot of it overboard. Even the showcase items were no prize—the "lobster" roll, for example, was more breadcrumbs and ground-up scallops than anything else.

Ted was a great man, in his way, and Zonis could get anything done. But no amount of optimism was going to change the fact that the cruises on the *Mardi Gras* were pricing at 20 to 30 percent less than those of the competition, and the damned thing *still* wasn't sailing full.

Everyone who cared was uneasy about the situation. In its first eighteen months alone, Carnival had lost about $8 million, and Ted's business showed few signs of turning around in the near future—that is, if it still remained his company. The balance sheets, sent regularly up to AITS in Boston, were a constant source of dread. Ted had twice now been nearly broken by situations where a partner had pulled his joint operation out from under him. His worst fear was that, if the company didn't start generating income, the same thing would happen with Riklis. School ties only go so far. The Kloster funds might have paid for most of the *Mardi Gras*'s purchase price, but there had been no reserves. As operational and upgrading expenses continued to accrue without a profit stream to pay for them, AITS—and Riklis—gained more and more of a hold over Carnival's decisions. With a familiar, sick feeling, Ted saw his fledgling company beginning to slip through his fingers.

When there had been no movement toward profitability by August of 1973, Riklis made one. Against Ted's wishes, he installed a new chief operations officer, a diminutive, acid-tongued young vice president at AITS named Bob Dickinson, who'd been overseeing Ted's finances (which he'd belittled as "inordinately optimistic") from the Boston offices. It could have been much worse; Ted actually had far less support from his old friend in New York than he realized. Riklis, Dickinson remembers, had actually wanted to install him as president, but the young executive, convinced such a coup would leave the small, intensely loyal organization in irreparable chaos, had talked him out of it and came in instead as the number two. Everyone but Ted—Zonis included—reported to him.

Predictably, Ted was deeply unhappy about the new arrival, as were Zonis and a few of the other top executives. Although many of the Carnival people regarded Dickinson as a Riklis spy and were cautious around him, no one really knew what to make of him. Sharp faced and skinny, he wore a pair of oversize prescription glasses, longish hair almost in a mullet and an out-of-place little moustache. Inexplicably, women fell all over him. Dickinson himself wasn't thrilled to be moving to Miami—it was a "cow town," as far as he was concerned—for he was a self-styled cosmopolitan, his personal style ranging from the flamboyant to the absurd. One particularly garish dinner jacket, referred to behind his back as "the tablecloth," was abandoned only after Dickinson caught the ventriloquist act on one of the *Mardi Gras* sailings: the dummy's outfit was a dead ringer for his own. Fair enough; Dickinson had an arsenal of one-liners to go with the getup. In later years he'd become famous for them—especially in his appearances on industry panels, where he consistently eviscerated the nonplussed executives unlucky enough to share the stage with him and which colleagues discussed with an enthusiasm typically reserved for minor blood sports. Disquietingly quick on his feet, Dickinson was especially tough on those who failed to grasp what he saw as self-evident realities of the business, which covered pretty much everyone, pretty much all the time. "What is it?" he'd ask a sputtering victim. "You just come out of an eggshell?"

Of course, the only thing that really mattered about this "nerd" from Boston was that he was a brilliant businessman. And he knew how to crack the whip; confrontations caused him no more discomfort than they did Zonis. The first thing he did was to sit down with his sales force. "I interviewed four of the sales reps and got rid of two of them right there on the spot," he remembers. "I mean, they were just buffoons." He replaced them with people who fit his own image of himself. "The sales force at that time definitely had my personality," he remembers. "It's also known as a very attractive sales force—generally the talk of the vacation industry, because if you were a Carnival sales rep you were generally a very good-looking young lady or a very handsome young man, or middle-aged man." By the start of 1974, he'd replaced much of the marketing and sales staff, and Carnival's losses had been halved.

Changes in the day-to-day tempo followed swiftly after. The drinking bouts continued—if anything, they picked up—but they no longer began at eleven A.M. "When Bob came in, I think there was a decision to kind of make things more professional," Micky remembers. Some of the steps were so remedial as to be absurd, but they were necessary all the same. "We put in a 'no drinking' rule in the company during lunch," Micky said. "Those kinds of things started going into effect."

Dickinson made another move that flew nakedly in the face of Ted's authority, by hiring Micky full-time over his father's strong objections. Not long before, one of Ted's senior people had brought his own son into the company. Things got very awkward when the hire didn't work out, and Ted had been left with a strong aversion to nepotism. He also worried that Micky was getting a little too fond of the shipboard lifestyle. As someone who'd walked away from his own inheritance to become a "self-made man," he didn't feel any compunction about denying Micky a job—especially when the kid could barely get himself through junior college. But something about the business called to Micky all the same, and he'd become a fixture at the Carnival offices. As Dickinson recalls, Micky's knowledge of the operation was just too valuable to give up at such a difficult time. "This is no time to stand on ceremony," he remembers insisting to Ted in what he calls one of their "early big fights." "Here we have a company that's drowning, and Micky knows the company, knows the industry. You do what you need to do." Micky himself remembers Dickinson's motivations a little differently. "Bob found it disconcerting that I'd be around the office and I was the one guy who didn't report in to him," he recalls. "So he offered me a job." And in fact the job Micky got tends to support his version over Dickinson's claim that Micky at that age was somehow indispensable to the organization, as he was sent to work the northern part of Florida's west coast as a very unhappy sales rep. It might as well have been Siberia. "To me, to be on the road, by yourself, knocking on doors, staying in hotels, eating in restaurants by yourself—it was murder. I hated it," Micky recalls. "I absolutely hated it. But I did it."

Along with Zonis, Dickinson would eventually become one of the twin pillars of the company. He transformed the way Carnival sold and thought about its product, embracing an unpretentious philosophy of advertising that was decades ahead of its time. The *Mardi Gras* was an embarrassment—nothing could be done about that—but promoting a run-down old ship as "the flagship of the golden fleet" was just preposterous. A competitor had been advertising its vessel as "the Happy Ship," and Dickinson decided he liked that approach.

"We called it the 'Fun Ship,'" he'd later remember, "really stealing the idea." Dickinson had a keen mind for marketing communications, and he could be as tightfisted as the best of them. All too aware of his limited budget, Dickinson stepped back and let his competitors do some of his work for him. They all sent their ships to the same places, after all; if the competition's ads were in the same newspapers as his, pushing the very same ports that were on his own itinerary, why should he waste his precious advertising dollars? Cruise ads had traditionally promoted the ports of call; under Dickinson, they concentrated almost entirely on the ship. "We made it an educational ad rather than just focusing on the ports," he remembers. "Because, obviously, we could say at the bottom, we go to these ports, and let the other people talk about them." He had his people step back and focus on big, basic questions. Forget the negatives, he told them. What did the *Mardi Gras* have going for it? Even figuring in the space taken up by the ongoing renovations, it was bigger than any other ship in Miami by almost a half, for one thing, with bigger cabins and much more public space on board. Carnival accordingly started running ads reading, "A Big Ship Makes a Big Difference."

Carnival didn't have the money or facilities to compete with NCL and Royal Caribbean on quality, so it stopped trying and went for the bottom of the economic pyramid instead—not only offering cruises to people who never thought they'd be able to afford one, but gearing the whole cruise experience toward them. The competition boasted of white-glove service and formal nights. Carnival went the other way, bringing belly-flop contests and beer pong to the high seas. "As long as you're not barefoot in the dining room," the new philosophy went, "you're pretty much all right."

Dickinson's success was doing little to ease Ted's concerns about getting pushed out. As business continued picking up, it seemed that it was only a matter of time. Then, in December of 1974, with Dickinson's remarketing taking hold and the company on the verge of profitability, Ted had another run-in with fate—and this time luck was on his side.

Riklis had indeed been moving in for the kill, but Carnival would never be more than a tiny part of his empire, even under Ted's most ambitious scenarios. The financier's hopes and attentions were then focused on what he believed was a far more glamorous and lucrative project, the Riviera Hotel and Casino in Las Vegas, future stage of Pia Zadora, which was under construction even as Carnival was finally beginning to show some promise.

Luckily for Ted, Riklis had the Nevada Gaming Commission to contend with. "To be a 'Fun Ship,' " Micky remembered, "we had to have gaming. And there was no way that Nevada was going to allow an unregulated casino to be owned by the Riviera. This company wasn't making any money anyway, so basically he said, 'Come on, guys, take it away from me so I don't have to deal with it when I'm doing my hearings in front of the Nevada Gaming Commission.' "

Overnight, Riklis sold the *Mardi Gras* and his multimillion-dollar debt burden to Ted for one dollar. "Ted," Riklis said, "if you ever make any money, send me a present." And off he went to Vegas. Years later, Micky's still laughing. "So he's gotten a lot of presents," he says. "And a lot of cheap cruises for him and his girlfriends."

The deal closed on a Friday in December. First thing the next Monday, feeling as if he'd cheated the hangman once again, Ted walked into the office—*his* office—past the crummy buildings lining the downtown sidewalk, up the crummy stairs and right past the crummy little video camera, and fired Bob Dickinson.

Firing Dickinson was one thing; getting him to leave was quite another. It wasn't that Dickinson had built up so much support among the other executives, really. They respected his success and some of them had even started to like him, but as far as they were concerned, Ted could do what he liked.

"I spent the next three days trying to talk myself into getting my job back," he remembers. From nine to noon, the pair would sit in Ted's office, going back and forth. Then they'd break for lunch and walk a few blocks to a nearby Howard Johnson, where they'd spend less than five dollars on their combined meals and set business aside. "Everything was social," Dickinson remembers. "How's the family, the kids, all that sort of stuff." After lunch, it was hardball time again. "One o'clock, we'd be right back in the negotiations. We did that until five-thirty, three days in a row."

The issue was simple enough; Ted wanted his company back, and he didn't want to worry about having to keep an eye on Dickinson. Ted wanted all of his division heads, who had been reporting to Dickinson, reporting back to him, and he was highly skeptical of Dickinson's ability to take a demotion and remain productive within the organization. "Personally, I think he had every intention of not firing me," Dickinson would later say with characteristic self-confidence. "But that was a way to get me to understand the new rules of the road. It was never an issue about the contribution I made; it was never an issue of whether he had someone else who could make that contribution. His big deal was that he wanted to run it, wanted to be the boss. And that I needed to understand what the new organizational chart was all about, and embrace it."

Keeping Dickinson turned out to be one of the smartest moves Ted ever made. Between him and Zonis, Carnival's bases were covered, and Ted was free to do what he did best—to think about the big picture. AITS had been something of a liability in two respects: first of all, as a tour operator, it had demanded a preferential commission and pricing structure from Carnival, which had siphoned off a significant chunk of Carnival's income. Especially after the Fun Ship marketing strategy started gaining traction, it became apparent that the problem hadn't been that the *Mardi Gras* wasn't making money, so much as it was that a questionable portion of its income had been flowing to Boston rather than remaining in Miami, boosting the AITS balance sheets at Carnival's expense. "That was our argument with them all along, that the numbers they were seeing from us were depressed by their own desire to show the margins in Boston," Micky recalls. "From the day that that broke, we gave them pricing equal to anybody else's pricing. They were moving, I don't know, 20 to 30 percent of the ship, some big number. So that profitability moved."

Secondly, dealing with an AITS subsidiary had been making travel agents nervous, which in turn had hurt bookings almost as much as the *Mardi Gras*'s shoddiness. Travel agents, the gatekeepers for the cruise industry, are by nature a skittish, suspicious bunch. They make their money from long-term relationships with clients who trust them to book their vacations and give good advice on where to go, and they guard those relationships jealously. Cruise lines didn't sell directly to the public in those days, but AITS did, and as long as Carnival had a parent company that the travel agencies saw as a competitor, bookings were going to suffer. With Riklis out of the picture, many agents who'd stayed away for fear of AITS poaching their customers began sending their clients to sail on the *Mardi Gras*. Here, too, Dickinson made a critical contribution to the future of the company. He took his attractive sales team on the road, assuring travel agents nationwide that Carnival considered them valued partners and intended to do everything in its power to protect them and help them grow—even to the point of honoring commissions on canceled cruises. His tart, direct style won them over immediately. It may have seemed like unwarranted largesse from a company that was still stretching its budget to buy rotten cheese, but the message got through, and as time went by the payoff would prove bigger than anyone had dreamed possible—not Ted, not Zonis, not Micky, and not even the motor-mouth with the funny moustache and the ventriloquist's tailor.

The month after Ted took over the *Mardi Gras*, in January 1975, a debt-laden but 100 percent Arison-owned Carnival Cruise Lines posted its first profit. There were congratulations all around, and there was big talk of the future. The light at the end of the tunnel, however, was still a long, long way off.

CHAPTER FIVE

LOVE . . . EXCITING AND NEW

Making money is art and working is art and good business is the best art of all.

—Andy Warhol

With companies like Royal Caribbean, NCL and even Ted Arison's struggling outfit all starting up in Miami within a few short years of one another, the cruise industry of the mid-1970s was shaping up as an enterprise with a future. On the West Coast, too, several operators were doing a humming cruise business, with Princess Cruises and a handful of smaller competitors running out of Los Angeles to the "Mexican Riviera," and Holland America up in Seattle developing the summertime Alaska cruise market.

In many ways, the industry was at an exciting juncture. New ships specially designed for cruising were proving stunningly profitable—and remarkably cheap to build, thanks to heavy subsidies from European governments desperate to support their civilian shipbuilding sectors at a time of rampant unemployment. At the same time, the near-total disappearance of the traditional liner trade was flooding the market with secondhand tonnage; big ships were selling for a fraction of what they'd been worth only a few years before. Registering ships in offshore tax havens boosted profit margins considerably, and a virtually infinite pool of cheap, third world labor propelled profits into the stratosphere. On the supply side, cruising was ripe for an explosive expansion.

The great uncertainty, however, lay in the market: how much capacity could the business sustain? The industry faced a fundamental obstacle in its image problem. For most of the American public, cruising was still tied to the old liner trade and all the cultural baggage that went with it. The symbols that invoked the industry most powerfully were all dinosaurs of questionable appeal. The widest popular exposure the cruise business had gotten in a decade was *The Poseidon Adventure*, a 1972 disaster film featuring an old-fashioned ocean liner overturned by a tidal wave—not exactly a beguiling image for the prospective vacationer. The new cruise industry that people like Ted Arison, Ed Stephan and Knut Kloster were building still had a depressingly low profile. Part of the problem, from a marketing perspective, was the nature of the product itself: the cruise lines' corporate offices may have been located in Miami, Los Angeles or Seattle, but their ships were usually in the middle of the ocean, where no one could see them. First-time cruisers were by definition making a purchase sight unseen. The vast majority of passengers were still from either Florida, California or New York, coastal regions where passenger ships had always been a familiar sight. Farther into the heartland, no one really knew quite what a cruise was.

When most people thought of cruises, the image that came to mind tended to be something out of a Cary Grant movie: days spent lounging in a deck chair with a blanket wrapped around one's legs and evenings wrapped in furs and diamonds. This world had little to do with the realities of cruise ship life in the 1970s, and more to the point, it had even less to do with the desires and tastes of the informal, middle-class passengers most of the new lines were targeting. The cruise lines were going to have to find a way to tell their story, but tiny operations like Carnival and Royal Caribbean could have pulled down profit margins of 100 percent or more and yet still have been unable to afford a major nationwide marketing campaign. As a result, cruising was enlarging, but slowly. Most companies, leery of outgrowing their markets, funneled their considerable profits back to owners and shareholders rather than spending on aggressive expansion. It was just too much of a risk; industry handwringers were still wondering whether they would survive another decade. Even the most optimistic maintained that there were only modest fortunes to be made.

Then, in September of 1977, with one of the great lucky strokes in the history of commerce, the industry's image unexpectedly took a quantum leap into prime time.

The Love Boat debuted as a weekly series on ABC to a fusillade of nautical puns from a scornful entertainment press. Several critics proclaimed themselves "seasick," while others called for torpedoes as they ragged mercilessly on television's new "unfathomable low." The *Washington Post* warned viewers that "it takes plenty of furious paddling to keep one's head above water when material gets this rock-bottom" and proclaimed that "Nothing is worth the boredom of the deep."

America loved it, of course.

Remember? There was Julie, the perky cruise director; fatherly Captain Stubing; the obsequious, goofball duo of Gopher and Isaac. There was lanky, womanizing "Doc" Bricker and the ex-wives that he could barely count on one hand; the loungey theme music; the stories beginning week after week in the lobby of the ship, where the passengers—and their problems—were introduced as they checked in. *"I'm Mrs. Baltimore,"* a typical guest star might huff as she stepped off the gangway and approached one of the crew, her hapless-looking husband stumbling behind her overloaded with their luggage. *"And this is my husband, who can't keep his hands to himself, I'm sorry to say."* *"Ah, Mrs. Baltimore, of course! You're in Aloha Deck 315, right through the elevator there. Have a great cruise."* Or: *"We're Mr. and Mrs. Smith. Do we look nervous? We're going to adopt a child from the orphanage in Mazatlan!"* And off we'd go.

The show ran for almost a decade and was syndicated in forty-seven countries; at its height, as many as fifty million households a week were partaking of *The Love Boat*'s unlikely Saturday night cocktail of syrupy morality tales and naughty innuendo. Put it on the short list for the single greatest product placement of all time; the more than $100 million it earned for its producers pales next to the untold billions it indirectly generated for the entrepreneurs in Miami and elsewhere who, by the time the show went off the air ten years later, would be well on their way to becoming genuine robber barons of the high seas. When the show premiered, an estimated 825,000 cruise passengers were sailing annually out of North American ports, up from about 500,000 at the outset of the 1970s. A decade later—inestimably boosted by what amounted to a free, weekly prime-time infomercial minus the truth-in-advertising obligations—the industry would be on the cusp of the three million mark.

The secret of the show—both as television and as marketing—was in the simple, schmaltzy, unvarying genius of its formula. Anchored with unrelenting cheerfulness by its regular cast, each episode revolved around the antics of the S.S. *Pacific Princess*'s passengers, played with relish by a parade of guest stars that included hundreds of has-beens, never-weres and a few legends. Burt Convy one week, Lana Turner the next. It was a phenomenon; once the show got going, even cultural royalty like Andy Warhol, Bob Mackie and the mercurial Halston put in appearances. As their backdrop, the show's writers created a happy, amnesiac world where the responsibilities and consequences of everyday life were abandoned at the gangway. The closest thing to a running circumstance in any of the regular cast's outside lives was the telegrammed demands for alimony checks the ship's doctor was always getting from his ex-wives.

Life on the "Love Boat" was a glorious, unapologetic schlockfest. Feuding fathers and sons were reunited; widows, clueless, found new love in elaborate schemes that turned out to have been orchestrated by their dead husbands; past-life lovers found their reincarnated soulmates; and overeager young men were gently relieved of their virginity, even as their overwrought middle-aged counterparts discovered the ship's miraculous properties as a seagoing impotence cure. For untold legions of Saturday-night babysitters, *The Love Boat* augmented the sex ed classes they were getting in school, and nobody seemed to mind. It was all so harmless, somehow, despite almost constant references to impotence, adultery, orgasm, virginity and the loss thereof. "If Disney did a porno flick," one comedian joked during the show's early days, "the result would be *Love Boat*."

The Disney reference was apt in more ways than one; *The Love Boat* was a merchandising bonanza. Along with the episodes themselves, uncounted *Love Boat*–branded lunch boxes, lighters, action figures, dinnerware sets, belt buckles, golf visors and commemorative coins—even travel insurance policies—helped cement the sitcom as an icon of Americana at its most trivial and entertaining.

Fittingly enough, it all started with a bad book review.

One afternoon in 1975 several pairs of influential eyes in offices around Los Angeles fell upon the same unencouraging book review in the *Los Angeles Times*. Under the knife was *Love Boats*, a raunchy tell-all written by a former cruise director named Jeraldine Saunders, a self-described "vibrant, vivacious and voluptuous Virgo from Glendale." Among the showbiz executives who'd noticed the article was Douglas Cramer, a TV producer who, though he'd had some successes under his belt, was overdue for a good idea.

"I had seen the review," Cramer remembers, "which said it was sort of tacky and trashy, and was about a cruise director who wanted to get laid, but that it was a fascinating idea, and it was too bad the book wasn't as good." Cramer was scheduled to pitch new ideas to the head of ABC movies over lunch the next day but didn't have anything showstopping. He handed the review to an assistant and sent him out to the nearest bookstore.

Cramer had been looking for something ever since his last big show, *Love, American Style*, had gone off the air. *Love, American Style* had been promising, but because it had been an anthology show—a series of vignettes built around an ensemble cast and a weekly crop of guest stars—it lacked the unifying element that every genuine hit needs. Aside from a common theme of romantic comedy, the segments had little to do with one another. With its vasectomy jokes, suggestively timed fireworks and trademark giant bed rolling through the streets of Los Angeles, the show had been risqué enough, but it had never broken number twenty-five in the all-important Nielsen ratings. "The network theory," Cramer remembers, "was that, because it was an anthology and was only bridged by those little vignettes, it would be a much bigger hit if we could find a way of doing it with running characters and a running thread that people came back to each week."

Saunders's book was a revelation. Taking considerable license, it described a sexy, exotic and very funny world that by definition whisked a constantly revolving cast of characters through a set that never changed. As Saunders presented it, the world of cruise ships was one giant sex party—"wild and wonderful floating bedrooms" ruled over by virile captains and their strapping officers. In stumbling but enthusiastic prose, she laid out a colorful taxonomy of cruise ship life that included groupies who followed ships to sleep with the officers ("Seagulls"); bombastic, impossible-to-please guests who terrorized shipboard staff with their demands ("Godzillas"); and perhaps most memorably, the "Diddler" and his more impressive cousin, the "Flame-eyed Tailchaser." The pages—though Cramer only had time to skim them before his meeting—were packed with stories of beauticians turning tricks on the side, little old ladies plying "sturdy young crewmen" with marijuana in hopes of luring them into the sack, and couples coming to extraordinary—and sometimes very public—sexual awakenings. The chapters had titles like "Bear Hugs and Bare Skins" and "It's Nothing but a Hangnail, Doctor. I Do *Not* Need a Pelvic!" In Saunders's world, the libido was so powerfully and universally affected by the magic of a cruise ship that the mystery of one likely young woman's baffling indifference to "balling" was resolved only when Saunders learned she was one of Los Angeles's most exclusive call girls, at sea for a little rest. "Well, I had to hand it to Natalie," the admiring author wrote. "There was a lady who when she took a vacation, really took a *vacation*."

It may not have been literature, but to someone who knew what to look for it had "hit" written all over it. By the time Cramer met his lunch appointment, his lawyers were already working out an option deal with Saunders—and not a moment too soon, as he quickly discovered. Arriving at the restaurant, Cramer tossed a copy of the book onto the table. "I'll be damned," he remembers the mogul saying. *He'd* just seen the same review, and had dispatched his own lawyers to inquire about it just before leaving his office to meet Cramer. With no way of knowing which of them had been able to secure the rights, the two hammered out a rough agreement right there at the table; whatever happened, ABC would shoot a two-hour special based on the book. If the ABC people had been successful, the network would own the show and Cramer would produce it. If Cramer's lawyer had made the deal, Cramer would retain ownership but the project would still go ahead on ABC. "When we got back and checked," Cramer remembers, "my lawyer had made the call and his hadn't. He often referred to that as the $100 million mistake. It was actually a bigger mistake than that, when everything was said and done."

A pair of two-hour specials eventually ran in 1976 and 1977 as *The Love Boat* and *The Love Boat II*. With them the basic formula and tone for the series were in place, as were the central characters who would propel the show through hundreds of episodes—the captain, the bartender, the cruise director, etc. Three sets of writers were hired to assemble different story lines for the show, each centered on one set of passengers: one tale of young love, one vehicle for comic relief featuring the middle-aged, and a warmhearted tale of senior citizens finding new romance. These three archetypes became the template the show would cling to unswervingly throughout its tenure on the airwaves—and none of them would prove more of a signature than the old-folks storylines, so saccharinely over-the-top that they quickly became known on the set simply as "the warmly."

Most of the actual scenes were shot on a soundstage, with the exteriors filmed on a ship belonging to Princess Cruises conveniently headquartered in Century City. Princess hardly regarded its participation as an opportunity; the cast and crew were booked on at full price—and only after long negotiations with a deeply skeptical management. The book was too racy, they demurred. They were still committed to the upscale market, and it wasn't the kind of image they wanted to project. That the show would open with their logo and reach audiences they couldn't hope to on their own didn't impress them. In fact, Cramer remembers that they very nearly didn't let him on board, so foreign was the marketing-driven frame of mind at that time. "It started out antagonistic," he recalls. "They were doing us a great favor, and we had to watch ourselves. And they were . . . not embarrassed, but they were very nervous about us doing the show, and they were nervous about the material and what was going in—and what we were suggesting would happen on the ship." Eventually, Cramer was able to convince the Princess people that he was going for a much tamer version of Saunders's vision; network censors would demand it, whether he liked it or not. Privately, however, Cramer was convinced the show's appeal would depend in large part on its ability to test sexual boundaries.

When ABC balked at producing a third movie-length episode, Cramer and his new partner Aaron Spelling sold it as a weekly series. With hits like *Mod Squad, Starsky and Hutch, Charlie's Angels* and *Fantasy Island* behind him, Spelling was at the height of his power at ABC and easily got a commitment for a pilot episode on the condition that he and Cramer deliver the finished show within ninety days. After having hired two entirely different casts for the movie-length productions, the producers started almost from scratch and hit on the winning combination that would remain largely unchanged for nearly a decade. Bernie Kopell, who played the skirt-chasing ship's doctor, and Fred Grandy, who played "Gopher," the ship's naive, bumbling purser, were the only holdovers. Gavin MacLeod, fresh from a starmaking run on *The Mary Tyler Moore Show*, came in to play Captain Merrill Stubing, a divorced recovering alcoholic whose twelve-year-old daughter lived with him aboard the ship. That left the roles of Cruise Director Julie and Isaac the Bartender. To play Isaac they found the mustachioed, semi-Afroed, eternally thumbs-up Ted Lange, a Shakespearean-trained actor who'd had some success on race-driven sitcoms like *That's My Mama*. Casting Lange meant yet another struggle with the Princess people, still worried about their image. Cramer remembers that they asked him "whether we really needed a black member of the crew." Lange stayed. The pivotal role of Julie remained uncast until a few days before shooting; the producers wanted a fresh face—a girl next door with sex appeal—and hadn't been having any luck. Finally, someone remembered they'd seen an extra on *Starsky and Hutch* who fit the bill. They finally tracked a flabbergasted Lauren Tewes down at a restaurant in the Valley, where she was working as a waitress to make ends meet.

Assembled at a frantic pace, the series aired halfway through the 1977 season, running Saturdays at ten p.m., in a nod to its racy content. Although the network had bought *The Love Boat* as an hourlong series, they'd also ordered several two-hour episodes to intersperse throughout the season. It was an old Hollywood trick; when a competitor was scheduled to debut a potentially threatening new show, ABC rolled out one of its "very special" two-hour installments, the second hour timed to coincide with the new show's starting credits in hopes of keeping rapt viewers from checking it out.

Although the critics were nearly unanimous in their pans, ABC not only ordered the show for another year, but bet heavily on its continued success. Cramer's people set about building a million-dollar permanent set on the 20th Century Fox lot, one of the biggest and most expensive ever built for television.

Of course, by any artistic measure, the critics had the show pegged; dreck they called it, and dreck it was. Its success had nothing to do with the quality of its writing or its acting—at least, not with how *good* they were.

The secret of *The Love Boat*'s success was its democracy. You could look at it as a sort of antecedent to today's reality TV. By staging it the way they did, the producers brought the viewer into their world—the Hollywood world—and that was something no one had ever really done before. This is a country that reveres its celebrities infinitely more than its political leaders; for the families tuning in all across America, there had to be a certain thrill in the notion that the antics they watched from their living rooms were happening somewhere out there on a *real* ship—and on a cruise advertised in their local newspaper, no less, full of people just like them. *All in the Family* had been revolutionary when it premiered six years earlier, replacing the idealized, antiseptic universe of *Ozzie and Harriet* and its ilk with that of the loudmouthed, bigoted Archie Bunker and his family, a group of schlubs that anyone could identify with. But this was something new. People may have taken great pleasure in recognizing aspects of themselves in Archie Bunker, but no one wanted to *be* him. Never before had a televised world been both this accessible and this exciting: *The Love Boat* wasn't about poking fun at the daily

grind; it was about an existence full of fantasy, sex and happiness that somehow, miraculously, had room for John Q. Public. The fact that so many of
the celebrity guest stars were winkingly, unabashedly playing *themselves* only
made it that much more fun. Because, really, they were playing us.

Everything about *The Love Boat* was participatory, inclusive. The show
pushed sexual boundaries; but at the same time, it was the safest thing in the
world. John Ritter in drag wasn't *Boys Don't Cry*, or even RuPaul. You didn't
have to be rich; you didn't have to be good looking. You didn't have to be
charming or witty. You didn't even have to be young. Setting sail, wrinkled
old paramours turned out the lights and purred things like "Let's make love."
Even Buddy Hackett got laid. No wonder the show became a guilty pleasure
for millions—even if many of them wouldn't admit to watching it.

This couldn't have been more different from hits like *Dynasty*, *Dallas* and
Falcon Crest, where the appeal came from the utter unattainability of the
worlds they depicted. The ultra-monied, Joan Collins–type existence of sta-
bled estates, oil platforms and personal helicopters might as well have been
happening on the Starship Enterprise for all it had to do with the folks back
home. The TV screen had always been an unbreachable barrier between fantasy and reality. And there was never any question about which side you were
on. People knew very well that if they should ever be so bold as to approach
a real-life version of the country clubs they watched so avidly on television,
they wouldn't make it past the front gate—that they'd likely as not be turned
away by someone just like them, probably making about their salary, while
their betters inside went on sipping champagne. *"No problem ma'am, just
someone off the street."*

But all you needed to get onto the Love Boat—champagne and everything—
was a few hundred dollars and twenty minutes with your neighborhood
travel agent.

The Love Boat positioned cruising as exoticism wrapped in a security
blanket. If you could get on the ship, the unspoken promise was—and you
could get on the ship—you, too, would fall under its therapeutic, nonthreat-
eningly aphrodisiacal influences. The crew, with its good-humored, gently
guiding presence, was like a combination den mother and pimp. Once in a
while, its members confronted tough issues like child abuse or racism or
property theft. On the whole, though, they passed no more judgment on
people's pleasures and embarrassments than a Vegas croupier or a hooker
with a heart of gold. You might walk away from your cruise married, recon-

ciled or just happily oversexed—maybe with an adopted child, or maybe only with a sweet, sexy memory to keep you company during those cold winter nights back in Anytown, USA. But you were going to walk away happy.

Conventional wisdom in marketing dictates that too attractive is just as bad as too ugly when it comes to attracting customers. Companies spend millions trying to cast spokespeople who can entice without being threatening or intimidating. In *The Love Boat*, the cruise industry hit an all-time jackpot in this respect. The show introduced America to the concept of the cruise vacation via a seemingly endless parade of fading Hollywood stars, whose charm and charisma were still intact but who'd become somehow gentler, more approachable with the onset of their twilight years.

A rising tide lifts all boats, as the saying goes. The entire industry benefited from cruising's unexpected new status as a pop icon. When possible, other lines got into the act, drawing the spotlight in their direction. Carnival scored a minor PR coup in 1985 when the campy mercenary-with-a-heart series *The A-Team* filmed a season premiere memorably featuring the mohawked, muscle-bound, fifty-pounds-of-gold-chain-wearing Mr. T working in deep cover as a wheelchair-bound passenger on one of its ships. But nothing came close to *The Love Boat*.

The amazing thing is how little the cruise lines had to do with it. Notwithstanding Princess's early reticence, it quickly became clear that the industry had a hit on its hands. "There was hardly a ship that you could go on, after a couple of years, without hearing the theme from *The Love Boat*," one Royal Caribbean cruise executive remembers. Princess ships, having the benefit of the inside track, would actually pipe the song through their public address systems when they sailed, blurring the line between TV land and the real world enough to keep a team of crack graduate students working around the clock for a decade. The other cruise lines had to settle for having their bands play the songs in their various lounges—night after night after night.

As Marshall McLuhan had predicted, the medium had become the message. The show and the actual cruise experience had become inseparable. When the producers changed the uniforms on the show, Princess changed them on the ships, as well; it got to the point where passengers, on learning that their cruise directors couldn't produce Captain Stubing in the flesh, sometimes demanded their money back. Casting Isaac as a black man might have been an issue for Princess in the beginning, but as soon as black passengers began buying tickets, he became their main man.

With *The Love Boat* a bona fide national phenomenon, the number of actual cruise ships sailing their way through actual sunny seas began exploding. More and more Americans were deciding to spend their vacations on the other side of the looking glass. Real life, however, sometimes deviated considerably from its sanitized prime-time depictions. As Jeraldine Saunders had suggested, things were usually quite a bit raunchier.

Even in the days when cruising had been largely an old-folks pastime, things could get surprisingly wild on board—or at the very least, incredibly surreal. Death from natural causes was so common on cruise ships during the early years that on the tiny island of Curaçao, often the first port of call after several consecutive days at sea, the coroner would typically be on call when cruise ships arrived. "Lose anyone?" the local ship's agent would cheerfully inquire of the crew when he came on board. Maintaining an adequate inventory of coffins aboard was a significant enough expense for the cruise lines that one struggling operator had to make the cost-cutting switch from zinc caskets to wood ones. Another line skipped that step altogether, finding a bit of grisly efficiency in dual-purposing the meat locker as an ersatz morgue— much to the dismay of at least one ship's butcher, who had to be sedated after unwrapping what he thought was a side of beef and finding a human foot. Douglas Cramer, *The Love Boat*'s coproducer, recalls just such a voyage on one of his shooting trips. "One time we were going through the Panama Canal, and so many people died aboard the ship that they'd filled all the lockers with frozen bodies," he recalls. "We were eating really kind of tacky food, because they had to pick it up along the way—they'd given up the space. It was really gory." Working on a cruise ship meant working with the problems of the elderly. One purser, for example, has a treasured memory of explaining to one very insistent older passenger that, no, she would not be able to retrieve the set of false teeth she'd accidentally flushed down her stateroom toilet—and that she probably wouldn't want them, even if they could. "But it was her only pair," the purser would later recall. "She had to gum it through the rest of the cruise."

So far removed was the shipboard demographic of *The Love Boat*'s early days from what the show's producers wanted to depict that they had to bring in extras—at great expense—to play passangers to create the right atmosphere. "It became a major job in shooting to clean up the people," Cramer remembers. "I mean, men in black shoes and short black socks around their feet, and fat, fat women. . . . Those who wanted to be extras, you could talk to, and send back to their room to change clothes. Or we'd bring along lots of scarves, and shoes, and wraparounds—cover."

One former entertainment executive for Holland America, which has traditionally had some of the oldest passengers and one of the stodgiest reputations in the business, remembers trying to help a down-and-out acquaintance, "an elderly gay gentleman," by getting him a job as a shipboard dance partner. "He was flat broke, had no job and no prospects, and I knew he was a good dancer and I knew he would love the travel," the executive recalls. "So when I was hiring people, I said, 'You've got to give this a try, you've got to just try this out.' He did, and one of the little old ladies goosed him. And he burst into tears and quit. He just couldn't handle it. He said, 'I can't be a sex object.' It was very sad."

Sex was somehow built into the experience from the beginning. There really was something about leaving shoreside life and all its burdens at the gangplank that made people behave in ways they never would at home. Mix the liberty of isolation with the madness of crowds, add abundant liquor, scanty clothing and mind-addling tropical heat, and something approximating cruise ship life in those days begins to emerge.

One story sums up the tenor of the era as well as anything. Passing through a crew hallway with the *Mardi Gras*'s second-in-command at the time, a senior Carnival executive noticed a young female passenger slipping out of an officer's cabin, obviously after a rendezvous. Even in those swinging days, this was a serious breach of company policy, but to the executive she was just another satisfied customer. "You see," the executive said, pleased, "she'll be back again." That was the mind-set: give the people what they want. "We have observed," Carnival's Bob Dickinson would later write, "that some captains, because of their social and sexual prowess, have contributed to the revenue occupancy of the vessel."

With *The Love Boat* bringing its promise to the heartland, new and younger passengers began taking to the sea in search of romance, and their quests were inevitably more . . . vigorous. Singles started cruising for the first time; so did younger couples looking to inject some fresh energy into their relationships. The typical new cruiser was middle aged and middle class—informal, comparatively uninhibited and out to have a ball.

Some did and some didn't. There was, for instance, an inevitable downside to having an epidemic of passengers cruising to save their marriages. It was all romantic enough when things went well, but as the *Love Boat* myth took hold, ships' crews found that significant numbers of their passengers on any given voyage had essentially signed on to spend a week in excruciatingly close quarters with a person they could barely stand. And then there are the sins of omission: one survey found that only 13 percent of spouses would jump overboard to save their mates, compared with the 25 percent who said they'd do it to save a favorite hat. Calamities involving embittered spouses, often comical but sometimes deadly serious, became a staple of the cruising life.

Security officers and room service, for instance, would often be called to the same cabin several times in a single night—in alternating order, as the flow of alcohol fueled appetites and tempers alike. Honeymoons often became divorces before the week was out. Some favorite anecdotes from over the years—impossible to confirm, but all of them with the ring of truth—serve as cautionary tales. Take the couple whose bickering grew more and more intense over the course of their Caribbean cruise. The exasperated husband finally threatened to jump overboard if his wife didn't leave him alone. "You're not man enough," she snarled back in the balmy, tropical night. Over the rail the poor fellow went—neatly ending the dispute, along with his life. At least one other passenger did more or less the same thing, although this one survived. "He took a running leap over the rail," remembers an officer on duty during the second incident. "It's pitch black—you can't see anything—so we stop the ship. His wife is screaming and wailing on the balcony, this guy is floating around out there and we're in the rescue boats trying to find him, and we ultimately found him." What would have been high drama anywhere else was just another day at the office. "He was drunk, I think." The officer shrugs. "We threw them off the next day. We just get these *yahoos.*"

Oftentimes the issues were extramarital. One longtime Carnival executive remembers a distraught woman, complaining at the purser's desk as the ship was leaving some sunny port, that she couldn't find her husband anywhere. Suddenly, she realized that the man next to her was saying the same thing about his wife. The ship returned to the harbor, finding the missing spouses standing sheepishly at the pier—caught red-handed, if not with their pants still down.

In the absence of statistics, anecdotes suggest that wives who went overboard tended to do so less voluntarily than the husbands. In one particularly bizarre case, a Santa Monica chiropractor on honeymoon strangled his new wife and dumped her body overboard. He initially claimed that she had been the victim of "a strong gust of wind" but later changed his story, insisting that the Mossad had been trying to kill her that night in retaliation for a self-published book he'd written entitled *Nightmare in Israel*, in which he'd claimed that he had "been arrested on false burglary charges in Israel and abused in a mental hospital." He'd only thrown his wife overboard in order to protect her from the assassins' bullets, he explained. Her body was later recovered, and an autopsy determined that she'd drowned while unconscious. A Los Angeles court convicted the newlywed of murder. Extreme incidents like this were rare, cruise ship workers say, but they happened. A senior officer aboard another ship remembers a similar incident in which a man had killed his wife, this time in their cabin. The couple's private balcony offered a perfect way to get rid of the body—or so the man thought. "Deck four sort of bulges out," the officer remembers. "He threw her over and she went splat on the deck."

Romances too fervently in bloom presented problems all their own. Only the most naive pursers don't know, for example, that a midnight request for a hacksaw almost certainly means an erotic mishap of one kind or another—sometimes handcuffs, sometimes more specialized equipment. Unfortunately for everyone involved, such an innocent happened to be on duty one night when the call came in: "I need a hacksaw sent up to my room." "What's it for, sir?" she asked. "What do you need to cut?" "I. Just. Need. A. Hacksaw. Sent. Up. To. My. Room." As a colleague remembers, this back-and-forth went on for some time. "He finally told her that he had a cock ring on that he couldn't get off," the colleague remembers. "Well, she didn't know what that was. They finally ended up sending up the nurse, and they had to use the hacksaw, but they put a piece of sheet metal in to protect him."

In an environment like that, even the most outlandish scenes faded into the background after a while. For veterans, the real action was with the crew. A cruise ship during the 1970s and 1980s was a wild place to work, full of strange characters of every type—some there for adventure, others on the run from lives and debts and god-knows-what-else ashore. In an era when most communication between ship and shore was still via telegram, the ships existed as countries unto themselves, far from the rest of the world and operating under their own rules. It wasn't an easy life, but the dirtiest work was done by third world laborers, supporting families back home, who generally had little time for frivolity. The jobs on the entertainment and social staff—

the *Love Boat* jobs—generally went to younger Americans and western Euro-
peans, and these members of the crew made the most of the work-hard, play-
hard life they'd signed on for. Among other things, they shared a nearly
universal drive to take advantage of their unique surroundings to the best of
their considerable abilities. For some, that meant seducing a different passenger each week behind the same palm tree on the same deserted beach, but it
could just as easily have meant turning a cruise ship into a launching pad for
an exotic bird smuggling ring.

Things were just different out there. With the captain of one ship's approval, the ice-sculpting staff was diverted from its regular duties carving
swans and dolphins for the midnight buffet to help prepare for a special
"Caligula Party" in the crew areas. Later that night, under the shadow of an
enormous, shimmering, melting phallus, a debauch worthy of ancient times
took place—complete with an "auction" of volunteer sex slaves. Content in
the knowledge that the proceeds were going to a charity in Ensenada, the
high bidders enjoyed the services of their temporary wards on couches strewn
around the precincts of "Rome," for all to watch. An "S&M Party" aboard
the same vessel provided another memorable night—complete with an inflat-
able sheep.

Though they might easily have imagined the reverse, the passengers
themselves were perhaps the most important source of entertainment for the
largely male crews of those days—if only by default. "In the beginning, there
were five hundred crew members, out of which fifteen were female," one former waiter remembers of the *Mardi Gras* in the 1970s. "If there was anything
going on with a female, it had to be a passenger." In fact, there were rules
about romancing the passengers—for one thing, such dalliances were a privilege of senior officers—but they were based on somewhat different principles
than the sexual harassment policies of today. Back then, it was more of a customer service issue than anything else. "Those times, they were so reckless,"
remembers one former cruise ship captain. "The officers were free to go to
the nightclubs and so on; they got a girlfriend, she didn't want to go to the
cabin with him, so he dropped her and went to another. That was absolutely
not gentlemanly behavior, so I was very severe with that, very strict." All the
same, croupiers and bartenders lost count of the times they returned to their
cabins at the end of a long night shift to the sound of outraged female voices
in the corridors. "Take me back up to deck," the refrain went. "I thought you
were a nice guy!"

For all the outrageousness, cruise ships at their core were—and are—rigidly stratified societies. At the bottom of the ladder were the Third World laborers, followed by the mostly Western cruise and entertainment staff. Ruling over all of them was the captain and his maritime staff, who were generally of a single nationality—usually that of the ship's owner. In some cases, officers were technically employees not of the cruise lines but of the holding companies that owned them and so belonged to a categorically different power structure. At sea, the captain had absolute power over every aspect of life, and his authority flowed through his officers into every aspect of shipboard life. Often, this elite didn't even have to answer to the American management ashore. Even at the more tightly run cruise lines like Royal Caribbean, the senior maritime personnel's direct link to their countrymen in Oslo or Piraeus or Genoa allowed them to bypass Miami entirely when they wanted to. They had tremendous power as a result, which was often abused even on the best ships. "We stroked the boys pretty good," remembers Pete Whelpton, Royal Caribbean's longtime hotel operations chief. Whelpton, rarely one to defer to anyone, nevertheless recognized the importance of keeping the Norwegian officers happy. "They got their bottles, and they got their special meals and certain kinds of special cheeses, and whatever they liked to get. But what happened because of that was, they created a double standard on board. And the double standard merely said, that if you were a certain nationality and you belonged to the 'deck and engine,' you could rape a woman, you could fall down the stairs, you could tell a hotel manager to piss off, and you'd get a smack on the wrist, and a 'Now, you behave yourself.' If a hotel guy did that, he's summarily dismissed."

One outcome of life in an environment so simultaneously freewheeling and totalitarian was that sexual politics often became very political indeed. For cruise ship veterans—and especially for the women, who as time went on became more and more plentiful on board—sexuality was a delicate, eternal exercise in strategy. For female—and, occasionally, male—crew members, the right relationship with the captain or a senior officer could mean a much sweeter life. When things were good, savvy paramours could expect assignment to better accommodations, champagne on tap and a significantly reduced workload. "You could get what you wanted," one longtime tactician d'amour remembers. "But in exchange for that you were going to be their mistress and do things their way. . . . You'd get a nice leather chair in your cabin. It makes things happen."

Of course, a lover with that sort of power can just as easily make life uncomfortable for his companion when things don't go his way. One young crew member discovered this double edge when she returned to her cabin after a particularly stormy lover's spat to find every piece of furniture removed; another fight ended with a dead fish placed in her ventilation duct. If her cabin was rendered uninhabitable, her influential lover reasoned, she'd have no choice but to return to him. But that was just the way things went; he was well within the bounds of his authority, if not technically within his rights. The best strategy, old hands among cruise ship women say, was to room with the captain's girlfriend. This way, you get most of the perks without having to sacrifice your independence—sexual and otherwise.

All manner of things went that way, mixing the dynamics of desire, commerce and control. Recreational drugs were as plentiful as everything else during the years of the industry's reckless youth, and they were consumed as brazenly. One former crew member remembers reporting to the cruise director for his first day of work. "And there was this rock of cocaine the size of a golf ball sitting right on his coffee table." In such a tight working environment, knowledge of who was doing what could often be as much of a currency as sex was. "It's just like jail," one former casino worker on Carnival ships asserts. "There's always somebody who can pretty much get you anything you want; once you figured out who that was, and who's doing the drugs, you get a certain amount of immunity. I was never one to call the shots, but a lot of times I was in messes where somebody else might have been fired, where I wasn't, because I guess certain people were afraid I would talk. If the casino manager's buying coke off of somebody, they're not going to want it to get out."

It was something of a golden age.

At the center of the cruising experience was the cruise director. For the audience back home, this critical function was typified by *The Love Boat*'s Julie, an adorable social hostess and administrator who spent her days wandering the ship with her clipboard and sweetly attending to the sundry organizational and emotional crises of her miniature community at sea. Real-life cruise directors performed Julie's functions and more, presiding over hairy-chest competitions, beer-drinking races and the evening's variety acts with courtly attentiveness and vaudevillian charm. Shtick was a prerequisite, and they all had their trademarks. One ship featured a pair of identical twin brothers as co-cruise directors. For the first few days of the cruise, their routine was to simply do their jobs, never letting on that there were two of them, and never letting a passenger see them together. "It seems like you're everywhere at once," the passengers would say. On the appropriate evening, the pair would mount the stage together during one of the marquee events, invariably inspiring a moment of stunned silence followed by a roar of appreciative applause at their elaborate joke.

You couldn't do the job without being an entertainer, but a good cruise director's best roles were performed belowdecks, at the heart of the underground economies that really drove life on the ships. And they made a killing.

The era of the credit card had not yet taken hold during the cruise industry's formative years, and when Ted Arison gained genuine control of Carnival in 1975, magnetic stripe readers were still on the cutting edge. It was only toward the end of the decade that major retailers like JCPenney and others began accepting third-party charge cards like Visa, American Express and MasterCard. As the new cruise lines were getting off the ground, major purchases like home furniture or airline tickets were still paid for with cash or personal checks. And while a check served for the advance deposits on the cruise tickets themselves, everything purchased on board the ships was paid for in currency.

When all the cocktails, cigars, shore excursions, bingo cards and souvenirs sold aboard were added up, the take on a good cruise could run into the millions of dollars—all of it flowing through the cruise director's hands. There was only so much oversight that could be done from Miami; record keeping was minimal, and shipboard workers in the right positions were able to take unbelievable advantage. "There were a lot of what we call 'partnerships,'" remembers one cruise line president. "Bar waiters would be a partner with us—we just didn't know it at the time." Years later, when the cruise lines finally moved to cashless, computerized payment systems on most of their ships, shoreside executives would be stunned at the amounts they were suddenly recapturing. As much as 3 percent of the gross onboard sales had been being diverted—even at Carnival, which was famous for its parsimony. In an investigation into corruption on the Miami waterfront during the 1970s, the FBI would record a Florida mobster explaining the setup at one unidentified cruise line to his disbelieving confreres from the north. "Every meal sold got a kickback," he told them. "Every quarter that went into a slot machine got a kickback. Every bottle of booze sold in the gift shop, or every bottle of per-fume, got a kickback. That one little vessel had enough kickback on it to put many thousands of dollars aside every ship. Right smack off the top."

It was a hustler's dream, and the cruise directors were in on almost all of it. There was a lot of off-the-books money to be made in the right jobs on board, but getting assigned to them could be costly. Complex systems of kickbacks and informal profit sharing ran through the cruise director's office; waiters would kick up to maitre d's in order to make sure they were assigned to the big tables where the tips were fat; maitre d's in turn kicked their share up to the cruise director. On some ships, the cruise directors had to pay the captains, but as often as not the captains were unaware of the ship's hidden economy—a byproduct of their power's insularity. Shoreside management tended to turn a blind eye to most of these practices—it only made the work-ers more efficient, after all—so long as they got their cut.

Micky Arison remembers a behind-the-scenes environment that resem-bled *The Sopranos* more closely than it did *The Love Boat*. "So much money was being siphoned off through this corruption; everybody knew that all this stuff was going on, but it was all cash, it was all undocumented," he recalls. "The bingo money used to be the cruise director's play money—and it was a lot. What I think people didn't realize in the early days was how much money it was."

The real gold mine for the cruise directors, however—the angle that turned the best of them into off-the-books millionaires—wasn't on the ships themselves, but in the ports of call. From the industry's beginnings, one of the major appeals of the cruise holiday was the chance to shop in the quaint, tax-free port towns of the Caribbean. And people came to spend, purchasing everything from transistor radios to cases of rum to loose diamonds. As pas-senger volume picked up, local merchants began to seek a competitive edge over their neighbors. That was where the cruise directors came in. They were the passengers' link to the islands, advising them where to go and what to do ashore. The "shopping talks" they gave before arriving at each port were so popular that they often had to stage them back to back, as the auditoriums were too small to accommodate all comers. For a price, directors steered their passengers to various shops and attractions in the various ports of call, and as their influence grew, they began charging simply not to steer traffic away. "Those that really knew the power of their word marketed that power to the local suppliers of services very clearly," recalls a former resort operator in the

Dominican Republic, now an executive with Royal Caribbean. "They made it clear that if the product was to really be successful, they needed to be involved in it. And if they were not, then you wouldn't be successful." Another longtime industry executive remembers, "In the old days, the cruise director was a very, very powerful person. It was like a symbiotic relationship where he'd go around and collect envelopes from all these shops. That was his big job in port, to collect cash."

Occasionally, shipboard excesses bordered on full-fledged organized crime. Prostitution rings sprang up from time to time; one worked through the ship's spa and beauty salon, while another gave new meaning to the term "room service." Drug smuggling, long a staple of Caribbean commerce, was rampant. Crew members—and sometimes passengers—secreted bundles of heroin, cocaine and marijuana in their bags. When customs started searching the luggage, they began stashing it in the ship's railings and ventilation ducts; when customs started searching the ships themselves, they welded oil drums onto hull bottoms, below the waterline. Millions of dollars' worth of contraband entered the U.S. in this way annually—and still does. It was dangerous work, however, and far more clandestine than the rest of it. In general, the income from the cruise directors' lower-profile activities was so good that their main interest lay in making sure they kept their jobs and avoided unwanted attention. Why get greedy?

Ultimately, this era put an end to itself. Many of the most effective cruise directors simply retired on the vast sums they'd stashed away. Others had inevitably failed to save, and when they succumbed to burnout from the hard-driving shipboard life, they took promotions into the shoreside management. Their practiced eyes suddenly on the other side of the table, they saw to it that most of the old loopholes were soon plugged up. Profits that had run to individuals began flowing into the companies instead, although many of the internal transactions and power structures between crewmembers continued. Along with the increasingly complex corporate structures the cruise lines had begun developing to deal with their growing operations, this migration signaled the beginning of the end for cruising's wild and crazy days. Like any thriving frontier, that era was ultimately a victim of its own success.

CHAPTER SIX

RUDE AWAKENINGS

I have enough money to last me the rest of my life, unless I buy something.

—Jackie Mason

A confluence of events had given the cruise industry the one thing no amount of hard work can guarantee: a magic moment. As the swinging seventies gave way to the "Me Decade," all the structural elements were in place for a textbook boom. The bygone age of transport-oriented passenger shipping was still recent enough to ensure the cruise lines a ready supply of cheap, serviceable ships—in mothballs, perhaps, but suitable for conversion to cruising. And, thanks to Hollywood, there was suddenly more passenger demand than the industry could hope to handle. From Miami, the road ahead looked paved with gold. But if the 1970s had been about proving that the cruise business was a feasible jet-age enterprise, the 1980s would be about determining whether operators in Miami and elsewhere had what it took to turn the industry into a major commercial success. It was about growing up, in other words: learning to play the game on the level of America's real power brokers. There were hard knocks ahead, and lesson one was that prosperity cuts both ways.

At Carnival, the new decade kicked off in much the same way as the previous one had: with a world of promise on the horizon and an episode that threatened to bury the company. For Ted Arison and his team, as for much of the burgeoning cruise industry, the spring of 1981 would be a season of harsh confrontations with the realities of success.

During the years since Ted had taken over the business in 1975, growth had been steady and encouraging. If ticket prices were low and the brand was still at the bottom of the barrel, profits were constantly improving. The bottom of the barrel, as Carnival was learning, was sometimes not such a bad place to be. Still uncertain about the future of the industry, most of Carnival's competitors had been funneling their profits elsewhere at year's end—in many cases using them to subsidize the less profitable cargo ventures of their owners, who still viewed cruising as a sideline. Ted had other ideas. Under Meshulam Zonis's miserly eye, every spare penny had been channeled into Carnival's future, first to upgrade the ramshackle *Mardi Gras* and then to buy other ships from their bankrupt owners in Europe. By the end of the decade, Ted's fleet of Fun Ships numbered four—including, to everyone's astonishment, the about-to-be-delivered *Tropicale*, the first new cruise ship built in almost ten years.

In Miami, Carnival's overworked management team felt that the company was finally seeing daylight. At sea, however, resentment had been simmering. Growing numbers of the crew watched the company expand and wondered where their share of the new prosperity was. On Easter Sunday that year, the pot boiled over.

The morning began like any other weekend day, filled with the ordered chaos of turning two cruise ships full of passengers around within the space of a few hours. The *Mardi Gras* was sitting bow to bow in the Port of Miami with Ted's second ship, the *Carnivale*, taking on passengers and supplies in preparation for a late-afternoon departure. But there would be no sailing that day. Instead, around midday, a group of nearly three hundred crew members voiced their frustrations in the most dramatic fashion. Without warning and without a plan, they seized the ships, initiating a standoff that would stretch out over the coming days.

No one remembers exactly what triggered the action. Some people recall a controversial firing; others point to frustration over the delay of yet another round of paychecks. A Miami attorney who came to represent the strikers points to an injury to one of the workers as the spark that set it all off. For the Honduran deckhands who made up the vast majority of the strikers, being far from home on the holiest day of their year was probably a factor. Among the Jamaican hotel workers who constituted the remainder of the group, many would have been influenced by the fiery politics of their homeland at the time, which blamed its economic desperation on a racist and imperialist United States, saw Havana as a better friend than Washington and spoke daily of legacies lost and stolen. At any rate, the incident itself was important only insofar as it underscored the frustrations with life belowdecks on the Fun Ships, with its long hours, low pay and racial slurs from the all-white officer corps, with a life lived in cramped quarters and at the mercy of the captain and no recourse to impartial authorities ashore. When a small cadre of workers started calling for a strike that afternoon, they found they had an attentive audience.

Confused, frightened passengers who'd barely started unpacking their bags in expectation of a dream vacation suddenly found themselves hustled from their cabins and over the gangway without warning or explanation. Many, including a large group of high school girls traveling on a school trip, were so quickly forced off that they lost their passports and birth certificates. Word reached the Carnival offices that something was happening down at the port, but even then no one grasped the magnitude of what was taking place: About a third of the *Carnivale*'s and *Mardi Gras*'s crews was in control of two-thirds of the company's fleet. And they were angry. The strikers gathered at the bow of each ship to form a strategy, fastening heavy lines between them to prevent towing and stringing thinner ones across the gap that they would use to pass notes back and forth. Inside, gangs patrolled the vessels, "making sure that no one else worked" and enjoying their newfound power in an environment where powerlessness had always defined their experiences.

From the outset, though, it was obvious that the action had not been well planned. There was no strategy: even as the crew vowed to hold the ships for as long as it took to win their (as yet unspecified) demands, the chefs who were cooking for them were being chased out of the galleys as scabs. Oratory from the Jamaican contingent, declaring the strike a victory for "Black Power," left many of the Hondurans wondering what exactly they were risking their jobs for. Evidence of a hasty, ill-planned venture was everywhere. As reports of the mutiny spread through the port and the news helicopters began circling in the sky above to get footage for the evening broadcasts, the cameras caught a misspelled sign among the dozens of waving workers seated on the decks, inviting people to "COME ON BOARD AND LEARN THE TROUT" about their working conditions.

Anyone who was familiar with Carnival's hiring policies would not have been surprised to see the poor spelling. As the fleet had grown, one of Zonis's chief recruiting methods had been to rely on word of mouth from existing workers—especially the Hondurans, who had proved to be diligent, reliable employees, seemingly all too happy to leave behind the dismal economy of their homeland. A long line of brothers, cousins and friends of the Honduran crew was always waiting in the wings as new jobs became available; the chance to help them get cruise ship work was considered a significant perk within the hierarchy of shipboard benefits. For Carnival's part, having a centralized recruitment apparatus and a labor force invested in long-term good relations with the company made a lot of sense—and for Zonis, the arrangement helped solidify the intangibles of influence that he prized so highly. As harsh management and poor working conditions on the ships diminished the company's reservoir of goodwill, however, the system also provided workers with a natural community within which they could nurture their discontent without fear of discovery. When the time came, it ensured that the strikers would be a close-knit and unified group.

Ashore, Carnival's management was caught completely by surprise. Hindsight would show that its attentions had been elsewhere. The late 1970s had seen a heavy focus on making changes within the company, beginning with Ted's surprise appointment of Micky as president in 1979. Barely thirty at the time, Micky was still much closer to the young man who liked to party a little too much than he was to the magnate he would later become. His long hair, tinted glasses and the wide-collared shirts he wore open to his chest were a far cry from a corporate president's typical uniform. His manner, forthright and comfortable one on one but painfully shy in public settings, did little to improve the image. In big rooms, Micky lurked around the edges.

Nevertheless, Ted had felt it was time to make the transition. Micky had been a success since he'd been hired over his father's objections. He'd worked his way up from that first sales route in rural Florida to a central role in the company's reservations department, and with every step the company had been the better for his advancement. He was due to move up again, but there was nowhere left to promote him within the existing management structure without displacing loyal, high-performing executives—something Ted was unwilling to do. So Ted got out, just like that. "He called me down to his office," Micky remembers, "and told me, 'I think you're ready.' " Ted would remain chairman, he explained, steering the company's long-term vision and keeping responsibility for building new ships, but on a day-to-day basis, the company was Micky's to run as he saw fit. In fact, Ted was moving his personal offices to a space he'd already rented downtown so as not to undermine the new structure. And with those words, Ted closed his briefcase, stood, and walked out of the room. "I was blown away," Micky recalls. "Completely shocked. I did not at all personally feel I was ready. It took me days, if not weeks, to get myself together." Once Ted had left, Micky shut the door of his new office in a daze. He didn't come out for the rest of the day.

Ted's decision was all the more extraordinary for the fact that he and Micky, never terribly close, had been "knocking heads" more and more often as Micky had risen in the company. "It's not like me and my father agreed on a lot of things," Micky remembers. "In retrospect, I give him a huge amount of credit. He recognized that I'd run the company completely differently than he did. He recognized that I didn't agree with most of his management. And yet he basically said, 'Okay, you've got it,' and good-bye. 'If you want my advice, give me a call, but I'm not going to interfere.'" Given the differences between their two personalities, a major shift in the tone of Carnival's operations was inevitable. If Ted was the great optimist, Micky was a worrier and moody; his instincts led him away from his father's cronies and toward a stricter management discipline. He could be very warm when he wanted to be, even ebullient, but to those who'd grown used to Ted's gentle, paternal manner, Micky could come off as aloof. Looking back, some of those observers now attribute that impression to his youthful shyness, but that accounts for only part of it. For all of the love beads and hippie sympathies of his younger days, Micky had a hard, competitive edge; he was more aggressive, less forgiving than his father. True to his word, Ted looked on from the sidelines in the following months as Micky reorganized much of the management structure his father had assembled, drawing the line only at a few top people—executives who'd been with him for years—who Micky wanted replaced.

As Micky struggled for traction in his father's old office, the tensions on Carnival's ships continued to grow unnoticed. Micky was surely overwhelmed, but he was also distracted. He was in love, for one thing—and in competition for his sweetheart's hand. The girl was in Monaco, and so was Micky's attention. "That whole fall," he remembers, "my focus was on how to get her from Monaco to Miami. My focus was not on running the company." Nor was it merely his mind that was wandering; one of his early acts as Carnival's president was to fly to Piraeus, in Greece, ostensibly to inspect a ship. Micky recalls it as the "first excuse for a date" of his tenure, but not his last.

And there was more than enough to occupy what attention he did have to spare for the business without getting into the finer points of shipboard morale. A salmonella outbreak earlier that year had forced the company to finally break with its cut-rate food and beverage concessionaire, who in turn did everything he could to sabotage the final voyages under his contract. The outbreak had been severe; the afflicted ship was out of service for an entire week. When Zonis got the news, the story goes, he pulled up at the pier in such a furor that he forgot to put his new Oldsmobile into park before getting out and running to the gangway. Away it rolled behind his back, creeping slowly toward the edge of the pier before tumbling, after an agonizing last-minute balancing act, into the water. Zonis blames a faulty transmission, an explanation that draws snickers to this day.

But the strike was Micky's first real crisis. Less than two years into his presidency, he had two ships out of service—potentially indefinitely—and a huge percentage of his employees in outright revolt. That he'd had to cancel the two cruises—which alone cost millions in lost revenues and refunds—was bad enough. Micky's real concern, driven by informants aboard, was sabotage, and as talks went nowhere, the chances of that seemed to be increasing by the hour. "Our fear was that they'd burn the ship down," he remembers. "That they'd do something really stupid." He was hearing "all sorts of talk about sabotaging the ship, breaking the toilets, lopping pipes and everything else." Something would have to give, he knew, but until then he was at the mercy of an angry crew—and patience was a luxury he could ill afford. "Whatever you're going to do," the warnings kept coming in, "you'd better do it quickly."

Zonis, of course, was beside himself, as many of the strikers were his own people. The world they were rejecting so suddenly and with such a fury was a world that he himself had shaped, a world he'd prided himself on knowing the ins and outs of. The situation was irreconcilable with his benevolent self-image as "the good guy that allowed so many Hondurans to be with their families, with their brothers, with their cousins, with everything." It was painfully clear that this was not how his workers saw it. "It was devastating," Micky remembers, "because they were revolting against his management. It was much more personal for him. It was to some degree a lack of sensitivity to the issues of those guys, but I think he felt betrayed by a lot of guys that he thought would have told him if there were issues."

But how could there not be issues? Carnival crews slept six to a cabin with little space or opportunity for recreation. Workdays could run in excess of twelve hours for uninterrupted months on end. The heavy workload and the crowded quarters clearly exacerbated the situation, but Carnival's real problem was people; similar conditions obtained on many other cruise ships, and none of them had experienced anything like the drama unfolding aboard the *Mardi Gras* and *Carnivale*. Carnival's officers—Zonis's officers—ruled with a heavy hand and without objection from the Miami office. "We weren't very diligent about crew relationships," Micky says. "There clearly was a, let's say, over-authoritarian middle management on the ship. These guys were not being treated the way they should have been." The strikers' action could have been perceived as an unfortunate but necessary move to draw senior management's attention to their plight. But they would not profit from their courage. It was regrettable that things had gotten so bad, Micky recalls thinking, but he had a business to build and he would be damned if he was going to let the unions get a stranglehold on him. "By the time they reacted the way they reacted, it was too late to deal with their issue," he remembers. "We decided to fire them and start again, and hopefully when we started again we'd do a better job of recruiting and training."

But the strikers still had his ships. The situation was already precarious; firing them outright might remove whatever hopes were still keeping them from causing serious damage.

Because the takeover had been a spontaneous expression of anger and frustration and not an organized union drive, there was no strikers' fund, no support from allied unions. But for the three hundred–odd men on the ships, neither was there any going back. As the initial euphoria of their audaciousness had worn off and it became clear to the strikers just how poorly they were situated, the atmosphere grew increasingly charged with fear and menace. As their demands wilted from bold calls for better working conditions to feeble requests for back pay before being shipped home, the threat of violence became more and more imminent. Everyone felt things slipping out of control. For many of the Hondurans, the close-knit community that at first had seemed such a source of strength had turned into a trap. Some among the strikers later said they'd contemplated going back to work but that they'd been threatened with reprisals if they did. "The key was that there were a couple of people that were ringleaders, and these ringleaders coerced other people to join them," one crewmember at the time remembers. "They were threatening families at home; it was really not nice. . . . And a lot of guys got roped into it not because they wanted to but because they were afraid not to be. I just remember it as being really, really sad."

By the end of the third day, everyone was haggard and frightened; on shore, Micky worried for his ships while the hundreds on board wondered bleakly what the future held for them and for their families at home who en masse would soon be receiving fresh mouths to feed along with radically slashed incomes. The big decisions had already been made; Micky had known from the beginning that he was going to fire them, and immigration officials at the port had long since agreed to deport the workers once they were removed. The strikers never had a chance.

When it finally came, Micky's move was swift and decisive. In anticipation of removing the strikers, he'd hired a small army of private security guards—a very intimidating group of "ex-paratroopers" rented from Wackenhut, the business that today runs prisons around the world and provides security for nuclear power plants and similar facilities. "These guys were Rambo-type guys," one crew member at the time—and not the only one to invoke Sylvester Stallone's iconic tough-guy role—remembers. "These guys were tough; they were really, really tough. They were scary guys." Big men every one of them, helmeted and armed with knives, clubs and sidearms, they were kept carefully out of sight for the time being. It was the morning of the strike's fourth day, but the decision to go in had already been made. The delay was simply a matter of tactics.

Hair-raising though it had been, the duration of the sit-in ultimately gave Micky his opening. After days of siege, things had settled into certain patterns and routines, and the assault team used that to its advantage. The Miami press had been following the story breathlessly, and the strikers had grown to expect the daily appearances of the television trucks and news helicopters. "What we noticed was that they had been cued to play to the cameras," Micky remembers. "We came up with a diversionary tactic."

What happened next could have come out of a Hollywood action movie. Micky sent word to the strikers that he was ready to negotiate and requested that the leadership meet with him ashore. After they arrived he sent a rented helicopter disguised to look like it was from one of the news networks—fake camera crew and all—for a flyby on the water side of the ships. As the bleary strikers clamored to that side to wave their misspelled signs for the umpteenth time, Carnival's private SWAT team crept silently across the gangway and onto the ship.

Leaderless, their defenses down, the strikers were sitting ducks. One crewmember loyal to the company remembers the point of no return. "An announcement was then made on the two ships that immigration was doing an inspection in such-and-such a lounge," he recalls. "What happened was, all the good crew members went to that lounge; all the bad crew members stayed on strike up on the bow. The bad guys were sealed off on the bow." The security force moved in.

Out of nowhere, the strikers on the two ships found themselves sur-rounded by dozens of heavily armed, masked and helmeted men. Shouts and threats came at them from every direction, but it was a highly disciplined ma-neuver. For the most part, the strikers were gentle working people who'd long since recognized that they were caught up in events that had gotten away from them. Any chance of their offering physical resistance evaporated as they broke into a panic. "Some of the crew just didn't want to move, and when these guys started yelling and screaming and threatening, 'I'm going to blow your head off if you don't move,' it's amazing how fast these guys moved," one witness remembers. "They were very threatening and very, very aggressive to get people to do what they wanted. I thought it was scary." The open space of the deck had been the only feasible place to make a stand. Once inside the winding gangways of the ships, the strikers found they had only one route open to them. "Every exit on the route to the gangway was covered by big Wackenhut guys," Micky recalls. "If they tried to go in an-other direction, there was no way."

If anything, the show of force at the gangway was even more over-whelming—a "mighty display of power," as the strikers' attorney would later describe it. The moment the operation on board the ships had gone into ef-fect, a fleet of rented prison buses pulled out of hiding and drove up to the gangway. Under the eyes of dozens of Miami-Dade County police officers, the rebellious crewmembers were hustled past waiting immigration officers and onto the buses. "They flew off that ship," Micky remembers. "Immigra-tion was there, stamping passports 'deported.' " But by that time, it was al-ready over. "Dade County put a double row of huge, riot-type policemen with big batons, big helmets, very intimidating," the attorney remembers. "They had a double row of them from the gangplank all the way out to these prison-type buses. And then they hired the private security guards, the rough, tough guys that will do what Dade County can't: go on the ship and break the strike. They picked them up, whether they wanted to be picked up or not, banged them around and marched them out."

For nearly all of the striking workers, the step onto the prison buses with their chicken-wire windows would be the last time their feet ever touched U.S. soil. The buses rolled in a convoy to the airport, where their occupants were loaded onto waiting charter planes cleared for takeoff to Honduras. A last-minute court fight kept the planes on the ground for several hours, but finally they took off. In a few cases, executives and ships' officers had been able to pluck a favorite worker or two out of the line before they'd had their passports stamped, but mostly cases there was no choice but to follow the hard line Carnival's young president had drawn. The entire ordeal was terribly painful for all involved; some of the deported workers had been with the company almost from the beginning and had put in countless hours of dedicated work to keep Ted's dream alive. Even Zonis, years later, wept while telling the story of the breaking of the strike.

As he watched his clients depart, the attorney found himself contemplating the meaning of what had just taken place. This, he thought, was the stuff of coal mines and auto plants, not of a local cottage industry. "Now," he would ask years later, "how do you get a customs guy to come down to the port at your private company's beck and call? How do you get armed riot policemen to come down here to do your private business? You do that by a lot of money and a lot of pull and a lot of power. It was a mighty display of power."

Carnival, in other words, was on its way.

The late 1970s had seen a sea change in the industry, and the name of the new game was growth. Everywhere, in those days, ambition and insecurity were hazing the atmosphere. Notwithstanding stagflation and a sputtering national economy, cruise traffic out of U.S. ports had been setting records almost every year since Ted Arison and Knut Kloster first teamed up to form NCL. With the war in Vietnam finally at an end, things promised to get better still. When the Carter administration deregulated the airlines in 1978, the feeling in Miami was that a world of expanding profits would not be far behind. New cruise ships were being built for the first time in nearly a decade; others were being hauled from the graveyard and cleaned up at a furious pace. New operators were coming in at every level of the market from bargain basement to ultraluxury, while the existing players maneuvered for position in what everyone sensed would be a coming roller-coaster ride. Things were simply getting too big for the cozy, catch-as-catch-can manner to which the industry had grown accustomed, and observers were unanimous on one point: the future lay with more and bigger ships.

This wasn't exactly news to Ted Arison; as soon as he'd gained control of his company, he'd gambled everything on the future and had never looked back. Others weren't so decisive. At Royal Caribbean, the trio of Norwegian firms who owned the company spent years agonizing over if, how and when to expand. Almost from the beginning, president Ed Stephan and the rest of the Royal Caribbean management in Miami had been pushing for new vessels to meet the growing demand, but as the 1970s began drawing to a close, there was still no decision from Oslo. Things had come to something of an impasse. Unlike most of its competitors, Royal Caribbean had begun its business with new, specially designed ships, and it wasn't about to start playing the salvage game. But what had cost $13 million to build in 1969 was now going for many times that. It never failed: every time two of the partners were feeling flush and optimistic, caution or finances led the third to balk at sinking that much money into the venture. Finally, the board settled on a compromise, albeit a bold one: rather than building a new ship, they would lengthen the ships they had, starting with the *Song of Norway.*

It was a radical notion and by no means an inexpensive one. The total cost of the operation came to $12 million—nearly as much as it had cost to build the original vessel, but a bargain compared with the $100 million or more that a comparable ship would have cost to be built from scratch. It also made a lot of sense in terms of the bottom line. The stretched ship would carry nearly a third again as many passengers as before, and with a minimum of extra crew and hardware. It was a poetic expression of the industry's new buzzword—a perfect "economy of scale."

Economies of scale, of course, were hardly unique to the cruise industry; the principle itself dates back to Adam Smith's writings in the eighteenth century. The essence of the idea is that, on a unit-by-unit basis, a system that builds one thousand houses in a year will do it cheaper than one that builds ten of them. Build ten, and each time you've got to make every nail, every plank and every shingle yourself, because with so little work, who can afford to specialize? Build one thousand, and suddenly there's enough to support entire side industries of blacksmiths, carpenters and masons, each of them finding ways to do his job better and with less expense as he perfects his craft. The greater the scale, the more efficient the economy.

It was the pursuit of these efficiencies that drove the industrial revolution and the concurrent rise of modern cities, eventually finding its purest expression in Henry Ford's assembly line, where everyone did only a single, highly specific job. Today, the principle is actively applied to everything from fast food to high tech, as manufacturers strive to minimize the costs of starting up and stopping production by standardizing products—or even components of products—as much as possible into a single, steady flow.

By the late seventies, economies of scale were so obvious an advantage in commerce that they hardly needed explanation. Cruise ships were a perfect manifestation of the principle. Whether carrying one hundred passengers or one thousand, a ship still had one captain, one power plant, etc. And what did a staff of fifteen highly paid European engineering officers care how many passengers were on board, so long as the ship they were running could hold them? The fixed costs were more or less the same; cabins don't burn fuel. Building for more passengers did mean bringing on more hotel staff to cater to them, but these workers came so cheap that they were almost free—all of them from the Third World, most working almost entirely for tips. Beyond a certain point, every extra passenger represented pure profit. As long as a company could fill the cabins it had paid to have built, there was no reason not to build as many of them as it could afford—and the cruise lines had been putting passengers on waiting lists for years.

The *Song of Norway* returned to Helsinki in the autumn of 1978 to the same shipyard where it had originally been constructed. Against a backdrop of the season's eerie half-light, sparks played though the acrid smoke of burning metal as workers inside a massive building shed literally sliced the ship in half with welding torches—room by room, cabin by cabin, cutting through the ceilings, floors and walls that held its honeycombed insides together. Once the incision was completed, a tug dragged the now-freestanding stern, floated on a pair of massive pontoons, out into the icy harbor. Another pushed the new midsection—already fitted with outer decks, windows, a new swimming pool and more than 150 finished cabins—in toward the half-ship. It was a weird, improbable sight: bulky, disembodied puzzle pieces bobbing along like *Fantasia* broomsticks. Putting the pieces back together was by far the hardest part of the process. "Each section floated at maddeningly different depths," a company history reports. "Engineers had to play a patient juggling game, with ballast tanks and winches, scrupulously aligning their trio of disparate floating craft into one seamless, horizontally aligned whole."

Adam Smith would have been proud: back in action, the lengthened ship began to generate soaring profits, and in 1979 Royal Caribbean sent the second of its three vessels, the *Nordic Prince,* for the same treatment. It was a bad time for building, however. The shipyards were no longer as desperate for business as they'd been even a short time before, and the best price Royal Caribbean could negotiate for the refitting was $20 million. The board went ahead with the procedure but balked at repeating it a third time. The moment for half-measures was past. Instead, the decision was finally made to finally order a new vessel, to be delivered in 1982 at a price tag of $150 million. The Norwegians knew a golden goose when they saw one: the ship's name would be *Song of America.*

After years of conservatism, Royal Caribbean was making a great leap forward. The completed *Song of America* weighed in at around thirty-seven thousand tons, compared with twenty-three thousand for the lengthened *Song of Norway* and twenty-seven thousand for the *Mardi Gras.* In keeping with president Ed Stephan's design philosophy, cabins were kept on the small side, although they received upgrades like full-size windows and individual thermostats. But there were many more of them, and greatly expanded public spaces, including Broadway-themed venues like the "Guys and Dolls Lounge" and the "Oklahoma Lounge"; a state-of-the-art arcade where "kids of all ages" could sample trendsetters like Space Invaders and Ms. Pac-Man; and a dazzling two-story dining room ringed with inward-facing balconies.

The entertainment on board remained squarely in line with the variety show theme that cruise passengers had come to expect—a sort of Borscht Belt on the high seas. Headliners included acts like Baron Bela, who performed the gypsy music he'd recorded for the soundtrack to *Doctor Zhivago.* Late-night fare might be more risqué, like the ventriloquist whose dummy went by the name "Kinky Kong." It could have been the Catskills, if not for the rocking of the ship. "Is that your wife," the dummy would ask hecklers, "or is this a business trip?"

Impressive as it was, *Song of America* was essentially a larger version of its predecessors. Its designs reflected Royal Caribbean's cautious optimism—the expectation, shared by most of the industry at the time, of profitable, gradual growth. It was a big bet, but a relatively safe one.

Under Knut Kloster, NCL took a different tack altogether. The Norwegian had built up his fleet steadily after his disastrous breakup with Ted Arison until he had four very profitable ships—but none with room for more than seven hundred passengers and none larger than twenty thousand tons. He was doing extremely well, but he'd envisioned greater things back when he'd stood at the edge of the still-unfinished Dodge Island almost fifteen years before. No longer young, Kloster had lost none of the philosophical fervor of his MIT days, and he was unhindered by his countrymen's conservatism. His maverick spirit restless, he was ready to make a splash.

In 1979, NCL purchased one of the last great ocean liners, the S.S. *France,* which had been sitting abandoned in a French harbor for five years, destined, it was universally presumed, for the junkyard. Kloster renamed it the *Norway* and instantly became the owner of the world's largest cruise ship, a distinction he'd enjoy for most of the decade. This was the revolution he'd been hoping for. When it was launched in 1980, one former NCL executive remembers, the *Norway* represented fully 40 percent of the total passenger capacity sailing year-round to the Caribbean; at sixty-six thousand tons, 1,035 feet in length—about six city blocks—and with space for more than two thousand passengers, nothing else came close. And even after adding $60 million in refurbishments to the $18 million purchase price, the price tag still came in at well under what it had cost to build the *Song of America.*

It was probably worth it for the free publicity alone. For the first time, a cruise ship featured a five-hundred-seat, three-story theater capable of mounting full-scale stage productions. The initial extravaganza, a sequined, flesh-and-feathers floor show entitled "Sealegs," might have struggled on the Great White Way, but passengers went crazy for it; subsequent years saw reprises like "Sealegs Goes Hollywood" and "Sealegs Goes Circus." A warren of discos and lounges catered to any number of tastes, from neon and strobe-light discotheques à la *Saturday Night Fever* to bookish, leather-covered sitting rooms, to cafés and bars full of retro designs from the mod 1960s. The art collection alone was appraised at more than $2 million, and the exterior paint may not have cost much less; it weighed more than thirty tons. Along with the usual swimming pools and sundecks, there was a paddleball court, an ice-cream parlor and even a driving range. Swooning reviewers swore that when on board, they'd forgotten they were on a ship.

"The *Norway* changed the industry," remembers a top NCL executive from the era. "It really opened people's eyes. The industry was growing, but the *Norway* brought in volume and increased the numbers dramatically."

Kloster may have done it more spectacularly than the rest, but the stage had already been set for a period of dramatic growth by the time he announced his acquisition—even, in fact, before Royal Caribbean had dropped the idea of stretching its ships and fully committed itself to the future. Ted Arison may not have had his old partner's expansiveness or Royal Caribbean's capital base, but he'd clear and away been the first one out of the gate when he announced in 1978 that he'd contracted for the building of the *Tropicale*. Ever since Carnival had first turned a profit, he'd stockpiled every spare cent that parsimony and guile could chisel out of its operating budget. As soon as he could afford to—before he could afford to, really—Ted had acquired two older ships in quick succession: The *Carnivale* in 1975, and the *Festivale* in 1977. The *Festivale*'s arrival in 1978 was a huge event in Miami. At thirty-eight thousand tons, it was a giant by the standards at the time; the industry's underdog, its bottom-feeder, suddenly had the biggest ship in town. The surprising turn of events was greeted with excitement, fanfare and no small amount of speculation as to whether Ted wasn't getting in over his head once again, expanding his rickety little cruise line at such a breakneck pace.

But he was still holding his real bombshell in reserve. Addressing an industry convention that autumn, Ted announced that he'd signed a $100 million–plus contract for a brand-new Carnival ship—the *Tropicale*. His competitors took in the announcement with stunned disbelief. This was back when stretching the *Song of Norway* was big news, a risky investment at a fifth of that amount. Nothing on this scale had been tried since Royal Caribbean's three partners had arrived on the scene a decade earlier, flush with profits from a Norwegian tanker boom, to build its three ships for an average of less than $15 million each. The skyrocketing interest rates and fuel prices of the intervening years had convinced most of the industry that building new cruise ships was all but impossible. Ted's whole *company* wasn't worth $100 million, and all of this was taking place just a few months before he handed the reins over to Micky. But there it was. Quietly, Ted had discovered an extraordinary financial vehicle to help him pull off the deal. What's more, he'd done it right under the Norwegians' noses.

"That," a grinning Micky remembers, "was a great deal." The key was the Danish government, which like much of Europe was fighting runaway unemployment, and for years had been anxiously watching the jet-age decline of its labor-intensive shipbuilding industry. Denmark was willing to go further than most, however; to save the jobs of its shipbuilders, it ended up paying for more than half of Ted's ship. The shipyard gave Carnival a low-interest loan, which it used to buy a raft of specially issued, high-interest government bonds from the Danes. "That's all it was," Micky recalls. "And what you did was, you just matched the debt with the bonds. So you take a $100 million project, and all of a sudden it's $40 million."

Even so, Ted had had to push his company to the limit to make it happen. Poor-mouthing may have been something of a habit with Carnival, but even in success it was still a small company, and $40 million was not an insignificant sum; Ted had just invested tens of millions of dollars in the *Festivale,* after all, and he'd barely started paying *that* back. The fact he'd managed to obtain a loan at all was remarkable, let alone a windfall like this. A landmark new ship was on the way, but things remained so tight at Carnival you would have thought the *Mardi Gras* was still sitting stuck on that sandbar. "When Ted was building the *Tropicale,*" the executive in charge of purchasing remembers, "he would call me and say, 'I need to make a payment; can you stall the suppliers for a couple of weeks?' " Carnival was juggling three or four bills for every one it could afford to pay. Even when the checks had been cut, they often sat locked away in desk drawers for months while the phones rang off the hook with calls from anxious vendors. Every penny counted—and was counted. And counted again. On the ships, big-ticket items like lobster and filet mignon were served on the same night, to keep passengers from ordering both. Bartenders were trained to count the number of maraschino cherries in a jar. "If you're going to serve a thousand drinks," their bosses drilled them, "how many jars of cherries should it take? And if you didn't serve a thousand drinks, where'd the jars of cherries go?" Life at Carnival, in short, went on much as it had before.

Keeping a close watch on the bottom line was only one aspect of survival during this era, however. At least as much depended on the Arisons' ability to keep the more destructive elements of the Dodge Island microcosm at arm's length.

It was an old story; organized crime is a fact of life for every waterfront city in the world, and Miami at that time was no exception. Before Fidel Castro came to power in 1959, the Magic City had been a favorite Cosa Nostra outpost: Al Capone's summer residence; the gateway to Meyer Lansky's Havana. But by the time ships like *Song of America* were on the drawing board, Miami had no more mob glitter than a garden-variety Baltimore or Hackensack. These were instead the salad days for labor racketeering. From New York, the Mafia controlled the International Longshoremen's Association, which gave them de facto control over most of the harbors up and down the eastern seaboard. Cargo ships could bring coffee beans from Africa, transistor radios from the Pacific Rim or designer clothes from Italy or France—the product didn't matter. Once they reached the U.S., their freight had to be unloaded; that meant being able to count on dockworkers, and *that* meant taking care of the ILA.

One of the very few unions deemed so thoroughly corrupt that it was kicked out of the graft-ridden AFL-CIO of the 1950s, the ILA was "virtually a synonym for organized crime in the labor movement," according to a report commissioned by the Reagan White House. Through kickbacks, extortion and hijacking, NBC reported in a 1977 broadcast, "organized crime and the Longshoremen's union have been able to put their tax on every item moving in or out of the ports they control." The film classic *On the Waterfront* portrayed the ILA in New Jersey during the 1950s; with Marlon Brando in front of the camera and Elia Kazan behind, the best picture of 1954 told the story of what happened when an individual took a stand against the union. Its brutal dominance over the bottlenecked inroads to the U.S. economy was worth untold millions.

Up until the late 1960s, Miami had been spared the worst of its excesses. Cargo traffic was what drew the real interest, and the city was a backwater compared with the Northeast's massive harbors. But boom times bring carpetbaggers of every stripe, and as the South Florida population explosion led to the building of Dodge Island and as the Port of Miami grew into a gateway to and from South America, notice began to be paid. Soon enough, the rules in Miami became the same as everywhere else: you had to pay to play. By the early 1970s visitors began showing up, one hand outstretched, the other in a fist. Boxes started falling off the backs of trucks. "Wary shippers reported no thefts," *Newsweek* reported about Dodge Island during this period, "even though they occur in broad daylight. 'It's like a jungle in those warehouses,' said one Miami seaport security guard, 'and we're not even armed. What am

I going to do if a longshoreman comes at me with a tire iron? Hit him with my radio? Forget it; it's their territory.' "

Those in the seaport business community who didn't give the newcomers what they wanted quickly saw their contracts evaporate. The ILA was a national power. The freight lines that did business in Miami were doing far more in New York and New Jersey, and they'd long ago learned not to work with anyone on the union's bad side. "It's not just Miami I got to worry about," shipowners would explain as they fired one or another contractor who'd competently handled their local business for years. "It's New York, and Boston and Philly. . . . Don't make *your* problems *my* problems. We can't afford friction with labor. You know how things are."

The cruise industry had two advantages when it came to the ILA. Most important was the simple fact that its ship carried people, not goods; there really wasn't anything to steal, and thus it took less to keep the powers that be happy. But they did have to be kept happy, if only by letting them know whose side you were on. The nonunion porters who'd been paying for the concession to load passengers' bags onto the ships were replaced with more expensive union people, for example. Royal Caribbean's treasurer at the time remembers an ILA representative showing up every Friday for his tribute. "Nice guy," the treasurer remembers. "Every week he used to come by Royal Caribbean, and they would load a satchel of cash into the back of his car. I think in today's parlance we would call it a 'facilitating payment'; it was to keep everybody happy."

The second advantage was Carmen Lunetta, Miami's port director. As a young civil engineer, Lunetta had been there with Ted Arison and Knut Kloster in the mid-1960s on the day they'd made the deal to start up NCL, and he'd been committed to the cruise industry ever since—"like the fifth man in the boardroom," in his words. In the mid-1970s, after years as deputy director, he took over the top job. To everyone on the docks, Miami was "Carmen's Port." His genius for doling out political favors, strategically timed municipal bond offerings and patronage jobs had given him the clout to run his port like a feudal baron, by turns avuncular and fearsome. For Lunetta, his cronies and "politicians of every stripe," the port was "a punch bowl into which they could dip at will," in the words of the federal judge who, nearly two decades later, would preside over the corruption trial that followed on the heels of Lunetta's hasty resignation. Although he'd end his meteoric career under a cloud of federal indictments, Lunetta for the time being was clearly on the side of the angels—no one wanted to see the port succeed more than he did.

His support often made the difference when the union started pushing too hard. "I had a close working relationship with the ILA," he remembers. "And I could pretty much do all the dirty work for the cruise lines and the cargo lines in bargaining their position, keeping peace between labor and management." The ILA may have had the shipping lines in a stranglehold, but they didn't have Lunetta. No stranger to the proverbial smoke-filled room, he used the carrot when he could; but he swung his stick, too. And with the county government firmly lined up behind him, his stick was a big one. "I used to walk amongst those guys—without a policeman, without any guards or anything else—and face the union leaders and shout them down in front of their own men, and things like that," Lunetta recalls. "I never felt that they were going to take my life or anything like that, but it got hairy from time to time."

One particularly tough labor negotiation during this era makes a good case in point. The ILA baggage handlers who'd replaced the concessionaires were pushing for bigger crews at the passenger terminal, and the talks had stretched into the late hours of Saturday morning with no end in sight. All around the country, would-be passengers—their deposit checks already cashed—were getting out of bed, ready to catch their flights and start their cruise vacations. Knowing that Saturday was the busiest turnaround day of the week for the cruise lines, the baggage handlers were threatening to strike.

Everyone feared the worst—including Lunetta, who was trying to broker the agreement. *We're going to have a major strike*, he remembers thinking. But at the eleventh hour, with Lunetta leaning on every pressure point he could find, the parties came to an agreement both sides could live with. Congratulating each other, the negotiators strolled outside into the breezes of the waning Miami night—smack into a sea of blue uniforms emerging from under the Dodge Island Bridge.

Diplomacy had succeeded, but the big stick had never been out of reach. "I already had seven hundred policemen in full uniforms—almost like a tank brigade—underneath the bridge, should anything erupt if we couldn't come to an agreement," Lunetta recalls, laughing. "If we had to pick the luggage up from the buses on the other side of the bridge and bring it to the ships, I was ready to do it."

With a strong port director on their side, dealing with the ILA was tolerable enough for the cruise lines. Corruption gave the longshoremen a certain predictability that stood in stark contrast to the young cruise industry's other labor nemesis, the National Maritime Union—or what was left of it.

Formed in 1937 when the United States still had a major merchant marine, the NMU had been instrumental in winning on-the-job protections and better wages for what was then a massive workforce of American seafarers. However, as taxes and wages rose during the postwar years, shipowners had stampeded offshore to register their ships in countries like Liberia, Panama and the Bahamas, where labor was all but unregulated and profits untaxed—"flags of convenience," as they're known in the industry. A force to be reckoned with in its prime, the membership pool of the NMU and affiliated unions had virtually disappeared by 1970. The NMU was a casualty of globalization decades before the phrase was even coined; for all intents and purposes, there were no oceangoing American shippers left even to strike against. Starved, it had deteriorated into a vengeful shadow of its former self.

As cruises aboard foreign-flagged, foreign-staffed ships based in Miami became an icon of American leisure and prosperity, the increasingly toothless union came to see the cruise industry as a metaphor for the system's unforgivable hypocrisy. What venom America's seagoing labor movement had left it directed at the cruise business through pickets, newspaper contributions and any other means its leadership could devise. Its profits were built on cheap foreign labor, they howled to anyone who would listen, even as its companies enjoyed every operating advantage of American corporations.

As far as the cruise lines were concerned, the union was little more than a nuisance. "They didn't accept this policy of having sixty different nationalities aboard like we did," remembers Royal Caribbean's then-president Ed Stephan, "making five or six times what they'd be making at home." Casting their practices in the most favorable possible light, Stephan and other cruise executives debated labor leaders on television, in print and even before Congress. Things at times got so heated that Stephan feared for his safety amid a barrage of threats: "We used to have to check under our cars in the morning." NMU members picketed cruise ships in New York and Miami, but to no avail; disruptive as their demonstrations could be for suburban couples looking to kick off a quiet week in paradise, there was little real pressure they could bring to bear on the cruise lines. And the interests of the two parties were so far apart, there might as well have been an ocean between them. "If they'd even wanted payoffs we'd have given them payoffs," Stephan remembers. "They just didn't want us to exist."

As it happened, it was actually the longshoremen who finally put an end to the industry's struggles with the maritime unions; those Friday-afternoon payoffs were worth something after all. "What the hell do we care about these seamen?" Stephan remembers ILA officials telling him. "They haven't got any jobs; they're not getting any income. You're at least giving us the income. . . . Quietly, if we'd have people picketing, I'd call New York," Stephan explained. "A couple of hours later, guys would show up on the pier and tell these guys to get the hell off or they'd be in the water." That was the power of the ILA in those days—so complete that it eventually took the largest undercover operation in the history of the FBI to break it.

While most of the waterfront was scrambling to keep the mobsters happy, Ted Arison and Meshulam Zonis had decided that the company simply couldn't afford to be extorted. When Fred "Fat Freddy" Fields, New York's man in Miami and by all accounts a dangerous fellow, demanded free tickets for a Christmas cruise in the mid-1970s, Zonis offered him a 10 percent discount. And the little Romanian knew exactly who he was dealing with; he recalls once asking the gangster about the pinky ring he liked to wear, about whether the "ILA" spelled out in diamonds on its surface stood for the initials of his union. "No," Zonis recalls him replying, a menacing chuckle jiggling his girth. "It stands for 'I Love America.'" Still, 10 percent off the price of a cruise was as far as Carnival was willing to go. "You will repent," Fat Freddy promised.

This turned out to be a rare exception from a man not given to empty threats. Just as it had everything else, Carnival survived the mob—thanks to a combination of luck and timing. No one knew it at the time, but when Fields started leaning on Zonis, the FBI had already had the port under surveillance for months, and Fat Freddy was in jail before he had the chance to deliver on his promise. But Ted and Zonis would have done the same thing in any case; they simply didn't scare easily. The way they saw it, there really wasn't that much that the ILA could do to them. The guy who handled their longshoring work had already taken all the beating that Fields and his cronies could dish out, and he was still in business—sort of. He'd once had the biggest dockside operation in Miami, but thanks to his intransigence, Carnival was now his only client. This was Mutzie Kratish, head of a family of self-described "tough Jews" and a man who made Zonis look like Neville Chamberlain when it came to making compromises.

It was Kratish, a fervent Zionist, who'd given Ted Arison space in his offices when he first came to Miami. And it was Kratish who got the contracts for Carnival's ships when things finally started taking off. There were no Cadillacs pulling up to Ted Arison's offices with empty trunks on Friday afternoons. A huge part of the ILA's Miami membership was black, and during the years when having a black face in Miami had meant police harassment, housing troubles and no job security, Kratish had been one of the few white employers to stand up for *all* his people. They never forgot it. When organized crime moved in during the 1970s, Kratish refused to play along. "The boys out of New York that came here to run the union, they tried to get tough," his son remembers. "We said, 'Don't get tough with us. You don't know us, we don't know you. You're no tougher than us. Leave us alone.' " Fat Freddie and his henchmen pushed back. The slip-and-fall death of a Kratish cousin was officially ruled an accident, but the family has its doubts to this day. As the union squeezed, Kratish's contracts—all but Carnival—quickly dried up, but his workers stood by him in spite of pressure from their union. As long as Carnival was still in business, he could make a living, and as long as he was making a living, guys like Fat Freddy couldn't do much to hurt Ted.

Made for each other, the Kratishes and Carnival went on in a sort of mutual limbo vis-à-vis the ILA during the late 1970s. Then, on June 8, 1978, the FBI agents who'd been building their case for months finally descended on the port. They arrested eighteen people, including a number of cargo executives and the presidents of two ILA locals on a seventy-count indictment charging that "businessmen, faced with extortion and intimidation, gave ILA officials kickbacks and payoffs of hundreds of thousands of dollars in cash, cruise ship tickets and other valuables." The resulting convictions reverberated from Dade County to Brooklyn, dealing one of the twentieth century's harshest blows to organized crime on the waterfront. The episode remains one of Zonis's proudest moments. "When they took everybody and everybody was walking down Biscayne Boulevard with the handcuffs, I was walking free because I not only did the right thing, but I also said the truth to everybody," he remembers. "They tried several times. I said, 'Discount? Yes, I'll give them a discount. Free? I don't get a free ticket for *nobody*.' "

Though at the time it was regarded as a salvation of sorts, the image of federal agents swooping down on Miami at the end of the 1970s is also a telling sign of the challenges the industry was beginning to face at the time. The days of the new cruise lines' troubles—and their opportunities—falling under strictly local jurisdiction were quickly passing. The FBI raid was the first of many times that the industry would cross paths with Washington in the years to come. Thanks to their rapid expansion and the efforts of the U.S. maritime labor unions, Washington was beginning to pay attention to the cruise lines. The industry, however, had not yet learned the importance of returning the favor.

One wakeup call came within months of Carnival's Honduran strike in the spring of 1981, when Congress blindsided the industry with a change to the rules for deducting convention-related travel as a business expense. Cruise operators had a significant sideline in hosting such events— trade groups, investment seminars, that sort of thing. For some of them, conventions accounted for as much as 20 percent of their bookings; Carnival alone had earned upwards of $18 million on such bookings in 1980. As far as Miami was concerned, it had been a win-win situation: the cruise lines got access to thousands of free-spending conventioneers, and the dentists or accountants or Amway reps got to write off a week in paradise. Congress didn't see it that way, and neither did the lobbyists for the hotel industry, who'd grown fed up with watching market share in the lucrative conventions trade go to foreign-flagged cruise lines offering fares they couldn't hope to compete with.

Under the new law, only conventions taking place within the U.S. could be deducted as a legitimate business expense; Jamaica, the Bahamas and sunny Mexico were no longer allowable. Nor were cruise ships, unless they'd been built in the U.S., were crewed by Americans, flew the U.S. flag and paid income tax on their profits. That the cruise lines would be targeted by such a bill was in itself unremarkable; critics had been hammering away at their flag of convenience advantages for years. That so important a law should take the cruise lines so completely by surprise, however, was proof positive that something was seriously wrong with the way the industry was doing business.

The fact is, there had never really been any such thing as a "cruise industry," per se. A lot of people were making a lot of money carrying Americans out to sea for their vacations, but they operated the way they always had—as affable but isolated competitors. There were meetings among the heads of various cruise lines each year, but they were as much social affairs as anything else. When issues of common interest were discussed, they tended to be local: docking fees at Dodge Island or problems at Miami International Airport. Beyond these relatively minor issues, there had never seemed to be much of a need for working together in a coordinated fashion. It didn't help that the principals involved were so disparate a bunch: Norwegian oilmen, Greek shipping tycoons, Miami hoteliers, convenience store magnates, an Israeli airfreight consolidator. In more ways than one, they just didn't speak the same language. The same promise of high cash flow and a negligible tax burden had drawn them all into the business, but that was pretty much where their common interests ended.

The industry's only collective representation came from the New York–based International Council of Passenger Lines, a holdover from the days before jet travel had changed the world. The ICPL was little more than a joke, still mired in the transportation-oriented mind-set of yesteryear and hopelessly out of touch with the concerns of the new industry. If the cruise lines needed a watchful presence in the capital, it certainly wasn't going to come from that corner. "The ICPL view was, watch and report in Washington," a top Royal Caribbean executive at the time remembers. "The chairman's office was in New York; some of us joked that he would go hide behind the lions on the capital steps and see what he could hear, but if anybody recognized him, he got the hell out of there as quick as he could. Because his view was, we don't have a constituency. We're foreign-flagged lines."

Whatever small amount of pull the industry had in Washington came from Miami's port director Carmen Lunetta, the same man who helped keep peace with the dockside labor unions. Lunetta had been thinking on a national scale from the beginning. From White House coffee klatches to municipal campaigns, he'd parlayed hundreds of thousands of dollars in unsupervised port funds into political influence on the local, state and federal levels—all of which he placed squarely behind the cruise industry, with one hand giving concessions to the cruise lines to entice them to Miami and the other reaping the fruits of his savvy lobbying in the form of federal infrastructure dollars. Lunetta made it his personal crusade to see Miami emerge as the "cruise capital of the world."

"Every ship that came off the line, I wanted here in Miami," Lunetta remembers. "We kept trying to grab as much as we could of the industry, and then building the facilities fast enough became the biggest problem: good government relationships, finding the dollars, getting the federal involvements that we needed, being able to have the federal agencies—customs, immigration, all the rest—be behind what we were trying to accomplish." In fact, when it came to involving itself with policymakers, Lunetta remembers that same haplessness and caution from the ICPL. "They didn't want too much exposure before politicos and what-have-you," he remembers, "so I guess I started assuming that role. Their posture was pretty much to stay way behind the scenes. I had to project for them what we needed at the port."

As the new tax law made abundantly clear, even the theoretically simple task of watching and reporting government trends seemed to be too much to ask of the industry association as it then was constituted. There had been signs of trouble brewing for some time, if anyone had been looking for them. Bogus tax deductions in the form of "sham vacations" had been getting more and more attention in the national press as the recessionary 1970s drew to a close, and the cruise lines were directly affected. With the nation's coffers severely strained, tax policy was a real story, and reporters loved to write about the more colorful ways in which the loopholes were put to use. Enterprising tour operators were doing a thriving business marketing Caribbean "seminars." All it took to get the write-off for a weeklong resort stay was thirty-four hours of videotaped lectures, seventeen on professional topics and another seventeen worth of investment advice. The screening rooms were no doubt packed with rapt orthodontists and divorce lawyers while the adjoining golf courses stood abandoned beneath the tropical sky. "For this you get a tax deduction?" *Forbes* marveled. "You really have to wonder: If these seminars can be put on videotape. . . . then why should the government subsidize trips to Hawaii to view them?" It was even harder to justify the write-offs taken by a "particularly large and visible number of American lawyers" attending the American Bar Association convention in London around the same time. Their problem wasn't that they'd deducted travel expenses to and from the conference; it was the fact that their chosen conveyances happened to be first-class cabins on the *QE2.*

In Washington's corridors of power, the rumblings had been audible for anyone to hear—anyone who knew what to listen for, that is. They'd been coming not from an outraged public, but from private lobbyists with their own interests at stake. The domestic hotel industry, already in a slump, was "struck with a sudden, chilling fear" for its own convention business and was fighting to close the loophole enjoyed by the cruise lines and other rivals. Hawaii, especially, stood to lose millions if cruise ships and non-U.S. warm-weather locales were allowed to compete. For Congress, the issue was a no-brainer. Every state relies in part on tourism revenues; here was a chance to earn points with local businesses with virtually no political risk. Who was going to complain? Jamaica? Certainly not the foreign-flagged cruise lines, which had only themselves to thank for their impotence on the Hill.

Spark Matsunaga, a Democratic senator from Hawaii, was the original sponsor of the new tax law. Ever sensitive to the concerns of his great state, Matsunaga was the founding chairman of the Senate Finance Committee's blatantly Hawaii-centric sugar and tourism subcommittee. "Pineapple," he'd later remark with a chuckle, "was not in need of federal legislation or assistance at that time." In 1980 the bill passed promptly and without fanfare. In Miami word quickly spread of the "eleventh-hour" vote. Speaking for the entire cruise industry, Carnival's Bob Dickinson complained bitterly that the new law had been "adopted without discussion or debate" and scoffed that "There is nothing worse than a legislator with only half the facts." The industry had been caught unawares, plain and simple, and that failure promised to cost it tens of millions of dollars. In retrospect, though, it was a bargain—a hard but effective lesson that over the coming years would return the loss to the industry a hundredfold or more.

Once it finally dawned on them that the high profile they'd been cultivating could cut both ways, the cruise lines adapted quickly. The embarrassment had fueled "a growing awareness that we were blessed and cursed by our visibility," as one cruise executive put it. "In the early days it was 'No one pays any attention to us: the press doesn't pay any attention to us, government doesn't pay any attention to whether we exist or don't exist.' Well, now they know we're there." Once it had been pulled into the game, the industry found that it excelled at it. Renaming their group the International Council of Cruise Lines, they moved its headquarters to Washington and began putting some genuine lobbying power behind it. Before long, senior lawmakers like Tip O'Neill, Dan Rostenkowski and Jim Wright were making fact-finding trips to Miami, lured in part by increasingly sophisticated public and private fund-raising efforts on the part of industry leaders. "That's when they put their political action committee together," Lunetta remembers. "They realized that there's all these attacks coming at them, that they had to band together with their resources to be able to fight these things. And that's when they started putting a good repertoire of their own together. They just couldn't rely on me to be carrying all those arguments for them."

Everyone makes mistakes; the trick is to make them only once. In subsequent years, as the industry's profile grew even higher and its treasured tax status came under fire from lawmakers as well as the press, the ICCL would come to serve as the flagship of a lobbying investment of many millions of dollars—and every penny of it well spent. Without it, the task of maintaining the comfortable arrangement to which the cruise lines had grown so accustomed might well have been impossible.

By the mid-1980s what the cruise lines needed most, however, was money—real money, the kind that gets $100 million ships built three or four or five at a time. With the exception of Royal Caribbean, nearly every company in the industry had gotten its foothold by acquiring older passenger ships at a steep discount. Now they were faced with two incontrovertible facts. As the era of passenger shipping receded further and further into the past, the pool of serviceable ships had dwindled steeply with it. Worse, the rash of ship construction during the early 1980s had dramatically slashed the profitability of those older vessels; with the exception of the heralded *Norway*, even the best of them couldn't hope to compete with the new crop. The ships that cost the most per passenger to operate were garnering the lowest ticket prices, and the disparity on both ends was increasing all the time. Even Carnival, which by 1984 had come far enough to declare itself "the most popular cruise line in the world," was still sailing a fleet that was three-quarters made up of secondhand ships. It was like trying to swim in quicksand. Everyone was eager to expand, but the very act of building new ships was tantamount to sabotage against the existing vessels whose profits were necessary to drive that expansion. There were only two possibilities facing the industry: grow radically, or die. Capital for building would be the lifeblood of the coming decade, and the kind of money the cruise lines needed came from only one place: It seemed that the future of passenger shipping was going to be in New York, after all.

Among the dominant players at the time, the only immediate contenders for major public financing at this point were archrivals NCL and Carnival. Despite the strength of its brand, Royal Caribbean was struggling under the weight of serious cost overruns and a fractious ownership, and Princess, though profitable, was wholly controlled by a massive British holding company that was not about to let it go. There were smaller lines that could point to investment-grade balance sheets, but their operations were so small that even a stellar public offering wouldn't bring in the money needed to build a large, modern fleet.

After revolutionizing their fleets at the beginning of the decade—Carnival with the *Tropicale* and NCL with the *Norway*—each had continued growing aggressively. In early 1987, both were maneuvering for offerings later that year. Nearly twenty years after Ted Arison's acrimonious departure from NCL, the two companies had followed very different paths. By the end of the 1980s NCL's founder was out of the picture. Ever the visionary, Knut Kloster had let himself be forced out rather than give up on what many of his colleagues and family considered a pipe dream—a supership, like nothing the world had ever seen.

While still at NCL, Kloster had code-named his scheme the "Phoenix Project." Nearly four times the *Norway*'s size, *Phoenix* was to operate as a combined vacation palace and business center, carrying a staggering fifty-two hundred passengers and an additional eighteen hundred crew—a number that rivaled the entire fleet capacity of any of NCL's competitors. Brochures spoke breathlessly of a ship designed for the twenty-first century: a "floating metropolis," a ship with a skyline. In a radical departure from conventional cruise ship design, *Phoenix*'s superstructure would consist of several towers, each of them eight or nine stories high, built atop a giant hull spanning the length of four football fields. If completed according to plan, Kloster insisted, the vessel would be more akin to a floating island than the cruise ships of the day. Cruise ships had miniature swimming pools; *Phoenix* would feature beaches, palm trees and a retractable harbor at which smaller ships could dock. Its amenities were to include nearly one hundred thousand square feet of convention space—about the size of the casino floor in a big Las Vegas hotel. Pumped full of earnestness and grandiosity, the venture had all the earmarks of a Kloster project. He saw it as a perfect fusion of enterprise and ideals wherein, as one brochure imagined, "On this particular day, CEOs of three Fortune 500 companies land their helicopters on the middle tower to join a conference on capitalism and third world development" as sun worshippers lolled at the ship's artificial shore. Early estimates put the building costs somewhere around $1 billion, however, and many within Kloster's own company saw the project as an obvious boondoggle. It was, in any case, not the sort of risk Wall Street investors new to the industry were likely to take.

In 1986, with his board of directors growing ever more convinced that a public offering was the only viable option for the company's future, Kloster was given a choice between abandoning the project and leaving. Bitterly optimistic, he went off on his own, leaving his brother in charge of the business he'd built and giving up a good chunk of his share of the family fortune in order to retain the rights to his beloved *Phoenix*. For the first time since his father's untimely death had thrust the family business upon him more than twenty years earlier, Kloster was a truly free agent.

In one of his final speeches to the industry as chairman of NCL, Kloster quoted, of all people, John DeLorean, the high-flying General Motors executive who went off on his own to build the eponymous car that today, if it's remembered at all, is known only for its cameo in the film *Back to the Future* and its spectacular failure in the marketplace. But then, Kloster was not seeking the conventional. "Morality has to do with people," he intoned on that occasion. "If an action is viewed primarily from the perspective of its effect on people, it is put into the moral realm. Business in America, however, is impersonal." The fact that he was right didn't change the fact that he was wrong; in spite of his commitment, the *Phoenix* would never get beyond the drawing board.

The years leading up to his departure might have taught Kloster that bigger is not always better—economies of scale notwithstanding. The *Norway*, so promising when it first came to Miami, had been a headache ever since—true-life confirmation of the old adage defining a boat as "a hole in the water that you throw money into." Power failures had left the ship dead in the water with a full passenger load more than once; tens of millions of dollars in repairs gave lie to any notion that the ship had been a bargain. Morale boosters around the NCL offices included T-shirts reprinting a cartoon that had run in a local paper depicting the *Norway* with a bristle of oars sticking out from each side of the hull. "We row together," it read. Worse still, it was a terrible distraction to the Miami management, who were having a tough enough time keeping up with the competition's steady stream of new ships without having their revenue and attentions tied up in maintaining a twenty-year-old cruise ship. Many felt the *Norway* had become a millstone.

While other lines were building new tonnage as fast as their finances would permit, NCL's expansion had continued primarily through acquisitions. In 1984 Kloster acquired Royal Viking, a well-regarded luxury cruise line in San Francisco that ran a trio of ships on various itineraries around the world. The move expanded his fleet to eight ships under the two brands, none of them built after 1973. Insult only added to injury with the media frenzy over a new Royal Caribbean liner, scheduled to usurp the *Norway* as the world's largest cruise ship on its completion in 1987.

In 1986, perhaps shaken awake by Royal Caribbean's announcement and certainly jarred by the precipitousness of Kloster's departure, the NCL board concluded that the era of opportunity was fast passing them by. The company's new leadership set about assembling a public face that it could present to the financial markets.

That November the directors took the company offshore and scrapped long-standing agreements protecting the ship's third world staff—something Kloster would never have sanctioned. Under a new charter as a Bermudan company, NCL began positioning itself for a public offering with an announcement that "The reflagging has allowed the company to reduce significantly its shipboard payroll of cruise operations." To combat the lackluster corporate image surrounding its aging fleet, NCL placed orders for two new ships, to be delivered in 1988. Einar Kloster, Knut's brother, aggressively billed the company as being on the lean, mean rebound from its former high-minded, high-cost incarnation. On October 6, 1987, NCL filed paperwork with the SEC announcing its intention to float an IPO "as promptly as practicable." If things went well, the press release said, the offering promised to net upwards of $125 million.

That optimistic outlook was surely influenced by Carnival's own blockbuster IPO earlier that summer. In the previous ten years, largely under Micky's management, Carnival had transformed itself from the industry's inside joke into its benchmark. Between 1977 and 1987 American cruising had seen annual growth of about 9 percent, increasing its passenger capacity from just under one million to nearly 2.5 million. Carnival's growth averaged close to 20 percent for the same period. By the time the company went public in July, its ships were carrying nearly six hundred thousand cruise passengers a year—a fifth again as many people as had passed through the Port of Miami in the 1970s combined.

Carmen Lunetta had watched it all unfold. "After the *Tropicale*," the port director remembers, "it was almost like Ted said, 'You'll never catch me.'" Ted's building the first new ship in almost a decade had instantly become a legendary moment within the industry, but it would soon be overshadowed by an even bigger achievement. When the ship arrived in Miami two years later to a hero's welcome, he'd motored his little speedboat out into the bay along with Micky to greet it. The newspapers had had a field day in advance of the event; Ted's boat was one of the hundreds of small watercraft in the harbor for the occasion. Trying to calculate the value of all the free publicity they were receiving, Micky leaned over to his father at one point with an idea for how they could generate some more. "We could really make some news today if we wanted to," he said. Listening to his son's plan over the roar of the engine, Ted nodded his agreement. As they expected, a pack of reporters was waiting for them when they returned to the pier. One of them, a journalist for the *Miami Herald*, shouted out to Ted; "What now? What are you going to do now?" Following Micky's advice, he shouted back, "Now I'm going to come up with three new ships!" A chorus of appreciative laughter greeted what they took to be a game joke, but back on shore, Micky explained to the press that Ted had meant every word. The next day they got their headlines, just as he'd predicted. And why not? There was no contract, no nothing. And as Micky had said when he suggested the idea, "Just the fact that I announce it at a press conference doesn't mean we *have* to."

Nevertheless, three new ships did soon come rolling down the line. In yet another bit of clever financing, Ted persuaded the banks to treat his vessels the same way they treated buildings; he didn't get investors taking a cut of his profits, he got long-term mortgages. It was another industry first. That money built a trio of "Superliners," weighing in at just over forty-seven thousand tons each, more than doubling Carnival's passenger capacity. The *Tropicale* had been a revolutionary move toward building big new ships, and competing lines had quickly signed on for the boom. But these new ships were simply off the charts. No one else was even close.

To generate enough traffic for the nosebleed expansion, Ted spent upwards of $10 million to launch the industry's first nationwide television campaign, recruiting a little-known on-air personality named Kathie Lee Johnson (the future Mrs. Frank Gifford) to star in song-and-dance commercials touting life on a "Fun Ship cruise." Years later, many people remember those spots even better than they do *The Love Boat*. Not that Ted put all of his eggs in one basket. Under Bob Dickinson, whom Ted had put in charge of marketing once he'd decided not to fire him, Carnival's sales force added a new arrow to its quiver. Sales reps began anonymously visiting travel agencies

around the country, walking in the door and asking for a blind vacation recommendation. If the agent suggested a cruise, the rep reached into her
pocket and peeled off a ten dollar bill. If the agent suggested a *Carnival*
cruise, the payoff was one thousand dollars.

As they found themselves increasingly involved in the business of raising
capital from private lenders, Ted and Micky realized that it was finally time to
stop conducting their day-to-day operations as if they were still running their
business out of the trunk of a car. Just because they were ahead didn't mean
they didn't need outside capital—and if they really expected to lure Wall
Street's dollars, a lot had to change. Bills would have to start being paid, for
example. "We realized that our credit rating was much more important than
hanging on to several hundred thousand dollars, or millions of dollars, or
whatever it was, on a monthly basis," a senior vice president remembers. "At
some stage the mentality changed. Let's not do it like this, let's do it better;
let's get our credit rating up; let's be on time, let's have vendors paid on time."
And it wasn't just the vendors. That same executive, who'd been with Carnival since the late 1970s, says he hadn't even realized the company was making
a profit until shortly before it went public—and even then he heard it as a ru-
mor from Ted's personal physician.

Unlike the management at NCL, Ted himself had harbored strong doubts
about whether to take Carnival public. One member of his inner circle remembers spending long hours at Ted's kitchen table during those days trying
to persuade him to go ahead with the move. Though not as shy as Micky, Ted
also dreaded the limelight. And he feared that public stockholders would
curb his financial freedom and his ability to take risks. As the friend remembers, "He didn't see other people having a good experience in public companies. He just didn't want to get involved if he didn't have to." But he did have
to. Like it or not, the income from a successful IPO was the only thing that
could take Carnival where Ted wanted to go.

Once their decisions had been made, the biggest problem for both Carnival and NCL was learning how to communicate with an investment community that little understood what their business was all about. Some firms sent
their cargo shipping analysts, others their tourism and leisure people, and still
others their gaming or airline experts. It was like a financial Tower of Babel.
Everyone was drawing on different experiences as they tried to make sense of
this quirky new industry and predict its future performance. Fortunately for
the cruise lines, 30 percent profit margins sound attractive even in Esperanto.

Although it would take years for its analysts to grasp the nuances that drove the industry, the investment community didn't have to study the numbers for too long to realize they were looking at something special—a "fine-tuned money machine," as one report put it.

Demand was at an all-time high, as it had been nearly every year since the 1960s, and the lack of capital seemed to be the only impediment to growth. Even as the supply of passenger berths mushroomed in the recessionary early 1980s, demand had outpaced it. The industry had embraced America's travel agents with fat commissions and seagoing training seminars, and the travel agents had hugged back.

Some analysts balked at the single, all-inclusive payment cruises required, fretting that "In a 'charge card society' where the cost of goods tends to be evaluated in monthly payment terms, advance payment in full is a serious deterrent to many potential cruisers and helps to reinforce the high-cost image." But the numbers proved them wrong. Agents, in fact, were so sure people would pony up for cruise deposits that they fell all over themselves to get more access to the available berths. In 1985, for example, a raft of travel agents on the West Coast got mailings inviting them to renew their membership in the "International Cruise Conference" for one hundred dollars. The only problem was that no such organization existed; the mailings were a clever hoax designed to cash in on credulous or greedy agents gripped by cruise fever. "Many," one trade publication lamented, "paid up without question."

Wall Streeters were perhaps not quite so prepared to set all caution aside when it came to the cruise business, but many of them were happy to march to the industry's tune. Salomon Brothers, the underwriter for Carnival's offering, was especially glowing about the industry's prospects, but it was hardly alone. Drawbacks were often minimized, so charmed were the new initiates. Recession, the bogeyman of the tourism industry, was interpreted as a boon for cruises: the values afforded by their tax status and low labor costs would drive newly budget-conscious vacationers into the industry's arms. Fears of overcapacity, the buzzword for new building that outpaced demand, were put to rest when the most effective cruise lines pointed to more than a decade of sailing at 100 percent occupancy or higher, even as new ships had flown off the line into a plummeting economy.

There was even an upside to a human tragedy like the 1985 hijacking of the *Achille Lauro* by PLO terrorists. That incident had gripped the country;

Leon Klinghoffer, an elderly, wheelchair-bound American celebrating his thirty-sixth wedding anniversary, was shot to death and dumped overboard as the ship sailed from Genoa, bound for Haifa in Israel. Anyone would have thought the killing would have exposed cruise ships as soft targets and hurt business, but Ted's optimism, finally, seemed to be contagious. "The lingering effects of the terrorism threat," a 1987 Salomon Brothers report on the Carnival IPO read, "continue to discourage European cruises and direct tourists to the Caribbean, Carnival's principal market." The industry seemed literally bulletproof.

Remember, this was the summer of 1987, when the seemingly endless flow of investment capital—and the pseudocash junk bonds that drove the greatest excesses of the go-go eighties—was still burning a hole in Wall Street's pockets.

Those who bet on Carnival that July won big.

Trading as CCL on the American Stock Exchange, Carnival netted close to $400 million from the offering while leaving the Arisons in control of some 80 percent of the company's voting shares. Quietly, and with astounding speed, the Arisons' wealth had surpassed that of such American dynasties as the Tisches, the Marriotts and the Busches. Some of the proceeds went to the banks, eliminating "virtually all long-term debt"—including the mortgages on the new Superliners. The rest was set aside against an even more radical expansion.

NCL was not so lucky. When it had announced its offering during the first week of that October, it had pledged to go ahead at the earliest possible moment. The date they set turned out to be the following Tuesday, one day after Black Monday, the stock market's worst day since the Great Depression.

The year had begun well enough, with the Dow Jones index breaking 2,000 points for the first time in history that January, then making its largest single-day leap later the same month. On the surface, things couldn't have been better—a spectacular opening to what promised to be another spectacular year. As the weeks and months wore on, however, the ground beneath Wall Street began to feel shakier and shakier. An SEC investigation into arbitrageur Ivan Boesky eventually led to his cooperation in bringing down Drexel Burnham Lambert's junk-bond pioneer Michael Milken, a case that ballooned until it enveloped the entire firm. Along with scandals at old-line firms like Goldman Sachs, Merrill Lynch and American Express, the Milken affair brought "insider trading" into America's vernacular. Through it all, the promise of easy money had overwhelmed the public's worry and the stock market had continued to climb. Finally, in October, reality hit.

On the two days following NCL's announcement of its intention to make an offering, the Dow plummeted a record 95 points—and another 58 the day after that. That Friday, Iran launched several missiles at an American tanker in the Persian Gulf, in the second major anti-U.S. incident in the region in less than six months. Come Monday morning, people couldn't sell their stocks fast enough. The resulting free fall dealt a crushing blow to companies and individuals around the world, but nowhere more so than at NCL.

"We were ready to roll," the cruise line's chief operating officer at the time recalls. "I think it was the Friday before Black Monday, the market went down, and that got everybody concerned. Lo and behold—Monday. That took care of that! Friday's concern was wiped out by Monday's sheer panic." Its grand strategy for the next decade shattered in an instant, NCL had no choice but to withdraw its offering. It would be nearly six years before the country was ready for another major cruise line to go public. And the intervening years would make all the difference in the world.

The crash turned out to be one of the best things to ever happen to Carnival. That it allowed them to buy back a huge, dirt-cheap chunk of the stock they'd just sold was the least of it. "It's not enough to succeed," Gore Vidal once said. "Others must fail." Carnival had gotten through the door to the capital markets, but what would forever change the industry was the way fate slammed the door shut behind it. Wall Street had become a sudden desert, and the Arisons were the only ones among their competitors with a well. Carnival's first annual report had nothing of the underdog about it. Sleek and richly illustrated, it spoke of dominating an incredibly profitable industry that was still in its infancy. And for once, Ted's vision had not outpaced his means. At the helm of a virtually debt-free company, father and son were carrying more than 20 percent of the cruise passengers sailing out of American ports. They had a war chest at their disposal that their nearest competition couldn't begin to match—and wouldn't be able to for years. All they had to do was decide what to spend it on.

Earlier that year, a team of investment bankers advising on the IPO had walked out of a particularly good meeting in Carnival's gleaming new Miami offices. The numbers were fantastic; they knew that they were all about to make a ton of money. But one lingering concern remained. Stepping into the elevator, one of them voiced what the whole group had been thinking. "About Micky," he said. "Who's going to tell him to cut his hair?"

Whoever was delegated that unenviable job, the message came through loud and clear. Come July, the days of Micky's playing the shy young CEO were gone forever. Vanished were the wide lapels, the funky glasses and all the rest of it. In their place was a tailored black suit, dark tie and a vintage late-eighties power haircut. Standing at his father's shoulder, staring confidently out from the glossy, boastful pages of his company's first annual report, the new Micky Arison was promising his stockholders a future worth billions— and meaning it.

CHAPTER SEVEN

A RUN AT THE COMPETITION

*I owe my success to having listened respectfully to the very best advice,
and then going away and doing the exact opposite.*

—G. K. Chesterton

Prior to the crash of 1987, there had been a sense that the industry was moving into a new, harsher phase: "consolidation," the economists called it, a sanitized name for what happens when industries give way to the law of the jungle.

In broad strokes, the cycle is the same in any business—the early years are defined by a wide range of small start-up companies, which grow steadily. As time goes by, circumstances, culture and performance produce a number of major players, and, as competition intensifies, scale begins to play more of a role, and size becomes an ever more important competitive advantage. As they are able, strong companies start to grow even more quickly by acquiring other companies, further fueling the consolidation process. It's not unusual, by the end of this cycle, to have more than 75 percent of a mature industry controlled by a handful of players: it's played out that way with entertainment, with the energy industry, in the fast-food industries and in any number of other areas.

But in the summer of 1987 this sort of future had seemed distant, almost abstract to the cruise lines. Most operators felt that there was still plenty of time to jockey for position before the carnage began: time to build more ships, time to tap into public financing. More than thirty cruise lines were operating in the U.S. alone, after all, and most of them were thriving. How bad could it be? Certainly, no one would have predicted that fifteen short years would see nearly 90 percent of the industry under the control of just two companies.

But down in Miami that Black Monday closing bell on Wall Street echoed like a starting gun. Recession tends to winnow out industries for the simple reason that, in tough times, it's harder to make a profit, leaving the weak to fall by the wayside. This was not the case for the cruise lines, however. The actual business of running holiday cruises was remarkably unaffected by the stock market crash and the recession that followed: the ships still sailed full, the passengers were still there. Just as the bullish analysts had predicted when they'd evaluated Carnival's IPO that summer, the industry's tax-free status and dirt-cheap labor costs insulated it from economic fluctuations shoreside to such an extent that its profits were virtually recession-proof. If anything, the crash actually helped the industry's marketing efforts, as people didn't necessarily stop taking vacations in lean times but just took greater care to get their money's worth. Ads comparing the value proposition of a cruise ticket with what could be purchased ashore for the same amount resonated that much more.

The crash was a galvanizing event for the industry not because it hurt the individual cruise lines, but because it removed the great strategic unknown of the preconsolidation era: access to the public markets—who was going to get it, how much it would bring in and what would be done with the money. Overnight, the features of the competitive landscape were locked into place.

As of October 1987 four players dominated the cruise industry, running fleets of big new ships. They were: Carnival, NCL, Royal Caribbean and, out on the West Coast, P&O Princess. A fat second tier consisted of about a dozen midsize lines running fleets of three to six older ships, and below that was any number of one- or two-ship operations, almost too small for the bigger fish to notice. Right up until the crash, some of the second-tier operators had been struggling to make it up to the level of the "big four," either through building new ships or acquiring competitors. In Florida, for example, an upstart line by the name of Premier Cruises had headquartered itself outside Orlando and had cleverly negotiated to be the official Disney cruise line, selling package tours mixing short cruises with stays at the theme park. Premier, a subsidiary of the $6 billion Greyhound Corporation, had been set to acquire another of its second-tier fellows—it planned to dissolve the brand and take the ships for its own fleet—when the market tanked. With Greyhound's financial clout behind it, the sky had seemed the limit for Premier.

Greyhound shrank in value by about $1 billion on just that one day—nearly 15 percent of the company's value—and the deal was pulled at the last minute. Premier's chairman at the time views that incident as a turning point. "We would have been playing with all of the big players," he remembers. "We might have been playing in the big leagues."

Close as it had been, Premier's moment—like those of other would-be cruise giants—had passed it by. The industry suddenly had a single superpower: Carnival, which thanks to its IPO now held literally enough cash to buy most of its competitors outright.

Aggressive as ever, the Arisons chose for their first target not one of the small-fry circling around the periphery of the industry but their nearest rival—Royal Caribbean Cruise Lines. For those who'd followed the industry over the years, the very notion was astounding; when the *Mardi Gras* was sitting stuck in Miami harbor on its maiden voyage, Royal Caribbean was already running three brand-new, purpose-built ships, revolutionizing Caribbean cruising in the process. But the intervening years had seen Royal Caribbean's ownership lose focus, growing soft and risk averse with success, even as an underdog like Carnival was making inroads into its business. While the second half of the eighties had been something of a renaissance for Royal Caribbean—by January of 1988 the company was fresh from a major corporate restructuring and basking in the glory of having taken delivery of the world's largest cruise ship—Ted and Micky still saw in it an unwieldy and cost-laden company that could benefit from their lean management style. They were confident they could squeeze dramatic new profits from the popular brand, and having negotiated secret deals with two of Royal Caribbean's three Norwegian owners, it seemed a done deal by the time it was announced in the summer of 1988.

But the industry's former underdogs were in for more of a fight than they'd guessed. By year's end, Royal Caribbean's remaining partner would be fighting Carnival off with a tenacity that surprised even himself—waiting, against hope, for the arrival of a white knight to save his company.

It may not have been obvious to outsiders—it certainly hadn't been to Carnival—but Royal Caribbean in the spring of 1988 was not the company that it had been even a few years earlier. It had indeed lost its way during the 1970s, thanks to the squabbling and conservatism of its fractious Norwegian ownership, but under new influences (if not new management) it was on its way back. By the mid-1980s, the partners had come to realize that a radical reevaluation of their business strategy would be necessary if Royal Caribbean was going to compete in the increasingly aggressive cruise market.

In the summer of 1984, as the future Kathie Lee Gifford was saturating the U.S. airwaves on Carnival's behalf and as *The Love Boat* was still carrying the Princess logo into millions of American living rooms each week, the Royal Caribbean board of directors gathered in Oslo to hear the report of a group of consultants they'd retained to assess their position. Like a doctor with a good bedside manner, the presenters began gently but wasted little time in getting to their diagnosis. "Royal Caribbean is a leading competitor in today's cruise industry," they told the board. "But Carnival poses a future threat." It was a gross understatement. By every important measure, Royal Caribbean was already being outpaced by its rivals—not just Carnival, but every other major line. Coasting on the early dominance of its brand was not going to suffice anymore. If the partners wanted to stay in the game, it was going to take aggressive expansion, a marketing overhaul and, most important, a thorough restructuring of the corporate organization.

The original setup, established when Ed Stephan had flown to Norway seeking investors during the 1960s, had called for splitting not only the cost of the venture but also the responsibilities for managing it. This was in keeping with good Norwegian common sense: if you want something done, do it yourself. It fell to the Skaugen family, the dominant partners in personality if not in equity, to hire and manage Royal Caribbean's maritime personnel. The bookkeeping and financial management fell to the Wilhelmsen family, whose Harvard-educated scion, Arne, had already begun to take over the family business. The third partner, the London-based shipping firm Gotaas-Larsen, took more of a venture-capitalist stance, content to remain a more or less silent partner in the arrangement so long as the profits kept rolling in. The Miami-based management under Stephan—who himself held no equity in the company—was there "to make the beds and cook the dinners and sell the cruises." Stephan's concept had been revolutionary, but the corporation that had sprung from it was a study in tentative entrepreneurship. Although it had offered security at the outset, the three-way arrangement spread out not only the venture's risk, but also its momentum and creative thrust. No party seemed responsible for the company's future plans; each had a sort of tunnel vision, based as much on whatever its independent agenda happened to be at

the moment as on any long-term considerations. Stephan, who hated traveling, flew to Oslo several times a year to report on the business; he'd often arrive in Norway on an early morning flight, report to the board and head back
to the airport that same evening.

The very structure of the partnership worked against promoting extended
investments; since the beginning, any profit at year's end was split up among
the principals. As a result, Royal Caribbean had gone from pioneer to borderline straggler in the space of ten years. While Carnival was spending more
than $100 million on the industry's first new ship in a decade, the partners in
Oslo were agonizing over whether to spend a tenth of that to stretch the *Song
of Norway.* By the mid-1980s, Royal Caribbean barely had a million dollars
in the bank.

Part of the problem was that two of the partners simply didn't like each
other. Tensions between the Skaugens, with their traditional shipping outlook, and the forward-looking young Arne Wilhelmsen hampered the company's agility. The owners bickered over the smallest details, and with a
charter that required unanimity on every board decision, major compromises
marked every turn. While his fellow investors were old-line shipping men,
Wilhelmsen prided himself on a broader outlook, seeking to expand his
family's holdings into such diverse fields as fish processing, prefabricated
housing and offshore drilling. Of the cruise line's original investors, he may
well have been the best suited to guide the company into the future, but his
voice was often ignored. "For a good number of years, in the three-company
partnership, Arne was kind of the odd man out," one senior Royal Caribbean
executive remembers. "And you could see that early on. I think a part of it
was that Arne asked questions. Arne wasn't a diplomat. He asked tough questions, and he was stubborn—just stubborn."

With the world changing rapidly around it, the company staggered along
in this manner until the late 1970s, when Royal Caribbean's third partner
started speaking up. The founder of Gotaas-Larsen, another Norwegian shipping man, had sold out a few years earlier to the Philadelphia-based holding
company International Utilities. IU's chairman and CEO Jack Seabrook, a
charming aristocrat who did not always view his business dealings in the
same light as the SEC, was something of a shot in the arm for the partnership. Initially, Seabrook had watched Gotaas-Larsen—which was only a
small part of the IU portfolio—ride high on a wave of oil-tanker profits and
saw little need to micromanage the cruise investment. "We didn't think of

our relatively small investment in Royal Caribbean as a profit center," he remembers. "Our main goal was to arbitrate between the two families, and
other than that we didn't really have a view as to whether the staterooms
ought to be green or purple."

By the mid-eighties, however, an increasingly troubled Gotaas-Larsen was
taking more and more of an interest in the goings-on at Royal Caribbean.
Seabrook had spun Gotaas-Larsen off from IU in 1979, under a cloud from
an SEC investigation into his corporate practices and personal finances, and
had followed the subsidiary into the haven of Bermudan registry as chairman. "We simply separated the two and took Gotaas-Larsen offshore," he recalls. "We spun it off and gave the creditors no claim on IU and its assets. I
won't go into the details, but it was hairy." Among the issues raised by the inquiries were allegations that Seabrook "diverted funds to bribe NYC politicians," that "Seabrook's personal lifestyle has been subsidized" by IU in the
form of nearly $1 million in personal legal fees for him and two other senior
officers and that "significant amounts were spent in IU in the United States
and Switzerland to disguise the existence of a Swiss bank account set up by
Seabrook." IU settled on the matter of the legal fees, but there was little question that he had to depart, and suddenly Seabrook went from commanding a
vast empire as one of America's best-paid CEOs to running a single company
with two major concerns—an ailing tanker business and a stagnant cruise
operation. Now, when he wasn't raising racehorses on his North Carolina estate, the newly independent Gotaas-Larsen had his undivided attention.

Up until this time, features like Royal Caribbean's complimentary Hershey bars, playing cards and other giveaways had been a huge point of pride.
"In Royal Caribbean's cabin, you'll receive fifty-two items," executives
boasted. "In Carnival's you'll get two: a washrag and a bar of soap." But Carnival was now surpassing Royal Caribbean in every respect that mattered—
something Seabrook understood far better than did the Norwegians, who'd
always regarded a too all-consuming emphasis on the bottom line as somewhat vulgar. Seabrook started using his "aggressive, harum-scarum flair" to
call for a reevaluation of Royal Caribbean's priorities, and the process that ensued was something of a shock for the Norwegians, who'd grown accustomed
to having a silent partner in Gotaas-Larsen. An executive present in many of
the board meetings during this period recalls a typical scene: "Seabrook got
up and said, 'You know, Royal Caribbean has without a doubt the nicest
ships, the best product of any of your other competitors. You cater more to

the needs of your passengers.' And on and on and on. He gave this speech and went on for ten minutes just off the top of his head giving all these accolades. Then he turned around in a split second and said, 'But I have never seen such a group of guys that just doesn't give a shit about making money!' And he went nuts."

Much of Seabrook's influence on the Royal Caribbean board was exercised through his somewhat more diplomatic lieutenant, a young Gotaas-Larsen managing director named Richard Fain.

Heir to a vast family fortune back in the U.S., Fain had followed Seabrook from IU, where he'd risen though the ranks since Seabrook had first given him a summer job between semesters at Wharton business school—a favor to Fain's older brother, then a senior executive at Bank of America and a very important contact for Seabrook. "If he had asked me at that moment, 'Could Richard Fain have married my daughter,' " Seabrook recalls, "I probably would have said yes."

The young MBA was nevertheless an exceedingly bright executive, and he advanced quickly to become Gotaas-Larsen's treasurer and then, after the spin-off from International Utilities, a managing director based in London. Like his boss and sometime mentor, Fain brought a dispassionate financial perspective to the eccentric, ego-driven tangle of the Royal Caribbean board. "Richard took a big role in what I was trying to do," Seabrook remembers, "which was to get them on more of an oatmeal diet rather than a caviar diet." Unlike Seabrook, however, Fain almost immediately discovered a genuine passion for the industry. "He fell in love with the cruise business," Seabrook recalls, and that passion in turn brought him much closer to the Norwegians than anyone had expected. At first, though, he was regarded as just a nuisance. "As I became more vocal at the board meetings, I was told that the company was set up with the understanding that everybody had a clear role," Fain remembers twenty years later, chuckling from the sofa in his elegantly appointed CEO's office at Royal Caribbean's Miami headquarters. "The Skaugens were responsible for the technical operation of the vessels. The Wilhelmsens were responsible for the finance and economics. And Gotaas-Larsen was responsible for keeping quiet."

Fain and Seabrook set about transforming the partnership into something resembling a modern corporation. At Fain's urging, Gotaas-Larsen made a condition of its share of the financing for *Song of America* on amending the articles of the partnership to require that Royal Caribbean have a minimum cash balance of $3 million before paying out dividends, thereby giving it an independent reserve to help weather hard times, and at least the beginnings of a genuine treasury.

That ship, with its incremental advances in design and amenities, arrived to rave reviews in 1982, and things continued much as they had until late 1984 when Ed Stephan approached the board with a proposal to build another, bigger ship—which he conceived of as a "larger *Song of America.*" By the time a board committee, under Fain's direction, had finished examining the proposal, Fain was spending more than a quarter of his time on the project; he was exhilarated. "It said that there was a vast, untapped potential there," he remembers. "That not only had we not tapped the potential of the market that was there, but with minor changes to the vessels we could significantly broaden the product we were offering and offer it to a much broader segment of the population."

As he got further into the research, Fain realized that he was uniquely suited to serve as an intermediary between the Americans in Miami and the board in Oslo. "Ed had good insight, but he wasn't presenting it in a format that all these weird people could relate to," he remembers, with what his critics would later point to as a trademark blend of superciliousness and genuine humility. "Part of what the committee's report did was summarize what management had been saying all along—and put it in a more coherent and understandable framework and document it better than just 'I have a feeling.' We had market surveys, we had numbers, we had demographics."

By the end of the process, the concept had grown under Fain's supervision into something different altogether: a strategy for revitalizing the company and bringing it into the new era with guns blazing. The board had realized too late that with the *Song of America*—built only after years of Stephan's prodding—it had "entered a middleweight contender into what had become a heavyweight bout." It was determined not to repeat the mistake.

The new ship was a quantum leap forward for the entire industry—perhaps not so grand as a pie-in-the-sky dream like Knut Kloster's 250,000-ton "*Phoenix* Project," but astonishing within the generally agreed-upon realm of the possible. At seventy thousand tons and a $190 million price tag, the vessel would be nearly twice the size of anything built within the previous thirty years. In the summer of 1985, the partners signed off on the plans for the new ship, to be named *Sovereign of the Seas*, with an energy they hadn't felt in years. *Song of America* had carried one thousand six hundred passengers; the *Sovereign* would boost that to two thousand three hundred.

Basic elements of ship design had had to be reconceived, so much bigger was the *Sovereign* than what had come before. For the first time, a single dining room was insufficient. Cruise ships had never had enough eating space for all their passengers at a single sitting; they'd always relied on a split seating system to help maximize space, assigning passengers to either the six p.m. main seating or the eight-thirty p.m. late seating. In addition to halving the per-passenger demands on dining space, cooks and serving personnel, that system effectively doubled the size of a vessel's other public areas as well, directing traffic in a subtle but efficient "clocklike motion" throughout the evening. As those in the early seating—older folks, mostly—munched on their shrimp cocktail and baked Alaska, for instance, their counterparts were in the various lounges and performance spaces watching the shows; when it came time for the late seating, the early diners would file into the rest of the ship for repeat performances from the same entertainers, passing their hungry counterparts bound for identical dinners from the serving staff they'd just left behind them. By the time the late diners were leaving the dining room, most of the older passengers had gone to bed, and the remaining night owls made for a lively crowd in the discos and casino. Half the *Sovereign*'s passengers, however, would be nearly as many people as the total capacity of most contemporary cruise ships. A dining area big enough to serve them efficiently would have had to have been enormous; the traffic in and out would have jammed the ship. Instead, designers opted to double up on the space, building a pair of two-story, 650-passenger dining rooms—one above the other, with a kitchen in between to serve them.

The *Sovereign*'s most ostentatious design revolution was its enormous five-story atrium, intended to be the heart of the ship. "It's all brass and marble, mirrored ceilings and circular stairways, fountains and foliage," *Playboy* gushed. "On the bottom deck, a quartet plays schmaltz on strings and a white baby grand." On the various floors of this "Centrum," passengers would enter the ship from the boarding gangway, arrange their affairs with the purser's desk, browse and buy shore excursions for the various ports of call and head into the ship's twin dining areas at mealtimes. Snaking corridors that contained gift shops, casino spaces and showrooms—more than twenty major public spaces in all, including a large new fitness center and "live" casino, where table gambling rounded out the slot machines that had been integrated into Royal Caribbean's earlier ships almost as an afterthought—all came to an end at the atrium's rails. Traffic moved up and down in glass elevators and along the sweeping balustrades of the "parade staircases" connecting the levels. One observer, getting perhaps a little carried away with the grandeur of it all, recalls watching the traffic flow through just prior to the early seating. "Like a flooding reservoir, the Centrum fills, its railinged margins awash—nay, cresting—with hungry passengers. Once the long-anticipated chimes have sounded, the Centrum's reservoir drains precipitously, its passenger torrents spilling down the lower stairs and surging aft on two levels."

Everything about the *Sovereign* was carefully considered down to the tiniest detail: the path each case of liquor would take from the storage spaces up to the bars, the route of each cartful of dirty sheets down to the laundry. *Song of America* became the engineers' laboratory, as "company spotters with stopwatches and clipboards were stationed all over the vessel, tabulating the occupancy of public spaces every ten minutes throughout the day and evening," the better to design the new ship for a comfortable flow. Finally, in January of 1988 the *Sovereign of the Seas* took its place as Royal Caribbean's flagship to an avalanche of free publicity. It was the biggest ship in the world, and the run-up to its launch was a skillfully orchestrated media event executed by a newly energized company. Reporters couldn't get enough of the "ultimate floating amusement park," the "ruler of the seas."

As the steering committee refined the *Sovereign*'s design, the company began to transform its organizational structure. The magnitude of the new venture demanded a stronger hand for management and an end to the supremacy of bush-league squabbling among the ownership. At the same 1985 meeting where the contracts for the *Sovereign* construction were finally signed, new partnership agreements were also drawn up; Royal Caribbean reincorporated under the auspices of a Liberian parent company, its articles amended to eliminate the unanimity requirement that had so often hamstrung the board. The chairman's office was not only given increased authority, but also moved from Oslo to Miami, where it could operate at the heart of the business. In keeping with its new, forward-looking attitude, the board voted to offer the position to Richard Fain.

But Fain decided the job wasn't for him. Notwithstanding a certain leeriness at the prospect of being caught between two feuding Norwegian partners, Fain was still on his way up at Gotaas-Larsen, and much as he liked the cruise business, he wasn't ready to leave. The firm was finally beginning to see the return to profitability that it had sought since Seabrook spun it off—shakily—six years earlier. Fain had been close to this recovery process from the beginning; closer even than he'd been to the *Sovereign*. Most recently, he'd pushed through the decision to build Gotaas-Larsen's first new tanker in years—a risky move, but one that he expected would pay off. Besides, he could hardly walk away now. At the meeting where the contracts were approved, Seabrook had announced that he thought it would be fitting to name the new vessel after Fain's wife; Fain had been touched at this uncharacteristic bit of tenderness from his boss—that is, until Seabrook finished the thought: "Because if this is as dumb an idea as I think it is, I want everybody to remember who was presenting it." Gotaas-Larsen also had a wholly-owned cruise subsidiary of its own, Admiral Cruises, in addition to its share of Royal Caribbean. Admiral was a small, low-cost operator, and although profitable enough, it had been strictly a back-burner concern for Gotaas-Larsen; repairs to one of its vessels, a former U.S. Army troopship, had left so many tons of excess concrete and steel in its hull that it had acquired a permanent five-degree list. But the line had been doing well in recent years, and there was talk at Gotaas-Larsen of contracting for a new Admiral ship, as well. No one was more excited by the changes at Royal Caribbean than he, Fain told the Royal Caribbean board, but now was not the time for him to leave Gotaas-Larsen.

The *Sovereign*'s arrival in January 1988 had been all that Fain had hoped for, and more. It had opened up a new world of possibilities for the company, and the board's Norwegian members approached him once again, this time with an offer he couldn't refuse. They offered Fain not only the posts of Royal Caribbean chairman and CEO—combined, in the American style, for the first time in the company's history—but gave him the option of taking the job on a half-time basis so that he could continue to participate in Gotaas-Larsen's recovery. The Skaugens and the Wilhelmsens had just agreed with Gotaas-Larsen to merge Admiral Cruises into Royal Caribbean; accepting the position would place Fain atop the combined entity, while leaving it would possibly take him out of the cruise business forever.

It was too good an offer to turn down. The establishment of Royal Admiral Cruises, Ltd.—Richard Fain, chairman and CEO—was announced on May 13, a Friday.

In retrospect, Friday the thirteenth was as fitting a birthday as any for Royal Admiral. The merged company was born under a bad sign. Throughout that spring, even as he'd been working out the details of his new position, Richard Fain had been carrying a stunning secret: Jack Seabrook and the Arisons were in talks to sell off Gotaas-Larsen's share of the business to Carnival. Fain wasn't exactly caught by surprise by the proposed deal; he'd been in the room for the meetings.

Carnival had made no secret of its plans for aggressive expansion, which is why Seabrook knew exactly who to go to when he made up his mind to sell. In the company's first annual report, Ted and Micky had prominently outlined a two-pronged strategy for adding an upscale cruise brand to their holdings—this in addition to a huge resort it had opened in the Bahamas, a commuter airline to service it and contracts for three new Fun Ships whose designs promised to rival the *Sovereign*. Since the IPO, Carnival's engineers had been working on plans for a possible trio of ships for a new high-end cruise line—"Project Tiffany," they called it. But starting from scratch was a fallback. Why build a reputation, after all, when you can buy one? The Arisons' preference was to acquire an established business. Holland America Line was actually their first choice. With its upscale clientele, one hundred–plus years of tradition and dominant position in the lucrative Alaskan summer market, the line complemented Carnival's mass-market, entry-level product perfectly. Speaking competitively, a merger would also have had the benefit of co-opting one of the industry's most promising midtier players just when it was on the verge of joining Carnival in the big leagues.

Micky and Kirk Lanterman, Holland America's president, understood each other very well, but talks with the line's owner, Nico Van Der Vorm, had left little hope on that front, much to Micky's disappointment: "Our preference at the time was Holland America, where we thought we'd be a nice match from a product point of view. But Nico Van Der Vorm showed no interest. He was working on a bigger ship project, had just bought or was just buying Home Lines, had just gotten involved with Windstar. He was in positive growth mode."

Royal Caribbean was therefore an imperfect second choice. "There was a lot of stuff about Royal Caribbean that we didn't like," Micky remembers. Royal Caribbean was also in "positive growth mode," of course, but unlike Holland America, it was at the mercy of its disparate ownership. And Seabrook wanted out. He made his move in the balm of a midwinter Miami evening—at the inaugural cocktail party for the *Sovereign of the Seas*, ironically enough. Ted Arison was there to pay his respects—to the competition in general and especially to Ed Stephan, whom he considered a friend and with whom he often shared evenings at the symphony when the two could find the time. Circulating among his fellow industry bigwigs at one point in the evening, Ted noticed a slim, debonair figure making his way toward him through the crowd. It was Seabrook; though the two men knew each other by sight, they had never met. Extending a well-manicured hand and smiling comfortably beneath a head of snowy white hair, Richard Fain's boss introduced himself, and the two began to chat.

Seabrook was growing restless with his cruise investment, although no one outside of Royal Caribbean knew it at the time. Already in his seventies, he was thinking about retirement, and with things improving on the tanker and the liquid natural gas side of the business, it was the perfect time to get his money out of Gotaas-Larsen. That meant selling the company, however, and *that* made Royal Caribbean an obstacle, under any circumstances. There just wasn't much a potential buyer could do with a one-third holding in a company like Royal Caribbean. "I knew from the beginning that I would have a very hard time finding a buyer who would be interested in the LNG business *and* the cruise business. They were two totally different things and people wanted one or the other, but they sure as hell didn't want both," he remembers. "The LNG business, there were a lot of people who might have been willing to buy it. But nobody wanted to get in bed. We could only sell one-third of Royal Caribbean, and to be a minority partner between two quarreling Norwegian families is not the right place to be."

Philosophically, furthermore, Gotaas-Larsen's investors saw themselves as having bought into a shipping company, and had never been particularly comfortable running a cruise line. They had had a hard time understanding the Royal Caribbean side of the business, and occasionally had shown themselves to be fundamentally suspicious of the whole endeavor. In the days following the 1987 crash, one of Seabrook's biggest investors, the legendary currency speculator George Soros, had placed three separate calls to Fain demanding that he cancel the order for the *Sovereign of the Seas*, then less than two months away from delivery. "George," Fain remembers explaining, astounded at the request. "You can't cancel the ship now—they're vacuuming the carpets!"

Royal Caribbean simply didn't fit into Seabrook's long-term plan. The previous year, he'd extended the offer to either buy out or sell to one of the other Royal Caribbean partners—he didn't seem to care much which it was, so long as he was either out or in control—but the overture hadn't been successful. And now here he was in the middle of Royal Caribbean's proudest moment, making defection overtures like a Soviet general at a U.S. embassy cocktail party. "He talked about the problems between the various partners and left us with the impression that he wanted to keep talking," Micky remembers. "He left us with the impression that he was a seller." Another meeting was quietly set soon after, to be held aboard another, slightly smaller vessel: Ted's personal yacht, the *My Lin IV*, anchored within sight of Rome for the occasion.

Overcoming Micky's and Ted's concerns about Royal Caribbean was no simple task. It simply wasn't as compelling a merger as Holland America would have been; Royal Caribbean might have been somewhat up the scale from Carnival, but it was still in the same price bracket and their ships still sailed mostly the same routes at the same times of year. A deal with Royal Caribbean was more a quick market share buy than it was anything else. Operationally, there didn't seem to be a whole lot for Carnival to learn. Seabrook was a smooth operator, however, and recognized that there were obvious advantages to gaining such a large share over the volatile, heavily discounted Caribbean market. And he knew just how to make the case that a bloated Royal Caribbean was missing out on millions of dollars in profits that Carnival's tightfisted, more aggressive management would be able to realize. "I had never felt that Royal Caribbean had been very efficiently run by the two families that were always quarreling," Seabrook remembers explaining. "There were a lot of things that I felt should have been done."

Throughout that late winter and spring, Seabrook and the Arisons hammered out the beginnings of a deal, meeting several times on Ted's yacht, far from prying eyes. "It was a hard, hard thing to get done," Micky remembers. Aside from the fact that they were far apart on price, the Arisons had made it clear that they had no interest in simply taking over Gotaas-Larsen's minority share; they had the same problem Seabrook did: they wanted a controlling stake in the partnership, they insisted, or nothing at all.

Richard Fain, bitterly opposed to the deal, sat through the talks and hoped they would fall through. "Jack was a seller, and it was obvious that Richard was pissed," Micky remembers. "Richard had just gotten the chairmanship of Royal Caribbean from the Gotaas-Larsen piece of the partnership, and he was not a happy camper." But Fain continued to hold his tongue, at least as far as the rest of the Royal Caribbean partnership was concerned. He was torn between several loyalties: to Seabrook and Gotaas-Larsen, who were still his employers; to Royal Caribbean's other partners; to his own vision for the company's future. Settling into his new CEO post, he put on a smile for the Wilhelmsens and Skaugens and hoped that his promise about the company's exciting new era turned out to be true.

In August, after months of discussion, Seabrook and the Arisons stunned the industry with news of a deal for Gotaas-Larsen's share of Royal Caribbean. As the details emerged, the Norwegians grew very nervous indeed. Most important, the proposed transaction appeared to circumvent a critical article in the partnership agreement that gave each partner a right of first refusal in the event of a sale. In theory, this was a stabilizing measure to benefit the remaining partners; it froze the value of the shares being sold, preventing an auction or other unpredictable events that a prospective buyer might use to play the shareholders off against one another. Carnival, however, insisted that it wasn't actually buying Gotaas-Larsen's shares in Royal Caribbean; it was merely buying the Gotaas-Larsen subsidiary that *owned* those shares and therefore not activating the right of first refusal. So what if those shares were that subsidiary's only asset? With the tactic, Carnival could maximize the effect of both its carrot and its stick, offering a high price to the second partner to sell while making it known that the third would be stuck as a minority shareholder. With the financial clout from their IPO, flexibility on price favored the Arisons, not the remaining Royal Caribbean partners.

Questionable as that maneuver had been, it wasn't the only aspect of the deal that raised a red flag. Carnival's purchase was announced as pending not only due diligence, but approval from the Carnival board. The Norwegians worried that Arison might not be genuinely interested in the deal—that he might simply be using the offer as a ploy to get into Royal Caribbean's books and throw the partnership into chaos. At the very least, both remaining partners saw the deal as little more than an effort to "pressure them to move the next step," without putting anything binding on the table in return. "If Ted Arison wanted the deal," Fain remembers an agitated partner fuming, "he can get board approval in the shower in the morning!"

But all of that paled next to the biggest concern surrounding the deal: legally speaking, it wasn't entirely clear precisely what was being sold to Carnival. As a corporate entity, Royal Admiral didn't really exist beyond the pages of the May press release that had announced it. The three partners had signed an agreement to restructure the organization, but as of that August, little had been accomplished to that end. No sale could be consummated until the exacting technical work of the restructuring was complete. But suddenly the partners had different and potentially contrary economic interests at stake, which were sure to be affected by the way management handled what remained of the Royal Admiral paperwork. Unless everyone involved somehow came out of this happy, it was a set of circumstances that all but promised a nightmare of litigation.

For Seabrook to get his deal, it had been necessary to catch the Skaugens and Wilhelmsens by surprise. It hadn't helped matters, however, for them to learn about it almost at the same moment as the general public. These were strong personalities that had been blindsided; press releases began circulating and attorneys fanned out from offices all around the world as everyone hunkered down for the coming storm.

The announcement, in fact, had sent the Norwegians reeling. Seabrook had been open enough about his willingness to sell, for the right price. But to Carnival? To Ted Arison, of all people? Ted's reputation in Oslo, where national pride runs high and memories long, was not good. Although his breakup with Knut Kloster was ancient history in Miami, it was still a fresh enough wound among the princes of the Oslo Shipping Club. Norway may have been one of the wealthiest nations in the world, but in many ways Oslo still ran like a small town—with no strangers and few secrets. "Someone would write a memo," a former Royal Caribbean executive remembers, "and it would get sent to Oslo—and a day later it would be in NCL's offices right across the street in Miami."

Ted wasn't merely an outsider in the Norwegians' eyes; he was an outsider who'd humiliated and betrayed a member of their insular shipping fraternity. Seabrook, difficult as he could sometimes be, had at least come with bona fides from one of their own. To the extent that Ted came with any character references at all, they were at the wrong end of a highly public lawsuit alleging embezzlement and graft. Worse, as the Norwegians saw it, he ran a shoddy operation. He may have been making significant money, but at what cost? Carnival was a low-class, penny-pinching, bottom-of-the-barrel product. When they spotted a Fun Ship on the horizon, Royal Caribbean cruise directors got on the public address system to inform their passengers that they were looking at the "Kmart of the Caribbean." The thought of such a fate for Royal Caribbean was understandably alarming. The king of Norway himself was a regular Royal Caribbean guest! Royal Caribbean ships had as godmothers such figures as the wife of a Norwegian prime minister and Scandinavian film legend Ingrid Bergman—not this insufferable Kathie Lee whatever-her-name-was. The *Sovereign of the Seas* had been christened by an American, but she had been no less a personage than former First Lady Roslyn Carter, with her husband standing at her side. Richard Fain was an American, but he'd been born to the aristocracy, and had been further refined by a decade in London. It was one thing to have a bunch of Americans running your ships for you, and quite another to have them owning the entire enterprise. Turning such a heritage over to a déclassé bunch from Miami seemed unthinkable.

Wilhelmsen and Skaugen had both agreed that Carnival's price had been low and that pooling their resources to buy out Gotaas-Larsen themselves was financially feasible. Assuming they could enforce their right of first refusal and keep the price frozen, both were confident they could find the cash, but that didn't change the fact that the two families could hardly bear each other by this point. "The Skaugens and the Wilhelmsens had a fair amount of discussions among themselves as to whether the two of them wanted to buy out Gotaas-Larsen," Fain remembers. "And basically that wasn't moving very quickly and didn't look like it was heading toward any kind of a resolution. It was fairly clear to our team that absent something to break the logjam, the path we were on was not leading anywhere." Gotaas-Larsen had provided the partnership with more than just its share of the capital. Particularly after the board abandoned its unanimity requirement, the publicly traded firm had represented a tie-breaking vote that both sides could trust—whether they agreed with it or not—was interested only in the bottom line. Absent the influence of that dispassionate capitalism, antipathy between the two family firms threatened to undermine all the progress the company had made since it began waking from its slumber in the late 1970s.

But the alternative was to abandon the business altogether at precisely the moment when it seemed to be turning a corner, and neither of them, the two parties assured each other again and again, wanted to do that. For the two weeks following the Carnival announcement, the two continued their negotiations, circling back over the same ground as they struggled to find a way to go forward together.

Carnival had set the partners up with a classic prisoner's dilemma: the suspense, in retrospect, was only a matter of who would crack first. From his uncomfortable perch at Gotaas-Larsen, Fain had watched the drama unfold. "Up until hours before the Skaugens' meeting at which they agreed to this, they were still working with the Wilhelmsens," he recalls. "It was very clear that the Wilhelmsen group felt that the Skaugens had stabbed them in the back—that in effect, that they were negotiating a peace treaty while, as they saw it, they were in effect preparing the assault." The ambush had been perfect. Wilhelmsen had learned of it only when the Skaugens canceled a breakfast meeting in Oslo at the last minute; they were in fact in New York, signing papers with Carnival's attorneys. "They didn't make a public announcement before we were informed that they had made a decision," Wilhelmsen remembers. "We didn't know that they were talking to Carnival."

But the Skaugens had demanded a powerful concession of their own before capitulating. They agreed to sell out to Carnival only on the condition that the Wilhelmsens be explicitly guaranteed the opportunity to exercise their right of first refusal with no further interference from Seabrook or the Arisons. From the date the Skaugens sold, the Wilhelmsens were to have forty days to decide whether or not to exercise that right, and then another thirty to close the deal at the price to which Skaugen and Gotaas-Larsen had already agreed. The condition was generally seen as an empty gesture; the Carnival and Gotaas-Larsen lawyers, who readily agreed to it, were sure that this was simply a matter of self-preservation. "Any litigation on this transaction was going to be years," Fain remembers. "You've got conflicts of law; you had different jurisdictions; you've got fifty different corporations. So, frankly, it was the view of the lawyers that the reason the Skaugens insisted on this was so that they had a clean deal."

But there was an element underlying the demand that had eluded New York and London. The Skaugens may indeed have been acting to protect their deal, but failing to perceive their true motivation turned out to be an expensive mistake for Carnival. Money only went so far in this instance. They wanted a clean deal, but they were also acting out of concern for a reputation that meant more to them than write-ups in all the world's business magazines: their reputation within the walls of the Norwegian Shipping Club. "I think they felt very strongly that they wanted to protect Norwegian interests," Fain remembers. "It quickly became clear to me that this was a matter of principle."

The Skaugens' turnaround, announced on August 31 in time for the next morning's papers, was reported on both sides of the Atlantic as the unofficial conclusion to a mildly interesting takeover struggle. The London-based *Financial Times*, more closely attuned to the shipping industry than the U.S. business press, reported that it was "virtually certain" that the Arisons, apparently now solidly in control of fully 70 percent of Royal Caribbean's shares, had won the day. "Wilhelmsen's position was unclear last night," reported one morning edition, "although the company was thought unlikely to try to raise the $550 million necessary to block the sale."

Back in Miami, Micky was by his own admission smug in the belief that only formalities remained. "At that point," he remembers, "I was parking myself in Royal Caribbean's offices. It was a done deal." Shortly after making his deal with the Skaugens, Ted had called Arne Wilhelmsen with essentially the same message. The conversation was a brief one. "Arison said that he was very pleased with the transaction and he looked forward to having a good working relationship," Wilhelmsen remembers. "Obviously, I was not interested in having a long conversation."

Still, there was that something they had all overlooked—something that only the Skaugens, perhaps, understood. Wilhelmsen's terseness wasn't sour grapes, but sheer fanatical concentration. Fain, who in later years would have the opportunity to get to know the Norwegians much better, assessed it this way: "The Americans all saw this fairly dispassionately. They said, 'It's a business transaction, and it doesn't make good business sense to risk your entire fortune to maintain your investment in this company.' But I think they underestimated the emotional attachment, and the willingness to take a risk for what the Wilhelmsens saw as a company which they had a large personal commitment to."

As the clock started ticking on the Wilhelmsens' forty days, word began trickling through the industry's grapevine: of meetings on Wall Street and in Chicago penthouses; of Arne Wilhelmsen stealing scant hours of sleep on Concorde flights back and forth across the Atlantic.

Royal Caribbean's pup was showing his teeth.

For everyone but Wilhelmsen, the next five or so weeks were a waiting game. Micky, who'd prematurely declared victory in Miami, did what little he could to slow Wilhelmsen down. The Skaugens and Gotaas-Larsen, not believing Wilhelmsen would really come up with the money, watched for actions on all sides that might derail their sale to Carnival. And Richard Fain, desperately wanting Wilhelmsen to pull the purchase off but under obligations of his own, began to walk an ethical tightrope with uncommon grace and skill.

Royal Caribbean's senior management had tremendous strain placed on them by the deal's competing demands. Whatever they did risked alienating them from a possible future boss: both the Wilhelmsens and the Arisons felt, not without reason, that management was beholden to them and ought to be working to help their respective deals.

At the sticky center of this web of overlapping allegiances was Fain, still wearing two hats as Gotaas-Larsen managing director and Royal Caribbean's chairman and CEO—and not, at the moment, a very popular guy. At one point during the process, Fain had been frozen out by almost everyone involved. The Wilhelmsens and the Skaugens, whom he'd cultivated assiduously during his time on the board and his brief tenure as CEO, had viewed him as a turncoat when news of the Gotaas-Larsen deal broke. Fain offered his resignation from Royal Caribbean at that point, but all three partners, he remembers, declined the offer—not out of affection, but based on the logic that any deal would require at least a short-term continuity of senior management. So he stayed, but there was no love lost. In Fain's own camp, Seabrook had grown increasingly fed up with what he saw as his insubordination. By August things had deteriorated to the point where Fain was not included in even the final Gotaas-Larsen meetings.

Meanwhile, the Arisons appeared to be holding all the cards. While

Wilhelmsen technically had the full seventy days to close on any purchase of his former partners' shares, the terms obligated him to express his intention to do so in a binding letter within only forty days from the start of the clock. In practice, he had less than six weeks from the day of the Skaugens' agreement with Carnival to come up with a solid half-billion dollars for the buyout; if he couldn't, Carnival would carry the day. Gotaas-Larsen and the Skaugens, furthermore, were both bound by a "no-shop" clause prohibiting their people—Fain included—from looking beyond Carnival for a buyer for their share of the company. That included helping Wilhelmsen find a new partner. Even if he could pull it off—a possibility so remote that the Arisons hardly gave it a thought—there was still the all-important matter of the Royal Admiral merger. Carnival's lawyers could make a solid case that the clock on Wilhelmsen's right of first refusal should continue to run regardless of whether Royal Admiral's legal status was resolved in time. If Fain didn't succeed in finalizing the new partnership agreements by the end of the seventy days, the company would go to Carnival even if Wilhelmsen somehow came up with the money. They might not have had enough to convince a court, but it was certainly a strong enough case to tie the company up in litigation for years, crippling and potentially destroying it in the process.

Initially, Wilhelmsen's likeliest bet had seemed to be the investment banking firm of Shearson Lehman Brothers in New York, where an acquaintance from Harvard Business School was putting together a proposal for a Lehman-backed leveraged buyout of the cruise line.

Originally known as "bootstrap deals," LBOs were at the height of fashion in the financial world in the late 1980s. On the surface, the structure offered Wilhelmsen a perfect solution. The basic logic was simple enough: in an LBO, a company's management or one of its principals uses money raised by a Wall Street partner to buy their company from the other shareholders. The new owners then "ruthlessly cut costs and sold unwanted businesses, freeing up every extra dollar to pay debts." After several years, when the debt is paid down, the owners take the company public again, netting millions, sometimes hundreds of millions. In *Barbarians at the Gate*, their classic account of the largest LBO in history, authors Bryan Burrough and John Helyar explained the tensions surrounding LBOs in the following way: "Critics of this procedure called it stealing the company from its public shareholders and fretted that the growing mountain of corporate debt was hindering America's ability to compete abroad. Everyone knew LBOs meant deep cuts in research and every other imaginable budget, all sacrificed to pay off debt. Proponents insisted that companies forced to meet steep debt payments grew lean and mean. On one thing they all agreed: The executives who launched LBOs got filthy rich." The LBO process had been pioneered in the 1970s as new financial mechanisms like junk bonds flooded the takeover markets with what was essentially free money at the same time low stock prices were forcing the massive conglomerates of the 1960s to rethink their viability. By the late 1980s it had become a favorite tool of the era's corporate raiders.

Lehman was one of the dozens of newcomers to the lucrative LBO trade and desperate to make a name for itself. It had raised a fund of more than $1 billion dedicated specifically to executing such projects and, eager to use it, was lobbying Wilhelmsen hard to take that tack—perhaps too hard. "I was surprised at the meetings with the Lehman Brothers LBO fund," recalls Fain, who participated in his capacity as CEO. "They seemed less interested in the specifics of the deal; it was more a question of them trying to convince us that we ought to go with them."

But there was a bigger problem with doing an LBO. The company was at a juncture where it needed to spend money, not save it—its very survival depended on bringing more ships like the *Sovereign* on line as quickly as possible. The crushing debt associated with any LBO, though it would almost certainly make Wilhelmsen fantastically rich, would just as surely stunt the company's development. Doing things Lehman's way essentially meant destroying Royal Caribbean in order to save it. Still, it was an option Wilhelmsen would rather have pursued than give his cruise line up to Carnival.

Finding a new long-term partner who could buy out the Skaugen and Gotaas-Larsen shares with equity rather than debt would be a far better solution. Only a few entities in the world have such resources at their disposal, and even fewer are willing to commit them on such short notice. Wilhelmsen had to knock on a lot of doors in the weeks after Skaugen's announcement, but fortunately he had a powerful ally in the French banker Paul Bequart, head of shipping finance at Banque Indo-Suez. In the tiny, capital-intensive world of shipping, Bequart served as one of the handful of nodes through which flowed the endless stream of building loans that made the business possible. An astute strategist, he recognized a potential fortune for his bank in the exploding market for new cruise ships—especially those built at the French shipyard where the *Sovereign of the Seas* had been completed just a few months before. Bequart had strong incentive to see Wilhelmsen succeed; his bank stood to profit tremendously if Royal Caribbean went ahead as planned with sister ships to the *Sovereign*. Wilhelmsen had made it clear that he would build the ships if he could; Carnival, on the other hand, was an unknown. Even if it did build more ships for Royal Caribbean, it was more likely to go with the Scandinavian yards it had used for its own vessels. And a Carnival shipbuilding contract could be a double-edged sword, in any case; just the year before, the Finnish shipyard where Carnival was constructing its three new *Sovereign*-size Superliners had collapsed under the weight of bad debt and poor investments—not helped, the grapevine said, by the intense financial pressure from the sharply negotiated Carnival contracts. Ted had flown immediately to Helsinki on his private jet to head the consortium of investors that bailed out the yard, and a new entity, MASA-Yards, was formed in its place. It was named for a Finnish entrepreneur, but the industry joke was that the new name stood for Mister Arison Strikes Again.

Bequart had been working the phones from the moment the Skaugens announced their defection, trying to drum up interest on Wilhelmsen's behalf among bulk shippers and other cruise lines. His search led him to one of the legendary names in American finance: Jay Pritzker, whose buying power dwarfed that of many nations.

The Pritzker dynasty, as the legend goes, began in the late nineteenth century when Nicholas Pritzker, a penniless young immigrant from Kiev, was given an overcoat at the Chicago hospital where he'd been treated for a cold. Reaching into his pocket, he found the tidy sum of nine dollars—his first investment capital. In the intervening years, Pritzker and his progeny had parlayed the windfall into one of the world's largest private fortunes. For his part, Jay, the patriarch of the family's third generation, had taken a single hotel and built the Hyatt empire. At various times, the family's holdings had included airlines, tobacco companies, sugar manufacturers, real estate investments across the globe and any number of other ventures and holdings. In the art of the deal, the family's law firm and in-house investment bank rivaled those of any collection of high-powered Wall Street concerns. "Pritzker," one of his many admirers summed it up, "is synonymous with smart money."

At the time, he was embroiled—along with Lehman Brothers and just about every other major investment bank in New York—in the largest takeover battle in American history, the fight for RJR Nabisco, later immortalized in *Barbarians at the Gate*. But Pritzker was not a man to overlook an opportunity simply because his attention was focused elsewhere. Never mind the fact that the amount of money Wilhelmsen sought was greater than any single investment in the family's history. As it happened, Pritzker had been considering another cruise investment earlier that year, but had ended up backing away from the deal. He liked the industry. Have Wilhelmsen come to Chicago, Pritzker told Bequart; maybe they could do business.

Bequart caught the next Concorde out of Paris to New York, where a frazzled Wilhelmsen kept him waiting for two hours in the gilded lobby of the Hotel Pierre while he was upstairs meeting with another in a long string of shipping firms and getting nowhere. The Pritzkers had been on a list of possible investors Lehman had come up with, but Wilhelmsen hadn't thought they were a particularly promising prospect. He'd initially dismissed Bequart's suggestion, in fact, saying that he didn't have time to make the trip to Chicago. Concerned that the deal was slipping away before it had even had a chance to be explored, Bequart called the Pritzkers. By the time Wilhelmsen came out of his meeting, a private jet was waiting on a runway just over the George Washington Bridge, at Teterboro Airport, ready to whisk the two of them to Chicago.

The meeting turned out to be everything you could ask for in a first date: dinner and breakfast. Wilhelmsen remembers being taken aback by how eager Jay Pritzker and his son Tom seemed to be to invest. Hyatt had been very good to them, they explained; the cruise business seemed like a good fit. "It was obvious that they were very interested in getting into this," he recalled. "We agreed that we should try to make a deal." The makings of an agreement were in place within a matter of hours, and by the time Wilhelmsen returned to New York the next morning, they'd come to a basic understanding. If the financing made sense, they said—and that was still a big "if"—they were prepared to move ahead. "That left us with a little more than three weeks," Tom Pritzker remembers. "The question was, could we put the financing together so that Arne could exercise his right of first refusal and be a buyer rather than a seller or a holder?"

And that's when things really started getting complicated.

The following evening, Richard Fain's home phone rang at ten P.M., Miami time. On the other end of the line was the unmistakable voice of Jay Pritzker. "Richard," he said. "Can you come to Chicago and talk to us about the business?" The two men had met three years earlier, when Pritzker had considered acquiring a stake in Gotaas-Larsen. He hadn't made that deal, but Fain had spent enough time with him during those talks to know that Pritzker was not a man to make idle inquiries. In that instant, all his doubts about Wilhelmsen's ability to pull this thing off dissolved. Fain was on the first flight out the next morning.

In a comfortable anteroom just off the entrance to Jay Pritzker's apartment, beneath a large Peter Max portrait of Pritzker's wife, Fain sat for several hours and discussed Royal Caribbean's inner workings with the Pritzkers, Eyal Ofer—heir to one of Israel's great shipping fortunes, a Pritzker partner and a likely coinvestor who'd flown in from London for the meeting—and financial advisers from the Pritzkers' in-house bank. For the Wharton grad with a love of long-winded presentations, Jay Pritzker's ability to get to the point was something of a shock. "His questions were scarily on topic," Fain remembers. "They weren't asking me what it cost to serve a cup of coffee; they were asking, strategically, where is Royal Caribbean going? What is Royal Caribbean's strategic direction?" Still, things moved quickly. "Richard, he came to us and said, 'Look, I think Gotaas-Larsen is making a mistake; I think this is a hell of a good business,' " remembers Tom Pritzker. "And he put together a wonderful presentation as to what he thought he could do with the company, and he said he would leave Gotaas-Larsen and do this full-time."

When Micky and Ted had made their deal with Seabrook, he'd assured them that Wilhelmsen would not be a problem. It hadn't occurred to any of them that Fain might be. Micky had noticed that the new Royal Caribbean chairman was "not a happy camper" at those meetings, but he'd still seen Fain as Seabrook's man—and bound by the same obligations to protect Carnival's deal. "Seabrook assumed that he would follow instructions and not solicit," Micky recalls, the irritation still evident nearly twenty years after the deal. "As a Gotaas-Larsen employee, he was not allowed to get into the picture, based on the agreement, and he went out and helped Wilhelmsen!" As the Arisons saw it, Fain's responsibility was to do what he could to facilitate the deal they'd made with his boss—which meant, if not actively trying to subvert the Wilhelmsens, then at least not flying out to Chicago on a moment's notice to give aid and comfort to the enemy.

From Fain's perspective, however, the picture was very different. The no-shop clause in the Gotaas-Larsen deal did prohibit him from seeking a new buyer for the firm's share of Royal Caribbean, but he hadn't been the one to contact the Pritzkers, and that was where his obligations to Carnival ended. He had a responsibility to Gotaas-Larsen and a responsibility to Royal Caribbean's shareholders; Micky was on his own. "I think Micky was thinking—and I think to some extent Jack may have given him some expectation—that I would side with Micky and I would work to make the Carnival deal happen," Fain remembers. "I think they felt that 'We have a deal with Gotaas-Larsen. Richard is Gotaas-Larsen, so Richard owes us his allegiance.' I never felt I owed Carnival my allegiance." Because of the right of first refusal, price wasn't an issue. Therefore, his responsibility to Gotaas-Larsen, as he saw it, consisted of protecting Seabrook's deal by making sure Wilhelmsen never had cause to bring a lawsuit in the event that things didn't go his way. Not that Fain couldn't have swung the deal Micky's way if he'd wanted to; it would have been easy. "Carnival had all the time in the world, so if I'd simply slowed down the due diligence then that would have probably made the Wilhelmsen deal less viable," he says. "The chance of getting the Pritzkers or anyone else to buy into a company on less than a month's notice without a CEO is probably going to be tough. For Carnival, they know this business inside out. They didn't need anything—they certainly didn't need any management."

Fain gathered that much at a lunch with Micky at the Intercontinental hotel in Miami shortly after the Skaugen deal was announced, a meeting that Micky remembers as a turning point and that Fain believes has been overblown.

"He basically fished to keep the chairmanship of Royal Caribbean, asking for a lot of money," Micky remembers. "And I was polite, and I said, 'Richard, I'll think about that.' And we had a very cordial lunch, a tense, cordial lunch, but I gave him no assurances—in all honesty, I didn't see any need for him. I was meeting with Ed Stephan every day." Ted, in fact, had already spoken with Stephan, quietly offering him the top job if the acquisition went through as planned. Royal Caribbean's longtime president, who considered Ted a close friend, demurred. "I've got one owner here," Stephan said. "And I'm responsible for seeing that he comes up with somebody on this, and we'll just see what happens." Ted took his unwillingness to help block Wilhelmsen's deal—no different from Fain's, really—as a sign of Stephan's characteristic integrity rather than a personal slight. When Stephan's wife gave birth later that month, her hospital room was deluged with flowers from every senior Carnival executive—a gesture Wilhelmsen learned about to his dismay. With Fain, it was just different; he and Micky were like oil and water.

And so Fain went where he was needed, and came in from the cold.

The question of potential conflicts of interest was soon moot, in any case. A little more than two weeks into Wilhelmsen's initial forty-day grace period, Fain stepped down as managing director of Gotaas Larsen. There's no way to determine for certain whether he indeed resigned, as the press release suggested or whether Seabrook fired him, as Pete Whelpton and other Royal Caribbean executives remember. "I wish there was some way I could be in two places at once," he quipped in its pages. "Unfortunately, technology hasn't yet progressed to that level and so I had to make a choice." Although with the price frozen Seabrook stood to make the same profit regardless of the buyer, he didn't take kindly to perceived disloyalty. Whelpton colorfully described his version of events. "Jack cut a deal," remembers Whelpton, who went on to work under Fain for another decade following the deal. "And Richard fucked with it. And Jack said, 'You motherfucker, get out of here!' Jack has no patience for people that do things that are opposite to what he wants." Seabrook himself was a little more circumspect in his account of the exchange, though not by much. "I was fairly rough with Richard," Seabrook recalls. "I told him, 'You're either with me or against me—and get out.'"

Things had gotten ugly, and the parties began turning toward contingency plans. The Pritzkers by this point had not only agreed to come into the partnership, but also to back building two new sister ships to the *Sovereign*. On the thirty-fifth day, fearful that Carnival might somehow make a last-minute bid to up the price, Wilhelmsen sent a letter to his two partners informing them of his intention to exercise his right of first refusal. That left him with thirty days to both formalize his financing and see the Royal Admiral restructuring completed. Whatever happened now was going to hinge on the legal fine points of the still-unconsummated Royal Admiral merger. Unbelievably, the clock was ticking, the Pritzkers were on board, but there was still no actual legal entity for them to buy.

"There were essentially worldwide batteries of lawyers ready to pounce, ready to arrest ships, ready to commence lawsuits, ready to kind of stop everything in its tracks," remembers one of Fain's deputies. "No matter who had ended up with ownership of Royal Caribbean and Admiral, it would have been potentially devastating to the business." What had previously been seen as a purely administrative matter was now a question of survival for Wilhelmsen.

Far from dragging out the Pritzkers' due diligence as Micky might have wished, Fain did the opposite. He put Carnival's own due diligence requests—which had called for a "truckload" of documentation from Royal Caribbean—on hold. During their lunch together, Fain had asked Micky to trim his requests to "more relevant" material in light of the many pressures on the company. Micky had refused, arguing that *everything* was relevant. Carnival's secret had always been in its ability to find a penny's savings in pools of millions of dollars. "He said something along the lines of, 'You'd be surprised how much money there can be involved in these kinds of things,' " Fain remembers.

If indeed Micky had snubbed him at that lunch, Fain gave as good as he got. He went to the board. "I said, 'It seems to me the Carnival deal has no time limit; the Wilhelmsen deal does,' " he recalls. " 'The priority ought to be meeting Wilhelmsen's needs.' " Carnival's requests, he argued, compromised his ability to do that. The board agreed, and flow of information to Carnival slowed perceptibly. Micky felt his deal beginning to slip away, and there was nothing he could do but watch it happen.

Wilhelmsen had accomplished more than anyone had thought possible, but Pritzkers or no, there were still plenty of chances for the deal to come apart. If the Royal Admiral restructuring couldn't be completed before the clock ran out, Wilhelmsen would still argue that the company was his—that he'd fulfilled the terms of his right of first refusal and that the Royal Admiral question wasn't his responsibility. Carnival, on the other hand, had left no doubt about where it stood. If Wilhelmsen couldn't consummate his deal by the end of the thirty days—for whatever reason—that was that. The legal issues were thorny, to say the least, as they involved competing claims regarding murky agreements that stretched across multiple jurisdictions. If the courts had to decide, it would be chaos.

Here, too, the lines between professional and personal obligations began to blur. Fain, to the dismay of the Pritzkers and many at Royal Caribbean, had hired two Gotaas-Larsen executives to be his deputies at Royal Caribbean—Bruce Seabrook, Jack Seabrook's son, and Adam Goldstein, the son of Gotaas-Larsen's chief tax attorney.

As officers of Royal Admiral only, the two of them were technically not exposed to the potential conflicts of interest Fain had to contend with. But both had been given key positions on the team assigned to see the merger through; doing their jobs meant working against a deal both of their fathers had made on behalf of investors at a company they'd been at for less than three months. Goldstein's position as Royal Admiral's corporate secretary in particular put him in the middle of the process. Were the newcomers working in Royal Caribbean's interest, Miami management wondered, or were they spies? "It was the most bizarre thing in the world," remembers Ken Dubbin, Royal Admiral's treasurer at the time. "It just didn't feel comfortable at all. And we were all suspicious of Adam. There were times that we would go off and talk without him, because we never understood where his loyalties lay." An early mistake in which Goldstein—in his own words, "either innocently or naively"—gave the wrong documents to the wrong party didn't help matters. Then again, recalls Dubbin, who went over to Carnival in 1999, "Adam was so green he couldn't get out of his own fucking way." Goldstein was not missed by many of his new colleagues when he disappeared for two weeks at the height of the frenzy to attend the Olympics in Seoul. But if Goldstein was conflicted, it didn't show in his work. Apart from his Olympic sojourn, he labored around the clock along with Dubbin and others.

Ironically, now that Fain was no longer at Gotaas-Larsen, his interests and Seabrook's were once again aligned; the only way for Fain's former boss to be assured of getting his money out of Royal Caribbean was now to see Wilhelmsen's deal succeed within the specified time frame. Any other outcome would almost certainly go to the courts. "About two weeks into it," Fain recalls, "I started getting calls from both Jack and the lawyers, worried that we weren't moving fast enough. 'You really have to get this done, and done now.'" But there were any number of stumbling blocks.

The dozens of freestanding partnership agreements that Royal Caribbean and Admiral had comprised had to be consolidated into a single entity. Old boards had to be voted out; new boards had to be voted in. Many of the subpartnerships had individual financing, and each change had to be approved by the banks holding that paper. At one point, one of the attorneys discovered that a forgotten cranny of the partnership's bylaws stipulated a board of nine directors—no one remembered why, but there it was. Royal Caribbean had been operating with twelve directors for more than a decade. Rather than risk a challenge later on, Fain had to chair more than fifty board meetings,

Miami's obsolete downtown port, a few years before Dodge Island's completion. In the upper part of the frame stands the first version of the Dodge Island Bridge.
(*Courtesy Lewis Fraser*)

"*Yarmouth Castle*, she's a dyin' and don't know it": Postcards for the *Yarmouth* and the *Yarmouth Castle*, the "Twin Fun Ships," published shortly before the fire and sinking that killed ninety-one people, all but two of them—a doctor and a nurse—passengers.
(*Courtesy Bård Kolltveit and John Maxtone-Graham*)

In the wake of the *Yarmouth Castle* tragedy, a modern ship like the *Nili* was big news—just what the local boosters were looking for. Little did the Frasers know, they'd be out of business in less than a year. *(Courtesy Lewis Fraser)*

Out to change the world: The back page of a self-published Knut Kloster pamphlet from the early 1970s.
(Courtesy Knut Kloster)

Royal Caribbean's founding partners, aboard the just-delivered *Song of Norway* in 1970. Harry Larsen of Gotaas-Larsen is on the far left; the last two on the right are Sigurd Skaugen and Arne Wilhelmsen.
(Courtesy Royal Caribbean Cruise Lines)

One of the few Royal Caribbean print ads from the early days. *(Courtesy Royal Caribbean Cruise Lines)*

"Each section floated at maddeningly different depths": Stretching the *Song of Norway* in the late 1970s; the operation cost nearly as much as the company had spent building the entire ship a decade earlier. *(Courtesy Kvaerner-MASA yards)*

What a difference a decade makes: Carnival's first three ships in the late 1970s *(above)*, and its three new "Superliners" *(below)* at Dodge Island in the late 1980s.
(Courtesy Carnival Corp.)

"I could pretty much do all the dirty work for the cruise lines . . . bargaining their position, keeping peace between labor and management": Longtime Miami port director Carmen Lunetta, one of the key figures in building the city into "The Cruise Capital of the World."
(Courtesy Carnival Corp.)

Moving on up: Carnival's new offices, circa 1990.
(Courtesy Carnival Corp.)

"As long as you're not barefoot in the dining room," Ted used to say, "you're pretty much all right." Pole wrestling *(above)* and beer-chugging contests *(below)* helped Carnival shake the industry's stodgy image.
(Courtesy Carnival Corp.)

On the cusp: Micky with Ted, staring confidently out from the pages of Carnival's first annual report.
(Courtesy Carnival Corp.)

"In the Morning, in the Evening, Ain't We Got Fun . . ." With three new giant ships on the way, Carnival went national with the industry's first major television campaign. The ads, starring a then-unknown Kathie Lee Gifford, were second only to *The Love Boat* in reshaping the way Americans thought of cruises.
(Courtesy Carnival Corp.)

Keeping the travel agents happy was a critical ingredient for the industry's success. Carnival's Bob Dickinson teaching the art of "Power Selling" on one of his many road shows for the trade. *(Courtesy Carnival Corp.)*

Nothing a new coat of paint can't fix: Ted's second ship, the *Carnivale,* arriving in Miami on New Year's Day 1976 *(left)*, and sailing out again thirty-eight days later *(below)*. *(Courtesy Carnival Corp.)*

Micky, Lin and Ted Arison, Meshulam Zonis and his wife, Clara, in 1978, a year before Ted's surprise installation of his son as Carnival's president. On the far left is a girlfriend of Micky's at the time.
(Courtesy Carnival Corp.)

A one-ship operation: The original sales team in front of the *Mardi Gras* in the early 1970s. *(Courtesy Carnival Corp.)*

Although the company was well capitalized, Royal Caribbean's first office was little more than a trailer.
(Courtesy Arne Wilhelmsen)

Welcome to Miami: Royal Caribbean's Arne Wilhelmsen, and Ed Stephan at Dodge Island in the 1960s with Miami port director Admiral Erwin Stevens *(center)*. Behind them, another new passenger terminal is going up.
(Courtesy Arne Wilhelmsen)

RCCL's first two ships side by side in Finland. *Song of Norway,* on the left, is nearly finished. *Nordic Prince* has a little further to go.
(Courtesy of Kvaerner—MASA yards)

A new leader for a new era: Richard Fain, early in his tenure as chairman and CEO of Royal Caribbean.
(Courtesy Royal Caribbean Cruise Lines)

Jay Pritzker, Royal Caribbean's white knight: "Once it was Pritzker," Micky Arison remembers, "the party's over, guys—if Pritzker is willing to write a check, the party's over."
(Courtesy Royal Caribbean Cruise Lines)

Fain, shortly after his and Wilhelmsen's victory over Carnival, celebrating the contract for two sister ships to the *Sovereign of the Seas*. The triplets, for a time, were the largest cruise ships in the world.
(Courtesy Royal Caribbean Cruise Lines)

A rendering of the world's first "Megaship." The three-story atrium in the center of the ship was a design revolution in the industry.

(Courtesy Bård Kolltveit)

Pete Whelpton *(far left)* and Ed Stephan *(far right)* at the inspection of the *Sovereign of the Seas* under construction in France.

(Courtesy ALSTOM Marine)

The "sunbowl" on *Song of America*'s upper decks. *(Courtesy Kvaerner-MASA yards)*

Rivals, more bitter with the passing of the years. Royal Caribbean passengers watch a Carnival ship sail past off Miami. RCCL cruise directors used to get on ships' public address systems at such moments, informing their passengers that "there goes the Kmart of the Caribbean."

(Courtesy Bård Kolltveit and John Maxtone-Graham)

A touch of class: sound advice from a Carnival sommelier.
(Courtesy Carnival Corp.)

"A day without wine is like a day without sunshine."

"Yes, I'd like to place a satellite call, please."

It's the fastest, clearest, most private way you can phone home.

Unless you ask for satellite service when calling ship-to-shore, you'll have to put up with the static, interference and delays of ordinary radio phone calls. So if you want a fast, private, static-free phone call ask for satellite service. And get through loud and clear.

COMSAT
Maritime Services
Clearly, the best choice.

Anyone in the U.S. can call you aboard ship. For instructions, have them call 1-800-826-8680.

Marketing to the yuppies at the end of the "Me Decade": High-tech communications (*right*) and expanded fitness centers (*below*) quickly went from being luxuries to necessities.
(Courtesy Carnival Corp.)

They keep getting bigger and bigger . . .
(Courtesy Carnival Corp.)

A world of promise: P&O Princess' chairman Lord Geoffrey Sterling and Micky in 2003 after closing the industry's last big deal.
(Courtesy Carnival Corp.)

At the end of an American Life: Ted's final birthday party. When he died, the *Jerusalem Post* eulogized him as "the richest Jew in the world."
(Courtesy Carnival Corp. and Lin Arison)

Emperor of the Waves: Micky in 2004, worth $5.3 billion and the thirty-second richest person in America, according to *Forbes* magazine—up seven places and nearly $1 billion from the year before.
(Courtesy Carnival Corp.)

one in each subsidiary, "ratifying every action they had taken in the last twenty years." Finally, on November 2, two days before Wilhelmsen's deadline, Fain convened an epic meeting in London to pull it all together: the Royal Admiral merger, the transfer of the Skaugen and Gotaas-Larsen shares to Wilhelmsen and the subsequent entry of the Pritzkers into the new partnership. As the meeting was brought to order, there were few among the Royal Caribbean personnel who'd slept at all during the previous thirty-six hours.

Attorneys and executives arriving at the London offices of Royal Caribbean's attorneys were greeted by a remarkable scene. "Every square centimeter was covered with paper," one of them recalls. "We just had table after table after table of papers and stock certificates of all the companies," Dubbin remembers. "There was one table that had to be fifteen, eighteen feet, and then there were subsequent tables. And there were actually other rooms, and while we were closing the deal there was another group of us going back and forth negotiating with the lenders to get the acquisition financed—we were literally drafting the loan." With so much going on, everyone involved was struggling to keep a handle on things. "Jack Seabrook and the Gotaas-Larsen lawyers were getting very nervous about the issue of the litigation," Fain remembers. "Because if they went too far in one direction, Carnival would sue on the basis that Gotaas-Larsen had not lived up to its obligations. If they went too far in the other direction, the Wilhelmsens would sue on the basis that Gotaas-Larsen had not honored its right of first refusal."

Fain had asked everyone to arrive first thing in the morning so as to be finished well ahead of the deadline. As the day unfolded, however, it became obvious that that had been wishful thinking. Morning turned into evening; evening into the dead of night. Calls from Carnival's attorneys were coming in constantly, becoming more and more aggressive as the hours dragged on. "We were getting these kind of badgering phone calls," Dubbin remembers. " 'You guys lost, you guys lost. We're coming. It's over.' " It wasn't. Finally, at around two-thirty A.M. on November 3 every partnership had been consolidated, every loan approved, every document signed. All that remained was the final transfer of funds, including $350 million from the Bank of Nova Scotia in New York.

"And then," Fain recalls, "we lost the money."

When the call came in, he couldn't believe his ears. Unbelievably, the transfer had disappeared in the bank's system. Representatives from the bank tried to soothe the dumbstruck group. "We handle three million wire trans-fers a day," they told Fain, "and once a week we lose one of them, and it just so happens this is a big one. It's here somewhere, but it'll take us a while to find it." As the agonizing minutes and then hours ticked by, constant updates were provided by the bank's data technicians. At about four-thirty a.m., less than twenty-four hours before Wilhelmsen's deadline was up, they reported that they'd "narrowed it down to a small area." Then, at five a.m., everything came to a halt. Back in New York, the bank's representative explained to the stunned executives that the bank's computers were all shut down for routine backup and the search wouldn't be able to continue for another two hours. The night turned into morning in an atmosphere of dazed unreality. No one could bring himself to leave the building. Fain, a little punchy, stood up at the conference table for a while and sang a few songs from *Oklahoma*.

When the money was finally located and transferred by an apologetic bank officer, the dawn's first grey rays had turned into the full half-light of an autumn London morning. The deal was finished. Wilhelmsen had con-founded every expectation. After a brief celebration, the Royal Caribbean people all stumbled back to their rooms at the Hyatt Carlton Towers, where their new boss had arranged for lodging at a modest discount.

For Carnival's father-and-son team, their first foray into the takeover world appeared to be a washout, despite that they walked away with a $9 million break fee—a fee Micky later regretted not forcing higher, calling it a miscal-culation on his part that may have cost him the deal.

But the Israeli immigrant and his college dropout son—billionaires now—were not to be outdone by a bunch of Ivy League "aristocrats." Even as the financial press was still speculating about a Carnival victory, backup plans were being set in motion. Public bluster notwithstanding, it had been appar-ent for some time before the closing that things were not going their way. "The key issue is, does the new guy have money or not?" Micky remembers thinking. "Once it was Pritzker, the party's over, guys—if Pritzker's willing to write a check, the party's over."

Around that time, however, with Carnival's $550 million offer for Royal Caribbean still on the table, an unexpected but very welcome call had come in from Seattle: it was Kirk Lanterman, Holland America's president, sound-ing a little agitated. When Nico Van Der Vorm had out of hand rejected the notion of selling his company the year before, Lanterman told Micky, he hadn't realized how rich a buyout by Carnival could be. "Are we talking this kind of numbers?" Lanterman asked. Perhaps Van Der Vorm might be interested in doing something after all—something Lanterman desperately wanted to see happen. "Kirk was dying to get out from under Nico Van Der Vorm," Micky remembers. "And so he came and met with me and came up with a strategy to get Van Der Vorm to the table."

This time, the negotiations sailed through, even as the fight for Royal Admiral continued to play out. On November 25, only three weeks after Wilhelmsen's deal had closed in London, Carnival announced formally that it had made a deal to acquire Holland America for $625 million, that Lanterman would stay on as president and that Nico Van Der Vorm would be joining Carnival's board.

Anyone would have forgiven the Arisons—especially the increasingly competitive Micky—for taking some time to lick their wounds after their bruising in the largest takeover fight in the history of their young industry. Instead, in almost no time at all, they'd turned around and *topped* it. For many in Miami, this was the first indication that Carnival wasn't just in a league of its own; *Carnival was playing a whole different ball game.* A nickname started to take hold: Carnivore Cruise Lines.

Even at its worst, the public side of the Royal Admiral fight never approached the level of rancor of Ted Arison and Knut Kloster's parting in 1972. But the collegial atmosphere at the Port of Miami's passenger terminals had nevertheless been irreparably damaged. Royal Caribbean's incoming leadership, under Fain, had been forged in a crucible of menace and competition with Carnival—a "tremendous rivalry," as Adam Goldstein put it. "Just zero desire to ever be a part, a division or a subsidiary of that company." Feelings on the Carnival side were just as strong. The old days were gone. "We competed, we competed as hard as anybody," Micky remembers of the relationship between the two companies before the buyout. "But we did it in an environment of everything being aboveboard and very much understanding that there was no point in hurting each other." No longer. "It only soured," he continued, "when Richard got involved, because we couldn't do the kinds of things we'd done in the past. There wasn't that level of trust, and there wasn't that level of believing that the other guy wouldn't lie to you."

It was not to be the last time Micky Arison and Richard Fain would go head to head.

CHAPTER EIGHT

HIDING IN PLAIN SIGHT

But in this world nothing can be said to be certain, except death and taxes.

—Benjamin Franklin

In October of 1990, several months after Carnival concluded the final details of the Holland America acquisition, Ted Arison decided that it was time to step aside for good. This time he was leaving not just the day-to-day operations of the company in his son's hands, but the entire enterprise. Micky took over as Carnival's chairman and CEO, and Ted moved to Israel to "retire." To say the least, it was an active retirement. Within a short time he owned the country's largest construction company along with various real estate, technology and financial holdings and had politely turned down an offer to become Israel's finance minister. In 1997 he led a syndicate to buy the country's largest bank from the government. But his Carnival days were behind him, at least officially.

Micky, after ten years in the president's seat, was more than ready to take over. There were, however, other motivating factors behind Ted's decision than the mere question of succession. At the age of sixty-five, death and taxes were both looming large for Carnival's founder. When Ted Arison—aging now and suffering increasingly from a variety of health problems—gave up the chairmanship of Carnival Cruise Lines, he also gave up his citizenship in the country that had made him rich. He'd arrived in Miami in 1965 with almost nothing. Twenty-five years later, no longer an American, Ted returned to his native Israel, where there is no estate tax, to wait out the ten-year period of "denaturalization," during which the IRS reserves the right to collect estate taxes. If you live outside the country for a full decade, the government's thinking goes, you've proven you didn't just do it for the tax break. "All I know is, my lawyer he told me, 'You'd better live for another ten years,'" Ted said in a 1996 deposition. "That's it. So I'm trying."

He almost made it, succumbing only a few months short of the deadline to the cancer that was ravaging his body.

In the intervening years, he continued to live in the manner to which he'd grown accustomed. His two-hundred-foot pleasure yacht was equipped with an office from which he could oversee every aspect of his empire from anywhere in the world. The food was especially good, thanks in part to the hydroponic herb garden Ted's personal chef had installed aboard. For local excursions, the side of the ship opened to reveal twin speedboats tucked away inside—"like a James Bond little movie boat," as one senior Carnival executive remembers it. He also continued to maintain the Boeing 727 he'd bought in the early 1980s, an airliner that in commercial use carries nearly two hundred people. Ted's customized model was equipped with fewer than twenty seats and a full-size bedroom—shower, king-size bed and all. The engines were souped up and the fuel tanks expanded so the plane could make the Atlantic crossing more quickly. A safe on board held tens of thousands of dollars in cash, there to ensure that fuel and spare parts would be available even in places where credit wasn't, where officials might make things difficult or where for security reasons Arison might prefer not to identify himself. The pilots did more than just fly the plane: they were, in essence, a well-supplied advance team, there to deal with whatever Ted might need on the ground. Once, upon greeting Ted on his arrival in Egypt, his host asked him if his pilots needed accommodations. "I don't take care of them," the tycoon laughed. "They take care of me."

In 1992, with a net worth of $2.8 billion, Ted appeared on *Forbes*'s list of America's hundred richest people. He'd long been one of the four hundred richest. When Arison finally did die, his funeral was news around the world. The *Jerusalem Post* eulogized him as the "world's richest Jew." Upon his death, his Israeli holdings—by a considerable margin the smaller part of his fortune—went to his daughter, instantly making her that country's richest citizen. Carnival went to Micky.

Ted may have been born in Israel, but it was America that had made his fortune possible, a fact that he'd apparently recognized when he chose to become a naturalized citizen of the United States. There's no indication that

Ted's ultimate renunciation of that citizenship came as the result of any disillusionment with the U.S. If anything, he had seemed to have been growing more and more closely involved with American life in the years before he left. As majority owner of the Miami Heat he'd taken a leading role in bringing a new professional sports franchise to the Magic City, and he had certainly not cut back on his investments in U.S. real estate. In 1987, when Carnival went public, Ted gave an extraordinary $40 million in stock to endow the New World Symphony in Miami, and he contributed generously to other charities as well. At one point he even bought in to a savings and loan, which turned out to be an embarrassing casualty of the quintessentially American fiasco that savaged that industry in the late 1980s. He also started an airline, which had initially been conceived to ferry customers to Carnival's Bahamas resort but which quickly took on a life of its own with routes up and down the eastern seaboard. With all this activity Ted had managed to keep a remarkably low profile for someone of his stature until returning to Israel. Perhaps he understood, as one member of his inner circle put it, that "the spouting whale gets the harpoon." But when the question of estate taxes came up, his American roots turned out not to have grown too deep to pull quickly.

Ted's life as an American, defined as it must be by that final act of rejection, is an apt metaphor for the entire cruise industry's relationship to the United States. It is a relationship, critics say, in which cruise lines enjoy virtually every benefit and protection of operating as an American company—and they have indeed become icons of Americana—without being asked to shoulder any of the responsibilities commonly understood to accompany the privilege. For all intents and purposes, they pay no federal taxes, and contend with no labor restrictions. Right or wrong, it is a brazen arrangement.

In industry shorthand, the system whereby shipowners can, for a fee, register their vessels in nations where the laws are less restrictive than in their own is known as "open registries," or flags of convenience. It is, as the writer William Langewiesche described in his remarkable book *An Outlaw Sea*, "free enterprise at its freest, a logic taken to extremes."

Sailing a commercial ship under the U.S. flag requires the fulfillment of certain responsibilities and legal requirements; one cannot simply run the Stars and Stripes up the flagpole. A U.S.-flagged ship must be built in the U.S. and crewed by American citizens. Its owners are expected to adhere to U.S.

law and pay taxes on their profits. Incidents on board, wherever in the world they happen, are subject to investigation by American authorities and resolution in American courts. A U.S.-flagged ship, in essence, is a little piece of America floating on the grey international sea.

In the context of the world labor pool, of course, the American flag becomes an expensive proposition, a liability, which is why most oceangoing vessels—cruise ships included—are instead flagged in the open registries of places like Liberia, Panama or the Bahamas. Under their flags of convenience, they operate as little floating pieces of places that are far less stringently administered than the United States. Even those laws that are on the books in FOC countries are seldom enforced when it comes to the foreign-owned ships they register. A shipowner's presence in one of these countries usually amounts to nothing more than a post office box or at most a brass plate in a lawyer's office. Ask a thirty-five-year Royal Caribbean veteran if he's ever been to Liberia, where until recently the company was incorporated and most of its ships were registered, and he'll give you a blank look. "There's no reason to go there," he'll say. And he's right.

FOCs are the product of a global economy in which money talks, preferably without interference from governments and other annoying impediments to doing business. "For better or worse, shipping is international business in its purest form," Matt McCleery, editor of the top trade journal *Marine Money* explains. "It's not uncommon for a ship to be built in Japan, owned by Greeks, manned by Filipinos, insured in Bermuda, managed from Monaco, financed in London and flagged [registered] on a tiny island most people have never heard of. While the majority of shipowners run first-class businesses, the opportunity for abuse within the system is simply breathtaking."

It's a system of sovereignty for rent. Liberia's registry, for example, is contracted out to a private company that operates out of Virginia. Panama is considered "old-fashioned" because it still handles its flagging affairs through a consulate rather than a contractor. Today dozens of countries operate open registries—some of which have so little to do with the actual business of shipping that it makes no difference that, as in the case of Bolivia, they're landlocked. In return for registry fees shipowners gain the right to do business as corporate "citizens" under international law—complete with the protection of a convention that accords tax-exempt status to most foreign-flagged vessels doing business in the United States. For nations with little or no large-scale domestic enterprise, the opportunity to earn significant amounts of hard currency in return for little more than a rubber stamp is likewise irresistible. In the admittedly extreme case of war-torn Liberia, for instance, registry fees added up to an estimated 17 percent of the government's 2003 revenue.

The FOC system has its roots in the early years of World War II, when the U.S., still neutral, was struggling with the conflicting imperatives of supplying Great Britain with arms and munitions while ensuring that America not be drawn into hostilities before it was ready. Direct military support of an enemy of the Third Reich might give Hitler cause to declare war; similarly, a sinking of an American vessel at the hands of the Germans would likely force President Roosevelt's hand. A proxy was needed, and it only made sense that America would turn to Panama and Liberia, two small nations with which it had historical links. Panama's ties came first and foremost from its famous canal, built by the U.S. under an earlier Roosevelt administration and operated for much of the last century as American soil. Liberia, on the Horn of Africa, had been founded as a modern nation in 1847 by freed slaves who'd migrated from the southern U.S. and had a constitution modeled closely on that of the United States. Congress accordingly passed laws allowing U.S. shipowners to "flag out" their vessels under foreign flags, and the newly massive Liberian and Panamanian-registered fleets kept the British alive. After Pearl Harbor, the question became moot. Existing merchant vessels returned to U.S. registry and hundreds more, known as "liberty ships," were built for the war effort. But the law stayed on the books.

When the war ended, the U.S. had the largest commercial fleet in the world. The ensuing decades, however, saw U.S.-flagged shipping reduced to virtual nonexistence even as the nation between two oceans grew to become the world's only economic superpower. The liberty ships were gradually replaced by anonymous fleets owned by Americans but flagged under a growing number of new open registries around the developing world. In a way, the wartime ploy had worked too well. If the FOC stratagem had been sufficient to get around a bellicose Germany, surely it was more than equal to the task of dodging the peacetime U.S. government as it raised taxes and the minimum wage and expanded the reach of laws protecting U.S. workers.

Inevitably, a race to the bottom ensued. As a rule, responsibilities for prosecuting most shipowners' offenses—often including crimes taking place within the territorial waters of another nation—fall to the ship's flag state. But here, even those countries with progressive domestic laws face a fundamental conflict of interest; unlike genuine nationals, the shippers can simply take their business elsewhere. Open registry nations over the course of the last fifty years have bid against one another to offer shipowners the most attractive possible labor, taxation and—tacitly—enforcement regimens until they've reached the point where such traditional functions of government become little more than empty formalities. When there is nothing to prevent a shipowner from transferring his investments back and forth among national registries, no questions asked, meaningful enforcement of international norms is all but impossible; it takes only a few rogue registries to undermine the entire system.

Flag of convenience shipping is one of the least regulated commercial activities on the face of the earth; every tension of capitalism is intensified as the decent and unscrupulous alike make their business decisions without the genuine constraint of law. "In the main, it's still made up of a majority of responsible operators, with an unscrupulous fringe just like any other industry," Matt McCleery comments. "But the nature of its capitalism means that the fringe is much more fertile ground; those who want to run shoddy operations can do much worse, much more often—and get away with it." The net result of all this is that the sea has become in the modern era what it was in ancient times: a wild, ungoverned zone. The twelve-mile offshore boundary, which for most purposes marks the beginning of international waters, has become the limit beyond which, as the old maps warned, there be dragons. Those who venture there, whatever their reasons, must fend for themselves.

The modern sea's worst stories unquestionably take place among the ships of the merchant fleet, where the absence of enforceable law often combines with an almost unimaginable isolation to create a dangerous, hostile environment. Well-documented accounts of workers living like indentured servants aboard flag-of-convenience ships, their passports and money in the hands of their employers, are common. Months can pass with back wages unpaid; seafarers far from home toil helplessly knowing little of their rights, such as they are, and having scant opportunity to invoke them. Malnourishment has been a problem. Safety is often virtually ignored. Under FOC registry, poorly maintained freighters can trade for years beyond what other countries would consider their safe and useful lifespan. "Rusting beneath their paint," they stumble from port to port through lackluster inspections, sailing on aggressive schedules dictated through agents by an unknown, faraway owner—

until perhaps one day, in the face of a particularly brutal ocean storm, they break apart and sink. Perhaps they take some of their crew with them; thousands of sailors were killed in the 1990s alone.

When a rotting ship breaks up at sea, who is responsible to its victims? Remarkably, it's a question that is sometimes simply left unanswered. Registering a ship under a flag of convenience is a bit like opening a Swiss bank account in that it provides the customer with a nearly impenetrable veil of anonymity. When disasters happen, the shell corporations that own the ship can serve as a wall of silence. Langewiesche reported in detail on the *Erika*, a twenty-five-year-old Maltese-registered tanker, owned by an Italian, chartered by a French oil company and crewed by Indians, which sprung a leak and eventually broke up and sank off the coast of France in 2000. More than 2.6 million gallons of oil were released, making the incident one of the worst ecological disasters in Europe's history. Yet despite intense political pressure, a monthlong inquiry by the French government failed even to determine who owned the ship; the owner, who was later tracked down by a well-connected industry journalist, said he had been in France for the five days following the accident, sitting in on damage-control meetings. He was "bemused" by the investigators' difficulty in locating him. "No one tried to contact me," he's reported to have said. The story made headlines in the French press for weeks. Ownership information, furthermore, is not the only category of basic information that FOC registries actively obfuscate. Between 1978 and 1993 the International Maritime Organization, the UN body responsible for legislating safety on the high seas, requested specific "casualty reports" from the governments of member nations on 1,239 separate accidents at sea. It received just over half of them.

Cruise ships are something of a different story. For one thing, the U.S. Coast Guard holds passenger ships plying U.S. ports to a higher standard, although in truth the inspection regime consists primarily of a handful of hours-long inspections each year, mostly scheduled weeks, if not months, in advance. More important, the very nature of the cruise industry prevents its operators from taking refuge in the deep and disquieting anonymity enjoyed by merchant shipowners. By the early 1990s U.S.-based cruise lines were collectively spending hundreds of millions in marketing dollars to make sure everybody knew *exactly* who was responsible for running their ships. As a result, safety in a strict sense has been a bright spot for an industry that is well aware that its survival depends on public perception. Maintenance may be expensive, but it's a bargain compared with the alternative. The industry's consolidation has actually improved the situation. More and more, by the time Ted Arison was conveniently reasserting his Israeli identity, the cruise industry was in the hands of a few major players who well understood that, on basic issues such as safety and seaworthiness, they would sink or swim together in the eyes of both travel agencies and Wall Street. According to the industry's trade group, which represents all the major companies operating in the North American market, no passenger has died on one of its member lines as a result of a maritime accident in twenty years—although the same, unfortunately, can't be said of crew members, a number of whom have perished in workplace accidents.

Of course, having better safety standards than the cargo industry isn't necessarily saying much. The industry remains largely self-regulated, and although fear of public opprobrium is a powerful motivator, the repeated rejection of NTSB recommendations for fire safety and other matters suggests, at the very least, a pattern of calculated risk. More than a dozen groundings, power failures and fires involving major cruise ships took place during the 1990s—not to mention several sinkings aboard smaller lines—most of them without loss of life or serious injuries. Thanks to helicopters and satellites, some of these incidents—as in the case of the 1998 laundry room fire aboard the Carnival *Ecstasy*—unfolded live on CNN. Officials found that its crew rose to the occasion, and luckily the *Ecstasy*—Finnish-built and less than a decade old—was also close enough to shore to get help from fireboats. Even then, the blaze spread to three decks and left fifty people hospitalized for smoke inhalation. Passengers aboard the *Scandinavian Star* in 1990 were not so lucky when flames broke out in the dead of night. The ship—still well within its operating lifespan at nineteen years of age—was in ferry service between Norway and Denmark at the time but only weeks before had been running Caribbean cruises out of Florida. Within the space of forty-five minutes 158 people died.

The following year another older ship, the *Oceanus*, began taking on water off of the South African coast. The captain gave the order to abandon ship and eventually took his own advice—boarding a helicopter in an effort, he claimed, to check on the well-being of passengers who'd already fled to the lifeboats. Hundreds of passengers were left without their captain when rescuers refused to return him to the ship. Incredibly, thanks to daring helicopter rescues by the South African air force, no lives were lost. The last passenger was carried off the ship a mere twenty-five minutes before the

Oceanus sank. It, too, had been running cruises out of Florida ports within the previous year, though neither the *Oceanus* nor the *Scandinavian Star* was operated by any of the majors.

If the cruise lines—the large ones, at least—exercise a high degree of self-discipline when it comes to maintaining safety standards, they take full advantage of their FOC liberties when it comes to labor. Squeezing the most out of workers in return for the least possible pay is one of the keys to the industry's profitability, and the cruise lines have had to become extremely adept at it. Royal Caribbean's *Sovereign of the Seas* carries a staff of more than eight hundred, largely unskilled workers hired for the hotel operation; today's largest ships carry nearly twice that—approximately fifty times the number of workers that were aboard the Exxon *Valdez* when it broke up in Prince William Sound in the spring of 1989.

They come to the sea to feed their families, fleeing desperate third world economies: maids, waiters, maintenance and kitchen workers working ten, twelve, sometimes fourteen or more hours a day for as long as ten months without a day off. At the end of their contracts they are sent home with no promise of a job when they return. One labor activist described a Carnival worker who'd racked up fifteen years' worth of six-month contracts and still had no more job security than the day he'd first signed on. Competitive salaries for this kind of work hover around $550 per month—including "guaranteed overtime." Wages can get quite a bit lower than that, however. The best jobs for third world workers, the ones that involve tips, offer a base monthly salary of fifty dollars but also the opportunity to earn a total paycheck approaching a Western payscale. That's a fortune for someone from Russia or Bangladesh or Jamaica. In many cases, such a worker is supporting an entire extended family back home.

The cruise lines themselves acknowledge that it's a tough life, with hard work, long hours and loneliness. For a cabin attendant, laundryman or waiter, the official job description itself is enough to give serious pause to anyone with options. And there is much that is difficult about cruise ship life that most workers do not learn until they are aboard. The belowdecks existence—and for the dozens of laborers for whom being caught in a passenger area is a fireable offense, that small piece of the ship can indeed be their entire world for months on end—might as well be a million miles away from the lido deck up above them. "On board a vessel run in a paramilitary manner, sound service management theory, which emphasizes empowerment and shared responsibility, can only have a limited role," Bob Dickinson says of his workers. "If they do not perform their duties in a prescribed manner, they are subject to discipline." The description of the cruise ship society as "paramilitary" may sound draconian, but it also suggests a certain reassuring sense of security, of order, of a tough life that is nonetheless well in hand.

The faux naval uniforms and the captain's absolute power over shipboard society notwithstanding, however, the military analogy would be more aptly applied to the former Soviet Union's fast and loose kleptocracies than to the starched and regimented corridors of NATO or the Pentagon. In the late 1970s and early 1980s the cruise lines may have taken over the cruise directors' lucrative schemes for extracting payments from Caribbean merchants, but that was hardly the end of the industry's underground economies. A web of bribes continues to extend into every corner of the ship: it is perhaps the defining characteristic of crew life. This flow begins with the envelope left for the passengers to stuff their tips into at the end of their cruise, but the overall process is a self-perpetuating and perhaps unavoidable cycle. Without paying the appropriate kickbacks, it's very difficult for a tip worker to provide the services passengers expect, without which they stand little chance of earning what they need to pay the kickbacks. And so on, ad infinitum.

Cabin attendants have to pay a fee to the laundry chief in order to get clean sets of sheets on time; waiters not only have to pay the cooks to make sure their food comes out hot, but also their maitre d' to secure a big table. Many jobs are so demanding that they are all but impossible for the crewmember assigned to them to do alone. Dipping once again into their envelope, workers often have to pay off-duty, salaried colleagues to help them complete their jobs. Employers look the other way or even encourage the practice. "There was an underground economy on the ship; it was a pecking order, and it would go all the way up the ship and then come shoreside," a longtime treasurer at Royal Caribbean, now at Carnival, remembers. "One of the hotel managers used to go on and effectively extort the crew. They would say, 'You want to stay? You want to keep your job? You've got to pay me X amount a week.' " Perhaps worst of all are the bribes sometimes extorted back home—crippling, illegal payments to local recruiters, known as "manning agents," paid in return for the chance to get the job at all. Although the laws and corporate policies against this practice seem in some cases to have been more strongly enforced in recent years, it continues to be common enough. It can take a worker months aboard a ship to cover the high-interest loans taken out to come up with such payments.

As Dickinson's metaphor suggests, the chain of command is indeed iron-clad. Here, too, the flow of money is often a favored instrument for enforcing discipline. Along with their authority to curtail shore leave or impose extra labor as punishment, officers are empowered to levy fines for infractions such as lateness or straying out of one's authorized areas. One worker claimed to have been fined fifty dollars for being caught in the wrong part of the ship. That works out roughly to thirty-three hours' worth of work. Another common punishment banishes a worker to clean up crew quarters or serve meals at the officers' mess, work that earns no tips, however well it's done, but can have dire consequences if done poorly. Most first-time workers have paid their employer in advance for their airfare home—again, often with money borrowed at usurious rates. As a result, the threat of repatriation at one's own expense—a devastating prospect with loans outstanding and no other way to earn income—is a real one. There have been discernable improvements at some of the major lines, but in practice low-level, Third World laborers continue to have little redress against arbitrary or unjustified dismissal. "I work in fear of being fired at any time," one worker injured aboard NCL's *Norway* said in court, speaking for countless silent colleagues out at sea.

And that's just during work hours. The possibilities for personal time on board are generally quite limited. The worst living conditions are found aboard the older ships, which were converted for labor-intensive cruise service rather than built for it. These overhauled liners, however comfortable their passenger accommodations, can be hellish ships to work on. Over-crowded crews live in areas designed for a third their number, sometimes eight to a room, for months on end. There is the example of the *Britanis*, an old but well-regarded ship belonging to the Greek company Chandris Fantasy Cruises, a long-standing family-run business that later invested in new ships and became Celebrity Cruises, owned today by Royal Caribbean. Aboard, one observer has reported, "seafarers slept in triple-level bunks, eight or ten in some cabins, and were provided no storage area. Books and clothing were stacked at the foot of the bunks. One bare bulb lit the entire cabin, and was being turned on and off all day and all night as the occupants went to and from their duties. The cabin had no ventilation, and smelled like a gymnasium locker room." The bathrooms were worse. "The toilet facilities were also repulsive," the observer went on. "International standards on new ships call for one shower for every eight people on board and one wash basin for every six. The filthy, broken showers and toilets on the *Britanis* were used by many more." Sometimes the showers and the toilets were difficult to tell apart, as human waste bubbled up from the drains. Meals were eerily similar to those consumed by the steerage passengers of the early twentieth century—unrecognizable stews and mashes, often as not taken standing up. Similar complaints have been made about Carnival's earlier ships—the *Mardi Gras, Carnivale* and *Festivale*—which had likewise been converted from liner service. Carnival no longer operates any of these ships—and, like Chandris, gets far higher marks for the vessels it's built itself—but the old *Carnivale* is still sailing today, and its former sister ships were finally retired only in 2004. The *Britanis* sank in 1997 on its way to the breaker yards on the coast of India, where it was to be sold as scrap.

As the industry boomed in the 1980s, newer ships brought with them major improvements in crew accommodations. Carnival, shaken by its experience in 1981 when hundreds of Honduran and Jamaican workers seized two of its ships, took care to provide certain amenities for workers as new ships were commissioned. Today its executives proudly point out that workers sleep no more than two to a room. Cruise workers on the larger, more modern ships have movie nights, discounted e-mail access at sea for communicating with their families back home and even special shore excursions for those members of the crew off duty when their ship is in port. Aboard Royal Caribbean ships, a dedicated human resources officer organizes any number of company-sponsored activities, including social get-togethers in honor of the national holiday of every country represented by the ship's crew. The real nightmares today tend to be reserved for the industry's fringe—the operations running one or two old ships in the Caribbean or Mediterranean, the ratty old "cruise-to-nowhere" gambling boats that get back to Fort Lauderdale before bedtime after a day's cavorting on the edge of international waters. There is no shortage of these.

At the same time however, the scalar economies so beloved of the cruise lines ensure that as the new ships grow larger, the ratio of passengers to crew grows higher—making already overwhelming service jobs even more de-manding for cruise workers even as it lowers the company's per-passenger expenses and fattens the bottom line.

Today's big cruise lines present themselves as models of enlightened self-interest. As evidence, they point to millions spent on improving crew accom-modations. They're in the business of making people happy, they'll tell you, and that's a function an unhappy, overworked crew can't perform. But "happy" and "unhappy" are relative terms, especially in the globalized, feast-or-famine world of the early twenty-first century. Objectively speaking, the average cruise worker's experience plays out more as a parable of domination and vulnerability than as a case study in striving and betterment.

At its best, the seagoing life can offer great opportunities in return for the hardships it imposes. With discipline and foresight, a waiter, bartender or cabin steward can save enough in five years to buy some property, or start a small business back home. Alternatively, he might spend an entire career working on ships, but also put an entire generation of his family through col-lege. However difficult the work may be, this kind of sacrifice is fundamen-tally logical to an American sensibility. But these are the shining examples. The raw economics of the arrangement can be deceptive, and beneath them are disturbing power dynamics at work.

For the laborers who drive the industry's profits, the journey toward a job on a cruise ship almost always begins at the end of a long line in one of the world's poor and desperate corners: India, Indonesia, Russia, Honduras, China, Haiti. Perhaps nowhere is the system more naked than in the Philip-pines, where income sent back from overseas laborers accounts for fully 10 percent of the country's gross domestic product.

In the Philippines, the job begins with a colorful advertisement in a local newspaper. The ad shows a cruise ship on a perfect Caribbean day and lists openings for jobs that promise wages that would be impossible to earn at home. The image of people having fun on the ship and the lure of all that money makes for a powerful combination; it brings hundreds into the re-gional center where the agent who placed the ad, one of many such firms around the world on contract to provide seagoing labor, is headquartered. The line of applicants—you could wait all day without ever getting to the front of it—ends at several waist-high windows within the building, like the ticket windows at a movie theater. There, employees of the agency take the applicants' passports, paperwork and any other certifications or documents they've brought in hopes of standing out from the crowd and read through them all slowly. The lucky few are given a date to come back for an "inside interview." The agency holds on to their documentation, including their passports, for the duration of the process.

The inside interview involves another long day, taking place perhaps a few weeks after the evaluation at the ticket window, with the crowd in the waiting room almost as large as the one outside had been. Like the day on line, there is no guarantee it won't be spent just waiting. "There is a large room with aisles of seats similar to a movie theater. There are always many seamen waiting, sometimes hundreds," one man who went through the process recalls. "The seaman is given a time to be interviewed, but normally he waits all day for that or is asked to return another day."

Finally, the lucky ones find themselves nearing the process's halfway mark. "When I passed this level," another Filipino cruise worker recalled of his experience at the same agency, "I was given a date in the future to come back. I was told to return in a coat and tie and to 'go upstairs' to be interviewed by a fleet manager of the crewing agency." When the worker passed this interview, he was given yet another date to come back to be questioned by a representative of the cruise line, an American who asked "tricky questions." Once the American signed off on him, the man was sent to a doctor for a thorough medical evaluation. If he'd been a woman, a pregnancy test would have been part of the exam. Any health problems that turn up in the examination must be taken care of at the applicant's expense before the process continues. Finally, in July, he was told to come in to the office to sign his contract. It was February when he'd first made it to the ticket windows in the front of the line, but he felt lucky.

"I was given a contract to be a bellboy," he remembers—a job that promised nearly one thousand dollars a month, maybe more if tips were good. "I was only allowed to check my name, the ship, the rate of pay, the duration of the contract. There were other documents beneath the one-page bellboy contract. The official lifted the bottom edge of my one-page contract and other pages and required me to sign some of the pages below, but I could not see them sufficient to read them and was not allowed to read them. He just pointed and told me to sign. Immediately after signing the bellboy contract and the other documents that I don't know, they were all taken from me. I was told to wait until I was called." Those other documents, as he later learned, included an agreement to "arbitration" in the event of any dispute with the cruise line, which explicitly precluded him from seeking redress in U.S. courts. They also stated that a five-dollar monthly union fee would be deducted from his paycheck and that he would be subject to that union's collective bargaining agreements. "I know nothing about a union," he would later testify. "I have never seen articles of any union. I have never signed any agreement to join any union. I have never attended a union meeting. I have never met a union representative before I was in the hospital, I have never had union benefits, rights or obligations explained to me." At the time, he just did what he was told, mindful of the long line of people waiting outside for the same job. When he was finished signing his name, he went home to wait for the call.

The call came nearly four months later, and it was bad news. Contract or no, the agent said, the bellboy job wasn't available after all. "If I wanted a job, it would have to be as a utility [garbage man] for less money," the worker recalled. "My contract for the bellboy position was thrown out and cancelled. I had no choice but to be a garbage man or nothing." After almost a year of waiting for this job, he had few options. "I knew that if I didn't sign the new garbage man contract I would be dismissed and another applicant would be called," he says. "At no time was I permitted to ask any questions, discuss anything or attempt to negotiate, or the process would be terminated and another seaman would be selected."

As far as such stories of "softening up" go, this worker's experience was mild enough. It's far harder when the switch is made after a new hire has already left home—a development regularly encountered by port chaplains, the clergymen who are often the only people seafarers can turn to when things go wrong. "They convince somebody that if he pays them all this money in Honduras, they're going to get this job making eight hundred dollars a month on a cruise ship," explained one Florida chaplain. "And then they fly them up here, stick them in a hotel, soften them up. And then, when they're desperate because the first payment on the loan that they took out in Honduras is coming due and they still don't have a job, they come along and offer them something for four hundred dollars a month. What's the guy going to do? It's a terrible evil. And everybody agrees it's illegal, and the industry looks the other way."

Cruise executives insist that if they're able to substantiate a claim of such abuses by manning agents, they "fire them on the spot." In practice, though, such policies are tough to enforce even with the best of intentions. And in any case, the system guarantees a docile and highly motivated labor force.

Race also plays its part in the cruise worker's dilemma.

To be precise, the issue is not so much race itself as it is a more general myth about the darker-skinned peoples of the world. It's an old story, repeated often enough in any number of variations: that the world's poorest, most disenfranchised people take the miserable jobs that they do not out of desperation but because they are so well suited to them. In the cruise industry, you encounter this mentality again and again. "The Asian seafarers, especially the Filipino, they can smile very nicely. They seem to have [been] born with a wonderful service culture. They always greet the guests and always smile. And they do it so naturally," one recruiter told a researcher from Cardiff University in the UK. "In comparison, European seafarers seem easy to get fatigued. After four months, their fatigue will show, and our guests don't like to see those who serve them look tired and cannot smile." Another agent halfway around the world shared the identical perspective with the interviewer—regarding an entirely different ethnic group. "We use many Indians aboard our vessels," this human resources official explained. "Believe me. They are wonderful people and they always smile." Comments from the industry's highest levels bear out the notion that fundamental prejudices are at work here. "Third World citizens hold these jobs in high esteem," Carnival's Bob Dickinson has written. "It is more difficult to find Americans who have a flair for service hospitality. The egalitarian nature and heritage of Americans tend to work against their ability to be motivated to serve others."

Royal Caribbean president Jack Williams speaks in even starker terms, seemingly unaware that he might be praising the worst aspects of the system. Williams—who goes by "Mr. Jack" when he visits the workers on his ships ("They know they can approach me," he says. "I'm very approachable, very accessible")—told the story of a conversation he'd had with a laundryman on one such occasion. "He had to be about fifty years old," Williams reminisced, "but he was the third generation in his family in the laundry room with Royal Caribbean International. He said, 'You know, Mr. Williams, my grandfather worked here, my father worked here and I work here, and my only hope in life is that my son can get a job here.' It was quite moving, it really was. And he meant it. He loves this company. He loves it."

Starting from the bottom may be a quintessentially American idea, but staying there is not. At a time when so much public discourse revolves around globalization's promise for the world's poor, Williams's anecdote highlights a striking disconnect. Americans have a long tradition of looking at striving and sacrifice as a means to an end. Benjamin Franklin once summarized the ethic with simple elegance. "I am a strong believer in luck," he wrote. "I find the harder I work the more I have of it." First-generation Americans are legendary for their ability to tolerate tough working conditions and meager pay; this was true of the Italians and Jews and Chinese of the early 1900s, no less than it is of the Pakistanis and Russians and Mexicans of today. Sacrifice and struggle, we all learned in elementary school, are the price of admission to the Land of Opportunity. But the idea that anyone would put up with it all only to have his grandchildren—his *great-grandchildren*—toil under the identical conditions would have been anathema. Poverty forces all kinds of compromises, but four generations of a single family toiling away for $1.50 an hour in the same sunless laundry rooms doesn't qualify as a success story anywhere in the world.

Racism in a stricter sense also abides aboard cruise ships. Some of the epithets that pepper daily shipboard life can be chalked up to a polyglot barracks existence when more than sixty nationalities might be found aboard a single ship. Along with the usual slurs, Filipinos in this environment become "flip-flops." Blacks, on some ships, become "sunburnt Norwegians"—a supposedly affectionate moniker. The cruise lines are quick to tout their "floating United Nations" as a sort of happy social experiment. In fact, the remarkable diversity of the workers on most cruise ships stems as much from a fear of organized labor as anything else. The industry still remembers Carnival's Honduran strike, and how it almost put the company out of business. Having survived that, the Arisons instituted policies—mirrored at other cruise lines—to ensure nothing similar could happen again, and the industry followed suit. "The whole thing was to not have a ship with 15 percent or more of one nationality," a senior Carnival executive explains. "And it's difficult, because we've got a lot of people from the Philippines today."

The one exception to these conditions is among the officers, who are well paid, usually come from the same country and are protected by strong unions. But the officers are the arm of shoreside management; as the authority figures on board, their ability to act in unison is clearly in the lines' interest. With the rare exception, Carnival's senior officers are all Italian; Celebrity's are Greek; NCL's and Royal Caribbean's are Norwegian; Princess's are British; Holland America's are Dutch. Across the board, entertainers and social staff are almost always American or from the UK. In the military style, officers eat apart from the crew; sometimes even in passenger areas, which is one of their privileges. Even in their own mess halls, they dine on the same food served to passengers, while the crew eats a separate menu designed for their presumably different needs. National identity is a powerful control mechanism. "Crew members from different nationalities on different vessels told me that they had been discouraged from speaking together in their own language when away from passengers, or even during their time off on board," one union-funded researcher—not the only person to make such a claim—reported in 2001. "Meanwhile those in higher positions on cruise ships use their own languages at will, even during working hours." One industry observer noted a historically specific undercurrent to the officer-crew dynamic while cruising on Holland America, where a large number of the crew are from Holland's one-time colony Indonesia. "It became clear that the traditional colonial relationship between the Dutch and Indonesian was replicated on these ships," he wrote. "The Indonesian staff was naturally reverent and deferential to the Dutch bosses, not just as their employer but also as the colonial power under which previous generations grew up." He recalled asking an Indonesian busboy about his working conditions. "The Dutchman," the crewmember replied, "is always watching."

Pete Whelpton, Royal Caribbean's longtime operations chief, remembers similar dynamics playing out aboard his ships, where a "double standard" for the Norwegian officers and an international crew broke down just as clearly along national lines. "There was at times what I felt was harsh discipline for offenses," he explains. "Little things, like they'd catch a hotel guy riding the passenger elevator, and they'd fire him. Catch a Norwegian seaman or deckhand riding the passenger elevator, and something would be done—but no one knew what. A Norwegian would get drunk in a nightclub, an officer, and something would be done about it, but nobody knew what."

Predictably, fights and feuds and factions among the crew often break down along ethnic or national lines. Sometimes this is relatively innocent, as in the case of the Korean waiters aboard one Carnival ship conspiring to hoard the early batches of clean silverware from the lunchtime cleanup for one another. At other times, as in the case of the knife fights one Royal Caribbean officer remembers breaking up from time to time, it reinforces just how distant this world is from the endless party taking place above.

But there is more at work here than the predictable cruelties of a clique society. In this system, there is often a clear message from the highest levels that people are valued differently, assigned to a caste based on their origin or appearance. In 2003 Holland America announced a new initiative for its "Pinnacle Grill," a specialty restaurant where guests pay a fee over and above the all-inclusive rate to dine on signature gourmet food. The Indonesian and Filipino waiters who staff the main restaurants, however, were not tapped for the new assignment, as a trade magazine breezily reported in 2003. "The Pinnacle Grill on the new *Oosterdam* is staffed by a dozen Hungarian waiters, and the line will transition to European service personnel in this specialty venue on other ships. 'There's no question our traditional staff are extremely competent,' says Stein Kruse, senior vice president of fleet operations. 'Employing European servers is simply a way of further differentiating the Pinnacle Grill from the main dining room.' "

When examined in the context of the worldwide shipping industry, cruise ships tend to be among the better places to work. Certainly, they are the safest. Similarly, in the context of the global pool of unskilled labor, even the worst of cruise ship life stacks up fairly well against the factories of East and South Asia, with their epidemics of mangled limbs and tales of children chained to the machines at which they slave. By the standards of today's world, if a cruise ship is indeed a sweatshop—and most of them probably fit the bill—it's a relatively benevolent one.

That said, these *aren't* factories—they're cruise ships. *Cruise ships.* "Disneyland for adults," as Micky Arison once put it. At the most basic level, these vessels exist to produce nothing but the immediate experiences of pleasure and satisfaction. Even factoring in all the economic promises for workers with little prospects back home, it's hard not to feel something disheartening in the notion that the world's extremes of poverty and entitlement are coming face to face with one another in this odd zone of international waters—in such a shiny, happy atmosphere—and failing to grasp one another's realities any better than they do with the vast Atlantic or the Pacific between them. In the age of the Internet and of the supposed "global village," it all brings the human cost of a globalized economy into sharp relief.

~~

As the industry evolved throughout the 1970s and 1980s, lawmakers in Washington attempted to address the flag of convenience system from time to time, but little headway was made. It's difficult, after all, to get people too worked up over something happening so far away and so completely out of sight, and even if would-be reformers had public outrage to motivate them, they would still have found themselves facing the staggering complexity of a system built not only on domestic law but any number of international treaties and arcane considerations.

In 1992, when Bill Clinton swept into the presidency after twelve years of Republican control of the White House, critics of the flag of convenience system saw an opportunity to push their obscure issue to the forefront of national debate. Fearing what they perceived to be Clinton's "protectionist bent," cruise industry lobbyists prepared for the worst.

There was good reason to believe that reform in one form or another might be on its way. Late in the campaign, rhetoric had grown heated over a Clinton plan for cracking down on foreign corporations dodging taxes on their business in the United States. Attack ads taken out by the Clinton campaign claimed that IRS enforcement had grown lax on Bush's watch and that billions of dollars were slipping through the cracks as a result. By going after the money, Clinton insisted, an additional $45 billion could go to fund his ambitious health care, education and infrastructure initiatives without raising taxes. No one disagreed with the premise, although skeptics predicted a windfall closer to $3 billion than to $45 billion and pointed out that the IRS under Bush had in fact upped its funding for enforcement aimed specifically at just these sorts of offenses.

The debate fueled public perception that foreign corporations were reaping fat profits at the expense of U.S. taxpayers. And *that* made the cruise lines nervous. Furthermore, there was widespread speculation that with Clinton's North American Free Trade Agreement straining his relations with his all-important union base, the White House would be looking to make conciliatory gestures as a matter of good politics. Foreign-flagged shipping seemed to be a prime target, and one that presented little threat of political backlash.

The measure that inspired the greatest fear in the industry was a labor reform bill named for William Clay, a Missouri congressman. First introduced in 1991, the bill proposed applying the Fair Labor Standards Act and the National Labor Relations Act to most foreign-flagged ships regularly calling on U.S. ports. In effect, this would have applied U.S. minimum wage, collective bargaining rules and other restrictions to the labor-intensive U.S. cruise industry as well as to the merchant fleet. In calling for support, Representative Clay made appeals to both nationalism and conscience. "An already meager U.S. merchant marine is increasingly being run off the high seas by vessels that are not subject to enforceable labor standards," he said. "We have heard of mariners being required to work eighteen to twenty hours a day for less than one dollar an hour, of living conditions so unsanitary they threaten life, of sailors forced to provide kickbacks to labor contractors for the privilege of being so abused, and of sailors abandoned in foreign ports and blackballed for seeking to improve conditions that all would agree are intolerable and inhuman." Adopting these measures was not mere altruism, supporters insisted, for such a bill would level a playing field that had been unfairly tilted toward flag of convenience registries. It could potentially restore thousands of vanished American jobs, they claimed. Clay defenders also argued that the lack of a significant U.S.-flagged merchant fleet put the country at a military disadvantage, limiting its ability to quickly mobilize seagoing supply lines in the event of a war. This last matter was in fact not purely theoretical. As recently as 1982, in the Falklands War, Britain had nationalized the *QE2*, painting its hull naval grey and putting it to use as a troopship.

None of these arguments had swayed the Bush administration, which insisted that an issue so critical to international trade was best handled in the diplomatic sphere. "Taking unilateral action," a Bush aide said, "runs the very real risk of isolating the U.S. from the mainstream of international commerce." And if the offshore nature of the industry suggested that there was little threat of a public backlash, it also guaranteed that there was little political hay to be made from embracing flags of convenience as a central issue.

The Democratic sweep in 1992 breathed new life into the bill, and it was reintroduced in 1993—although perhaps prematurely, as events would prove. The cruise and shipping industry's respective trade publications bemoaned its resurgence, denouncing the legislation as "onerous," "reviled," "notorious," "controversial" and "unpopular," among other things, and taking pleasure in referring to its "feet of clay." Richard Fain, Royal Caribbean's chairman, invoked Ronald Reagan's three-stage formula of government's relationship to business: first it taxes, then it regulates and finally it subsidizes in order to repair the damage from the first two. The cruise industry, Fain brazenly suggested, was in a fight to keep from being pushed into the third stage.

Internationally, the Clay bill drew appalled protests not only from flag of convenience countries but also from many important trading partners, sparking serious concerns in Washington, especially at the State Department. It's one thing when the Charles Taylor regime in Liberia, little more than a criminal gang, accuses the United States of trespassing on its national sovereignty. It's quite another when the United Kingdom, the European Union and Japan issue similar statements. One official in the UK's transportation department summed up the tone of the objections: "We wish to warn the U.S. that if they persist with these measures they run the risk of endangering international shipping." Dire predictions of "swift retaliation" in the form of a trade war were hardly lost on a White House that had come to power on the motto "It's the economy, stupid!"

For all the concerns about national sovereignty, an exemption in the Clay bill revealed that the real aim of the legislation was not to impose American law on the high seas per se, but to clamp down on a "runaway" flag of convenience system that seemed to be posing its own challenges to the viability of international law. If the bill was enacted, ships that were 51 percent owned and crewed by nationals of the country where they were flagged would not fall under its restrictions. Critics pointed out that, although the spirit of the exemption was honorable enough, it was poorly conceived from an enforcement standpoint. Then as now, the open registries were well known for their opacity when it came to giving up just such ownership information. Everyone agreed that administering such an exemption would be a nightmare.

The cruise industry, represented by the International Council of Cruise Lines, issued dire if not entirely credible warnings. "I am here to tell you that this industry will relocate if the bill is passed," the ICCL president testified to Congress. "Do not underestimate the effect of adverse legislation on this industry. We will seek out a favorable political and economic climate in which to operate." It had been a busy year for the ICCL, which had also been ensconced in the fight against another bill—introduced by a Florida congressman, of all people—intended to discourage European and Asian governments' subsidies to their commercial shipyards. Named for its author, Representative Sam Gibbons of Tampa, the bill proposed to effectively deny the crucial American market to subsidized ships by mandating that vessels calling at U.S. ports be taxed in amounts equal to the subsidies received under construction. If, in other words, it was determined that a ship built in France had been subsidized by the French government in the amount of $10 million, that ship would not be allowed to dock at a U.S. port until its owner surrendered that $10 million to the United States or otherwise expiated the subsidy. Although not as terrifying as the Clay bill, this was a major concern for a cruise industry whose furious expansion had been fueled in major ways by the sometimes absurdly advantageous terms offered by subsidized European shipyards. As the Clay bill began gathering momentum in late 1993, however, the ICCL opted to turn its attention to the more fearsome of the proposals staring it down.

In retrospect, it needn't have bothered. With such strong objections coming from the State Department, the presidential support so critical to the Clay bill's success failed to materialize. The legislation went back on the shelf, and there it has remained ever since. The Gibbons bill did ultimately pass in a milder form, but in this context it was not so bitter a pill to swallow.

Even if it had passed, the Clay bill would have left intact the other fundamental pillar of the flag of convenience system: the privilege of doing business tax-free.

Bilateral tax treaties between Washington and nearly every nation in the world have established special rules for the international transportation industry. Shippers and airlines doing business in the United States aren't taxed on their operations here so long as the nations where they are registered extend the same courtesy to U.S. companies carrying passengers or cargo across their borders. This agreement applies equally to major foreign companies, such as British Airways, and to the countless anonymous, one-ship operations registered under flags of convenience. And there is sound logic behind the practice, especially for a nation whose borders include the two largest bodies of water in the world. Upwards of 95 percent of the manufactured goods and raw materials imported into the United States arrives by ship. Airlines from nearly every country in the world fly in and out of our cities, carrying business travelers, tourists and government officials. Facilitating the reliable, swift and easy international movement of goods and people could not be more clearly in the national interest. Furthermore, the premise underlying these treaties assumes that the companies involved are being taxed in their home countries, just as American transportation firms operating abroad are taxed by their own government. Taxing the same income twice would be unduly onerous, the thinking goes.

This premise holds true today in the case of the airlines. On the high seas, however, the emergence of open registries has turned shipping into something it was never intended to be: an industry that is all but tax-exempt everywhere in the world. Representative Peter DeFazio of Oregon, ranking member of the House Transportation Committee, has called it "an illogical extension of our trade policy." Neatly summarizing the situation, DeFazio says, "You can become an international corporation, operate in America, and pay your taxes elsewhere. . . . And if that elsewhere doesn't require you to pay taxes, then, well, you don't pay taxes." In retrospect, this state of affairs seems almost inevitable. As new countries with little to lose began operating flagship registries during the 1970s and 1980s, the same race to the bottom that guaranteed shipowners lax enforcement of international labor and safety laws saw to it that any real taxation regime in the FOC nations would never come to pass. In shipowners, it turned out, these nations were competing for transient fee payers, not long-term corporate citizens. This unexpected new manifestation of international competition turned a sensible structure for easing international trade into a loophole big enough to sail a supertanker through.

As the State Department successfully argued when it opposed the Clay bill, however, there is little that can be done about the system without upending diplomatic relationships around the globe and risking an avalanche of trade sanctions and retaliation. One cannot, as a practical matter, recognize some national registries and not others; there are other trade, military and diplomatic considerations as well. Worse, when it comes down to the actual legal work of it, flag of convenience registries are difficult to define. Opaque ownership makes the 51 percent test impractical, and failing that it's difficult to say whether or not a ship's registry is in fact legitimate. One thing is certain, however: international law demands that the flag itself must be respected. The freedom of the high seas, as set forth by the UN, is a right of every nation, whether or not it has a coastline.

The multilateral route, through the UN's International Maritime Organization, is equally difficult. Leaving aside the dubious administration of some open registries for a moment, one runs headlong into the fact that a country's voting power at the IMO is determined by the amount of tonnage registered under its flag. This gives Liberia, which today scarcely exists, a voice more powerful than that of the United States when it comes to matters of law on the high seas.

One of the many ironies here is that the U.S.-based cruise lines that enjoy this arrangement are part of the shipping industry in only the strictest technical sense. The general consensus has been that, in the interests of global commerce and good diplomacy, flag of convenience shipowners will simply continue to get this free ride—a frustrating situation, perhaps, but far easier to bear than any plausible alternative advanced so far. Like other shipowners, the cruise lines have taken advantage of this legal anomaly: the marginal boost the tax exemptions provide has been a key to their rapid expansion and high profitability, perhaps second only to the savings they garner by using cheap international labor. Their business, however, although legally identical to that of cargo lines, is in reality a different enterprise altogether.

If this profoundly American industry is in fact somehow not American, it is also *not shipping*. In fact, the story of the modern cruise business has as much as anything been that of its steady and prosperous retreat from the transportation industry. The marketing mantra that "the ship is the destination" has grown truer and truer as the industry has matured. Today, exotic itineraries notwithstanding, cruise ships in a very real sense hardly go anywhere at all. With very few exceptions, cruises out of U.S. ports today are round-trips. Carnival and Royal Caribbean, which together account for more than 85 percent of the North American cruise industry, have achieved something truly remarkable. As public companies headquartered in the United States, traded on the New York Stock Exchange, earning the vast majority of their revenue from U.S. citizens making round-trip voyages originating in U.S. ports, they have managed to maintain, for tax purposes, the status of foreign corporations engaged in the international transportation of people and goods. With certain exceptions, such as subsidiaries like Carnival's Holland America and Royal Caribbean's Celebrity Cruises, which pay taxes on land-based tour assets and operations they own in Alaska, they pay no federal income tax on their U.S. operations.

In response to claims that they are effectively being subsidized by the U.S. government, industry spokespeople point to the economic contributions they make in their "homeports," the cities where they embark and disembark passengers. Billions of dollars annually, they say, are generated not only by port fees and the money spent on labor and goods during the turnaround but on the millions of people the industry draws to American port cities every year en route to its ships. "We have looked at the amounts of money that we bring into the U.S. economy," ICCL president Cynthia Colenda said in a 1999 interview, "and last year it was significant." According to the ICCL, the industry pumped $6.6 billion into the U.S. economy in 1997, generating more than 170,000 jobs. In 1999, it paid $66 million in port fees. But no federal taxes. Critics find this argument "absurd," in the words of DeFazio. "I mean, any other American corporation could make the same arguments they're making, which is to say, 'Well, gee, because we buy food from caterers, we buy advertising, we buy this, we buy that, we shouldn't have to pay taxes. Look at all the economic activity we're generating.' Well, yeah, but you're not carrying your fair share."

As the industry dons its shipping hat for the benefit of tax authorities, individual lines have been actively making a very different case to Wall Street. Over the past fifteen years, the big cruise concerns have become more and more dependent on the public markets to finance their aggressive new building regimes. Executives, through road shows, conference calls and countless meetings, have gone to great pains to convince analysts that the shipping industry, with its low profit margins and highly volatile business cycles, has little relevance to cruise business at all in any real economic sense. "They learned that this was a different business," recalls Howard Frank, Carnival's vice chairman and Micky's self-described alter ego. "This was not the shipping business, this was the vacation business. It took years."

To say that this best-of-both-worlds arrangement has served the industry well is a fantastic understatement. Comparing leading companies from the cruise and cargo sectors side by side, it quickly becomes clear that, if the cruise industry is indeed shipping, it's shipping on a boatload of steroids. In terms of sea traffic, cruising accounts for a tiny fraction of global shipping— well below 5 percent. Yet Carnival, based on its 2003 financials, is about thirteen times bigger than the world's largest publicly traded cargo shipping company. *Thirteen times.* It's a whole other league; the industry's unique status has catapulted Carnival well into the ranks of the two hundred largest companies in the world—bigger than Target, Honeywell, Allstate, General Motors and McDonald's, to name a few. And with profit margins that crest at 28 percent during the past ten years, one could be forgiven for thinking there might be enough money floating around to foot a tax bill.

Admittedly, Carnival is something of an anomaly. Royal Caribbean's financials, sometimes considered sluggish by Miami standards, would merely make it the world's biggest bulk shipper by a factor of three—if Royal Caribbean actually were in the shipping business, that is. Which it isn't, of course—except that it is.

In 1999 the *New York Times* estimated that the United States was losing hundreds of millions of tax dollars annually from the still rapidly growing U.S.-based cruise industry. Based on their filings with the SEC, Carnival and Royal Caribbean's combined income tax, figured at the standard corporate income tax of 35 percent, would have been about $518 million in 2003 alone. That's just under half that year's EPA budget for Superfund cleanups, nearly twice the funding for the Peace Corps and enough to cover a state college education for approximately 27,400 students. This figure, furthermore, doesn't take into account sales taxes, payroll taxes, Social Security contributions and the other usual costs of doing business in the United States. It's worth remembering that nearly everything that gets loaded aboard a cruise ship in Miami or Galveston or Los Angeles or New Orleans or New York is considered an export, and as such comes to the cruise line duty-free despite the fact that most products are sold on board at U.S. prices—another neat little sleight of hand.

The cruise business actually represents a significant government expense—and all the more so in a post–September 11 world. Its ships are potentially attractive targets for terrorists not only from a mass-casualty perspective but also because they symbolize so powerfully American consumer culture—irrespective of the flag they fly. Millions of federal dollars have helped fund port security initiatives, many of them designed to safeguard cruise ships. Approaching U.S. ports, the vessels are escorted in by Coast Guard and local law enforcement patrol boats. Once they are tied up, the waters surrounding the ship are constantly patrolled by armed speedboats and shoreside security personnel, government employees, all. "They go buy their ships elsewhere, staff them with cheap, third world labor, then enjoy all the benefits of doing business in America," Representative Gene Taylor, a Mississippi Democrat, has marveled. "When their ships caught fire, did they sit around and wait for the Liberian coast guard to show up? What if there is a hostage situation? Will they call in the Panamanian navy SEALs? Who incurs all of these responsibilities and pays all these costs? The American taxpayer."

One possible short-term solution to this loophole would limit the seagoing commerce entitled to the privileges of FOC registry by type rather than by ownership. Under such an arrangement, nations like the U.S. and its trading partners might redefine the relevant conventions to exclude vessels that fail to discharge 51 percent or more of their passengers or cargo before returning to the same harbor—Miami, for example. Such an approach would keep thinly disguised domestic corporations from making the use of tax and legal exemptions intended to facilitate international trade without discriminating against any nation or requiring impractical enforcement regimens based on the identity of a ship's owners or a company's investors. Perhaps most important, it would not inhibit the swift and affordable movement of goods around the globe.

This plan would require the cruise industry to shoulder an unaccustomed burden, however—one that would surely cut significantly into its profit margins. Then again, the industry can certainly afford it. To get an idea of how far outside the mainstream the cruise industry's arrangement is, consider the fact that if it were earning at Carnival's margins, the retail giant Wal-Mart in 2003 would have made an unheard of $65 billion in profits, an amount greater than those of the world's four most profitable companies: Exxon-Mobil, Citigroup, General Electric and Bank of America—*combined.*

Then compare that with the $8 billion in income Wal-Mart reported here on planet earth—*and* paid taxes on.

The tax question brings us back to Ted Arison and the last years of his long and remarkable life. He celebrated his seventy-fifth and final birthday on the Israeli coast aboard his yacht, the *My Lin IV,* which today belongs to Micky. The party was by all accounts a remarkable and skillfully organized affair. Guests were flown in on chartered planes as early as a week before, "in order to get over the jet lag." Brigades of jeeps with drivers and tour guides took them around the Israeli countryside. In their "Welcome to Israel" kits they learned of incidents in Ted's life that were new to many of them, such as the time an eleven-year-old Ted had "run guns for the Israeli underground, smuggling a revolver in a bouquet of flowers right under the noses of the occupying British army." Ted, struggling, attended what events he felt up to. It was, his wife remembered, "a week in which he had to marshal his resources." Finally, the evening of the party came. There was dancing and singing long into the night. Guests dressed in turbans and flowing bedouin garments distributed by the ship's costumed crew. As they lined up to pay their respects to a happy Ted, most observed the instructions from his bodyguards "not to shake Ted's hand or hug him because he bruised so easily." A few could not resist and took the frail old hand into their own or draped their arms around his skeletal frame.

There was much to celebrate: first and foremost, that Ted was still alive and up to seeing everybody. Two months earlier, it seemed doubtful that he would make it. Also, business was very good. In the years since he had turned the Carnival board over to Micky, the company had grown at an unbelievable rate. With the acquisition of the venerable Cunard Line that May, Carnival was the industry leader by an extraordinary margin. The company that had begun with the *Mardi Gras's* ill-fated maiden voyage now controlled Holland America, Windstar, Costa, Cunard and the ultraluxury Seabourn lines. Although he would not live to see it become official, it was already clear that 1999 would be the year in which Carnival's profits first broke the $1 billion mark. "Micky made me more money than I ever made for him," Ted said in 1996. "I think he did a better job than I did."

It's fitting that the party was held on the yacht—and not just because of Ted's career in ships. A yacht like the *My Lin* is the embodiment of a wealth and power that is without permanent allegiance: attached to solid earth only temporarily, and then only by a few thin ropes. All in all, not a bad metaphor for the last years of Ted's life—or for the industry he pioneered.

Nobody likes taxes. Ted Arison was certainly not the first U.S. citizen to renounce his country in order to preserve his fortune for the next generation of his family—and certainly, many among that number gave far less in their life than did Ted, who was by all accounts a generous and charitable man. But then, he could afford to be—even his considerable philanthropy never approached what the company he owned would have paid in taxes. And in Ted's case, at least one of the usual excuses does not apply. He was not born an American. He *chose* the United States out of all the countries of the world.

The country, for its part, made him rich beyond the dreams of even very wealthy men and women. When he turned in his passport in the fall of 1990, it's hard not to think, as his beloved Boeing 727 traced its arc up into the sky and out over the wild Atlantic, that Ted Arison had done his best to play a cynical joke, at the expense of the American Dream.

"Death *and* taxes?" one can imagine him chuckling from beyond the grave. "What do you think I am, anyway, Mr. Franklin—some kind of sucker?"

CHAPTER NINE

CARNIVAL IS A CARNIVORE

I know what you want, Rocco. . . . You want more.

—Humphrey Bogart, *Key Largo*

But 1999 is getting ahead of the story.

Nine years earlier, with Ted on his way back to Israel, Carnival's fate was squarely in Micky's hands. From that moment on, the company pressed forward even more aggressively than before, if such a thing was possible.

The ascension suited Micky well. Gone was the hulking, butterfly-collared, reserved kid hiding behind his thick-rimmed, tinted glasses. In his place was a fiercely competitive executive, if a somewhat unorthodox one. Micky ran his company with little concern for convention or outsider expectations, and although he'd mostly overcome the awkwardness of his younger years, he still kept a low profile and was nonconfrontational to a fault in many situations—a "dominant, shy guy," as one senior officer at Carnival described him. Just six years earlier, a guest at a reception celebrating Carnival's newest ship had mistaken a wallflowering Micky for someone who'd sneaked in from the street. Now, the transformation complete, no one was surprised to hear that Micky—not Carnival, *Micky*—owned an airline and a national basketball franchise in addition to the cruise business. Tanned, well fed and tailored impeccably, he was finally looking the part of a genuine magnate.

Although the Miami Heat was initially a sideline he'd inherited when Ted skipped town, the team quickly became an all-consuming passion, and Micky rarely missed a game. During basketball season, employees heading up to the tenth floor and into the corner office for a meeting with "El Jefe" made sure to check the sports pages before getting in the elevator. They knew that if the Heat hadn't won the night before, they could be facing a cranky audience. Basketball became something of a metaphor for the urges that would drive his professional life as it entered its prime. One comment seems to say it all. At a game with one of his top executives, Micky suddenly turned away from the action on the court to pose a rhetorical question. "Wouldn't this just be boring as shit," he said, "if there was a game going on and no scoreboard? It's just like business."

He'd seen clearly enough that the company his father had built was facing a moment of truth. In the nearly twenty years since the *Mardi Gras*'s disastrous first voyage, Carnival had gone from a shoestring operation to a public company with annual revenues in excess of $1.2 billion. Its first takeover attempt had been an embarrassing affair in which Royal Caribbean's owners had gotten the best of the Arisons, but Micky and Ted had recovered with incredible speed to announce their takeover of Holland America, which closed in 1989. To many people's minds, it was an even better match, and that deal had been an extraordinary success by any measure. Micky knew, however, that it was the events of the coming decade that would define Carnival's legacy, and his own. Everything else had merely been setting the stage; the real drama was just beginning.

Some form of consolidation would have been inevitable in any event, but the usual process was happening with unusual speed—intensified, like everything else in this business, by an abundance of cash and a minimum of outside interference or oversight. The entire cycle, from a diverse, fledgling industry to one in which three players controlled nearly 90 percent of the business, would take barely thirty years to complete. To put that time frame in some perspective, consider the Las Vegas gambling industry. Thirty years after the gangster Bugsy Siegel effectively kicked off the Las Vegas boom in 1946 by building the Flamingo Hotel and Casino, gaming revenues for the entire state of Nevada were just passing the $1 billion mark for the first time ever, and the strip was still a collection of independent operators. Today it's controlled by a handful of big companies, but it's been a long road to get there. Thirty-five years after NCL kicked off the Miami cruise boom, Carnival and Royal Caribbean together accounted for 86.4 percent of the North American cruise market. Their combined revenues for the year came to around $11.4 billion.

But again, that's getting ahead. Back in 1990, as Micky was settling in behind his father's old Formica desk, the show was just beginning.

The big lines kept bringing out their new ships more and more quickly. It was getting to the point that there was nowhere left in this business for a little guy to hide.

Traditionally, smaller lines had been able to nibble around the industry's edges, surviving at a lower price point with older ships while the majors commanded fat premiums for their new, modern ones. But the new tonnage was steadily changing the rules of the game. These vessels were not only easier to market, but were also far more efficient to operate. And there were so *many* of them. In 1981 the industry had about forty-one thousand berths sailing out of North America, a figure that had doubled by 1990; twelve thousand new berths had come online that year alone, at a price tag of about $1.4 billion. Unless you wanted to run two-hundred-person ships to the Galapagos or Antarctica, there wasn't much of a niche left to carve out. The big lines could charge less and less per passenger, making phenomenal profits even as they forced the pricing floor lower and lower for their increasingly hapless competition. For the midrange players, "discounting" became a dirty word, a symbol of their growing helplessness.

The industry's golden rule is that a cruise ship has to sail full if it's going to make money; everything else flows from that. The specifics vary widely, but as a general matter the first 65 percent of the passengers on a modern cruise ship are simply paying for the fixed costs—fuel, labor, capital expenses, etc. From an occupancy perspective, anything below that is a disaster: the flip side is that anything above the break-even number is pure profit, and usually tax-free. And it's not just the ticket sales, although they continue to represent a majority of any line's revenue. Onboard spending is crucial to the equation. An empty cabin on the sailing date means that for the duration of that cruise, the two people—or three, or four—who would have been staying in that cabin will not be buying drinks at the bar or shore excursions or souvenirs. Nor will they be paying the tips that sustain much of the crew in lieu of a salary. At the last minute, therefore, there's little incentive for a cruise line not to more or less give its remaining cabins away.

The cruise lines experimented with different approaches to deal with the problem. Royal Caribbean, for example, would market aggressively around the country, and use nearby Florida as a "dumping ground," easily moving their last-minute empty cabins by selling them cheap to customers who were already nearby. In those days you could still see senior citizens loitering around Dodge Island on Saturdays waiting to see if anything came up. The ones who knew their way around could live at sea for less than it cost them to stay ashore.

There was an obvious catch, however: passengers do not like finding out that the person sitting next to them got a better deal than they did. And they do find out. There's a timeless industry truism about this phenomenon: When people sit down for dinner, the first question is "Where do you come from?" The second is "What'd you pay?" The real problem was not that the passenger who'd paid more would get upset, although that was unfortunate. The real problem was that a disgruntled passenger would then go home and yell at her travel agent for not getting a better deal. The agent in turn would reasonably conclude that the cruise line's erratic discounting had made a fool of her and would certainly be wary of selling that company's cruises in the future.

A cruise may seem like a pedestrian enough holiday, but for first-time cruisers it's a significant departure from their past experience—and fifteen years ago it was even more so. In 1990, according to industry estimates, only a tiny fraction of Americans had been on a cruise. The experience was familiar and unfamiliar at the same time. It all took place in the middle of the ocean, after all, and in extremely close quarters. The very notion seemed to suggest seasickness and claustrophobia—*and* you're expected to pay for the whole thing up front. Even if the bottom line added up to a bargain, it was a big check to write. Selling a cruise, in short, was not something you could do with a brochure. People had questions; you needed a face, a voice, a pitch. The cruise lines moved upwards of 95 percent of their bookings through travel agents, which made them indispensable to the industry's profitability. At a time when simply surviving meant cajoling hundreds of thousands of new passengers onto the high seas every year, keeping this constituency happy was a top priority.

Fortunately for the cruise lines, there were strong incentives in the early 1990s for travel agents to sell cruises. For one thing, the deregulation of the airline industry in 1978 had begun a squeeze that threatened the fat airfare commissions agents traditionally relied upon. The smart ones were looking to develop new revenue streams, and saw that cruises held great promise. Cruise vacations were among the biggest-ticket items a travel agent could sell and the easiest to process by far. No need to hound various airlines, hotels and other businesses for paperwork. It was all one receipt, sent directly from the cruise line by a contact person who, if you sold any number of cruises regularly, likely as not knew your name and the names of your kids. The cruise lines even handled the airfare booking—and paid commissions on it, even when the airlines didn't. In short, it was more money for less work—and that doesn't even count the freebies: the cruises, the *shrimp*. Put travel agents on a ship with a bucket of shrimp cocktail in front of them, old hands say, and they're just about the happiest people alive. It's just one of those things, some sort of hard-wired predisposition science hasn't yet managed to explain. It got so that shorthand for schmoozing travel agents became "eating shrimp," as in, "No one ate shrimp with the travel agents better than Rod."

Discounting, however, was a real problem. Local travel agents depend on repeat business above all else. The fact remained that, as attractive as cruises might be to agents, if cruise lines' pricing strategies risked costing them customers, all the shrimp cocktail in the world wasn't going to make it worth their while.

Throughout the furious expansion of the 1980s and early 1990s, the industry walked the discounting tightrope. The need to sail ships full inevitably trumped other concerns, and the unpredictable pricing persisted. "The cruise industry had gotten to the point where it was like buying a car," one executive remembers. "You had the sticker price and nobody paid it, and it got kind of shady. There was a lot of wariness and skepticism by the distribution."

The big lines soon recognized the need to have their houses in order when it came to discounting and came up with a variety of approaches to deal with the problem. The most successful was to simply disguise the discounts. Since the cruise lines arranged the door-to-door vacation experience, elements like airfare were a highly effective way of aiming discounts at specific markets while keeping the overall "sticker price" of the cruise itself relatively even for everyone. Somehow, as long as they were all paying the same thing for the cruise itself, people who would have been outraged to learn they'd overpaid by three hundred dollars didn't feel cheated when they heard that the couple across from them got a ninety-nine-dollar airfare to Miami from Chicago when they'd paid four hundred dollars from Baltimore.

While deregulation may have forced the travel agents into the cruise lines' arms, it was also the one area where the gospel of scale worked against the industry. As airfares kept getting cheaper for individuals, they got more expensive for the cruise lines. The lines had always bought big blocks of seats far in advance, and shuffled them around as bookings came in. This had worked well when fares were fixed by law, but under deregulation the airlines were free to take advantage of the cruise industry's total—and totally predictable— dependence on their services.

If you need to get six thousand people into Miami during a six-hour window on a particular Saturday, there's not a lot of room for flexibility. "At the end of the day, they know that we need our flights," one Carnival executive explained. "They know that we can't arrive at 10 P.M. when the ship's going to sail at four." Increasingly, passengers began booking their own airfare for less than the cruise lines could provide, denying the industry what had been a valuable veil over the discounting process.

Stripped of a key component of their marketing strategy, the lines looked for other ways to hide discounts, and the late 1980s became the years of "promo-mania." Ten days at sea sold for the price of seven; two people could sail for the price of one; the cabin price would include "free" coupons for on-board purchases. Upgrading already booked passengers to more expensive cabins on "softer" sailings—those with weaker demand—allowed operators to put the cheaper, faster-moving cabins back on the market without under-mining their pricing. In some cases, boosting commissions to top-performing travel agents motivated agents to boost sales by giving discounts of their own—a move that although effectively subsidized by the cruise lines, was not publicly tied to them. "We had every gimmick imaginable," one marketing executive recalls. Instead of discounted airfares, the lines began offering bargains of land-sea packages. "You had 'Rail & Sail,' 'Surf & Turf,' 'Sea & Ski.' " Things could sometimes get out of hand. When NCL offered one par-ticularly aggressive package in the spring of 1991, Carnival's Bob Dickinson publicly dismissed the move as "premature price ejaculation." Several weeks later, when Carnival offered the same deal, the NCL team sent over a pair of boxer shorts, with Carnival's own splashy promotion sewn onto the front.

The helter-skelter of the old days' gut approach to pricing was fast giving way to the science of revenue management. The infrastructure and personnel required to oversee it all represented a significant investment. The major lines spent millions developing ways to predict demand—and that was on top of the tens of millions paid out every year in marketing costs and padded com-missions. By the mid-1990s, Royal Caribbean was bringing in a team that included NASA engineers to develop complex algorithms to predict demand—

a huge investment, but also a resounding success. Imagine the frustration when Carnival, true to form, hired much of that team away within a few years of their arrival.

It was an untenable environment for the smaller lines, forced to almost blindly discount the old, inefficient ships they were already operating at the low end of the market, where margins were the tightest. Even the best of them were a big step behind, as one Royal Caribbean executive recalls. "We'd look at their brochures and their prices would be identical to ours— identical," he says. "Even when we did something stupid, they copied us. I can remember once, we had a misprint on a gateway, and they did it—we made a mistake, and they copied it."

The big question had ceased to be whether or not the small players would be able to survive; no one believed they would. The question now was, which of the big players would eat the little ones up? And, what would happen between the majors as the bankruptcies and acquisitions changed the face of the industry?

By the middle of the decade, a number of spectacular collapses had already driven the point home.

Contrary to the poet's advice, some of them went gently, like Majesty Cruise Lines. The upscale offshoot of the budget operation known as Dolphin Cruises, Majesty had been doing a good business with its single ship, the *Royal Majesty.* Dolphin had bought it new from a Finnish shipyard in 1992 at a rock-bottom price when the company that had ordered it went under. Nonetheless it was a stretch for the little company, which ran a trio of older ships back and forth between South Florida and the Caribbean, the world's most heavily discounted cruise market. But Dolphin, along with many of its competitors, was facing the inevitable fact that its ships would soon be too old to operate. Discounting pressures had all but precluded the possibility of making enough money to enter the new building game; it had been a minor miracle that the opportunity to acquire the *Royal Majesty* had arisen at all. Dolphin's management decided to launch it under a new brand—a clean slate, so to speak. "We hoped that we could continue and grow the company, little by little, and sell the ships of Dolphin and phase them out," recalls Dolphin's president at the time, Paris Katsoufis. "It was evident that the future was with the new ships."

The *Royal Majesty* was, by all accounts, a lovely little ship. Smallish at just over one thousand passengers, it served top-notch food, and instead of show-girls, the management brought real actors on board to perform repertory theater, to "add intellectual value." And the hardware was as good as the "software" provided by the service staff—or at least it was supposed to be. Somehow, the *Royal Majesty*'s up-to-date, computerized satellite navigational technology didn't keep the ship from running aground off the coast of Nantucket in June of 1995 with a full load of passengers on board. No one was hurt in the incident, but "it was a very traumatic experience for a young company that was ready to take off," Katsoufis remembers. Repairs were expensive, but the real pain came from refunding tickets, offering incentives to the inconvenienced passengers and canceling future cruises for the duration of the work. Worst of all, the grounding had taken place at the outset of the lucrative summer trade—the bread-and-butter months for the upscale lines, when the warm weather makes it possible to get out of the Caribbean and take advantage of the higher rates passengers will pay for seasonal destinations like Alaska, Canada and Europe. The total impact was estimated at $7 million—catastrophic for such a small company.

The repairs got done and Majesty made it through the year, albeit limping. Without any further disaster, Katsoufis reasoned, they'd be able to get back on their feet. But no one had accounted for the weather. The following year's hurricane season was unusually intense, and it claimed the struggling Majesty as one of its casualties. "Some hurricanes in that year reached all the way from Miami up to Halifax," Katsoufis remembers. "And it was one after the other. In some cases, you avoided one up in Halifax, but you had another waiting for you in Bermuda." It was just the sort of unpredictable, nobody's-fault scenario that companies must be able to endure, but it was too much for an already struggling Majesty. The rough seas made life aboard the little ship unpleasant, and meanwhile the bigger lines were offering their passengers full refunds—plus 50 percent off another cruise, in some cases. Majesty had no choice but to match them. "The big guys, they could suffer," Katsoufis says. "But for us, it was straining us more and more." It wasn't long before Majesty couldn't make payment on the ship's mortgage. The shipyard—struggling itself—took equity in the company, and things began sliding downhill from there. By 1997 the *Royal Majesty* had been sold, stretched and overhauled for incorporation into the NCL fleet. Dolphin's ships went onto the open market.

Especially during so rich a decade as the 1990s, such collapses were sad; others, however, were spectacular. Perhaps the most colorful—and disastrous— of these was that of Regency Cruise Lines. Regency, in the words of the trade press at the time, "abandoned its ships at sea, turned on an answering machine at its New York headquarters, and left several hundred passengers to fend for themselves, in one of the most ungraceful business shutdowns in history."

Toward the end, the line had become a specialist in the so-called "cruise from hell," as the management failed, capital dried up and the crews were left to stall the inevitable as best they could. On one ship, the refueling hose broke while it was suspended over the gangway, of all places. "Passengers are walking under it," remembers Randy Johnstone, a former Regency purser who spent several years with the line rotating through different ships. "And the shit just exploded, covering everybody in this thick crude oil—nasty, nasty stuff."

When the toilet system on one of its ships went down, most lines would have concluded that there was no way to continue with the cruise. Not Regency, whose passengers had to make do with the dozens of portable toilets that were brought onto the *Regent Sun* and lined up on the aft deck. When the air-conditioning system aboard the same ship failed, the solution was even more brazen: they just lied about it. Embarking passengers who inquired about the stifling heat were told it was due to all the open loading-bay doors during the provisioning. Once the ship got under way, the crew insisted, the air-conditioning would kick in and things would cool down. What were the passengers going to do, anyway—jump overboard? Their tickets clearly stipulated a no-refund policy. "So we fed this line to everybody that came on board for seven weeks running, that everything was fine," Johnstone recalls. "Then we had them on there for a week with no air-conditioning and prayed they never passed anyone at the airport who was coming on the ship." Perhaps most memorably, when Honduran authorities arrested a *Regency* vessel on behalf of a creditor, the hotel manager, desperate to continue the cruise, unsuccessfully offered as collateral a lifeboat and one of the ship's room stewards.

Regency died as it lived. In the weeks leading up to its 1995 collapse, its crews went unpaid, although of itself that was hardly evidence of things being out of the ordinary. Even when one of its ships was abruptly sold, management insisted that it was simply a matter of the company tightening its belt. Then, the day before Halloween, hundreds of passengers arrived at docks to meet ships that either weren't there or weren't sailing anywhere. In total, about thirty thousand passengers, all of whom had paid in advance for tickets, found themselves at the end of a long line of creditors.

Johnstone had been aboard the *Regency Spirit* in Nice when the word came down. Dumbfounded passengers were turned away, as the abandoned crew struggled to figure out what to do. Most of the concessionaires had packed their people up and left as soon as they'd heard the news, which left about eighty crew members on board the *Spirit*—dancers, cruise staff and third world maritime and hotel workers—Johnstone included. None of them had been paid in weeks. "We appointed two guys to be the cooks for the crew and took money out of the safe," he remembers. "We went to the equivalent of a French Costco and bought bags of rice and pasta." During the ensuing weeks, workers with nowhere else to go simply waited aboard the abandoned ship. "Their singers and dancers weren't going to get paid, so they took their DAT machines and costumes out into the street and pawned it all, just so they could have some money in their pocket," the purser remembers. "People were stealing television sets and anything they could get their hands on to make money."

There were other failures during this era—though few as spectacular as Regency's—as well as any number of minor mergers that went belly-up in turn. As of January 1992 the industry's nine leading lines accounted for 47 percent of the cruise traffic through American ports. By now, the story of the industry was no longer a tale of scrappy, risk-taking entrepreneurs but had become instead a saga of corporate dominance—giants competing for tiny advantages on vast, exclusive playing fields.

From a pure business perspective, the consolidation process seemed to promise the best of both worlds—at least for the survivors. For a well-run operator snapped up by a larger company, the thinking went, the stronger infrastructure and presumably more sophisticated financial management would support the smaller lines' shipboard operations and marketing efforts. Wall Street loved the idea, since having the stream of new ships managed by fewer players held out the hope of stabilizing—"rationalizing"—the volatile discounting that dragged stocks down with the ticket prices. The theory played well in the industry's boardrooms, and the relevant buzzwords helped obscure the human cost of the consolidation process. The trouble with mergers, of course, is that however good they look on paper, they often yield unintended consequences. The annals of business abound with tales of theoretically sound deals soured by culture clashes and personal conflicts, from RJR Nabisco to Time Warner. Applied to the cruise industry, where companies are often defined by idiosyncratic family ownership, rigid shipboard cultures and strong national identity, such factors were especially significant.

Carnival, however, was developing a corporate philosophy that would allow it to take advantage of the era's opportunities without falling into this trap. It was simple: where subsidiaries were performing well, it was gospel not to meddle in their affairs. This tenet has since been celebrated as the secret of Carnival's success—its greatest management showpiece—but it first took shape as a happy accident, a product of the unique circumstances surrounding Carnival's acquisition of Holland America.

If Micky had succeeded in his pursuit of Royal Caribbean in late 1988, things might well have taken a different shape entirely. Although it had appeared to be a consolation prize, Holland America was actually in much better financial shape; all it really needed was more capital. One of the world's oldest continually operating passenger lines, it was also one of the most profitable, thanks in large part to Kirk Lanterman, who as president had played a major role in turning the formerly ailing company around. Geography played a part here, too. With Royal Caribbean headquartered only minutes away from Carnival's Miami offices, the temptation to interfere in its business on a day-to-day basis—to "Carnivalize" it—might well have been irresistible for a company with no prior merger experience. Holland America, on the other hand, was headquartered far from Miami, in Seattle, the better to administer its lucrative Alaska trade and its huge network of hotels, buses and railcars. Micky kept an eye on things but left the Holland America group intact and largely autonomous. And why not? The entire point of the acquisition, after all, had been to gain entrée into the higher-end segment of the cruise market, an area in which Carnival's down-and-dirty Fun Ships team admittedly had little experience.

Lanterman himself was a strict numbers man who prized results and had no tolerance for failure. At a board meeting he once quizzed a new treasurer on an arcane point of one of his ships' mortgages. When the man, three weeks on the job, responded that he didn't know but would get back to him with an answer right away, Lanterman snarled. "Don't ever come to another board meeting unprepared," he said. "Or you're out of here." He knew his business, however, and he got results. The grapevine had it that he even intimidated Micky a little.

The separation between the brands also enabled Micky to encourage the nascent rivalry between Lanterman and Carnival Cruise Lines's emerging chief Bob Dickinson without fear of creating a rift within the organization. He carefully kept the two of them apart, making sure to give neither of them power over the other's semiautonomous territory. And then he pushed them—just a bit—to keep them on their game. The mantra of senior management was simple and came directly from the top. There were exceptions, of course, but at Carnival the answer to most questions was "Sure, as long as you hit your numbers."

Micky had further defused the disruptive potential of the merger with his choice of deputy. Uncharacteristically, he'd declined to promote from within, thereby taking both Dickinson and Lanterman out of the running and leaving them to focus on their respective brands. Well aware that his company was turning a corner, Micky decided he needed someone who knew his way around the world of finance, a world whose language and customs he himself was not yet familiar with. In 1989 Micky brought in Howard Frank, a partner at the national accounting firm that had landed the Carnival account just prior to the IPO two years earlier.

Hiring PricewaterhouseCoopers had itself been an unusual move for Carnival, which at the time was still run very much as a family business. In one way or another, most of the company's relationships dated back many years, having their roots, as Micky put it, in Ted's "cronies" from the early days. Nationwide firms like Pricewaterhouse were simply not used. Of his predecessor, Frank would later say, "I'm not sure what his competence was, other than he would never spend money. I know this because I could never get my bills paid." Carnival had been using a local firm for years, but Ted and Micky had agreed that shepherding the company successfully through an IPO would require bigger guns. Frank, who'd already done some work for Royal Caribbean (also a client) and had a passing knowledge of the industry, took over the account. As his team worked through the complicated business of carving out the cruise business's finances from the tangle of Ted's various other investments, Micky had plenty of opportunity to watch him work. When the attempt to take over Royal Caribbean began to fall apart in the following year, it was Frank who flew out to Seattle on Carnival's dime to head up the Pricewaterhouse due-diligence team. Shortly thereafter, Micky brought him on as senior vice president for finance. Within three years, he was chief operating officer of the corporation and was sitting on the board as vice chairman.

Frank was a great counterweight for Micky. Where Micky had stumbled through community college before trading the University of Miami for a staff job on his father's ships, Frank had graduated from the University of Rhode Island and gone on to make partner at one of America's top accounting firms. Micky was the strong, silent type, with an impulse to withdraw and sulk rather than express displeasure outright. Frank, though he could be as tough as anyone, knew how to wheedle and whine behind closed doors if that's what it took to get what he wanted. Outwardly, he prided himself on an aggressive, all-business persona. Hearing on one occasion that a speech he'd made had reminded an observer of Gordon Gekko (the fictional corporate raider immortalized in Oliver Stone's 1987 film *Wall Street* with Michael Douglas sporting a bad attitude and a memorable power haircut), Frank leaned back in his chair and despite himself let slip a contented chuckle.

Frank brought formality to the finances of a company that had not too long before been run more like a local butcher shop than a major corporation. He took responsibility for communicating with Wall Street, although as time went by Micky grew more comfortable in that role, as well. "I don't think I would characterize it as mentoring," Frank says of their relationship. "I would say Micky recognized that he needed to have somebody who comes out of a more disciplined background and with certain skill sets that he didn't have, and didn't particularly want to have or felt he needed to run his business." Yet the two men shared a strong instinct for quick decisions. With either of them, senior Carnival people say, "Let me think about that" tended to mean "No."

Today Frank says he's Micky's "alter ego." Others have compared them to an old married couple. "We read each other so well, when we go into a negotiation with a third party, just by eye contact we know what we're doing. It's a very unusual relationship, but we're very close from that standpoint," Frank says. "He recognizes my strengths and weaknesses, and I recognize his strengths—god forbid he should have any weaknesses."

With Holland America and Carnival Cruise Lines established as semiautonomous divisions, the company's corporate group under Micky and Frank was free to concentrate on other matters: financing and negotiating new ships, building relationships with the investment community, scouting for acquisitions, trolling the operations for new savings and efficiencies—all without disturbing the established management rhythms of the all-important product. They developed into something between an M&A hit squad and in-house consultants, alternately looking outward for opportunities and combing the organization for ways to save money. Within the industry, they inspired a combination of fear and awe. "If Carnival is Israel," it was said of Micky's strategic planning people, "they're the Mossad." If executives at Royal Caribbean and elsewhere in the industry are to be believed, the corporate arm's repertoire came to include the black arts of disinformation and sabotage. "If you go back and look at every public offering we have done," a top Royal Caribbean executive says, "in the weeks leading up to that, Carnival has made a lot of negative comments about the state of the industry. And there are those who believe that was not unintentional."

It's easy to imagine that the Arisons and their team were somehow unstoppable from the beginning. There's a good case to be made, however, that Carnival owes much of its success to that first lucky failure in the big-time. Had the Royal Caribbean deal gone through in 1988, if Carnival's first acquisition hadn't laid the groundwork for what would eventually be known as its "portfolio strategy," who's to say what sort of company would have taken shape?

As it was, the stage was set for an aggressive expansion not only through building existing brands, but through voracious acquisition. And if the corporate hit squad preferred to work behind the scenes, that didn't make them any less conscious of their public image. In 1993, after taking on a 25 percent stake in the small ultraluxury line Seabourn, Micky changed the company's name from Carnival Cruise Lines to Carnival Corporation. A small gesture, perhaps, but the new name was nevertheless a public expression of the organizational philosophy that had been taking shape for some time. Ted Arison's little start-up was fast becoming the cruise industry's first conglomerate.

By necessity, Royal Caribbean had evolved in the opposite direction. Richard Fain and Arne Wilhelmsen had kept the company out of Carnival's clutches, but only barely. To pull off their coup, they'd had to take on extraordinary leverage: once the dust settled, more than 75 percent of the company's market capitalization was composed of debt. At the same time, while rearranging the old partnership's scattershot accounting systems into something U.S.

investors—and the SEC—could recognize and understand, it became clear that the company's slim profit was the first it had made in years. Survival meant quickly paying down that debt even as the company brought new ships on line—and *that* meant an aggressive new focus on the bottom line. Just as some sharks cannot breathe unless they're in motion, a cruise line in the early 1990s lived or died on its ability to expand at a pace equal to that of its competitors. Failure was a real possibility; within a few years, well-established lines—many of them not much smaller than Royal Caribbean had been when Fain took over—would be dropping regularly.

Fain's ascendancy—like Howard Frank's—represented the industry's new emphasis on financial and corporate sophistication. There was a difference, however. Frank had been brought in to round out Micky's skills; there was never any question as to who was running the show or whether the entrepreneurial guts of the organization would remain in place following his arrival. Fain, on the other hand, was a blueblood Wharton grad coming in as a new sheriff—replacing in Stephan a beloved, self-made founder who'd overseen every detail of the business since he'd first sketched it out on his own living room floor some twenty years earlier.

Stephan stayed on as president under Fain, and for the year or two following the foiled Carnival deal he continued to exercise more or less the same degree of control as he had before. Fain knew that he had to learn the business before he could really step into Stephan's shoes, and didn't pretend otherwise. His stated first principle on taking over was "Don't screw up the brand."

"Richard was not ready to run the company in 1988," recalls Ken Dubbin, who served as Royal Caribbean's treasurer from 1985 until his defection to Carnival in 2000. "Richard only understood what he learned as a board member; it's a lot easier to coach than to play. I think it took Richard two or three years with Ed before he felt comfortable to cut Ed loose."

Fain had little choice: he had to destroy Stephan's creation in order to save it. The industry had changed, but Royal Caribbean was still organized like a small company. Stephan was an operations man at heart, not a strategist. As late as the early 1990s, Royal Caribbean executives say, he still read every passenger comment card that came off his ships, because that was what he loved. The man didn't have a corporate bone in his body. "He didn't understand, you know, dealing in the capital markets, or how to get a company ready to go public, or a lot of the administrative things," Dubbin says.

"He didn't have those kinds of skills, which Richard had. Ed wasn't a formalized strategic thinker, per se. Ed understood things, Ed had a vision. Ed was an entrepreneur. There's always somewhat of a clash when you put an entrepreneur with somebody who's got a Wharton MBA."

Stephan was loved and even revered within the organization, but he was not the man to bring a growing company into the twenty-first century. "If Ed had owned the company it would have never gone anywhere, god love him," remembers Pete Whelpton, Stephan's friend and longtime right-hand man. "He would have still been doing the books out of his pocket. But he was a great, great builder." It was not an easy transition, although reports of "titanic struggles" between Stephan and Fain seem to be exaggerations. Fain, after all, had the clear allegiance of the board, and that was the end of it. For the first two years or so, longtime colleagues found themselves in the awkward position of reporting to both Stephan and Fain for fear of doing the wrong thing. As time went by, however, it became apparent where the power now lay. People coming into Stephan's office expecting approval for relatively minor initiatives—a change in the uniform, for example—found their old boss balking. "Why don't you run that by Richard," he'd say.

As Stephan was eased out of the decision-making process, Fain's people began assuming positions of power. Adam Goldstein, the "green" young MBA and attorney who'd taken off for the Olympics during the Carnival merger fight, was asked to come up with a long-range plan. The future of Royal Caribbean, his report concluded, lay not in acquisitions that it couldn't afford, but in becoming a "megabrand," a product that operated around the world and catered to many different demographics.

It was an entirely new archetype. For the first time in the history of the company—perhaps for the first time in the entire industry—corporate-speak crept into the managerial lexicon. Pete Whelpton and the other department heads had grown used to being "little kings"—autocratic, but always running their decisions by Stephan, whose office included a small anteroom packed with fabric samples, silverware, bedding and all the other minutiae of the ships he loved. He was happier there, his colleagues say, than he ever was behind his desk. Fain both delegated and formalized the functions Stephan had guarded so jealously. He insisted on memos, reports and management-wide debate in committee meetings. But once a decision was made there, it was finished. Senior executives remember coming into his office with what they considered to be an important decision about the operation. "I don't understand," Fain would say. "Why are you bringing this to me?" The perception was that Fain liked to "fly at thirty thousand feet." "Richard didn't want to deal with the operations side," a longtime Royal Caribbean executive remembers. "From a ship design standpoint, yes; he loved that. But from, How do you get the steaks from galley to the plate hot or the rooms made—that, he didn't. And he didn't particularly have a tremendous affection for the people Ed had running that." At the same time, however, executives working under Fain complained of what one called his "selective micromanagement," a tendency to swoop in from on high and focus on a minor detail.

However diplomatic Fain tried to be, the kind of transition he envisioned was impossible without a considerable degree of tension and discontent. "We early on had an agreement among the management . . . that it needed to be a fundamental shift," he remembers. "That didn't mean we didn't still have very strong arguments." Accounts suggest that's something of an understatement. Although he outwardly praised the previous management, Fain was taking the company through a top-to-bottom overhaul that didn't necessarily leave room for the old guard. "Work smarter," for example, was a new management mantra with a clear enough subtext: *Your way isn't working.* Structural changes further weakened the old guard. In the hotel department, for example, shipboard supervision was decentralized and moved to the individual ships, a move that was tantamount to a purge. "What they did at Royal Caribbean was, they took the support staff for the ships and got rid of all of them. And said to the ship, 'Here, you do it,' " Whelpton remembers. "That was a cost-cutting move—get rid of those people, because we need to be more like Carnival." Most of the positions that were cut had been taken by people who'd worked their way up from the ships over many years—decades, in some cases. Older now, they weren't about to go back to sea, and for better or worse, they left. A considerable part of the company's soul, personality and collective memory went with them.

Fain's reliance on outside consultants only exacerbated the tensions. Many longtime executives were indignant at what felt like an unspoken suggestion that outsiders with Ivy League degrees would know their business better than they did. "Richard would hold these meetings about controlling costs," one former top manager remembers. "That would normally be followed by him going out and spending a couple of million bucks on something that nobody thought made any sense: research projects." Many felt that Fain's beloved consulting projects did little but generate paper and stifle creativity with empty buzzwords. The process perhaps culminated when Stephan was eased out of the president's office in 1996, stepping down to take on a more or less emeritus function as vice chairman. Having come in as something of an outsider himself, Fain's choice of successors showed just how deep the changes would be. In January of 1997 Stephan's job went to another outsider: Jack Williams, a regional vice president for American Airlines who'd never worked a day in the leisure business.

Carnival loved it. Taking their cue from Micky's own aggressive stance, Carnival executives heckled the new Royal Caribbean style—not exactly publicly, but freely enough. "Carnival doesn't use consultants," they'd crow. "Micky *trusts* his people." It could sometimes get quite a bit more personal that that. "If we produced Richard's results," one Carnival VP unguardedly mocked during a press interview, "every one of us would be fired." Meshulam Zonis, who for Carnival's sake had faced down the Mafia and who spent a lifetime squeezing vendors "until they scream" by knowing more about their businesses than they did themselves, spoke in his heavy accent about Williams's appointment. "With Jack Williams, I didn't have any deals," he said. "I knew, from the first time I shook hands with him, that I can't have no chemistry with him."

Always Carnival loomed as a constant, goading presence. Their efficiency, their profitability was a taunt. Reading the prospectus for Carnival's public offering had been an epiphany for everyone at Royal Caribbean. "We were so flabbergasted by how much money Carnival made, we thought we were in a different business," Dubbin remembers, "Every afternoon, Ed and I sat for two or three hours at a time in his office and tried to analyze the Carnival financial numbers to compare them to Royal Caribbean, to find out what the heck these guys were doing to make so much damn money. We couldn't figure it out." Fain himself wielded Carnival's "bombshell" numbers "shamelessly," in his words, using them as proof that Royal Caribbean could do better—and as a reason for bringing in yet another team of expensive consultants.

How *did* Carnival manage to achieve such remarkable results? For one thing, its cabins, larger than those on the Royal Caribbean ships, could accommodate groups of three or four, giving a significant boost to occupancy rates and consequently to profit margins. But the biggest difference was that Royal Caribbean had simply never evolved Carnival's mania for keeping costs down. Coming into the world well funded, it had never faced the same degree of economic pressure at the operational level. Carnival's mantra was "Never give the passenger something they're not willing to pay for." Stephan had built an organization focused on providing passengers with the best product possible—period. While fearful about cheapening that product, Fain was intent on establishing a culture where his people not only cut down on what they bought, but paid less for it. He also began the painful process of bringing some of the major concessions in-house—something Carnival had been doing for years.

Trimming the costly passenger accoutrements Royal Caribbean had become known for was a delicate process. Despite the fact that Carnival and Royal Caribbean charged comparable prices, Royal Caribbean had a difficult time thinking of itself as a purely mass-market option, and clung to the idea that it had one foot in the more upscale market as well. But Carnival was competing for the same customers without thinning its profit margins by paying for the giveaway playing cards, Hershey bars and other special touches that had been a point of pride for Stephan. And not only did Royal Caribbean buy more goods, but vendors regularly got away with charging Royal Caribbean more than Carnival was paying for the same items. At the negotiating table, Royal Caribbean's people lacked the ruthlessness and surgical precision that enabled executives like Zonis to turn apparent miracles into matters of routine.

The megabrand strategy helped to galvanize Royal Caribbean in the short term. The new concept produced an extraordinary parade of new ships, but also some inspired thinking about what the cruise experience could be. That thinking focused on appealing not to a single demographic, but to a broad range of people who would come together in a single floating resort. "We have flown in the face of marketing convention, and our objective is to be all things to all people—within certain boundaries," a top Royal Caribbean marketer has said. And the strategy worked, up to a point. Saturating the airwaves with a campaign promising viewers that "You've got some Royal Caribbean coming," the line became the cruise industry's biggest broadcaster. Inevitably, setting the vagary of "megabrand status" as a defining goal also intensified the corporate rivalry with Carnival, which throughout the 1990s irksomely continued to carry more passengers on its flagship brand alone than any other cruise company in the world. And that was just fine: if nothing else, having Carnival remain his company's chief rival helped Fain maintain the new focus on costs.

Where Carnival saw itself as the emerging General Motors of the cruise industry—operating a number of brands targeted to serve various sectors of the passenger market—a true Royal Caribbean megabrand demanded a single product that was as good as or better than almost every one of those disparate brands. In pursuit of this ideal, Admiral Cruises had been dissolved almost immediately after the merger. With the exception of the new vessel that Admiral had under construction, its ships were all sold off and most of its people let go, lest they taint the Royal Caribbean brand. No one had much missed Admiral, and there was little question that the new thinking had served Royal Caribbean well in the years since. From 1992 to 1993 profits shot up from a pitiful $4.3 million to more than $60 million with the addition of two new *Sovereign*-class ships—and three new ships were on the way in the largest single order ever placed.

As Fain steadily turned Royal Caribbean's finances around, and then in 1993 took the company through a successful public offering of its own, the competitive landscape began to look quite different. The megabrand approach, formulated when Carnival Cruise Lines seemed the most aggressive rival, had succeeded brilliantly; Royal Caribbean was handily keeping pace. But Carnival Cruise Lines was just one of the brands under Micky's umbrella; *Carnival Corporation* was leaving Royal Caribbean in the dust. It was incredible; the beast seemed to be expanding laterally into other brands by the minute, even as new Fun Ships kept rolling off the line like Model T Fords. In Royal Caribbean's corner offices, thoughts turned begrudgingly to mergers, and with only a limited number of desirable midsize operators out there, time was running out.

One possibility was Europe. A long-standing industry dilemma was becoming more acute by the day: it was getting tougher and tougher to make a profit operating the older ships in North America. It's not that they weren't in good shape, but they'd been built at a time when Americans thought of cruising as long, quiet days in a deck chair and evenings in the bar—not skating rinks, mud baths and a dozen different restaurants to choose from. Another of consolidation's side effects was that, just as a generation of formerly cutting-edge ships was passing out of their prime, there were fewer and fewer of the midsize lines that had traditionally bought and operated such vessels still in business to pick up the slack.

The industry needed an unexploited market into which the majors could funnel their older tonnage, gaining extra years of profitable life from them at the same time as they served as "pathfinders" to open up new passenger sources for the future. Europe, where vacation time averages from two to three times what people get in the U.S., was the best prospect in this regard. Both Carnival and Royal Caribbean had looked to Asia without success. Fiesta-Marina, a Carnival venture aimed at creating a Latino cruise market, took the nearly forty-year-old *Carnivale* out of the Fun Ship fleet and ended up offending the very customers it sought with the notion that there was something specifically Hispanic about the out-of-date vessel.

But in Europe, where itineraries were based on short hops between excursion-intensive cultural capitals like Istanbul, Rome and Barcelona instead of the self-contained "floating-resort" sensibility that dominated cruising in the Caribbean, the plan could work. P&O Princess was developing products designed to enter the German and UK markets. Carnival had gotten its first front-page write-up in the *Wall Street Journal* when it announced a partnership with Club Med to use Carnival's older ships and Club Med's European brand recognition to create a new European cruise line. That idea collapsed, as did a similar attempt to create a Greek cruise line in 1995. But the concept was feasible, as was the belief that whoever moved first would enjoy a strong advantage. In addition to its other ventures, Carnival had already bought a 25 percent stake in a major British tour operator with an eye toward learning to navigate the European business environment. Fain realized that Royal Caribbean remained an essentially American product, notwithstanding its global self-image and the considerable amount of international business that it did. But if it could trailblaze with a success in the Old World, it could significantly narrow the nagging gap between itself and Carnival.

But Fain's casting about in the name of diversification also threatened to become a liability. This would be the company's second major philosophical upheaval in less than ten years; the news was greeted with excitement by some among senior management, but with ambivalence and confusion by many more.

The initial target was Costa Crociere, a family-controlled Italian cruise line that traded on the Milan stock exchange. Costa had been operating out of Genoa since the family it was named for had branched out from the olive oil business in the nineteenth century. An erratic performer over the years, the line had recently undergone a major expansion with an eye toward solidifying its fortunes. As of 1996 four of its nine-ship fleet had been built in the 1990s. But Costa had perhaps been overreaching. As one trade magazine put it at the time, the spree "was a bid to compete head-on with the Carnivals and Royal Caribbean Internationals of the business, which in turn left it susceptible to a powerful suitor." It was no secret, in fact, that Costa was open to a deal.

The head of the company—and of the Costa family—was getting on in years. A concert cellist who played in the Genoa Philharmonic Orchestra when he wasn't running a cruise line, Nicola Costa had a good reputation in the industry, but it was widely thought to stem more from his personality than his business acumen. With a challenging balance sheet to tackle and no clear successor, putting the company in the hands of a better-capitalized parent seemed to be the best move to protect his family's investment and legacy alike. Approaching Royal Caribbean, he let it be known that the Costas would be pleased to sell the whole company; if it would make the deal go more easily, however, they'd be willing to retain something in the range of a 20 percent stake.

What followed was a classic failed negotiation, full of faulty assumptions and ham-fisted politics. Costa had early on quoted a high price; Fain countered with a noncommittal response. "He gave them the Japanese 'I understand,' " Dubbin remembers. "Which means, 'I understand but I don't necessarily agree.' Then he said, 'But let us do due diligence, and we'll decide what we're going to do.' " Apparently under the impression that things were going forward on terms along the lines of those he'd set forth, Costa permitted what Rod McLeod, Royal Caribbean's longtime top marketing executive, eventually termed "Costa's undue diligence." Teams of analysts went through Costa's operation "like commandos," Ken Dubbin recalls. "They just took over Genoa."

The project, code-named "Michelangelo," would not be remembered as one of Royal Caribbean's finest moments. "They didn't deserve what we did to them," McLeod says. "There were people in the organization who would just shudder at the thought of getting assigned to the Michelangelo teams that were constantly being formed to study this and study that." The main concern was the obvious one. A Royal Caribbean–Costa merger would have combined two major debt loads, for one thing—a big risk to take in a market that was not yet fully understood. After agonizing debate among management and on the board—Stephan ultimately voted against the deal—Fain went to Costa with a proposal that many of his executives believed to be worse than no offer at all: to buy less than 20 percent of the company at a price well below what Costa had suggested. It was a transparent bookmark offer, designed to prevent another line from buying Costa without Royal Caribbean taking on the risk. The Italians were understandably less than thrilled. "If you show me your car and say you want twenty thousand dollars for it, and I basically indicate interest and I say, 'By the way, can I drive it for a couple of months?' and then I come back and say, 'Well, I think it's worth five,' you'd be pretty pissed off," Dubbin analogized. "At the end of the day, the Costa people, if they didn't say it, they certainly thought it: basically, *va fungulo*. And Carnival was on it just like that."

The industry seized on the affair not only as high gossip, but also as an emblematic moment. Royal Caribbean's new focus on costs, some felt, had caused it to be penny-wise and pound-foolish. "The attitude at that point in time," remembers one executive with years at both Costa and Royal Caribbean under his belt, "was that it's not so important to gain the strategic advantage or to expand your market share as it is to get a good price for what you're buying."

That seems to be an exaggeration, although not entirely innaccurate. The concerns about Costa's finances were genuine; the acquisition would have made sense only if it had meant a new infusion of capital, and Royal Caribbean was simply not well positioned to gamble so heavily. "Our risk profile was a lot different from Carnival's risk profile," Dubbin remembers. "Things that we regarded as issues, Carnival probably said, 'They're there, but they don't trouble us as much.' " Micky had harbored similar reservations about the purchase of Costa and only went ahead at Frank's strong urging. Even then, he only agreed to do the deal as a 50-50 partnership with Airtours, the British travel operator Carnival had bought into several years earlier. Within a few years, however, Micky held the full 100 percent.

At that time, Costa had been one of only two midtier players still operating with a strong presence in southern Europe. Carnival's takeover of it left only Celebrity Cruises—one of the best-regarded smaller lines in the industry, and one of the newest—with any serious foothold in the crucial market. "It was always on the cards," the trade press wrote, "that after failing to do a deal with Costa last year, a failure which led to the Italian company ultimately being swallowed up by Carnival, Royal Caribbean would sooner or later be in the market for another midsize company to swell its ranks." The obvious move was Celebrity, and Fain moved fast. The merger was announced mere weeks after Carnival closed its deal with Costa.

If Celebrity had entered the business just a little earlier, it might have had a chance at making it on its own. It certainly had amassed a respectable enough record in the short time it had existed. In the seven years between its launch in 1989 and the day it was taken over in 1998 the company grew from two ships to five, with an operation worth well over $1 billion— not bad considering that its growing pains had included a worldwide recession and the first Gulf War. It had been a remarkable ride, but like Costa, Celebrity was feeling the inevitable financial hangover on the heels of its rapid expansion.

Celebrity had grown out of another of the oldest passenger shipping companies still in business, Chandris Lines. Owned and managed by the Chandris family—"a Greek shipping family so ancient and powerful," the *Atlantic Monthly* once wrote, only slightly tongue-in-cheek, "that they apparently regarded Onassis as a punk"—Chandris Lines was facing the same problems as the rest of the industry by the time the mid-1980s rolled around. As commercial jet travel replaced passenger shipping in the 1960s and 1970s the company had done more than simply survive the transition into cruising. At its peak in the late 1970s the Chandris fleet had grown to fourteen ships— this at a time when Carnival was proudly operating its newly acquired third vessel and Royal Caribbean was debating whether to stretch the *Song of Norway*. They were able to achieve this in part because the family-owned shipyard in Greece performed the regular refurbishments their older vessels required; even Carnival had never seriously thought about bringing *that* side of the business in-house. But its moment quickly passed, and Chandris soon found itself becoming old news.

As the Miami-based lines had continued ramping up their construction throughout the 1980s it was clear to John Chandris, the patrician young head of the company, that he had to either join the fray at a new level or get out. The British-educated Chandris thought of himself as an innovator— something of a business radical, even, despite his lordly tailoring and upper-crust diction. In 1989 Chandris decided to go ahead with building new ships, but not for Chandris Lines. If he was going to build, he decided, it was going to be for an entirely new cruise brand—a brand unlike anything that had been seen before.

Chandris wanted to go after younger, wealthier passengers, people who had not yet taken to cruising in large numbers—who would, in fact, not be caught dead on a cruise ship. Upscale lines like Cunard and Holland America did well at the upper end of the market, cruising to Alaska, Europe and elsewhere, but their passengers were mostly older people. They had the reputation of delivering an elegant but stodgy experience, and that's exactly what they did. "We took what was typically thought of as a mass-market, banquet kind of a concept," Chandris remembers. "You have mass feedings, mass herding of people and so forth and so on, and we took that and we really looked at every avenue to break it down. Yes, we had large ships, but how do you move people within that large environment so it does not become a mass feeding, a mass moving of people?"

Chandris grasped the importance of intangible status symbols to his market—of suggestions, subtle associations. Celebrity's ships offered revolutionary fitness facilities—not only fitness centers, but glamorous spa treatments featuring mud baths, herbal wraps and other exotica. Their showpiece menu was to be designed by Michel Roux, one of the world's great chefs. In 1989 Chandris had asked Roux to cater a family wedding in Greece, and the 750-person affair had come off beautifully. If Roux could orchestrate food like that for so many on shore, why not on a ship? The relationship became a big selling point for the new cruise line. The aesthetic—and marketing savvy—went right down to the circuit boards, as a few years into the venture Celebrity negotiated a deal to showcase Sony's cutting-edge interactive television technology. But nothing got better press coverage than the art. Celebrity's ships were filled with museum-quality collections curated by Chandris's wife, Christina, and boasted works by Picasso, Warhol, Jasper Johns, David Hockney and many other of the twentieth century's artistic blue chips. The unusual display of sophisticated art aboard a cruise ship did wonders for the industry's stodgy, old-fashioned reputation.

It was all very personal for the Chandrises, a labor of love. One trade journal's prescient reporter gushed that Chandris "brought a European style of management to the company, one in which loyalties to people and to other companies extended beyond dollars and cents." As nonexecutive chairman, Chandris and his brother routinely sat in on low-level meetings to make sure things were being handled the right way. He spent one Christmas Eve shaking hands with each of the nearly 650 crew aboard one of his vessels. The ships' smokestacks said it all. Dark blue and angular, they were marked in white with what looked like an enormous X. The symbol was an elegant, rakish touch—suavely piratical, maybe—but it was in fact the Greek letter chi, without which you can't spell "Chandris."

Celebrity began operations with two thirteen-hundred-passenger ships, both built in Germany according to Chandris's specifications, and a completely overhauled vessel from the old Chandris fleet, the former *Galileo Galilei*, renamed *Meridian*. By 1995 it was taking delivery on a brand-new two-thousand-passenger vessel, and a pair of sister ships was due for delivery in 1996 and 1997. By the time the third ship was delivered, however, the company would be out of Chandris's hands.

There was just no getting around the realities of the business. That Celebrity had happened at all had been a triumph; in terms of capacity, the line had grown as much in seven short years as Royal Caribbean had in its first two decades—and in a far more challenging business environment. It had simply gotten into the game a little too late to make it on its own with the capital available to it. In 1992 Celebrity had brought in a partner to help fund the expansion: Overseas Shipholding Group, a tanker company headquartered in Manhattan and traded on the New York Stock Exchange. The tanker markets had once again taken a turn for the worse in the intervening years, however, and by 1996 OSG was, in John Chandris's words, "obviously keen to streamline" its balance sheet. "OSG was concerned that it wasn't showing to the market the sort of performance that it needed to show, and effectively, Celebrity at that time wasn't helping their results," he remembers. In theory, a public offering for Celebrity in 1998 or 1999 was a possibility, but when a serious offer came in from Royal Caribbean in late 1996, the opportunity was hard to resist.

It began with a telephone call from Richard Fain. He was going to be in London on other business, he told Chandris. Would Chandris meet with him and Jay Pritzker to discuss the possibility of doing some business together? Fain, in fact, had no particular plans to be in London. He was calling fresh from a series of sessions with his executive committee in which they'd been formulating a strategy for growth in the wake of the Michelangelo debacle. In some ways, a deal with Celebrity would be just as problematic as one with Costa would have been. Both lines had similar balance sheets, with heavy debt loads stemming from a rapid expansion. Celebrity, in Fain's words, was "run very much in the style of an old shipowner company." It was more expensive than Costa and more tenuously connected to Europe. Royal Caribbean's financial situation certainly hadn't changed in the months since making its offer to Costa; in fact, Fain voiced fears to his board that taking on Celebrity's debt risked a downgrading of Royal Caribbean's own bonds but urged going ahead with the deal anyway. Nearly everything that had raised a red flag the year before was suddenly deemed manageable. With the opportunities shrinking dramatically, Fain's risk profile had changed. He was determined to get Celebrity if he could.

Chandris was wary but agreed to meet, as he remembers it, "with diplomacy and interest, but with a certain amount of cool reservation." Chandris and Fain had never had much personal chemistry, for this was not the first time Royal Caribbean's CEO had approached him in this manner. Previous talks, both with Royal Caribbean and Carnival, had gone nowhere. "We met, we talked, they said what they were prepared to pay for a company of our size, and we said that that was simply completely uninteresting," Chandris remembers of earlier discussions with Fain. "Micky had previously indicated what he would have been prepared to pay in terms of multiples. It was even less interesting." It couldn't have been easy for a man as proud as Chandris to contemplate such a sale. He'd been one of the investors approached as a possible white knight for Royal Caribbean in 1998, but he'd passed in order to focus on Celebity, and now the tables were turned.

The clincher, for him, was the fact that Jay Pritzker would be present. Like many in the business world, Chandris was in awe of the legendary financier and considered him to be a "consummate dealmaker." "You mustn't forget, in retrospect, the considerable charisma and charm of one man, who brought this deal together: Jay Pritzker," Chandris would later explain. "Jay articulated really rather splendidly the benefits of merging, rather than selling—you see, he was courteous enough to use the word merge—our two companies together for the greater benefit of both companies. And he was the catalyst, effectively, or the protagonist, that brought the two companies together." For Chandris, so emotionally invested in every aspect of the business, confidence that his vision would endure was essential. Pritzker and Fain reassured him. "Celebrity was not in a position to expand, to take the position that Royal Caribbean had taken, to go after being one of the major players," Fain remembers. "It didn't have the capital to do so. And so I think he saw, I argued and I think he shared that vision, that as part of Royal Caribbean we could build it into a brand of greater critical mass."

That lunch produced nothing concrete, but the two sides agreed to continue talking. Fain needed numbers, but Chandris worried about opening his books to an outsider—Royal Caribbean more than anyone, after the way things had gone with Costa. The process dragged, with one executive comparing it to a game of Twenty Questions. Royal Caribbean's negotiators also worried that they were being lured in as a foil for Carnival, to boost the sale price by creating an open auction. They couldn't have known it at the time, but it was an unnecessary concern; as far as Chandris was concerned, Carnival was not a factor. For one thing, Carnival's aggressive, take-no-prisoners style of doing business offended the courtly Chandris.

And then there was the Bob Dickinson incident.

Acerbic, quick witted and highly opinionated, Dickinson was still the verbal gladiator he had been during his early days in the company. Audiences tended to look forward to his performances at industry panels with the enthusiasm of sports fans. It was generally in the spirit of good fun, but he occasionally took it too far, and on a bad day in 1995 his mouth may have ended up costing Carnival the opportunity to bid for Celebrity. Sitting on this particular panel with Dickinson was Al Wallack, Celebrity's senior vice president and head of marketing. Dickinson had arrived that day already livid, believing that Wallack had sneakily torpedoed one of his initiatives for an industry-wide advertising campaign in the trade association of which both were members. He went up on the stage furious, wanting to draw blood.

Descriptions of what came next all seem to rely on culinary metaphors, one way or another. Dickinson "filleted" Wallack up on that stage, as one witness recalls. Another remembers that Dickinson "put him in a blender." He began playfully enough—"I feel like I'm watching Tom Sawyer paint the fence," he said at one point in response to a Wallack boast—but the harsh undertone was immediately perceptible, and people shifted uneasily in their seats. By the time the verbal assault peaked, mouths were hanging open in the audience. "If Bob takes after you verbally," Howard Frank would later say, recalling the incident, "you're like dead meat. He can tear you apart." By the end of the session, Wallack had been thoroughly humiliated in his capacity as a Celebrity representative; Chandris was enraged.

Micky had not only apologized, but had ordered Dickinson to track

Chandris down and do the same. Officially, it was all water under the bridge, but Chandris was unmollified. "He took it against our whole company," Micky recalls. "Instead of saying, 'Bob's an asshole, he shouldn't have done what he did,' he took it against our whole company." This was not, Chandris felt, the way civilized people operate. Celebrity was *not* going to go to Carnival—not if he and his 50 percent stake had anything to say about it.

Chandris's team finally agreed to sell the company to Royal Caribbean for a total of $1.3 billion. The combined entity would be under the Royal Caribbean board, which Chandris would join, but Celebrity would be run by Rick Sasso, who had been with the company since it was founded and had served as president since the beginning of 1996. The Royal Caribbean brand would stay under Jack Williams, and both executives would report to Fain. Just before the press releases went out, Celebrity's top management was summoned to their Miami headquarters boardroom. The deal had been kept quiet, but it was clear that something was up: they'd been told to show up with jackets on. An exhausted Sasso broke the news with Chandris at his side. "We viewed it as very positive, getting the strengths of another organization behind what was then a new brand," one of the executives present remembers. "It was exciting, because naturally we were a very young organization." Chandris then introduced Fain to enthusiastic if slightly shell-shocked applause, and the two of them exchanged gifts—Fain a set of Royal Caribbean cuff links, Chandris a Celebrity pin. Fain, warming to the crowd, joked that he wished his own people would give him so gracious a reception.

Micky was furious when he heard the news. It was worse than just being blindsided; he'd been confident that word would get to him if anything serious was going on with Celebrity. Believing he had a reliable source on the OSG board, he'd let his guard down.

OSG, as it happened, was, like Carnival, owned by Israeli shipping magnates—a relatively small circle—and the two families, the Arisons and Recanatis, knew each other quite well. Only a few months earlier, one of the Recanati sons, Oudi, had asked Ted to speak at a benefit he was hosting in Miami. Ted had become a fund-raising icon in the city over the years, and if he hadn't been sequestered at the time, fighting off his cancer on the private top floor of Memorial Sloan-Kettering hospital, it would have been a routine matter. Under the circumstances it became something more. "He went to my father, who's got cancer—is sick as hell—and my father accepted," Micky remembers, still agitated years after the fact. "I told him he was nuts, but he accepted anyway." Medical team in tow, Ted was wheeled out of his hospital room in New York, taken to an air ambulance and flown to Miami, where he addressed the audience from his wheelchair. The Miami elite in attendance that night were shocked to see the great man so weak; faces in the audience streaked with tears as Ted strained to talk. When he was finished, he was rolled off the stage and flown back to his hospital room. It was unquestionably an extraordinary gesture on Ted's part.

"And then we hear this," Micky fumed. "I called Oudi and said, 'Don't you think I deserved at least a phone call from you?'" Recanati, who sat on OSG's board, explained that he was bound by a confidentiality agreement, but that only made things worse. Such matters, Micky felt—for people like him and his father—were formalities. Legal or not, *he should have gotten that call.* "I went nuts," he said. "I was so infuriated that the guy would do that. So we instantly decided that we're going to get this company or we're going to make it more expensive for Royal Caribbean."

Among other things, this story reflects a sense of entitlement that has defined every contested deal of Micky's career—real competition, for Micky, seems to demand a bad guy. In 1988 it was Richard Fain, supposedly betraying his allegiance to Gotaas-Larsen. And now the scene was being replayed, this time with Oudi Recanati and, to a lesser extent, John Chandris in the villain's role. Whatever the underlying psychology, the competitive juices were undoubtedly flowing during the Celebrity deal. Micky, normally circumspect, remembers taking "three seconds" before deciding to move on Celebrity. He was not without recourse, he believed. Chandris, who would not return Micky's urgent and repeated calls, may have been free to do what he wanted with his share, but OSG's management had a public company's obligations to its shareholders. If Carnival was to go to them with a more valuable offer, Micky reasoned, they might be forced to accept it. And what was the worst thing that could happen? As far as he was concerned, it was happening already.

Ultimately, Micky didn't get Celebrity, and while the score between him and Fain may not have become a tie, at least it was no longer a shutout. For his part, Chandris felt he had made a deal and intended to honor it. When he finally spoke to an "incandescent" Micky, he was on vacation on his own private yacht. Unwilling to accept a rejection, Micky refused to end the conversation, wheedling and pushing again and again. "Because they had shown a previous interest, they had expected us as a matter of course to tell them. But why should we?" Chandris recalls. "I remember thinking, if this conversation continues too much longer, my cellular is going to overheat." Carnival did succeed, modestly, in bumping up the price for Royal Caribbean. Although OSG's fiduciary obligations in this case were murky at best, with 50 percent of the company in the hands of a staunch opponent of a Carnival deal, OSG went to Fain with a face-saving request: a $15 million increase, which worked out to a little more than 1 percent of the deal's value. Fain agreed, and the deal closed without further incident.

Chandris would come to regret his decision, if not his pique, at the course of subsequent events—at least if his colleagues and friends, and the wistful smile that accompanied his "no comment" on the matter, are to be believed. Once the deal was done, it quickly became clear that his vision for the merger would not be realized. "It wasn't how I had expected the deal to develop, quite frankly," Chandris admitted. "I think, unfortunately, corporate politics had their role to play, and did so. And it was more a question, for a number of years, of who would dominate Celebrity than whether Celebrity would be allowed to develop exponentially."

What unfolded couldn't have been further from Carnival's strategy with Holland America; that much became clear when Celebrity's headquarters were shut down and its personnel moved into Royal Caribbean's Dodge Island office building. In a feverish search for the synergies Fain hoped would boost Royal Caribbean's profit margins and justify the merger to Wall Street, Celebrity departments were folded into their Royal Caribbean counterparts almost from day one. In some instances, as with the casino, the blending was relatively seamless and in fact made good business sense. Others were disastrous; perhaps none more than the integration of the two sales forces. The brands had completely different approaches to selling their product, and Celebrity suddenly found one of its most crucial functions forced into a box that didn't fit it. "Royal Caribbean having been already a twenty-five-year company, they'd become more of a marketing-driven company—it's the images and the things that they paste out there, the big marketing scheme that makes people buy them," Sasso remembers. "Ours was really more home-grown, one-on-one; that's how we got our business. I told you to buy me because *I* proved to you it was good. I did it homegrown; and when you have a model like that, you can't turn it off overnight."

Celebrity's European sales offices were likewise dismantled, which was particularly stinging to Chandris. It was a network he'd been proud of and which had ostensibly been part of the deal's strategic rationale. Even the new ships would be built differently with Royal Caribbean in charge. Over the objections of Celebrity's management, the contracts for a new class of ninety-thousand-ton ships went to a French yard rather than to the yard in Germany where all of the previous Celebrity ships had been built. The bids were the same, but the French yard had offered a shorter timeline. When the vessels were completed, there were serious problems with their propulsion systems; years later, a lawsuit over the cost of repairs and canceled cruises is still working its way through the courts. The effect of all this on morale was brutal. "We lost our identity," Sasso remembers. "There was no name 'Celebrity' on a building anymore, and our people got lost in the shuffle, for the most part."

In almost any merger, the smaller company can expect to suffer somewhat as it is absorbed. But this was a bad union from the very beginning—from even before the beginning—and Chandris had never seen it coming. Even as he and Richard Fain and Jay Pritzker had been discussing the glorious future of the Celebrity brand over lunch in one of Pritzker's London hotels, top executives at Royal Caribbean had been actively lobbying to "paint the ships white and call them Royal Caribbean" after the acquisition. Some of this sentiment stemmed from a continuing commitment to the megabrand strategy, which the merger seemingly undercut; a lot of it was pure politics.

Celebrity had been acquired by a company that was itself still in the throes of a profound transformation. The deal closed in September of 1997—barely nine months into Jack Williams's presidency. According to Ken Dubbin and others, Williams viewed the introduction of a new brand with another president as a threat. He'd come on as the second-in-command of a company with a clear hierarchy, and suddenly, the organization had an entire arm that didn't have to answer to him. "Jack stayed as president of Royal," Dubbin remembers. "But he immediately viewed that as a demotion. He was pissed off. He did not want to help Rick, and all of the central services that Rick had to rely on were put under Jack's jurisdiction. Jack jerked him around unbelievably. He wanted him to fail."

That's a strong allegation, and one that Williams categorically rejects. "They built a great little brand," he says. "It's a good solid management team that became part of a bigger compnay, and then the world changed." But there's no getting around the fact that the new regime was tough on the

Celebrity team, and that as more and more functions were taken over by Royal Caribbean counterparts reporting to Williams, Sasso had a harder time doing his job. "I think we didn't handle the integration as well as we might have. You had fairly strong personalities, and there was conflict," Fain would later say. "And I think there was a fair amount of feeling among some of the people at Celebrity that they were seen as the poor stepchild."

Department heads from each brand gathered for intense sessions, ostensibly to pool their strengths, but everybody knew that they were fighting for their jobs. "We were asked to meet our counterparts and basically take off the gloves and fight it out, so to speak," one former department head remembers. "It was very different. It's a very structured type of environment." One witness described the process as "psychological humiliation." Certainly, it was a world away from the genteel environment in which John Chandris had invested so much of his own personality. There was heavy pressure to use the merger as a vehicle for cutting costs in the short term—pressure that inevitably took its heaviest toll on the Celebrity people. "The little company had to swim with the big fish, and the little fish don't swim as fast," Sasso recalls. "They don't understand the ocean as well, that big ocean—they understand their pond. So the guys who are swimming in the big ocean, they obviously have a better feel for what's going on. So when there's this attrition that's going to take place, where do you think it happens? The little guy." For the Royal Caribbean people, making cuts in the Celebrity staff was a matter of survival. When Pete Whelpton decided that the Celebrity hotel team ought to remain in place, Williams applied pressure. "Jack looked at it from the point of view that 'If you want to keep the Celebrity group, fine. Then get rid of a bunch of your guys.' So we ended up doing that," Whelpton remembers. "I think I eliminated thirty-two people on the Royal side, and about six or eight on the Celebrity side. But I kept most of Celebrity's people. They melded in quite nicely with the office."

But Whelpton, a stubborn brawler in the midst of his own struggle with Williams, was the exception. For the most part, it was Chandris's people who were terminated. Six months into the merger, earlier than planned, Chandris stepped down from his transitional role. Within a few short years, a single senior executive remained of the nearly twenty Celebrity vice presidents who rose to meet Richard Fain that day in 1997. Williams may have wielded the axe, many felt, but Fain had simply sat by and watched the butchery unfold. "I don't think it was Richard per se," one recalled, "but he didn't play a sufficiently active and dynamic role to stop it." Ken Dubbin, observing from the Royal Caribbean side, summed it up more bluntly. "Richard," he said, "was not a good referee. He didn't stand in and say, 'Hey guys, play nice.' "

Sasso finally left in 2001, and Williams brought the brand under his authority. "I tried to run Celebrity the way I thought it needed to be run," Sasso would later recall. "And I did it for four years in a merged environment, which I give myself a lot of credit for." Like Carnival, Royal Caribbean doesn't disclose financial statistics for its individual brands, but industry insiders say Celebrity has been struggling mightily to make a profit ever since the merger—although several recent marketing drives seem to be improving its performance. "I'm not here to indict the previous guys and gals that were here; that's not the issue," Williams says. "The fact of the matter is, I think the board of the company just felt I could do a better job at this stage by taking it under one chief operating officer, letting me manage both brands, so that you had that differentiation." Williams's commitment to Celebrity's success, at any rate, is no longer questioned by anyone. One Celebrity executive remembers calming some of his middle managers when Sasso left with just that assurance. "They felt that they had lost the person who maybe could protect them," he recalls. "I remember explaining to many of them that what they have to understand now is that, with Jack in charge, nobody wants Celebrity to succeed more than Jack Williams." Since Sasso's departure, Williams has separated the sales teams and some of the other departments that had been joined together so violently. "They've since tried to undo that," Sasso says. "There are dedicated Celebrity sales people now. It may be a little late. I hope not."

By most accounts, Fain's first victory over Micky in the acquisitions arena has rung somewhat hollow—more a cautionary tale than a success story. Even Arne Wilhelmsen, founding board member and as strong a supporter of Fain as one could hope to find, sees mostly gloom in the way the deal played out. "By hindsight," he says, "maybe we would have been better off building more ships of our own than taking over Celebrity."

Carnival, meanwhile, prepared for the next contest. In 1998, just over a year after acquiring Costa, Arison brought Cunard into the fold. One of the most famous names in shipping, Cunard in 1998 was at best an aging beauty, long past its glory days in the transatlantic trade. Its once legendary vessels were old and its service lackluster, thanks in part to a series of distracted own-ers. The ships of the Cunard fleet were "like dirty underwear in a beauti-ful antique chest of drawers," as one marketing executive put it. The only thing worth having was the *QE2*—and the brand, of course. That *brand*—someone could do something with the name alone, if he had a mind to it.

The runaway success of *Titanic* on movie screens across the world the pre-vious year had only made the idea of Cunard more attractive: who knew there was so much interest in the old ocean liners? Talk had even been float-ing around Miami about building a full-size replica of the ill-fated *Titanic* as a cruise ship, although good taste and a dose of healthy superstition kept that from coming to pass.

Cunard had fallen into the hands of the parent company of Kvaerner Masa-Yards, Europe's biggest shipyard and the facility where Carnival—and almost everybody else, for that matter—builds many of its ships. Ted had bailed the shipyard out when it went belly-up in 1987 with two Carnival ships under construction. Kvaerner was about to close on a deal to sell Cu-nard to a group of private investors when Micky decided he wanted it. Fresh from his experience with Celebrity, he was not in the mood to be put off and dispatched Frank to lean on the yard as heavily as he needed to; Carnival, af-ter all, meant a lot of ships for them. The bargaining process evokes the im-age of an old-world Mafia chieftain more than it does a boardroom. "We called the Kvaerner people and said, 'I think it's important for you to con-sider our offer,' " Frank remembers. "The chairman was a very difficult guy, but I think we put enough pressure on that he said okay." Carnival walked away with the company for less than the price of a new cruise ship.

Cunard was the end of Micky's pursuit of the midsize brands. There were a few left that might be worth a shot, but he wasn't interested—which is not to say he was planning to bench his acquisitions squad. As 1999 began, the industry was down to four big players: Carnival, Royal Caribbean, NCL and P&O Princess.

Micky's eye was now on the big game.

CHAPTER TEN

INDECENT EXPOSURE

Let it flow . . . it floats back to you!
—*The Love Boat* theme song

Around the same time as Arison and Fain were orchestrating their power plays in Miami, newsrooms and law firms around the country were finally beginning to take a closer look behind the image that the cruise industry had tirelessly cultivated for itself over the years.

For cruise executives, managing the press had traditionally been a matter of making sure the right people got free tickets on a new ship's inaugural cruise or disseminating fact sheets about the latest disco, specialty lounge or athletic facility. Bad things happened from time to time, of course. There had always been the occasional "man overboard" feature in the local press detailing a strange disappearance—a mystery of shoes, perhaps, set down neatly by the railing before the leap—or the particulars of a dramatic rescue. There was the case of the former navy frogman, for example, given up for dead after falling off a Carnival ship late one drunken night several miles offshore. His friends learned the next day that he'd sobered up on contact with the water and had simply swum back toward the light of Miami. Stories like that came along in a slow but steady stream. Reporters also loved writing about the drug mules routinely busted on returning cruise ships by customs officers in Miami. The two men who tried to smuggle fifty-eight pounds of marijuana inside the cushions of their wheelchairs—one of them actually was handicapped—was a favorite, as was the twenty-three-year-old woman with $1.8 million worth of heroin in her suitcase. Most prized, for the cloak-and-dagger imagery they conjured up, were the tales of the cocaine-filled "blisters" that divers sometimes found welded to a cruise ship below the waterline. The cruise backdrop made for some evocative reportage and a nice change of pace from the usual rhythms of the law and order beat. Customs initiatives in Miami or San Juan with catchy names like "Operation Cruise Control" were a cinch to get written up in newspapers as far afield as Toronto.

But these stories hardly qualified as bad press, as far as the cruise lines were concerned. Such events transpired in a parallel universe from the one in which their passengers frolicked, and isolated incidents of smuggling little reflected on the companies running the ships. Frankly, the notion that one's waiter or pool attendant might in actuality be an international smuggler was a little titillating, "thrusting a high-stakes, illegal activity into an atmosphere associated with pleasure and escape from the grittier side of life," as one reporter wrote. The same went for the overboard stories; readers and reporters alike were drawn to such incongruous morbidity—that was all there was to it.

But as the business grew, the media inevitably started looking into the companies themselves. In the 1990s, for the first time, major news outlets began examining the industry in a systematic way—its finances, its labor practices, its impact on the environment. "They were flummoxed," remembers one reporter who covered the industry at the time. "They didn't really know how to deal with negative stories." Of course, that was about to change, as one spectacular scandal followed another during the mid- and late 1990s. From a fatal outbreak of Legionnaires' disease aboard one ship to shipboard sexual assaults covered up, to criminal investigations into bad environmental practices, a string of public relations disasters battered the industry's image.

Suddenly, on television and in print—in the *New York Times*, on the TV newsmagazine *60 Minutes* and even in local weeklies—journalists around the country were asking the dreaded question: "Are they safe?"

One November morning in 1998 more than one million *New York Times* readers looked down at the morning paper to see a big white cruise ship staring back at them from the front page. It being early winter, and a chilly Monday morning at that, many of those readers would have been harboring daydreams of a warm-weather getaway of their own. "Sovereign Islands: A Special Report," the headline read in boldface type. "On Cruise Ships, Silence Shrouds Crimes." The next column carried a companion piece, headlined "For Missing Woman's Family, No Answers," profiling a twenty-three-year-old woman from Virginia who'd disappeared while on a Caribbean cruise with her family. The report was the first installment in a yearlong examination into the cruise industry by one of the paper's top investigative reporters, a series that would run the length of a short book as it probed the industry's underbelly.

The journalist was Douglas Frantz, a former Istanbul bureau chief who'd been named *Times* investigations editor not long before. He certainly had dramatic material to work with: allegations of violent rapes by room stewards, of bartenders drugging passengers for the same purpose, of teenaged girls plied with drink and taken advantage of by crew members. What Frantz uncovered, however, wasn't so much that cruise ships were particularly dangerous places; it was the astonishing extent to which they functioned as privatized societies, ruled almost solely by their own corporate policies. While acknowledging that most cruise vacationers did have a safe and happy time at sea, Frantz revealed that when things did go wrong, passengers who'd assumed they were governed by the same laws and standards that protected them in the U.S. found themselves instead trapped on a tiny piece of Liberia or Panama or another flag of convenience country. He went on to paint a startling picture of an industry operating its ships essentially as private city-states, as "sovereign islands."

"An examination of sexual assault cases," Frantz wrote, "found a pattern of cover-ups that often began as soon as the crime was reported at sea, in international waters where the only police are the ship's security officers. Accused crew members are sometimes put ashore in the next port, with airfare to their home country. Industry lawyers are flown to the ship to question the accusers; and aboard ships flowing with liquor, counterclaims of consensual sex are common. The cruise lines aggressively contest lawsuits and insist on secrecy as a condition of settling."

A smuggling arrest was one thing; the systematic cover-up of assaults on passengers was quite another. Avoiding negative publicity, it seemed, was a higher priority than seeing justice done. The FBI has jurisdiction over crimes involving U.S. citizens that are committed on a ship that has sailed from a U.S. port—even if the vessel flies a foreign flag and the crime took place in international waters. The catch is, the law does not require that such incidents automatically be reported to the authorities; it's the responsibility of the victim to alert them. Based on court records, interviews with former cruise employees and alleged crime victims, Frantz documented a pattern whereby lines like Carnival and Royal Caribbean actively discouraged sexual assault victims on their ships from filing reports. Requests to contact the authorities were never turned down, but for an already traumatized passenger in a strange environment—often under the calming influence of sedatives prescribed by the ship's doctor—the cruise lines' apparent standard operating procedure could be quite compelling.

"You don't notify the FBI," one former Carnival shipboard security chief, who was a sheriff's deputy in Texas before taking the job in 1991, told Franz. "You don't notify anybody. You start giving the victims bribes, upgrading their cabins, giving them champagne and trying to ease them off the ship until the legal department can take over." In cases where the FBI was notified, alleged crime scenes were often cleaned before agents were able to come aboard to evaluate them. A documentary produced the following year by the History Channel, for which Frantz was a source, quoted a former detective for Scotland Yard who'd worked aboard NCL ships for six years, echoing these accounts. "I have sealed cabins or rooms that have been the subject of an alleged offense, and the next moment, when I've gone back in there, bed linen or clothing has been disposed of," he recalled. "The captain or the hotel director, who would be in daily, minute-by-minute contact with headquarters, would do things like offer you free holidays, just for you or your family. I've even known one person who was offered ten cruises."

Perhaps most aggressive in its coverage of sexual assaults aboard cruise ships was the *Miami New Times*, an alternative weekly that had targeted the industry, and especially Micky Arison, with a series of critical stories. In February of 2000 the *New Times* reported in detail on one such "cover-up," this one involving a middle-aged woman identified in the article as "Mary," a pseudonym.

As the *New Times* reported it, the woman was taking her first vacation after a year in which she lost her husband and her father and during which her daughter had had a miscarriage. With her daughter "Janice" in tow, she booked a Caribbean cruise aboard the Carnival *Fascination* in the summer of 1998. On the first evening of the cruise, the woman would later claim in court, she was sitting alone in her room while her daughter was out exploring the ship. Her cabin steward entered unexpectedly, forced her to the bed and raped her.

After the attack, the woman went to the ship's security personnel, who questioned the steward and recorded his denial. With no rape kits aboard, the ship's doctor administered a pelvic exam and prescribed sedatives; the woman and her daughter prepared to visit shoreside authorities when the ship docked in the Bahamas the following morning. "Officers handed Mary and Janice a bag containing the only evidence they had collected: the dress and underwear Mary had worn the night before," the *New Times* wrote. "They hadn't interviewed any passengers, nor had they removed the sheets from Mary's bed. A taxi took the two women to a doctor's office, where they waited for hours without seeing a doctor. Finally the cabbie drove the women to a hospital, where a physician did a second exam. Hospital workers kept the bundle of clothes." Arriving in Miami with the ship after spending the remaining three days of the cruise under sedation in her cabin, the woman spoke with FBI agents. "The investigators listened to the women's stories and determined the outlook was not promising," the story said. "Potential witnesses were not interviewed, valuable evidence was not gathered, the crime scene wasn't secured, and the clothing had been left behind in a foreign land. The lawmen decided they had no choice but to drop their probe." The steward was flown back to his home country on "medical leave," and at the time of the article's appearance in February 2000–eighteen months after the alleged incident—authorities in the Bahamas reportedly had still not released the results of the rape tests she underwent there.

A similar story reported by both Frantz and the *New Times* contained many of the same details but would have further-reaching consequences. Before it was over, a federal grand jury would be examining the possibility of criminal charges against not only the alleged assailant, but Carnival as well, for its handling of the investigation. It was another rape case, this time of a ship's nurse who'd reported having been assaulted by an engineer. The attack itself could have happened anywhere. Taking off work because of a knee injury, the twenty-seven-year-old nurse, an American, was spending the evening in her room when there came a knock on the door. It was the engineer, an Italian man who'd made sexual advances before but had accepted her rebuffs in a civilized enough manner that she now considered him a friend. He made another move, she would later testify, begging for a kiss, but when she put him off, he raped her over her hysterical protests. "It only lasted a few minutes," the *New Times* quoted her as saying. He left her room in the early hours of the morning, demanding a kiss good-bye.

After speaking with a friend, another nurse, the victim reported the incident the following afternoon. From this point, the accounts diverge. Carnival's attorneys would later insist that security personnel encouraged her all along to report the incident to the FBI, and that she demurred. The woman, on the other hand, claimed she was kept off balance, intimidated, pressured to make an immediate decision. "I was with her the whole time," her friend would later tell the *New Times*. "They didn't encourage her to report it. They just kept saying, 'What are you going to do? What are you going to do?' I kept telling them that she doesn't need to make a decision right away."

By the time the ship pulled into Miami, less than thirty-six hours after the alleged attack, the woman had decided to contact the FBI. She headed for an area hospital, where agents interviewed her and subsequently contacted Carnival to request a meeting with her alleged attacker—now the FBI's prime suspect in a violent felony investigation. But that interview would never take place. By the time the FBI called, he was already booked on an evening flight to Italy; following the allegation, the man had immediately been fired, ostensibly for being drunk on duty. Losing the job meant he also lost the work visa that allowed him to remain in the United States, and Carnival lost no time in complying with its duties to get him out of the country. Corporate security staff was to escort him to the airport and see that he got on the plane. FBI agents arranged to question him before his flight in the customs offices at Miami International, but he never appeared. Instead, Carnival's people had escorted him directly to the departure terminal—and out of the country. Carnival claimed a mix-up, and insisted that it was the FBI who'd failed to explain that they'd be waiting at the customs facility, and not at the gate. Absent the agents they were expecting, the company's security staff simply did its job. "The FBI never showed up," a senior executive would later insist in a deposition. Pressed by Frantz, the U.S. attorney's office would not confirm an investigation into the incident, but acknowledged that "Carnival raised some eyebrows when they whisked him to the airport moments ahead of the posse." The victim's friend, who had cooperated with the FBI, had been two months away from the end of her contract at the time of the assault. It was not renewed.

In the course of a lawsuit filed by the nurse, a Florida judge ordered Carnival to release a list of all incidents within the previous five years in which crew had been accused of sexual assaults—an order that was carried out only after it was twice upheld on appeal. The number, which didn't include alleged assaults by passengers, totaled sixty-two incidents ranging from allegations of rape to claims of inappropriate touching, to more innocuous complaints such as crew members brushing against passengers while helping them with bags. All in all, the claims suggested an incident rate of little under one a month—this for a fleet that carried millions of passengers during the time period in question. It hardly painted a picture of a system out of control, but it was a public relations fiasco nevertheless; Carnival's management came out of it looking indifferent to the well-being of the very people they'd drawn to their ships with promises of "the experience of a lifetime." To government officials, it was a demonstration of an utter contempt for U.S. law. Nothing formal came of the grand jury, but it was a performance the Justice Department would not forget when it came to its dealings with the industry.

The following summer the International Council of Cruise Lines announced that its members were adopting a "zero tolerance" approach to crime on board their ships. It was a remarkable concession to the power of the press—especially given the extent to which cruise operators had despised the *New York Times* series. Many, in fact, had been genuinely offended by the coverage, which they felt was one-sided and selective, and ignored the industry's own legitimate concerns. Carnival's people claim that *Times* editors not only signed off on slanted reporting in hopes of snagging a Pulitzer-winning investigative piece but that the editorial board refused to meet with industry representatives to hear their objections and that the paper repeatedly declined to print letters to the editor sent in response to the series.

If the *Times*'s depiction of the industry rankled, however, the response it elicited didn't place an onerous burden on it: the new zero tolerance policy was little more than a voluntary commitment to automatically report criminal allegations involving Americans to the FBI, rather than solely at the victim's request, and to "consult" with U.S. law enforcement agencies on evidence-collection procedures. Enforcement of the policy, skeptics pointed out, was to come from the ICCL itself. But the industry was growing far more media savvy than it had been in the past. Sticking to its message, the ICCL was successful in making the initiative sound like something more than an empty gesture. "This policy establishes a single industry standard that requires allegations of onboard crime be reported to the appropriate law enforcement authorities which, for vessels calling on U.S. ports or crime involving U.S. citizens, would include the Federal Bureau of Investigation," Micky Arison, Richard Fain and other industry leaders wrote in an open letter announcing the policy. "We will continue to cooperate with the authorities to ensure that perpetrators of crime are brought to justice." The ICCL put out a release assuring the public that

"A passenger is safer on a cruise ship than in urban or rural America. A review of FBI annual crime statistics reveals that the number of reported shoreside aggravated sexual assaults occurring in urban or rural communities is at least twenty to fifty times greater than the total number of all reported shipboard assaults of any type." Finally, the release assured the public, all this talk of "sovereign islands" was simply overblown. "All passengers embarking or disembarking a foreign flag vessel in the United States," it promised, "have recourse to civil actions in U.S. courts."

That last statement is technically correct, but only because the cruise lines had failed in a tort reform campaign two years earlier that would have made it almost impossible for passengers and crew to bring legal action against them in the United States. Not that such an action was particularly easy to bring to begin with; most cruise tickets have long included a "forum selection" clause in their fine print, stipulating that any legal action against the cruise line in question must be brought in Florida—regardless of where the voyage began or ended or where the passenger comes from. Obstacles like these, along with the challenges inherent in collecting sworn testimony from witnesses—especially crew—who may be halfway around the world, already made suing the cruise lines an expensive proposition. Nevertheless, as more and more passengers were taking cruises, well capitalized Florida attorneys lined up to take promising cases on a contingency basis, and the lawsuits began to pile up.

Rather than fighting expensive legal battles one at a time in the courts, the industry had decided to go directly to the law itself. In 1996 Representative Don Young—an Alaska Republican, congressional power broker and staunch ally of the cruise lines—slipped a trio of eleventh-hour, cruise-specific tort reform provisions onto a standard budget bill. The first of the measures, ultimately passed into law, indemnified the cruise lines against any injury sustained by passengers at the hands of shoreside physicians over the course of a voyage—at a local hospital in the Caribbean, for example. The other two measures were far more controversial. The first of these would have denied non-U.S. cruise workers the right to sue their employers in U.S. courts for workplace injuries. The second would have allowed passengers to claim emotional distress or suffering against a cruise line only if they could prove "substantial" physical injury—essentially barring shipboard rape victims, who often do not suffer major physical injuries as part of their attacks, from the courts. Though all three measures had slipped quietly through Congress, the last two raised a firestorm from women's groups, labor unions and trial lawyers and were ultimately blocked in the Senate. Hence the ICCL could claim, without fear of contradiction, that "Cruise ship passengers are afforded greater protection by Congress and the courts than any other vacationers in the world, and cruise lines consequently have a greater interest in deterring any wrongdoing on board their ships."

The industry might have felt unfairly singled out for a handful of negative incidents among the thousands of wonderful experiences each year on its ships, but in a way it had no one but itself to blame; by the late 1990s the cruise lines had more than earned the skepticism of regulators and the press.

The sexual assault issue might not have resonated quite so strongly, for example, had it not followed on the heels of a Justice Department investigation into illegal cruise ship pollution that uncovered practices so outrageous as to almost defy belief—complete with secret piping networks designed to bypass the very filtering systems the industry was touting as evidence of its commitment to environmentalism. The investigation had centered on Royal Caribbean, where it ultimately led to the imposition of $27 million in fines and left senior executives all the way up to Richard Fain discussing the possibility of prison. It also raised the industry's profile for journalists and watchdog groups, highlighting the implications of flag of convenience registry and revealing the sleek, luxurious white ships to have the same potential for abuses as any coal mine or chemical plant.

Royal Caribbean bore the brunt in this instance, but in reality it was no worse than any of the other major cruise lines—all of which would face convictions for illegal dumping during the 1990s. During the ten-year period beginning in 1993 the industry as a whole would pay nearly $50 million in fines to the U.S. government. The nature of Royal Caribbean's offense, however, along with the shameless strategy the company employed to defend itself, persuaded investigators to make an example of it. The case became a symbol for an industry that was amassing a fortune by running its ships "inside our waters and outside our laws." It was this incident, more than any other, that was responsible for forcing the *Love Boat*'s smiling and carefree world into the harsh lighting of the evening news.

The first signs of trouble came in 1994 in the waters outside Puerto Rico when a Coast Guard surveillance aircraft flying over the inbound *Sovereign of the Seas* noticed a three-mile-long trail of oily water slicking behind the ship. Upon docking, the vessel was boarded by Coast Guard investigators to interview the captain about the spill. Even as a second Coast Guard team was out at sea taking samples from the slick, the captain not only denied any dumping but produced logbooks to prove it. The suspicious investigators descended into the sweltering expanse of piping and machinery that was the ship's engine room. There they saw evidence—sludge, oily rags—indicating that oil had been dumped, but lacking the authority to keep the ship from sailing, they had little recourse but to videotape the scene and alert their Miami counterparts to their discoveries. That tape, along with another taken of a now cleaned-up engine room by investigators in Miami four days later, would become the heart of the government's case against Royal Caribbean, attempting to prove that the filthy engine room investigators first encountered in Puerto Rico—and not the pristine space that greeted them in Miami—represented business as usual for Royal Caribbean. Prosecutors would successfully argue over the coming years that the difference between the two images was proof of a companywide conspiracy to break the law.

The Exxon *Valdez* had already demonstrated that the American public could get up in arms over environmental abuses at sea. This situation differed, however, in two respects. First, as bad as the pollution on the *Sovereign* and other cruise ships was, none of these incidents represented a single, obvious cause of major environmental destruction. Unlike the *Valdez*, the *Sovereign* and other cruise ships were doing their damage a little bit at a time, and consequently didn't stir up the sort of outrage that inspired many Americans to drive past Exxon stations for years following that disaster. The second difference is perhaps the more critical one: the dumping documented by the Justice Department was anything but a drunken accident. Rather, it was part of a consistent and deliberate scheme aimed at breaking basic environmental rules that had been on the books for decades.

The oil in the *Sovereign* case had not leaked from a ruptured holding tank but had been intentionally released from the ship's fully functioning bilge, the cavity in the lowest part of any ship where seawater, oil and other fluids inevitably accumulate in the course of normal operation. The nasty cocktail that results is known as bilgewater. The problem with bilges is that they must regularly be emptied, in part because the oil and other chemicals in the bilgewater can present a fire hazard if they're allowed to accumulate. Today, there are nearly one hundred thousand ships one hundred tons or larger in the world merchant fleet, the smallest of them three to four times heavier than a fully loaded eighteen-wheeler and all of them with bilges requiring emptying on a regular basis. The damage done by any one such dumping incident on any single ship might not be dramatic, but the collective impact is so serious that the problem has been discussed since even before World War I—at a time when the world fleet was a tiny fraction of what it is today and when the environmental movement barely existed. Today it is possible to filter the bilge fluid so that the water, which makes up most of its mass, is clean enough to release into the ocean. The remaining sludge and oil then can be safely stored aboard the ship and processed ashore.

Since the 1930s European governments have enacted laws restricting bilgewater discharges in their territorial waters, and in the early 1950s the UK spearheaded an attempt to establish international conventions on the matter. But the great leap forward didn't come until 1973, when the UN's International Maritime Organization instituted its International Convention for the Prevention of Pollution from Ships, generally known as MARPOL. One stipulation of the convention—to which all of the flag of convenience countries where the cruise lines register their ships are signatories—states that "All ships of four hundred gross tons and above must be equipped with oily-water separating equipment, or a filtering system for discharges from machinery space, together with onboard tanks for retention of oily residues from separators and purifiers." Furthermore, "Vessels in excess of ten thousand gross tons must be equipped with oil discharge monitoring and control systems." This convention was adopted two years before Ted Arison bought the 27,000-ton *Mardi Gras* for one dollar, back when Royal Caribbean still had its hands full with a fleet of three ships that together were barely the *Sovereign*'s size. It's not as if the industry hadn't had time to get used to the notion.

In fact the *Sovereign* did have the necessary filtering devices, known as "oil-water separators," aboard that morning outside San Juan. Every other ship in the industry had them, too; they just didn't bother to use them consistently. For those imagining a transgression along the lines of forgetting to separate paper and plastic when putting the trash out—or even deliberately omitting the step because, like working with oily bilgewater, it's a "dirty, smelly, thankless job," in the words of one top Royal Caribbean manager— consider the following quote, which is an excerpt from the confession that Royal Caribbean president Jack Williams would ultimately sign on behalf of the company as part of its 1998 plea agreement in the *Sovereign* incident. The account picks up, a little sheepishly, after the Coast Guard crew left with their videotape and the ship sailed away.

"Shortly after the *Sovereign of the Seas* left San Juan, a senior officer aboard the cruise ship ordered the crew to work through the night to dismantle a bypass pipe used to circumvent the oil water separator and to discharge oily bilge waste overboard. The pipe was cut into small pieces and placed in a Dumpster in Miami, Florida, on October 29, 1994. The bypass pipe was removed and destroyed because crew members of RCCL's cruise ship believed that the Coast Guard had not discovered its true purpose and intended to prevent the Coast Guard from making this discovery when the agency's investigation continued in Miami."

The biggest charges that Royal Caribbean ultimately faced were in fact not directly related to the dumping; enforcement of environmental law on foreign-flagged ships remains challenging even today, and it's almost certain that the dumping itself would have brought little more than a slap on the wrist. (The fine levied against Royal Caribbean for the discharge alone was a mere four thousand dollars.) The company's real crime, in the law's eyes, wasn't dumping the oil so much as it was lying about it to the Coast Guard by falsifying logbooks the agency was entitled to inspect. It later came out that Royal Caribbean officers commonly referred to the discharge logs as the "eventyrbok," a Norwegian word that translates to "fairytale." Destroying the bypass pipe before arriving in Miami, furthermore, amounted to evidence tampering—a charge that was compounded when the company in its plea also admitted to ordering an engineer to give false testimony about shipboard practices before a federal grand jury.

In the face of overwhelming evidence, Royal Caribbean executives had insisted that the dumping and cover-up had been an isolated incident The investigation, however, quickly turned up evidence of similar doings on four other Royal Caribbean ships—one of them less than a month after the *Sovereign* was caught on tape. As far as prosecutors were concerned, they were dealing with an ongoing companywide conspiracy to pollute the environment and mislead the United States government in the process.

It was a conspiracy Royal Caribbean admitted to, but only at the end of a two-year courtroom fight during which the company hardly bothered to dispute the facts of the government's case. Its lawyers, who included two former U.S. attorneys general, instead made the astonishing choice to contest the government's right to prosecute at all. They argued that international law called for pollution cases to be adjudicated by the ships' flag states. It's not hard to see the appeal of that tactic for Royal Caribbean; out of 111 U.S. dumping cases referred to relevant flag states between 1989 and 1992, a congressional study found, fines had been levied in only two. Unfortunately for Royal Caribbean, the judge didn't see it that way. The company had placed itself squarely within the purview of the U.S. government when it lied to the Coast Guard; the case was going forward, which left Royal Caribbean with only one option: a guilty plea.

Even as they agreed to damning and detailed confessions, Royal Caribbean officials were privately convinced that the dumping had been the result of a culture clash—not a corporate conspiracy. The favored explanation was almost folksy: a story of old-school Norwegian sailors who'd been raised in a world where the oceans were seen as an infinite and indestructible resource and who were now struggling to adapt to the new environmentalism. "I don't believe that any of this has been created by pressures to cut costs. I don't personally believe that at all; I think it has been more, maybe, a result of some of the traditions," one senior Royal Caribbean executive would later say. "The world was changing, the regulations were changing. They felt that . . . there was no one really watching and that they were *almost* doing everything right, and they didn't really understand the seriousness of what they were engaged in."

Yet there were factors this theory fails to take into account. The increased pressure to keep costs down had not been accompanied by any increased oversight for the company's largely autonomous technical department—a holdover from the days when the Skaugens paid Royal Caribbean's maritime personnel directly and often bypassed the Miami management entirely. Certainly, the dumping was not the result of any deliberate policy from the top, but at the very least the problem was fueled by a staggering negligence from the company's executive suites. The savings were coming in, and no one had bothered to ask from where—no one had wanted to know. Justice Department calculations suggest that Royal Caribbean saved millions by the dumping—as much as $425,000 a year on unused replacement filters alone, not to mention the fees that would have gone to shoreside processing facilities if Royal Caribbean had complied with the law.

～～～

Again, as with the *New York Times* investigation into shipboard crime, the most profound shock of this incident lay not in the violations themselves but in the industry's utter lack of accountability. Nowhere was this more in evidence than in Royal Caribbean's so-called "sovereignty defense" against the pollution charges, in which it claimed to be outside U.S. jurisdiction. The strategy proved to be a major error, a taunt that the company's attorneys should have known was certain to provoke a devastating response. Pollution was one thing; taking on the government in this fashion only enraged prosecutors and brought the darkest aspects of the flag of convenience regime out of the shadows and into the spotlight. Holland America pleaded guilty to similar charges the same year as Royal Caribbean's initial guilty plea when a whistleblower reported being ordered to dump illegally. That fine was a mere $2 million, compared with Royal Caribbean's $9 million and five-year probation. But the government wasn't finished with Royal Caribbean. The following summer, Williams was back in court, pleading guilty to a new battery of charges for dumping incidents and cover-ups that took place *after* the company had been informed of the Justice Department investigation—one of them as late as 1998. This was in addition to the "unprecedented charge that it deliberately dumped into U.S. harbors and coastal areas many other types of pollutants, including hazardous chemicals from photo processing equipment, dry cleaning shops and printing presses."

Many of the flagrant offenses weren't even taking place under cover of the open sea. Nearly half of the second Royal Caribbean fine stemmed from "deliberate and routine midnight dumping of harmful quantities of waste oil into the waters off the coast of Alaska," including along the Inside Passage, an environmentally delicate national treasure that, to quote Royal Caribbean's own promotional literature, "captures so much of what people love about Alaska" with its "glaciers the size of Rhode Island" and "misty rain forests and ghostly blue fjords." Once again, Royal Caribbean proved a record breaker: Uncle Sam's penalty this time came to $18 million. U.S. Attorney General Janet Reno herself made her feelings known in no uncertain terms. "Royal Caribbean used our nation's waters as its dumping ground, even as it promoted itself as an environmentally 'green' company," she said. "This case will sound like a foghorn throughout the entire maritime industry."

And for a while the pressure indeed heated up. The plea certainly couldn't have come at a better time as far as the *New York Times* was concerned: Royal

Caribbean's $9 million sentencing took place barely a month before the first installment of the paper's "Sovereign Islands" investigative series appeared. Less than a month earlier, the *Miami Herald* had published its own in-depth report, catchily titled "Slick Justice." And the media had begun to pick up on other stories of cruise ship dumping as well. As beach cleanups up and down both U.S. coasts turned up cups, shampoo bottles and other debris embossed with the logos of various cruise lines, it became apparent that the dumping wasn't just a matter of oil, but that lines in many cases were simply tossing their trash overboard. A CBS news segment reported that there had been twenty such incidents within a two-month period in 1993, including one aboard a Princess ship where a passenger videotaped crew members throwing garbage bags overboard. The clip, complete with clear audio of cans and bottles inside the bags clattering as they hit the water, played nationwide on CBS's morning show.

With environmental regulation largely logjammed at the federal level, much of the effective response came from state and local communities stepping into the breach. During the same period as the Royal Caribbean dumping trial, the state of Alaska levied hundreds of thousands of dollars in fines for air pollution from cruise ships' smokestacks. Juneau, its thirty thousand residents feeling frustrated and overwhelmed by the six hundred thousand cruise passengers passing through each year—and, in Frantz's words, by the "ships whose smokestacks send a hazy pollution snaking around the mountains that cradle the town"—held a referendum in 1999 on whether to levy a five-dollar-per-person tax on visiting ships. Just three years earlier a similar proposition hadn't even come close to passing. Now nearly 70 percent of the ballots cast were in favor of the measure. The string of bad press was taking its toll, and quickly. Discharges in the San Diego and San Francisco bays as well as outside Fort Lauderdale sparked local outrage; the national media covered the city of Monterey's lifetime ban on the upscale cruise ship *Crystal Harmony* in 2003.

Remarkably, though, the vast majority of the American vacationing public seemed indifferent to these abuses. The pollution story just didn't resonate, somehow. In the years between Royal Caribbean's indictment in 1996 and its first guilty plea in 1998, profits more than doubled, from $151 million to $331 million. And the following year, in the face of a second felony conviction, massive fines and an ongoing cascade of highly critical coverage, revenues and profits dipped only a fraction. It was, in fact, a banner year for the entire industry. Carnival's profits broke the $1 billion mark for the first time, and, despite an $18 million fine of its own—and many smaller ones—in the upcoming years, the company would continue to grow at a pace that did the glory days proud.

All the same, the industry understood that it was facing a potentially devastating public relations problem. In Washington, where Senator John McCain leaned in to his microphone during one hearing to cut off the obfuscating testimony of an industry representative with the sharp reminder "You've got a credibility problem right now," it felt particularly urgent. Just weeks after Royal Caribbean's 1999 plea, desperate to halt the regulatory momentum building on Capitol Hill, the ICCL came out with what was emerging as its cure-all strategy for dealing with adverse public attention: more voluntary guidelines. These were followed up with "memoranda of understanding" between the industry and the environmental protection agencies of various states, stipulating guidelines for discharges and other environmental impacts and reaffirming that the industry was "dedicated to preserving the marine environment and in particular the pristine condition of the oceans upon which our vessels sail."

The only thing lacking, amid all the earnestness and hand-wringing, was the force of law.

A 2000 report to Congress found that while dumping incidents had decreased, the inspections system remained seriously flawed. Coast Guard agents still spent two hours or less a year inspecting any given ship for environmental compliance—and this during visits that were scheduled weeks or more in advance and, notwithstanding the lessons of the Royal Caribbean conviction, were generally limited to checking unverified paperwork. Of the illegal discharges detected between 1993 and 1998, only 18 percent were discovered as a result of inspections. Thirty-seven percent of violations—the largest single category—had come to the government's attention only when the cruise lines themselves reported the incidents. The industry, remarkably, continued to be largely self-regulated.

It was cruise shipping's good fortune that its scandals had been mostly complicated stories, full of arcane jurisdictional issues. Not unlike the financial scandals on Wall Street in the late 1980s, the sheer complexity of the matters involved was itself a sort of protection in the arena of public opinion. As far as the pollution cases went, dramatic conspiracy charges didn't change the fact that the oil dumping itself was an affair of parts per million and chemical analyses—not of poisoned, oil-covered pelicans and seals dying on untold miles of ruined beachfront. A CNN story on Royal Caribbean's landmark 1999 guilty plea—the second felony conviction within twelve months—was one of the network's few reports on the entire case to make it out of the travel section. It ran a little over 250 words, just under half the length of a typical wedding announcement in a major metropolitan newspaper.

The outright trash dumping, when documented, provoked a more visceral response—and made for better television. Some clever and effective producing on CBS's part, for example, cut back and forth between the clip of workers dumping trash bags overboard and images of a sperm wale that had washed up dead on a Carolina beach the month before after swallowing several plastic bottles. But the violations played out as a series of isolated incidents. The same was true when it came to shipboard assaults and the "cover-ups" surrounding them; those in which courtroom settlements didn't compel silence and deny the news media the story altogether tended to hang on competing claims that were all but impossible to verify. The real story was the law itself, and the law was obscure. Even the potentially far-reaching tort reform attempt in 1996 was a minor story as far as most media outlets were concerned. Missing from the equation was the black-and-white clarity—the "strong lead"—that good TV news seems to require.

Most important, no one was claiming that cruise lines posed a fundamental danger to consumers; no one was suggesting that they presented an easily understandable menace. The patterns documented by investigative reports, though disturbing, were indictments of corporate ethics at a time when such matters carried relatively little weight in the public imagination. The stories all had the flavor of local news reports filed from a place where nobody lived.

Ironically, the industry would sustain some of its most damaging public relations hits in the public health arena, where by the late 1990s the major lines were actually doing an excellent job. The culprit was gastroenteritis, a medical catchall category for intestinal distress from causes ranging from salmonella, to garden-variety stomach flu, to the now-infamous "Norwalk-like virus," which has come to be so closely identified with cruise ships in recent years.

This was a story the popular press could sell: boatloads of Americans supposedly sailing off on the vacation of a lifetime, instead trapped for days aboard a floating vomitorium. It was an unbeatable combination, affording newsreaders a Naderesque patina of consumer advocacy even as it delivered the exquisite schadenfreude of a mental image of a stricken army of fleshy, sunburnt vacationers seized by the panic of upchuck. It's understandable, then, that a CNN report on such an outbreak would run to more than three times the length of its coverage of the Royal Caribbean convictions. It's not every day a reporter gets the chance to rechristen the world's most famous passenger liner "The Good Ship Kaopectate," as one *Newsday* scribe happily did in 1987 when fifty passengers and crew aboard the *QE2* took ill.

Even at their mildest, major shipboard outbreaks of gastroenteritis are truly unpleasant affairs, usually involving "vomit squads" racing around in an attempt to stanch the tide. Food poisoning or a stomach virus, furthermore, though rarely dangerous for healthy adults, can pose a potentially fatal health risk for older passengers. From an epidemiological standpoint, the potential for contagion in the close confines of the shipboard environment is nearly limitless. This has long been recognized: from plague scows denied docking privileges in ancient times through the lice-infested steamers quarantined outside of Ellis Island, ships have always been regarded as incubators for disease.

On cruise ships, outbreaks typically have two possible sources. The first is contaminated food or water—devastating in an environment where as many as five thousand people are eating meals made from essentially the same ingredients and drinking from the same source. The vast majority of outbreaks, however, can be traced to viruses brought aboard from shore, either before the cruise or at one of the ports of call. These are the scenarios that keep cruise ship operators up at night; the only thing that can be done to prevent them is to quarantine those with suspicious symptoms, aggressively disinfect surfaces in public areas—from roulette wheels to deck chairs—and encourage passengers to wash their hands thoroughly after using the bathroom and before they eat.

If a more serious disease enters the shipboard environment, however—as in the case when a faulty Jacuzzi filter turned one of a Celebrity cruise ship's whirlpools into a breeding ground for Legionnaires' disease during the summer of 1994—it is prone to the same rapid spread. One person died in the Celebrity incident, and another developed a fever so extreme that it caused brain damage. There's no way of knowing how many more would have suffered serious injury or death if not for the remarkable fact that one infected passenger happened to seek treatment from a member of the team that had originally discovered the disease twenty years before in the air-conditioning ducts of a Philadelphia hotel.

News coverage tends to cast shipboard outbreaks as more of an industry-specific phenomenon than they actually are. On sea as on land, viruses are inevitable realities of life. Unlike other environments that foster contagion—nursing homes, elementary schools, movie theaters—a cruise ship's controlled environment makes the spread of illness easy to track. And, because any illness affecting 3 percent or more of passengers or crew is reported to the Centers for Disease Control, it leaves the sort of paper trail that for many editors automatically justifies a news story. The industry insists—and the CDC agrees—that such incidents happen no more regularly at sea than on land and that they receive a disproportionate amount of media attention.

For once the government has taken a strong and effective hand in the affairs of the foreign-flagged cruise industry, and the benefits are clear. For all the narrative appeal of such outbreaks, their incidence has been greatly reduced with the stricter preventive measures instituted since the CDC's Vessel Sanitation Program began inspecting cruise ships in 1975.

When the CDC launched that program, the industry's public heath standards were indeed nothing short of abysmal. The mid-seventies were a time when most cruise ships were still old passenger liners, many of which had had become home to any number of vermin during the course of their decades of service. Two weeks' worth of food came from ingredients loaded on the first day of a voyage, and aging or inadequate refrigeration systems often ran too hot to prevent spoilage. The same, unfortunately, could not be said of the dishwashing machines, which often rinsed dirty dishes and silverware at lukewarm temperatures before they went back out for table service.

The only good thing you could say about the failure rate for the first year of inspections was that it was a nice round number: 100 percent. The *Norway*, for example, arrived in Miami in 1980 to much fanfare from the travel press but considerably less enthusiasm from the CDC. In an inspection where 86 was a passing score, NCL's new flagship scored 8 points out of 100. Its lapses included kitchen handwashing stations without soap, "dirty" meat slicers, and "greasy" cookware. The floor was littered with cigarette butts, and the cooks were spreading mayonnaise onto sandwiches for the lunch buffet with paintbrushes.

Inspectors' authority over the cruise lines was both far-reaching and severely limited. Practically speaking, they lacked the authority to prevent a cruise ship from sailing. Absent circumstances dire enough to mandate a Coast Guard quarantine, the strongest measure available to them was a "recommendation" not to sail.

Not to be put off, the CDC brought the fight into the public relations arena. Inspectors in the late 1970s developed what became known as the "green sheet," a summary of the inspections and a list of individual vessels' performance which the agency made available to travel agents nationwide. Themselves heavily dependent on repeat business from their clients, agents were hesitant to risk recommending ships with poor health records. It was a savvy improvisation for a government agency that, despite a lack of statutory authority, recognized the importance of its mission. Their reports only became more effective as technology improved, evolving during the 1980s into broadcast faxes dispatched to thousands of travel agencies with the push of a button and more recently into a dedicated Web page.

The green sheets gave inspectors power their counterparts on land could only dream of. Take the beef industry as a reference point. Even today, government officials lack the authority to order a company to recall shipments of contaminated meat and depend instead on voluntary responses from meatpackers. The inspectors from the CDC, on the other hand, scrutinized every aspect of the ships' operations until standards exceeded those of shoreside restaurants and hotels. And although they resisted at every step, the cruise lines had little choice but to acquiesce.

Now only knives with one-piece solid handles were allowed, for fear food particles might get stuck in the seams between the handle and the blade. Hinged tongs were forbidden for the same reason. In one case, an inspector ordered Carnival to replace the entire dishwashing system aboard a brand-new ship because he didn't like the manufacturer. The machines were made by Electrolux, one of the world's leading appliance producers, but the inspector preferred Hobart. Carnival went along. As time went by, the CDC and the industry began cooperating more fully and something of a partnership evolved, with inspectors traveling to the European yards where Carnival's ships were built in order to identify problems early in the construction process.

Back in Miami the inspections—twice yearly and, unlike the Coast Guard's, unannounced—were serious affairs, with four inspectors spending a full day on a ship the size of the *Sovereign* examining everything from the chlorination levels inside the water tanks to the contents of the various freezers and refrigerators. Then as now, shipboard personnel invariably did what they could to make the necessary adjustments at the last minute. A flurry of activity preceded inspectors as they moved through the ship. "Of course, if there was a public heath inspection," remembers one Carnival executive, "I used to try to see which way the inspector was going and get in front of him so I could quickly see if there was anything that really was untoward. If it was something major you couldn't change it, but if it was something minor, you could maybe say, 'Clean that up,' or 'Get that out of the sink.' " To this day the employee, now Carnival's senior vice president for operations, has a pair of the contraband tongs that he was able to stuff into his jumpsuit at the last minute on one such occasion, just ahead of the inspector. "I still use them, by the way," he says. "Although my wife has bought me a nice big pair."

The scrutiny paid off. By 1980 the failure rate was down to a little less than half of the seventy-one ships inspected; by 1990 it was down to 27 percent of eighty-six ships, with the overall median score at 89 out of 100 points. And the improvements would continue though the next decade, even as the cruise fleet exploded with more and bigger ships. By 2000 the CDC was inspecting 130 cruise ships each year; fewer than 8 percent of those failed, and the average score had risen to 93 points. Outbreaks did happen from time to time, although they diminished as industry's performance improved and they typically originated somewhere outside of the ships. However, those outbreaks that did occur now took place in a media environment dominated by cable news channels desperate for the content they needed to fill their twenty-four-hour news cycles. These incidents, furthermore, fell into the here-today, gone-tomorrow category of breaking news rather than investigative reporting, and the overall trend toward cleaner, safer ships tended to get lost in the pressure to obtain a scoop.

A more pressing life-and-death health concern that attracted considerably less attention during this same time period—although the *New York Times* did cover it extensively in its investigative series—was the state of shipboard medical care. This was yet another area in which the lines operated largely beyond the reach of the U.S. government and its standards. International law held that shipowners were legally bound to provide doctors for their crew but not for their passengers. Nevertheless, *Love Boat*'s Doc was not a complete fiction. All cruise ships had physicians aboard to treat passengers, but their work was typically all but unsupervised, and courts in the U.S. had repeatedly held that since physicians were technically independent contractors, the cruise lines they worked for could not be held responsible for their malpractice or negligence.

A 1999 survey conducted as part of Frantz's *New York Times* investigation found that fewer than 60 percent of the doctors aboard Carnival Cruise Lines ships had the credentials required to work in any U.S. hospital. Royal Caribbean, with its history of refusing to skimp on the "Royal Caribbean Experience," reported that fully 85 percent of its doctors had such qualifications. Unsettling as these numbers are, they actually reflect a marked improvement. Frantz collected his data three years after the industry had adopted yet another set of voluntary guidelines, this time in response to the American Medical Association's decision to bring its own considerable lobbying clout to bear on the situation.

The AMA had been spurred to action after a medical journal published the results of a survey a pair of Florida doctors had conducted after one of their fathers, himself a physician, died of a heart attack on a cruise. There was a portable defibrillator aboard, but it hadn't been used. The son began to wonder whether his father had received competent treatment, and decided to look into the situation, ultimately discovering that more than a quarter of doctors and nurses at the eleven major cruise lines operating at the time lacked advanced training in dealing with heart attacks and that fewer than half of them had been trained to deal with traumas. Among the nurses—and anyone who's been in a hospital will tell you that, often as not, it's the nurses who really get things done—barely a quarter had undergone trauma training. Pacemakers, ventilators and crucial blood-test equipment were all in short supply.

There were exceptions, notably at the upscale lines like Holland America and Princess, where the passengers tended to be older and consequently in poorer health. But the mass-market lines had no shortage of senior citizens among their customers. Cruising in general remains an industry that, as of 2002, considered its median passenger age of fifty-one to be proof of its success in reaching younger markets. Cruise ships, with their endless parades of older passengers overeating, drinking too much and engaging in unaccustomed levels of activity and excitement under the hot sun, are places where heart attacks can occur at any time. That so many of the industry's physicians wouldn't be competent to treat the single biggest killer of its prime demographic—or even be equipped to do so—was astonishing.

It's impossible to know how many deaths could have been prevented during the thirty years before the AMA intervened, back in the days when cruises, as the old chestnut went, were for "the overfed and the nearly dead." These questions, however, made the joke considerably less funny.

In 1998 the AMA's pressure had led to the ICCL's adopting a set of guidelines "with input" from the American College of Emergency Physicians. These were the prototype for the voluntary policies that would later come to cover shipboard crime and environmental practices. Although guidelines were surely better than nothing, as *Consumer Reports* pointed out the following year, without enforcement they carried little weight. "Neither ICCL nor ACEP enforce those guidelines or inspect ships that are on record as having adopted them," it reported. "In a phrase: no oversight."

The new (unenforced) guidelines had indeed led to some progress when it came to equipping the ships for medical emergencies, but as the subsequent *New York Times* investigation established, serious questions about the competence of the doctors and nurses administering the care remained. In one case, a forty-seven-year-old woman had a heart attack misdiagnosed as bronchitis. In another, a diabetic passenger went into coma and suffered brain damage when the ship's doctor misread his diagnostic equipment and administered a near-fatal dose of glucose instead of the insulin she needed.

When a Carnival doctor appeared to misdiagnose a fourteen-year-old female passenger's appendicitis with near-fatal consequences, the liability question reached something of a watershed. The doctor had repeatedly insisted to her parents that the girl had the flu—even, according to the girl's mother, after she asked him "point blank" if the girl's appendix might be the problem. " 'No, no, it's not,' " she says he told her. " 'I'm not sure what it is. I'm sorry your vacation has been ruined.' " As the infection from the rupture spread throughout the girl's body, her family said, the doctor prescribed antibiotics designed to treat a stomach virus. It later came out in a lawsuit that Carnival had not followed up on any of the doctor's references when he'd applied for the job. This was in 1997, a full year after the new guidelines had gone into effect. In the process of filing suit, attorneys for the girl's family found that the doctor had left town.

In court, Carnival turned to a familiar and traditionally effective defense. The company's lawyers argued that the doctor—who was paid a cash salary every two weeks in addition to a percentage of passenger medical fees—was an independent contractor, and that because Carnival's executives "don't have the expertise to control a doctor in the practice of medicine," the company wasn't responsible for his misdiagnosis. Carnival won the first round before a Miami-Dade County judge, but a federal appeals court overturned the ruling in August of 2003. "The cruise line's duty to exercise reasonable care . . . extends to the actions of the ship's doctor placed on board by the cruise line," the presiding judge wrote. "The practical realities of the competitive cruise industry and the reasonably anticipated risks of taking a small city of people to sea for days at a time all but dictate a doctor's presence." Since doctors wear the uniform of a company officer and their services are advertised as part of the cruise package, the judge ruled that, fine print notwithstanding, "the ship's doctor is an agent of the cruise line."

The ICCL adopted a public relations strategy similar to the one it would maintain on shipboard crime—that cruise ships were no less safe than the average small town. In this case, it argued that medical care was likewise comparable to what one might find in such American hamlets. It was a clever rhetorical bait and switch, substituting a debate over how often things go wrong for the actual issue of what happens when they do. The fact remained, however—and the industry still has no real response to this—that its "small town" is in the middle of the ocean: its hospitals, jails and every other public function are administered entirely by a single figure—the captain—whose allegiance is to the company, not the passengers. Such arrangements have had their day on land; despotic factory towns around the country had been run that way with results ranging from the utopian enclave of Hershey, Pennsylvania, to the black-lung epidemics and strikebreaking constabulary of the coal-mining towns just a few hundred miles to the west. It's a system that breeds abuse almost by definition, and one that, on shore at least, has largely been left in the dustbin of history.

At any rate, the "small town" argument is somewhat specious on the medical front. For the inhabitants of actual small towns in the United States, after all, there is almost always a well-equipped hospital within driving distance. And even the folksiest country doctor in the United States is board certified.

The inquiries and challenges of the late 1990s didn't stop at the waterline. Back home in the Port of Miami longtime port director Carmen Lunetta, revered as one of the cruise industry's indispensable pioneers, was suffering through his own fall from grace at the hands of the federal government.

For decades Lunetta had championed the cruise business; a functioning Port of Miami without him had been unthinkable. He'd been there from the very beginning, present at the Dodge Island construction site as a young civil engineer when the port director at the time had helped persuade Knut Kloster to bring his ship into Miami and start NCL. Since 1978 he'd presided over the port's emergence as a center of cruise tourism and as an international cargo hub. Lunetta's tireless campaigns to expand the port's infrastructure and his skill at luring federal dollars to the region had made him a hero to Miami's business community. Throughout his tenure at "Carmen's Port," Lunetta worked twelve hours or longer each day, six days a week. Often he financed his construction projects through bond offerings so aggressive that they fit the profile of a private corporation more closely than that of a government agency.

The port ran on Lunetta's handshake. Thanks to the political machine he built up around him, this public servant managed it all with less oversight than the average candy store owner has to contend with; financial records were sometimes kept only in his head. He made things work, and for decades that was all anyone needed to know. When the county commission held its periodic hearings on fee increases at Miami International Airport, for example, representatives from every airline in the region attended, turning the session into a pitched battle. Seaport hearings, on the other hand, ran smoothly, Lunetta having always negotiated the relevant deals to everybody's satisfaction beforehand, well out of the public eye, the cruise and cargo lines often didn't even bother to show up. He made the county commissioners look good, and they in turn left him alone.

He was a remarkable figure, among the last of the old-time regional barons whose immense political power flowered in the areas where America's public sector, industry and labor unions overlap. But he stayed too long, and it all came crashing down.

It began in the fall and winter of 1996 as news broke that a longtime Lunetta associate was under investigation in "Operation Greenpalm," an FBI sting aimed at the kickbacks, bribes and other incidents of government corruption that had been rampant in South Florida politics for years. Thrust into the spotlight was Calvin Grigsby, a San Francisco investment banker who had brokered millions of dollars' worth of municipal bond offerings for Miami Dade County over the years and who was slated to handle the financing for a wastewater treatment plant, an $80 million highway project and a new downtown sports arena, among others. The FBI allegedly had Grigsby on tape in a San Francisco hotel room, discussing a $300,000 kickback with a Dade County commissioner.

It didn't take long for the investigation to be broadened into Carmen's Port, where a separate Grigsby-owned concern had held a key contract for nearly twenty years. The venture, little more than a shell company, was named Fiscal Operations, and it had control over the enormous gantry cranes that loaded containers on and off cargo ships. Lunetta, prosecutors would later argue, had actual control of Fiscal. Millions of dollars allegedly failed to make it into Dade County coffers as Lunetta and Grigsby had used the company to turn the seaport into "their own personal bank" to finance personal expenditures and keep Lunetta's political machine humming smoothly.

Lunetta made it through that spring, but the pressure was mounting.

His autocratic ways had always been tolerated; this was the man, after all, who'd helped make Miami into the cruise capital of the world, breaking both passenger and cargo records year after year. It now came out that, far from being the source of income to Dade County most people believed it was, the port was deep in the red, owing $22 million to the county's general fund and struggling to service the debt on hundreds of millions of dollars' worth of municipal bonds. As auditors went through the port's books, a disturbing picture began to emerge. "They found accounts receivable in a shambles," one report on the audit read. "Contracts and leases broken or ignored, cash management systems in disarray and millions of past-due dollars owed by companies run by longtime pals of Port director Carmen Lunetta." Among the questioned transactions was a 1992 deal to expedite the expansion of two cruise terminals for Carnival Cruise Lines, in which Lunetta had ordered construction to go ahead despite the absence of necessary permits. "I didn't have six months to stand in line over at the county building department waiting to get permits," Lunetta scoffed with characteristic disdain. Such defiance had always made him seem like a maverick before; now people were calling him a crook.

In April, as a federal judge was ordering Fiscal Operations to turn its records over to Dade County auditors, the *Miami Herald* reported on a pair of loans to the construction company Lunetta owned with his brother. It came out that the Lunettas had accepted a five-hundred-thousand-dollar letter of credit the previous year from an offshore holding company registered in the British Virgin Islands and controlled by anonymous owners. Lunetta claimed that he himself didn't know the precise source of the money—a remarkable admission for a public official whose duty it is to avoid conflicts of interest. He vowed to discover the source of the loan, but nothing ever came of it. In any event, the whole arrangement—with its secret account-holders, offshore financial dealings and "No Comment"s from lawyers along the way—had the *feel* of impropriety, whatever the reality might have been. Within weeks of that revelation, the *Herald* learned of a 1989 loan for $745,428 from a savings and loan owned by Ted Arison—made at a time when the port was financing a major renovation of Carnival's passenger terminals. None of this was illegal, exactly, but it cast a suspicious light on Lunetta's allegiances yet again, and at the worst possible time for him.

The calls for resignation began to come in, but Lunetta held fast. At the age of sixty-six, he insisted he still had at least five more good years in him. On May 12, a Monday, still pushing the $163 million port expansion plan that was his latest pet project, Lunetta went before the county commission to report on the seaport's finances with his customary optimism. The commissioners tore into him, citing a litany of inaccurate budget projections, raging debt and barely existent financial controls as his political allies stood helplessly by. "All Lunetta could do," wrote one observer, "was hang his head and quietly agree that perhaps some form of oversight was in order for the port." On Friday, the *Herald* obtained copies of the documents Fiscal Operations had released to the county the month before. At eleven P.M. that night, Lunetta faxed his resignation to the county commission. The revelations contained in those records, he knew, would be more than any public official could withstand. Four days later, federal investigators announced that they had expanded their probe to include Lunetta himself. In a little over a year, Lunetta and Grigsby would be defending themselves against charges of embezzlement, money laundering and campaign fraud involving more than $1.5 million in port funds.

Within days of the resignation, a stunning portrait of life at Carmen's Port had begun to emerge. The Fiscal Operations documents suggested a reckless-

ness beyond anything that even Lunetta's most vocal public critics had imagined. The public learned of lavish spending on events ranging from golf tour-
naments to Super Bowl tickets, to luxury car leases. Between 1994 and 1997
alone, $150,000 had gone to charity golf tournaments in which Lunetta—
described by the *Herald* as "a duffer with a 19 handicap"—played and
brought guests. He brushed the golfing off as a "promotional expense," despite the fact that his guests included a retiree, his pastor and several pro
golfers.

Lunetta justified exceeding county spending caps by claiming it was Fiscal
Operations that had paid for the events, not the port itself. The question of
just whose money it actually was, however, would soon be one for the courts.
Since 1988 the company's budget had been subject to Lunetta's approval, and
Fiscal Operations' money had paid for a lot of things during those years, as it
turned out. The junkets, or even the maintenance on Grigsby's yacht back in
San Francisco, were the least of it. In 1994 the company had lent one of its
vice presidents, Fred Darden, $75,000 to make a down payment on a house
Lunetta owned, along with a thirty-thousand-dollar salary bump to cover
mortgage payments. "Lunetta took the money," the *Herald* reported, "but
never gave Darden the deed." And in 1990—two years after Lunetta had
gained veto power over Fiscal Operations' budget—the company invested
fifty thousand dollars in Ristorante Buccione, a power-lunch spot in Coconut Grove favored by the Miami political establishment. Among the
restaurant's investors were Lunetta and Grigsby; the investment went on the
books as a "marketing and promotion" expense.

Day after day, the reporters in the front rows of the coutroom were re-
galed by stories of an unstoppable political machine. "The government has
provided substantial evidence of greed and public corruption, the placement
of private interests over those of the public," a federal judge declared on the
last day of Lunetta's trial in 1998. "Accountability was nonexistent; financial
controls were ignored, even disdained. It is also evident that misconduct
went beyond these defendants to past and present elected and appointed officials who viewed the Port of Miami . . . as a place to obtain under-the-table
loans, political contributions, jobs for relatives and friends, and favors of all
kinds." Among the incidents the judge was referring to were an $85,000 loan
by Fiscal Operations to a county commissioner "funneled through a Puerto
Rican trust account" and never repaid; a $120,000 contribution to the
Democratic National Committee made in $15,000 installments within a

two-month period by a port tenant who was reimbursed by Fiscal Operations; a $39,000-a-year no-show job for an area city councilwoman whose salary, along with seven others, was paid by Fiscal Operations; and $8,000 that started in the port and allegedly ended up in the coffers of a Saint Louis politician with ties to Grigsby. A longtime secretary for Lunetta testified that at his direction she'd spent hours soliciting political contributions from companies that did business with the port—as well as for the ill-fated Ristorante Buccione. The judge added that "the defendants, as well as politicians of every stripe, used Fiscal Operations, Inc. and its collection of crane user fees as a punch bowl into which they could dip at will."

That rebuke, stinging as it was, could only be welcomed by Lunetta and Grigsby; it was the prelude to their acquittal.

The vitriol was a sign of the judge's frustration: the jury would not get to decide the case. The prosecution had failed to prove a crucial point—that the money in question in fact belonged to the port, and not to Fiscal Operations, at the time that it was spent. Fiscal Operations, the defense successfully argued, had been accused of a legal impossibility—stealing money that, under the terms of the agreement, already belonged to it. It hardly mattered that the contract itself was so complicated that Fiscal's own CFO testified that he'd never been able to understand it. "I honestly looked at it as a game between Carmen and Calvin," he said on the stand not long before the trial was cut short. Common sense and good business practice dictated that the money collected from the crane operations belonged to Dade County, but Lunetta and Grigsby were sheltered by a contract that stipulated otherwise—and when it came to the law regarding municipal contracts, the statutes governing what was acceptable and what wasn't were "maddeningly vague," as the *Herald* put it at one point. Since 1982 Fiscal Operations had had the right to collect the crane revenue and take out expenses along with its fee; what was left over went to the county—but, in a tortuous turn of legal logic, it wasn't considered county money until the county received it. The agreement was strong enough to hold up in court. The judge, hamstrung, ruled that the case could not proceed.

Grigsby's other corruption charges, based largely on FBI tapes, also stunned the city by ending in acquittal. Grigsby walked free and clear; the county commissioner accused of taking bribes in return for steering bond issues his way was acquitted of all but one of the counts he faced, that sole conviction based on a videotape in which he could be seen accepting an envelope stuffed with cash and saying, "This is a wonderful country."

The following year, stymied state prosecutors brought new charges against Lunetta—campaign fraud, this time, based on evidence he'd illegally spread a total of twenty thousand dollars among dozens of Florida politicians between 1993 and 1996. They were filed five days before the statute of limitations ran out. Lunetta, exhausted by what he felt to be a witch hunt, pleaded no contest and was sentenced to six months of house arrest, fined five thousand dollars and ordered to reimburse the state $8,500 for its investigation.

It was, as the *Herald* put it, "the final chapter in a tainted political life," but it was also more than that. For the cruise industry's top players, it was yet another sign that the frontier where they'd come of age was being civilized. Lunetta had escaped the most serious charges against him, but with his disgrace the world he had constructed was gone, never to return. In the corner offices of Carnival, NCL and Royal Caribbean, the industry's captains had suffered no direct effects from the scandal. Nevertheless, they soberly marked the passing of the era.

In the long run, these potential crises were all apparently manageable for the increasingly powerful cruise lines. Voluntary initiatives to improve crime reporting, to bring higher standards of medical care and to exceed federal rules on environmental matters seemed to placate lawmakers. Lunetta's downfall, although symbolic for insiders, hardly registered outside Miami, and even there it wasn't seen as particularly connected to the cruise lines. They'd weathered each of these storms and had emerged with barely a bruise. No one, even in the darkest moments of these scandals, had raised serious objections to the industry's prized tax or labor arrangements. The signals from Washington suggested the industry was correct in considering their various travails to be primarily public relations issues. And as American vacationers voted with their wallets, the cruise lines seemed justified in assuming the situation was nothing they couldn't handle.

There was, in fact, one challenge during this period that truly threatened the industry's long-term bottom line, but that crisis played out far from the newsrooms and courtrooms of the American mainland. The big scare, instead, came from the sunny and unhappy islands of the Caribbean itself.

CHAPTER ELEVEN

TROUBLE IN PARADISE

*For to be free is not merely to cast off one's chains, but to live in a way
that respects and enhances the freedom of others.*

—Nelson Mandela

As the island nations of the Caribbean and the cruise industry have had ever
greater contact with one another, their relationship has evolved into a complex
symbiosis, full of contradictions, resentments and hope. For a glimpse into the
paradoxes that define the relationship, one needn't go further than one of the
region's prime exports and its most widely recognized symbol: its music.

The upbeat rhythms of a reggae or calypso song are so infectious that it's
easy to overlook the fact that the lyrics often tell a very different story. Although we tend to associate them with rum drinks and poolside afternoons,
those carefree island beats are actually a vehicle for complex and powerful political sentiment. Harry Belafonte's songs are typical; he sings of his "Island in
the Sun," but for him the palm trees and beaches are only a backdrop. That
island is a living place, where "My people have toiled since time begun."
When he looks at the vista, he sees the "woman on bended knee, cutting cane
for her family" and the "man at the waterside, casting nets at the surfing
tide." This cast of characters has no place in the tourist paradise that "Island
in the Sun"—transformed through countless recitals by steel-drum bands in
frilly pastel shirts—has come to signify. Yet this region is their home, the cane
fields and the shallows, though it has been reinvented as a playground for
strangers. Bob Marley is another case in point. *Legend,* his greatest hits collection, has sold ten million copies in the United States alone, because Marley's music *feels* like happy music, music for everyone. A song like "Could

You Be Loved," one of his most popular, never fails to get the people moving, dancing, smiling. But "Could You Be Loved" is not a happy song at all—it's a political song, an angry one about race, empire and oppression. Its politics are neither subtle nor indirect; they are right there on the surface for anyone to hear:

> Don't let them fool you
> Or even try to school you, Oh! No
> We've got a mind of our own
> So go to hell if what you're thinkin' isn't right . . .
>
> Don't let them change you
> Or even rearrange you, Oh! No
> We've got a life to live
> They say only, only
> Only the fittest of the fittest shall survive
> Stay alive

But when the song comes on the radio, the people keep tapping their toes; there's just something about those rhythms. In this respect, the Caribbean is not unlike the music to which it has given birth. Its landscapes of perfect beaches, balmy waters and coral reefs, its cloudless skies and almost absurdly beautiful sunsets all blend into such a happy syncopation that the darker truths of its day-to-day existence often go unnoticed.

Cruise travel is rapidly becoming the dominant mode of tourism in the Caribbean region. In 2000 cruise ships brought some thirteen million passengers to the region, about a quarter of its total tourist traffic. If you take away Central America, Mexico, Cuba and the Dominican Republic, however, cruise passengers account for almost 55 percent of all tourism in the Caribbean islands. And because cruise passengers are a different breed from the tourists who actually come to stay in the hotels and resorts of the West Indies, the islands have had to adapt to serve them. The mayflies of the Caribbean, cruisers come to town for only a day. The big white ships that carry them sail into various island ports of call in the morning and stay until five P.M. or so; in the meantime, passengers meander ashore, either on excursions organized by the cruise line or on their own, to experience the "paradise" they've paid to visit. "Dreams become reality when you find yourself floating through the warm, welcoming waters of the Caribbean on one of our award-winning five-star ships," the promotional literature promises. "Your place in the sun, sand and surf on a picture-perfect island is there for the taking." But the experience, so brief and superficial, virtually ensures that a cruise passenger will not penetrate the glamours cast over the places they visit. He or she is one of perhaps three thousand from a given ship—and as often as not, three other ships just like it are anchored in the same harbor. By sunset, it's back out to sea for another night of American-style gambling, dining and dancing before waking up in another little "paradise" the next morning to do it all over again.

"Fantasy" is the operative word here. Tourism marketing can be broken down into two major models: what might be called the "Roman Holiday" model, in which people are drawn to a locale because of the distinctive, specific attractions that make it special, and what could be called the "Disney World" model, in which an entire environment is remade to conform with a preexisting idea of what people want. Travel to the Caribbean on a cruise ship, and you're about as likely to experience the *Roman Holiday* version as you are to see Audrey Hepburn or Gregory Peck riding past you on a Vespa. Beginning with the marketing of the islands themselves, much of the Caribbean cruise tourist's experience is as tightly orchestrated an affair as any Disney World trip, with the locale nothing more than beguiling scenery.

This Caribbean is more a simulation than a genuine place—a real-life theme park composed of resorts sealed away behind fences and armed guards, of air-conditioned touring vans whose pith-helmeted drivers and guides whisk you through the places where local people live en route to this beach, or that charter boat, or this "colorful" straw market where ladies in bandannas hawk "local" crafts, with not a local customer in sight. Indeed, most of the major cruise lines have taken long-term leases on private islands where they can treat their passengers to a version of the Caribbean "as it's meant to be" without any inconvenient interruption from the locals.

Not that Caribbean cruises are actually marketed as opportunities to learn about the places themselves. Leafing through the glossy brochures, one would never guess that the region's nearly forty million people share an economic, military and social history that, from slaves, sugar and rum to the Monroe Doctrine and gunboat diplomacy, is inseparable from that of the United

States itself. Nor would one have any reason to infer that this history has brought together cultures from India, Africa, England, Holland, France, Spain and even China and as a result has spawned religions and art forms unique in the world.

The Caribbean's allure, instead, is presented as generic, an opportunity for "castaways" from the United States to let their hair down for a week in a carefully constructed Eden—to leave behind the stresses and complexities of their everyday lives. To the extent that a sales pitch mentions the character of local life at all, it's usually to paint a picture of a touchingly simple folk, who for all the world appear to hold no dearer wish than to welcome yet another tourist to their unthreateningly primitive world—and put an umbrella drink in his hand. Tucked away, out of the frame, are the armed guards patrolling the beachy borders of this wonderland, there to protect visiting eyes from the far less photogenic reality: of unemployment rates as high as 20 percent, of political frustrations nurtured by centuries under corrupt, inept or cruel rulers, of the resentments held by peoples who after two generations of political independence are still hopelessly unequal players in the arenas of international trade and diplomacy.

There is much that is charming and good about island life, some of which is not so far out of line with the fantasy sold to prospective tourists back in the United States and Europe. Rather than showcasing the culture and natural beauty of the islands, however, franchise attractions along the lines of the ubiquitous "dolphin encounter" have come to dominate island tourism in recent years. For about $145 a head, as the name suggests, cruise passengers are bused from the pier to "swim with dolphins," an activity that primarily entails standing thigh-deep in a fenced-off lagoon while trainers put the dolphins through their paces. It's one of the most popular and profitable excursions that the cruise lines sell, and it would be no less authentic in Orlando or Coney Island than it is in the West Indies. Certain types of porpoises are indigenous to the region, but the playful bottlenose dolphin featured in the encounter—remember Flipper?—is not among them. Like the mostly young, white and good-looking marine biologists from Europe and America who tend to them, the dolphins in these fenced-in swimming areas are usually imports.

This artificial Caribbean has become so vivid to tourists that even the most innocuous detour into real island life can be startling. The experience of one group of cruise passengers in Antigua is a case in point. After their dolphin encounter, they were being shuttled back to their ship in a minivan when the driver, a local, pulled over to the side of the road and stepped out to speak with a friend standing on his front step—a common enough practice there, as it is in many of the world's small towns. Among the van's passengers, however, the fear level suddenly rose. The circumstances could hardly have been less menacing; it was the middle of the day in the center of a sleepy town, and the driver had ambled to a spot less than twenty yards away. Unlike Jamaica, where a visitor might reasonably fear violence, Antigua is a mellow place where street crime is still the exception, not the rule. But back in the van, the people sensed danger—not merely the city-dweller's impatience with the slower clock of rural life, but the beginnings of genuine fear. When the driver returned after less than two minutes and resumed the journey back to the ship, the passengers shot each other surreptitious looks of relief, obviously feeling they'd had a close call.

The dolphins are just one example of the pseudoreality that is everywhere in evidence where cruise ships dock in Caribbean ports. Even the conventional water sports have become dumbed down, with popular attractions that include motorized underwater tricycles, yellow submarines and jet boats. The sheer scale of the traffic is such that even the authentically local attractions are overwhelmed. The natural wonder of the Cayman Islands known as "Stingray City," for example, is daily overrun with hundreds of cruise tourists crowding in to see the rays swarm their natural habitat. Erosion is becoming a problem. Rather than raise fees or limit traffic, however, the government of the Caymans is looking into the feasibility of creating a Stingray City II.

In the Jamaican city of Ocho Rios—a major cruise port—the downtown area is gritty and poor, full of beggars, drug pushers and sundry discomfiting realities of island life. Even on a good day, a stroll through Ocho Rios tugs at the conscience; on bad days, it can be frightening. Of those cruise passengers who opt not to pay for an organized tour into the beautiful waterfalls and jungles inland, many forego a downtown visit in favor of a stop in "Island Village," a themed warren of retail shops and bars located alongside the terminal facility. A policeman idles outside the entrance; the décor is rustic "Caribbean." Inside, faux bamboo huts lining the boardwalks hawk souvenirs of all kinds: carved walking sticks; T-shirts reading "No Problem, Mon," or "One Tequila, Two Tequila, Three Tequila, *Floor*"; novelty skullcaps patterned in Jamaica's national black, green and gold, with fake dreadlocks attached; portraits of Bob Marley. The high point is "Jimmy Buffet's

Margaritaville," where fans of the singer can order the "Cheeseburger in Paradise" right off the menu. On the far side of the restaurant, the ocean view is dominated by one or more cruise ships. There's a tiny beach where people can rent lounge chairs or swim in a roped-off area about twice the size of a backyard pool.

Perhaps the only genuinely Jamaican experience in Island Village is folded into the upbeat rhythms of the four-man reggae band giving a free show near the entrance: dancing in front of them is a young woman dressed up like Aunt Jemima, a fake Carmen Miranda fruit basket on her head and, beneath her dress, great big pads to simulate a plantation "mammy's" enormous rear end and bosom. As the passengers shuffle appreciatively past the twenty-first-century minstrel show, none hears the dreadlocked singer's words. *"Oh God,"* he sings as they pass, heads bopping in time to the song. *"Look what they're doing to my soul . . . Oh God! Oh God! Oh God! Look at how they take control . . ."*

It is understandable that a proud Jamaican might bristle. Such abstract indignities, however, quickly give way to more concrete concerns when the ships come to town. The strains on local infrastructure can be enormous. In the tiny British Virgin Islands, for example, locals often simply stay out of the capital city on cruise days, when the sidewalks are overrun and the streets jammed with minibuses taking passengers to excursion spots around the island. Still worse, in a socially conservative country with more churches than bars, visiting passengers show little respect for local propriety, ambling into banks and business offices in spandex, bikinis or shirtless. Even hiding out at home, locals may not be able to escape the cruisers' presence; it's not uncommon to step into one's own shower only to find the water pressure reduced to a trickle, so much of the municipal water supply is diverted to the ships. Of course, by industry standards the British Virgin Islands is an out-of-the-way cruise destination. The Cayman Islands hosted 1.6 million cruise passengers in 2003, or thirty-seven times its local population. A visitor-to-resident ratio like that in New York City would mean almost a half-billion visitors a year.

Not surprisingly, tensions have arisen. During the politicized 1970s, when all but the youngest children knew life under a colonial power firsthand, radicalism flourished in the islands as elsewhere in the third world. Islanders demanded to be taken seriously and not treated as commodities in marketing schemes developed in the very countries that had ruled over them. The occasional "YANKEE GO HOME" signs would greet cruise passengers; the hostility was often palpable on the street. The dynamics of a service economy just didn't play well in societies where the legacy of slavery was still a subject for contemporary debate, and "to hell with paradise" was a common mantra. But times changed, and the political climate eased somewhat as cash-strapped governments grasped the undeniable economic benefits of a robust tourism industry.

As the 1990s dawned, however, the Caribbean nations once again found themselves rethinking their relationship with tourism. This time around, it wasn't the result of a Cold War–era political philosophy, but of questions of where, in the new global marketplace, the benefits should fall. Instead of "Black Power" and "third world justice," the phrases on people's lips were more along the lines of "Show me the money." And for the cruise lines that was an infinitely more threatening notion.

In the spring of 1993 the member nations of the Caribbean Community— CARICOM for short—fired a shot across the cruise industry's bow. At its annual conference that July, CARICOM announced its intention to levy a minimum head tax of somewhere between ten dollars and fifteen dollars per person on cruise passengers visiting its members' ports. Furthermore, the group was looking into the possibility of establishing a regional licensing body to regulate the cruising trade in the Caribbean Sea. For the Miami cruise lines, it was an alarming development, and the tax as such was the least of their concerns. Bargaining power in the hands of a coordinated regional body theatened to upset a balance of power that for years had tipped steeply toward the industry.

Back in Miami, cruise itinerary planning had become something of an art; the trick was to balance big-ticket "marquee destinations" necessary to entice passengers with the cheaper, more out-of-the-way islands that charged less in port fees. Marquee ports—like the Bahamas, a stone's throw from Miami, or Saint Thomas, with its reputation as a prime shopping destination— could charge quite a bit more than the proposed minimum tax for their services, and the cruise lines were happy to pay because there had always been a surplus of the critical "second-layer" ports clamoring for new business and willing to take whatever they could get. Some had even been letting cruise ships dock for free, so desperate were they for the business. The contrast could be extreme. Even Barbados, a well-known tourist destination, had been charging a mere three dollars for years, until it finally doubled its tax in the summer of 1993—while isolated Bermuda to the north, thanks in part to its proximity to Northeast homeports like New York and Boston, commanded sixty dollars per person and actually went so far as to restrict the number of cruise ships it allowed to visit.

This disparity was the key to the industry's regional strategy. The cruise lines had become masters at leveraging their ships' mobility in negotiations with the various ports. Their ability to simply pick up and leave was a constant, underlying threat. But CARICOM's new initiative threatened to undermine that system. The lines could live without any single destination, and the islands all knew it; but surviving without the cooperation of the region as a whole was another matter altogether.

The Caribbean's location and climate make it a natural cruising ground. Its year-round perfect weather, its multiple destinations in close proximity to one another and its easy access to homeports in population centers up and down the East Coast of the United States all make it ideally suited to the cruise vacation format. If anything, the Caribbean had become even more important during the early 1990s as the industry began concentrating on the market for shorter and more profitable "getaway" cruises, ranging from a week to a single night. From a purely geographical standpoint, the Hawaiian Islands are a close second, but long-standing U.S. law prohibits foreign-flagged vessels from transporting passengers or goods between two U.S. ports unless the voyage includes a stop in another country. The nearest such stop, Fanning Island in the tiny South Pacific republic of Kiribati, is some twelve hundred miles and a two-day sail away from the nearest Hawaiian port in each direction, making any cruise shorter than ten days impracticable. Farther into the Pacific Rim, airfares become so expensive as to moot the savings that make cruising an appealing vacation option in the first place. And Mexico, while it does a good cruise business, lacks the island paradise image that sells so many tickets. During the summer months, cruise ships ply their trade all around the world—in the Mediterranean, in the Baltic and the fjords of northern Europe, in Alaska and in Canada and New England. In fact, these voyages tend to be among the most profitable in the industry. But come October, the ships all head back to the Caribbean; there's literally nowhere else they can go.

Rather than forcing the cruise lines to compete with one another for the opportunity to make use of the Caribbean countries' unique natural resources, the island nations had traditionally eagerly sought to lure the cruise ships, undercutting one another on price. This was an ideal situation for the industry, but several things had begun to change in the years leading up to the CARICOM initiative. The original negotiating dynamic had taken shape during a time when only a handful of cruise ships sailed the Caribbean, carrying relatively small numbers of affluent passengers. By 1993, however, cruising had become a squarely middle-class vacation, and the region was playing host to dozens of ships, with dozens more on order in the shipyards of Europe. The vessels themselves were far bigger, and creating the deepwater harbors they needed required major investments on the part of local governments. At the same time, with the bigger ships came new marketing schemes billing the ships themselves—and not the ports of call—as the "real destination" for passengers, an approach that made the locals nervous. Of greater concern were the industry's efforts to boost onboard spending—up from a per-passenger average of fifteen dollars in 1987 to thirty-five dollars in 1990—leaving a smaller slice of the pie for the ports. Granted, larger ships meant more passengers and more hard currency flowing through local economies, but more people also generated more waste and took a heavier toll on local infrastructure, offsetting economic gains and creating new strains and social costs.

Finally, bigger ships meant bigger cruise lines—with more passengers, more money and more leverage, and the islands soon found themselves negotiating with a handful of behemoths whose formidable resources and bargaining power dwarfed their own.

Shoreside businesses, moreover, had been undergoing a consolidation of their own. Increasingly, transnational retail franchises had been springing up to cater to cruise passengers in the various ports of call; from Antigua to Saint Thomas, duty-free outlets like Columbian Emeralds and Diamonds International were dominating the Caribbean's new cruise terminals, pushing local retailers out of the lucrative duty-free market and relegating more than a few of them to the harder and less profitable work of hawking T-shirts and trinkets.

This process only intensified as the lines took over the onboard "shopping talks" that had traditionally been a lucrative, if unofficial, sideline for cruise directors. For years the cruise directors had collected money from local merchants and tour operators in return for steering passengers their way. It was all done under the table, and in a place where bribery was the norm, it was generally understood to be an accepted part of doing business. During the 1980s, however, the increasingly budget-conscious lines cracked down on the practice—after a fashion. Rather than eliminate the arrangement, they turned the payoffs into a formal, centralized corporate function, moving the responsibility from the cruise directors on the ships to the offices in Miami. Where before they had negotiated one-on-one with cruise directors as the ships came through, local merchants now found themselves contending with franchise operations that not only had the resources to make the Miami trip on a regular basis—if they didn't already have a permanent representative there—but had the volume to offer terms that local businesses couldn't hope to compete with. Many such merchants watched in consternation as the passengers passed them by, directed elsewhere by flyers that had been placed in their staterooms the night before.

The same was true of many of the smaller tour operators who traditionally took visiting passengers on local excursions. At a markup of 100 percent or more, these trips had grown into a major profit center for the cruise lines, and they found that using the larger companies was simply more efficient. Economies of scale took hold, and smaller businesses once again were left in the dust. "Small operators like us do not have the financial resources, infrastructure or contacts to approach the cruise lines in Miami," one scuba guide from the Cayman Islands complained. As frustrations mounted, some began questioning long-accepted assumptions about the industry's benefit to local economies.

A backlash was inevitable. Just as skyrocketing profits had drawn the unwanted attention of lawmakers and regulators back in the United States, the cruise lines in the Caribbean faced the prospect of becoming victims of their own success—what Voltaire would have called an embarrassment of riches. As lines like Carnival and Royal Caribbean went public, observers from Wall Street to Washington found themselves wondering—either admiringly or with chagrin—just how they'd been able to make so much money. For their part, Caribbean stakeholders wondered where their own share of this new prosperity was.

It didn't help that the industry was also in direct competition with local hotel and resort operators. The hoteliers, one of the most potent political forces in the islands, resented the cruise ships' ability to profit from the region's attractions while sailing free from the constraints imposed on land-based businesses by labor unions, high import costs and heavy tax regimes. In the spring of 1993 they decided to make their play. Leveraging the influence of their industry association, the hoteliers tapped former Jamaican prime minister Michael Manley to head up a task force under the semigovern-mental auspices of the Caribbean Tourism Organization with a mandate to assemble data on the cruise industry's impact in the Caribbean and recom-mend a regional tax and licensing scheme to CARICOM.

Depending on your point of view, Manley was either the best man for the job or the worst. Few politicians in the region had a higher international pro-file. For most of the previous two decades, Manley had been the radical voice at the center of the Caribbean's efforts to define its economic relationship to the United States and the fast-changing global economy. During his first term, from 1972 to 1980, Manley's government moved toward a centralized, state-run economy while he—a graduate of the London School of Econom-ics—steered the ship of state decked out in a bush jacket styled after Che Guevara's. Virulent anti-American pronouncements and party platforms with titles like "Ten Steps to Socialism" did little to endear him to those who feared increased Soviet influence in the Western hemisphere. At a time when the so-called "nonaligned movement" gave third world nations an unprece-dented degree of geopolitical importance, Manley took his flair for oratory to the world stage, and with his searing critiques of the International Monetary Fund and other mechanisms of international finance, he "built himself a reputation abroad out of all proportion to his country's size—and to his own achievements at home," as the *Economist* once put it.

Having led the country to the brink of bankruptcy, he was ousted in 1980 by an opponent from Jamaica's Labour Party who swept into office on promises of deregulation and economic liberalization during a chaotic week that saw more than 750 people killed in election-related violence. But in 1989, capitalizing on public anger over the new government's cuts to educa-tion, health care and other social services, Manley returned to office, a new man. "His trademark open-necked safari shirt has been replaced by a sober, dark blue business suit," *Time* magazine noted approvingly. "Stressing prag-matism over idealism, he has purged the left wing fringe of the People's Na-tional Party, toned down his relationship with Fidel Castro and reassured jittery business leaders with talk of continued economic stability and the need for private investment." Manley spoke, furthermore, of a "new beginning" with the United States, and in 1990 he visited the White House, where President George Bush declared him to be doing a "first-class job"—an assessment that would have been unthinkable during his previous term. Poor health had forced him to step down in the spring of 1992; not long after, he agreed to lead the cruise study.

The cruise lines despised him, of course—not only for his politics, which even in their reformed incarnation were irreconcilable with the virtually tax- and regulation-free environment they favored, but also for his business ties to the hoteliers, their rivals. From Miami, his appointment looked like a gross conflict of interest. Even as he was conducting the study for the supposedly neutral CTO, cruise industry representatives maintained, Manley was collecting paychecks as a consultant from the decidedly biased Caribbean Hotel Association as well as Gordon "Butch" Stewart—chairman of Sandals, the regional empire of all-inclusive resorts, and a heavy hitter in his own right. Both had much to gain from measures restricting the cruise industry, which Stewart during this period described as a "giant sea serpent which is gobbling up the region's plant, personnel and profits."

Manley was a formidable advocate, though, and he was lending his stature to the cruise ship issue at a time when there seemed to be an unprecedented common political will among the typically fractious and disorganized CARICOM members. The fact was that the region badly needed an economic victory. The new cruise initiative was coming just at the advent of NAFTA in the United States and the new global free trade prerogatives enforced by the World Trade Organization had visited a series of humiliations upon the Caribbean—notably a devastating ruling by the WTO, made after the U.S. trade representative raised the issue at the behest of the Dole Corporation, to strike down longtime European Union trade policies designed to subsidize the Caribbean's struggling banana farmers.

It was, in short, a perfect political backdrop for someone with Manley's talents to raise the cruise ship question and to highlight the attendant issues of economic and regional sovereignty. The general consensus was that if CARICOM couldn't unite to seize the upper hand under these circumstances, it never would.

The cruise lines were facing the very real possibility of losing their chief negotiating strength in the region. Even worse, they knew CARICOM was ready for a fight. The previous year, in 1992, members of a CARICOM sub-group, the Organization of Eastern Caribbean States, had pushed for their own unified minimum tax on cruise passengers. Led by Saint Lucia, which had been charging $2.50 per passenger, OECS pushed its head taxes up to a minimum of $9.25. Saint Lucia bumped its fees to five dollars almost imme-diately, with plans to quadruple them to ten dollars by October of 1994. The industry response was Machiavellian. "When they did that, I pulled our ship out of Saint Lucia because that was one that came out first—it was the fore-runner," Royal Caribbean's Ed Stephan remembers. "The others were saying, 'Let's talk it over, blah blah blah.' Saint Lucia said, 'No! We're doing it right away.' Okay. Good-bye." Along with Royal Caribbean, Celebrity and Dol-phin also took Saint Lucia off their itineraries. With its leader slapped down so suddenly and so hard, the coalition crumbled almost immediately. Al-though the other OECS nations had threatened to boycott the relevant lines in response, several were soon making conciliatory offers to the very ships that had pulled out, and by October Saint Lucia had rescinded much of its increase. The island's audacity would prove costly; years would pass before its cruise traffic reached former levels. It was a classic example of the industry's divide-and-conquer strategy, as Rod McLeod, Royal Caribbean's top market-ing executive at the time, explained. "Let's say that five islands form an al-liance, and we have no way around the alliance. We decide that, instead of calling at three of them, we're going to call at two—and we pick which ones. The other members of the alliance are going to get pissed at the other two; that's been the case before that, and that's, I think, what didn't allow the is-lands to go forward. . . . They like to blame it on us, but the fact was that be-cause of their own individual interests, they couldn't get it together—they couldn't make it."

Saint Lucia's defeat had seemed a devastating blow, but less than a year later the islands had regrouped and again seemed ready for a fight. Working to face down the new initiative, the cruise lines sought out the coalition's Achilles' heel: CARICOM's charter required a unanimous vote to take ac-tion. The lines had to persuade but one member to back out, and the entire scheme would fall apart. And that was a game they knew how to play.

As spring turned into summer the situation grew increasingly con-tentious. Through its regional lobbying group, the Florida Caribbean Cruise Association, the industry insisted that the hoteliers were looking to blame someone else for their failures and were using CARICOM as a shill. The

FCCA cited a study it had commissioned the previous year from the auditing giant Pricewaterhouse, which found that the industry provided fully $2.7 billion in economic benefit to the region. Caribbean governments might be taxing their hotel industries into oblivion, they insisted, but that was hardly the cruise industry's fault. For its part, the Caribbean Trade Organization maintained that the report was premised on a significant overestimation of cruise spending in the region. The Caribbean Hotel Association further accused the industry of displaying a "cavalier disregard for the governments and peoples of the Caribbean" and of treating the region's future "like a bargaining chip in corporate negotiations." The debate cut to the emotional heart of Caribbean identity. Saint Lucia's prime minister touched on powerful sentiments when he railed that the Caribbean would "no longer accept mirrors and baubles for the use of its patrimony."

The two sides seemed to be at an impasse. In 1993 CARICOM cited its environmental concerns, worrying that stricter regulation in the United States might induce ships to dump more in Caribbean waters, where enforcement was spottier. The industry scoffed. "We have invested millions to grind and crunch and compact everything we need to be doing in excess of the regulations," a Royal Caribbean spokesman responded. "We don't want to pollute the environment." Within a year, a U.S. Coast Guard plane would catch the *Sovereign of the Seas* dumping oil into the Caribbean Sea off the coast of Puerto Rico, setting in motion a chain of events that would eventually lead to $27 million in fines and a felony conviction on charges arising from a "fleetwide conspiracy" to empty waste into the sea.

Finally, in late May the FCCA suspended its membership in the CTO, citing its "failure to publicly repudiate the Caribbean Hotel Association's misinformation campaign about the cruise industry." The CTO fired back that its bylaws had no provision for self-suspension by a member, but indicated the FCCA was welcome to withdraw entirely.

The moment of truth was to be the annual CARICOM summit, scheduled for Barbados in early July. At the end of June Jamaica had announced its intention to raise its head tax from ten to fifteen dollars, equaling the Bahamas for the highest in the region. With its most famous elder statesman leading the CARICOM charge, the move put the region's largest English-speaking country, long a top cruise destination, squarely at the epicenter of the fight. But bold as its posture was, the Jamaican government was struggling mightily under the weight of its international debt—and the cruise lines knew it. Desperate to find new revenue sources, it had just announced unprecedented tax hikes and was looking to the cruise fee as a key component of its budget plan. And so it was on Jamaica, both strong and vulnerable, that the hammer fell.

Even as the CARICOM heads of state deliberated in Barbados, NCL announced that it would drop Ocho Rios from one of its ships' itineraries. NCL denied the decision was connected to the meetings. "Companies move itineraries all the time," a spokesman said. "The timing is coincidental." In fact, according to one longtime industry executive and FCCA committee member, there was nothing coincidental about it. Rather, it was part of an unspoken "rotation" between the cruise lines—a system that allowed them to maximize their ability to collectively play hardball with the islands while distributing the ill-will and negative publicity that accompany a pullout. U.S. rules prohibiting price-fixing and other collusion between companies made this a delicate matter, to say the least. "None of us," the executive remembers, "wanted to get called up to testify in front of an antitrust judge." But the end result was clear enough. "It wasn't so much 'It's your turn,'" he explained of the system. "Royal Caribbean would say, 'We've taken our stand, and we've got to have some friends left.' The implication was that if something's going to be done about it, it's got to be NCL or Carnival."

It was a powerful gambit and a well-chosen target. Memories of Saint Lucia's experience the year before were still fresh. Ocho Rios is a household name in the U.S. as a marquee port. The message was unmistakable: if a big player like NCL was willing to drop a major port, no one was safe.

The pullout was only half the game, however. The action that NCL was taking in Jamaica might well have pushed the CARICOM nations even more firmly into one another's arms—and the cruise lines knew that, too. They accordingly approached a weak link: Barbados, where, ironically enough, the summit was being held and where the CTO was headquartered. Only a few months earlier Barbados had celebrated the grand opening of a new $3 million cruise ship terminal—an enormous building project by its standards. To help pay for it, the government had been negotiating an increase in its own head taxes, and in the run-up to the vote, the cruise lines made a generous deal, agreeing to double its fees to six dollars a head. "Was it linked to what was going on with CARICOM? Sure!" McLeod remembers. "Our view was that we would be better off having a deal with Barbados, and that that might bring the others to their senses." Barbados, unable to resist the temptation of the new revenue, unilaterally scuttled the measure. "We have recently moved our passenger tax to six dollars, and that is where it will stay for some time," the Barbadian prime minister announced at the conference's end. "We will not be moving now to the new ten dollar minimum." Without the unanimity needed to move against the cruise lines, the summit concluded with a weak agreement to implement a minimum tax "in principle," but without a time frame for putting it into practice the resolution was an empty gesture.

Barbados's defection had weakened CARICOM, and the supposed agreement notwithstanding, the collection of island nations were no less vulnerable than they had been beforehand. During the moments when the initiative had appeared to be going well, observers had praised the welcome and unexpected departure from the regional powers' typical petty squabbling. Now, in the clarity of hindsight, failure took on the dull tones of inevitability. By the following March several of the CARICOM states had still not brought their charges in line with the ten dollars they'd agreed to "in principle." Among those that had implemented it officially, most had established discounting schemes that all but negated its effect on the cruise lines.

As if to underscore the victory, the FCCA in November informed the CTO that it was dropping out of a nonprofit marketing consortium it had helped establish the previous year to counter heavy advertising from other regions like Hawaii and Europe. The program had been hailed as a great step forward for cooperation and mutual understanding between private industry and the region's governments. The FCCA was to have contributed $1.5 million, about 13 percent of the entire budget. Now, writing off the five hundred thousand dollars it had already paid, the FCCA was unequivocal in its position: the CTO was being punished for its transgressions against the industry. That letter would be one of the only communications between the two groups for nearly two years; the heat of the battle had given way to a major frost.

Realizing that it had won a battle only, the FCCA launched a campaign to improve its public image in the region. That was no small job, given recent events, and any rapprochement was further hampered by the fact that the FCCA had traditionally played the "bad cop" role for the industry, as one committee member active at the time put it. "The industry needs someone to apologize for," he explained. "Somebody who can go and say something at times that is not politic and who will be tough. Then the lines can come in behind that person and say, 'Well, she's a little rough.' But the point is made. You get hit in the nose, you remember getting hit in the nose. Then the person who paid to have you hit in the nose comes in and says, 'She may get carried away a bit; that's not quite our position.' "

Having the CTO as an enemy likewise didn't help make the job any easier for the FCCA. On a panel at the cruise industry's annual convention in Miami that March, the industry brought in several island ministers to stand in for the CTO officials who would have otherwise been present. Intended to highlight "the positive relationship between the cruise industry and the Caribbean destinations" at a time when there was none, the panel quickly degenerated into invective so bitter that one trade journal was prompted to note that "None of the speakers . . . seemed to have read the script."

That October, still hoping for a better reception, the FCCA unveiled an updated study of its members' economic contribution to the Caribbean, also conducted by Pricewaterhouse. It was, as the British journalist Polly Pattullo observed in *Last Resorts,* her 1996 study of Caribbean tourism, "a timely occasion for the cruise industry to rebuild its relationship with the Caribbean after the difficulties arising out of the head tax row. The problem was that not everyone accepted these statistics." Pattullo cited a stinging critique of the study penned by Klaus de Albuquerque, a sociologist at the College of Charleston in South Carolina. Comparing the 1994 Pricewaterhouse study with the one issued two years earlier—along with data he collected from national tourist boards and research conducted by staff at the *Economist* in London—de Albuquerque concluded that the FCCA had dramatically inflated its new numbers. The 1994 report pegged the industry's total economic contribution to the region at $3.9 billion, up nearly 60 percent from the previous estimates. Deployment of new and bigger ships might have accounted for this jump in the economic total, but at a time when the cruise lines were aggressively working to increase passengers' shipboard spending, claims of a 55 percent increase in local expenditures by individual passengers during the same period seemed suspect. And that was just the average; in the U.S. Virgin Islands, de Albuquerque pointed out, the FCCA numbers for individual passenger spending were fully 80 percent higher than those from two years before, and fully 270 percent above what the *Economist* had estimated in 1993.

There was some genuine improvement. One of the provisions debated by

CARICOM the year before would have conditioned a portion of the head tax on the extent of a cruise line's participation in the local economy—not just the tourist trade, but purchasing of food, fuel and local services. The lines may have frozen communications with the CTO, but they'd never stopped listening. Increasing local spending was a relatively painless investment in public relations, and in 1994 the FCCA reported a total of $71.3 million in spending on Caribbean goods and services, up from $51.2 million the year before. Fuel, spare parts and chemicals accounted for about two-thirds of the expenditures, with local products and services like sugar, rum, milk and coffee and jobs on the region's docks accounting for most of the rest.

In its quest for the hearts and minds of regional policy makers, the FCCA in 1994 also launched an annual conference to bring local Caribbean officials together with senior cruise line executives. The industry worked hard to persuade the powerful hotel lobby to think of them not as competition, but instead as a powerful resource. It was a neat bit of spin—and not without its logic. Estimating that as many as 25 percent of cruise passengers returned to the Caribbean for stays on land, the FCCA argued the position that cruise ships gave them the opportunity to showcase their destination to millions of visitors each year at virtually no expense to themselves.

Shying away from the browbeating that had characterized many of her organization's earlier interactions with the locals, FCCA president Michelle Paige departed somewhat from her own combative style, taking on a persona that seemed more suited to a self-help guru or a presenter of late-night infomercials than a high-powered industry lobbyist. Phrases like "the winning edge" and "proactive collaboration" began to appear in FCCA promotional materials as Paige encouraged destinations to "proceed on the road to success"—a journey, presumably, that would end in a "win-win situation for all." In 1993, with government relations in shambles due to the rift with the CTO, Paige introduced an "Associate Member Programme" for port authorities, vendors and other members of the private sector. In 1998 she rolled out the FCCA's "Platinum Associate Member Programme," which conferred upon a lucky few the opportunity to attend "exclusive" luncheons and other events with senior cruise officials held several times a year, as well as VIP treatment at the annual conferences—the heart of it all, to hear the FCCA tell it, although participation arguably came at a price well beyond the reach of most small-business owners. Platinum membership was closed out at just sixty-six members. "Our conference," Paige announced, "is the yellow brick road that leads each delegate, through persistence and perseverance, to the opportunity to attain their goals and enjoy a more prosperous future."

If the tone was new, the message was not; "success" was a matter of doing well by making the cruise lines happy, of creating the imaginary world the lines were selling to their passengers back in the states. "Passengers visiting Caribbean destinations," Paige solemnly reminded prime ministers and community leaders, "are expecting to see a tropical paradise, one free of debris."

The FCCA reactivated its membership in the CTO in January of 1995, with Paige's begrudging acknowledgement that "If we don't work together, we will not be able to have a sufficient tourism product in the Caribbean." To complement the conferences and the increased focus on local purchasing—and perhaps in part to deflect attention away from a concerted lobbying effort to keep individual countries from implementing the unified tax that was still technically on the CARICOM books—the FCCA embarked on a series of charity programs ranging from hurricane relief to medical and educational grants to a Christmas toy drive. Through its Foundation for the Caribbean, the FCCA estimates that it has spent nearly $2 million on such gifts between 1995 and 2004. That number, figured generously, works out to the equivalent of about forty-four cents for each passenger that cruised the Caribbean in 2004. As befits such an effective lobbying group, these expenditures are carefully calculated to achieve maximum political effect—not unlike the voluntary guidelines the ICCL was simultaneously implementing to placate regulators in the U.S. One FCCA flagship program is the annual environmental poster competition for schoolchildren. Coordinated with local governments, the competition is based on the theme "The Nature of the Islands: Plants and Animals of the Caribbean." Winners in each age group receive scholarships ranging from one thousand to twenty-five hundred dollars; first-place winners are flown to Miami to accept their awards at the FCCA's annual gala. Making children, parents and local leaders all look good, the program generates goodwill worth many times its cost. Likewise, it's not hard to acknowledge the benefits that accrue by getting teachers around the region to encourage their students to submit an entry to the FCCA's annual children's essay contest, in which kids are asked to expound on such topics as "What Steps Can We Take As a Cruise Destination to Make Cruise Passengers Feel More Welcomed While in Port?"

Disney Cruise Line, with its expertise in marketing to children, used a variant of the poster competition to celebrate a new stop in the already over-crowded Cayman Islands, where on a busy day the number of cruise passengers rivals the entire population of Grand Cayman, its economic and cultural center. Conceived in part to ease local grumblings about the heavy passenger traffic, the theme of Disney's poster competition is "Mickey at My Favorite Tourism Attraction in Cayman," with the grand prize being a free cruise for a family of four and a special visit to the winner's school in which Mickey and the gang tell the assembled children about all the good things the cruise industry does for their parents. The 2002 winner was a beach scene featuring Mickey and Minnie, lovingly emblazoned with the words "DISNEY AND CAYMAN . . . MAKING DREAMS COME TRUE."

Behind the scenes, the arm-twisting continued, but the FCCA was working hard to keep the industry's public image burnished. Decisive as its victory over CARICOM had been, there was no sense in unnecessarily antagonizing the people of the islands. Pete Whelpton, who for decades was Royal Caribbean's hotel chief and an active member of various FCCA committees, has experienced both eras. "There are new politicians and people in the islands now that look at cruise ships, and some of them say, 'It isn't worth the aggravation,'" Whelpton says. "They say, 'The ship comes in, they dump three thousand or four thousand people on the island, they wear out our roads doing sightseeing, they don't pay anything for it. We have to fill in the potholes, we don't have the budget for it. What are we doing here?' That may explain why the FCCA has become a lovey, do-good organization—because they *have* to be."

Some Caribbean-driven initiatives did succeed in the years following CARICOM's disappointment in 1993. Perhaps most prominent among them was a $1.50 per person levy passed in 1998 by the OECS, proceeds from which fund a series of new waste disposal stations designed in part to handle cruise ship garbage. Although this tax applied to both land- and sea-based visitors, the FCCA resisted it fervently. This time it was Carnival threatening to pull its ships out if the tax was enacted, as NCL and Royal Caribbean sat it out. Once again, Paige insisted that cruise passengers already paid their "fair share" with their purchases and existing port charges: "They all contribute toward the development of the tourism product." With the land-based operators having already agreed to the fee without a fight, the cruise lines' opposition "was regarded as yet another example of their unwillingness to make a meaningful contribution to the development of Caribbean economies," in the words of one generally procruise trade journal. Locally, many of the criticisms that had been aired in 1993 resurfaced; Saint Vincent's prime minister accused the industry of "not behaving like good tourism industry partners." The FCCA once again played the divide-and-conquer game so well that some of the islands were on the brink of offering to pay the $1.50 themselves rather than risk losing ships; others were mulling over the possibility of once again agreeing to the levy in principle but without imposing a time frame.

The cruise lines backed down only when the World Bank got involved. Bank officials—who were Washington-based, connected and the kind of people you want to keep on your side if you do as much business on Capitol Hill as the cruise lines do—explained that the fee was a condition of the $54 million loan it had made to fund the waste disposal project and that the governments were obligated to collect it. With a genuine power player in the game and with FCCA members at the time facing major environment-related prosecutions by the U.S Justice Department, the industry beat a strategic retreat.

But a 2003 attempt by CARICOM to revisit the unified head tax—this time a proposed twenty dollars, and without World Bank participation—went nowhere. It was déjà vu all over again, to quote Yogi Berra. Once more, the initiative gathered momentum in the face of fierce FCCA opposition over a spring and summer, only to fail when it came to a vote that fall. This time, the weak link was Antigua, which not long before had spent $22 million on a new cruise pier. "Any decision we make must be consistent with that investment," its tourism minister announced in October. "We have looked at the situation and we are not convinced that the U.S. $20 levy is in the best interest of Antigua and Barbuda at this time." In one of the bitter little twists of fate that seem to dog Caribbean politics, it was now Barbados lamenting the group's inability to collectively withstand pressure from the industry. "I understand that some people may already be starting to break ranks," the Barbadian tourism minister said plaintively. "What we cannot have is a situation where we continue to have one destination being picked off against the other. . . . We must, in a formal setting, agree collectively and stick to our guns, whatever that decision may be."

In the political and social paradox that is the Caribbean, ten eventful years had seen great change—and none at all. For all the skirmishes, the region's nations remained at the mercy of the cruise industry, unable to sustain a strong, united front.

The situation was—and remains—a classic Catch-22. With the pressures of a globalized economy whittling away at the region's meager domestic agriculture and manufacturing sectors, tourism development was no longer just an major economic priority—it was the only source of growth. Once a small government invests in a major port project, it's on the hook. Financing for such projects is contingent on projected income from cruise passengers, and once there's debt to be serviced, that revenue quickly changes from a short-term opportunity into a long-term obligation. In 1998, for example, having undertaken a $14 million cruise terminal project, Saint Lucia saw the income from its $6.50 head tax add up to less than $2 million. But problematic as the cruise ships may be, no government in the region can afford to turn away the hard currency they provide. In every way, the local governments come to the table at a disadvantage.

The prime minister of the Bahamas summed the situation up in a 2002 address to fellow regional leaders. "While we rant and rave about what the cruise lines are and are not doing, they are busy deciding how to extract the maximum from the Caribbean for their shareholders and at the lowest possible cost," he said. "On the other hand, even though Carnival Cruise Lines competes with Royal Caribbean and Celebrity Cruises, each month and nearly every day they are spontaneously cooperating and coordinating their efforts through the FCCA. . . . There can be no reinvention of Caribbean tourism," he continued, "without our daily intent to cooperate."

This power imbalance has only become more pronounced as the Caribbean cruise industry has expanded at the same time the region has continued to founder. By 2003 Carnival's revenues alone were more than 8.5 times the combined government budgets of the nine members of the OECS, where the push for a unified tax had originated back in 1992. Carnival, Royal Caribbean and NCL today control nearly 90 percent of the North American cruise industry; more than half of the CARICOM nations' most vital economic sector is in the hands of just three Miami-based companies.

CHAPTER TWELVE

THE PRINCESS'S HAND

Never interrupt your enemy when he is making a mistake.

—Napoleon Bonaparte

Bedeviling as the scandals of the mid-1990s had been, they largely remained battlefield dilemmas for trusted deputies. What kept the CEOs awake at night in those days was strategy, not tactics. There were fewer and fewer of them left, and with the industry having arrived at a moment of profound uncertainty, success or failure seemed to hang on a single misstep.

At the dawn of the new millennium, only four companies—Carnival, Royal Caribbean, Princess and NCL—accounted for nearly 90 percent of the $13 billion North American cruise business. So extreme a concentration of power in such a young industry was testimony to the ambition, focus and ruthlessness of the handful of men who'd built it.

Analysts on Wall Street had all but worn out their vocal cords over the years praising the lightning-quick consolidation of the industry during the 1990s. They loved the process for its promise to "rationalize" the industry's pricing; with midtier operators and their older ships forced out of the market, the theory went, pricing would begin to rise to keep in line with the remaining cruise lines' more expensive land-based competitors, and profits would see a corresponding increase. The industry actively encouraged this line of thinking, but in the executive suites of the big four, there was a more pressing concern. Rational or not, the plain fact was that with the industry under the control of an ever-smaller handful of players, the balance of power at the top had never been more precarious.

Throughout the 1990s, cruise lines had grown in two ways: through the aggressive but relatively uniform introduction of new ships, and the wild card of expansion through mergers and acquisitions. The ships continued to come, but now there were no little deals left. Of the lesser lines that remained, many of the midtier players were failing, and the niche operators had little to offer the majors. None of the acquisitions that remained for the big four had the potential to fundamentally transform the competitive landscape. Carnival still dominated by a wide margin, but for the first time in nearly two decades its position was vulnerable; a merger between any of its rivals could knock it off the top slot. Likewise, the others knew that any hope of presenting an effective challenge to Carnival rested on just such a deal—and that only one more major acquisition by "Carnivore" Cruise Lines would in all likelihood forever deny them the opportunity to do so.

The die was cast on November 20, 2001, when Royal Caribbean and Princess announced an agreement to combine their two operations in a deal valued at a little over $3 billion. From the moment the news broke, all eyes were on Carnival, eager to see how Micky Arison would respond. The proposed transaction was barbed with defenses to keep Carnival from forcing its way in, and was to all appearances bulletproof. But then, nothing's ever completely bulletproof.

Richard Fain, though he'd shepherded Royal Caribbean from a well-liked but inefficient, debt-ridden enterprise into a strong second-place position during his tenure as CEO, had never really gotten credit for his accomplishment. Even after all these years, many in Miami still thought of him as an outsider. For all his faults, Micky was regarded as someone who walked on water, but Fain's legacy within the industry continued to be overshadowed by what many saw as a series of strategic and managerial blunders during the mid-1990s. His greatest victory, the hotly contested 1996 acquisition of Celebrity Cruises, had failed to raise his stature; Fain had intended Celebrity to be his inroad to Europe, but the brand had strained under the pressures of corporate infighting while Costa—the deal Fain had walked away from—had sailed on to unprecedented success under the Carnival Corporation umbrella. A successful merger with Princess would put the company in a stronger position than anyone had ever imagined, and would be the ultimate vindication of Fain's leadership.

Micky, for his part, had everything to lose. Since his father started Carnival in 1972, he'd gone from living the life of a slacker scion to corporate princedom, and finally he had become an emperor. It was Micky who'd led

Carnival to its greatest successes, but he had never let himself forget that Ted had left him with all the tools; Carnival may have outpaced Royal Caribbean, but Micky had started with a Formula 1 racer while Fain had inherited an aging Cadillac in need of a tune-up. Micky, whose competitiveness had only grown with success, despised the press accounts that often cast him as a street-fighting college dropout locking horns with Royal Caribbean's sophisticated chairman. And yet here they were again. Suddenly he was facing the prospect not only of being overtaken by a man he didn't believe to be his equal, but—unthinkably—of being forced into second place for the first time since he'd begun taking his inheritance seriously so many years ago.

If the story of the cruise industry from the late 1980s onward is the story of its leaders' intense and often heated contention in the Dodge City business environment of waterfront Miami, the Princess acquisition was set to play out as the High Noon shootout, the showdown without which no true Western can end.

The ultimate outcome of the contest, however, would turn not on Micky's and Fain's decisions, but on those of Princess's CEO, Peter Ratcliffe, who would cunningly play the two suitors against each other.

Like the company he ran, Ratcliffe had entered the new millennium in something of a queer position. He was an Englishman who'd embraced the American style of doing business, a numbers man with an eye for grand strategy, a key player in the cruise business for more than twenty years who nonetheless kept himself firmly planted outside the sometimes incestuous culture of the Miami industry, dividing his time between London and Los Angeles. He was, above all, an outwardly modest man who colleagues say nevertheless held a near-infinite regard for his own intelligence.

Ratcliffe had been running Princess since 1993 but had enjoyed the independence of CEO status for scarcely a year when he and Fain announced their deal that November. Prior to 2000 Princess had been a subsidiary of the storied UK conglomerate P&O, an icon of Britannia in its day and one of the last of the great old passenger lines, a company with a pedigree dating back to 1840, which "once helped bind together the British Empire." The P&O of the mid-1990s remained a broad and formidable operation, with interests in container shipping, port operations, oil field operations, construction and ferries, along with its cruise arm and other ventures. At its head was Lord Geoffrey Sterling, a towering figure in Britain's contemporary business world. Sterling had elevated himself from modest origins on the tough streets of London's East End to the very pinnacle of British society. Among other honors, he served as chairman of the committee to organize Queen Elizabeth II's Golden Jubilee celebration. As the new century began, Lord Sterling was on his way to gracefully ending a legendary career.

Like the empire that spawned it, P&O's interests had, if anything, grown too broad with the passage of time. Princess, having been under the P&O umbrella since 1974, was feeling stifled in the sprawl—and understandably so. The industry had never seen a more promising brand than Princess Cruises, thanks to *The Love Boat*'s unexpected success on the American airwaves in the late 1970s. The marketing potential of that moment remains unparalleled. It was the infomercial of all infomercials, except that it reached a much wider audience and was subject to none of the truth-in-advertising restrictions. The company could have gone anywhere.

And Princess had done well by most standards, sliding into a strong third-place slot in the 1980s and holding it ever since. Steadily, as some competitors fell away and others exploded into wild success, the company's British ownership had fed its expansion. Being part of a major corporate structure had its advantages—especially at a time when the industry's potential was still unknown, and the public markets showed little interest in providing the massive amounts of capital required to grow a successful cruise business. But it also served as a brake on the wild outlays that had propelled lines like Carnival and Royal Caribbean to the top of the heap. "The problem with Princess was that we were the subsidiary of a British company, and the business over here had the potential to far exceed the size of our holding company," remembers Ratcliffe, who first came to Princess in 1986 as CFO. "We were always limited by how fast we could expand as an independent company. And we tended to expand more slowly than our competitors at the time."

As a result, Princess had for the most part sat out the tempestuous mergers of the 1990s, and it's a testament to the strength of the brand that it managed to maintain its third-place position even without the acquisitions that fueled so much of the growth at Carnival, Royal Caribbean and NCL. Yet there was no escaping the feeling that Princess could have been so much more. "If we had been independent back in 1989 and we had been a public company, we'd have just expanded like mad," Ratcliffe remembers. "We were always bigger than we were able to be."

Ratcliffe sometimes wondered whether he was looking at the same world as everyone around him. Periodically during the expansion of the 1980s and 1990s, the business press would take notice of the growing cruise sector, and articles profiling the cruise lines would show up on the pages of *Forbes, BusinessWeek* or elsewhere. Puzzlingly, it was as often as not the same gloomy story. Year after year, the same publications chimed in with stories of the glut of new ships being turned out by the shipyards of Europe and waxed pessimistic on the cruise market's supposedly imminent implosion due to an overcapacity threat. It was almost as if the reporters hadn't bothered to check the archive before they began writing. Year after year the ships sailed full, and the lines that weren't swallowed up or driven out of business posted record profits. Ratcliffe, who saw Princess as being "brand-heavy and capacity-light," read these dirges as the years went by and—in his careful, cultured, British way—seethed with frustration at the sheer irony of it all.

It was Ratcliffe's good fortune—and Princess's—that by the late 1990s the times were changing to favor nimbler businesses. Following a string of difficult years, Sterling was taking P&O in a new direction. In early 1999 he announced a new strategy to sell off the conglomerate's noncore assets, shrinking its size considerably but giving it a new clarity of financial and strategic purpose. The plan had initially been to focus the company around the so-called jewels among its holdings: its port and container operations, its ferries and the cruise business. But as things developed Ratcliffe saw the opportunity for something he'd spent years hoping for: an independent Princess Cruises. And he got his wish. By autumn 2000 P&O's cruise operations—Princess, along with a number of smaller lines servicing the European market—had been spun off as a separate company to be traded on the London Stock Exchange under the name P&O Princess Cruises. In the European style, Sterling was to serve as non-executive chairman. Ratcliffe would go on running the line, now as CEO. The cruise operation by this time represented fully half of the conglomerate's value.

The move instantaneously injected a radical new element of unpredictability into the industry. Conventional wisdom had it that all the major deals had been done—that, from a merger and acquisition standpoint, the industry was settled and mature. Although lines like Carnival and Royal Caribbean had traded publicly for years and were theoretically vulnerable to a takeover, their ownership structure meant that they operated in an essentially hybrid form. In a strategic sense, public life had offered the best of both worlds to the big cruise lines. Being listed gave them access to vast amounts of new capital even as the continued concentration of large blocks of stock in the hands of a small number of shareholders with close ties to management—often a few families, and in Carnival's case, the CEO himself—made hostile takeovers and shareholder revolts a practical impossibility.

All that changed with the Princess demerger. The largest shareholder in the new $3.6 billion company barely held a 4 percent stake. "Suddenly, overnight, there was a company that was 100 percent owned by public shareholders," Ratcliffe remembers. "And that changed the landscape, because it meant you didn't have to meet and negotiate—you could put in a bid."

Someone would be coming; in a cash-rich industry where market share topped the list of competitive priorities, Ratcliffe could be sure of that. The only questions were who, how, when—and just how much they'd be willing to pay. It was a moment of dangerous opportunity. Almost immediately, Ratcliffe set about looking at ways to control the situation.

The first step was to hire bankers to assemble a reliable assessment of where things stood—an assessment based on numbers, not just gut instinct. Ratcliffe had two main criteria for selecting his advisers: he wanted Americans, who would understand the competition's thinking, and he wanted bankers that hadn't worked for Sterling and P&O, who would see the company through the lens of his vision alone.

Throughout the spring, the bankers analyzed every aspect of the competition's businesses, while a team of lawyers pored through European and American antitrust rules. Certain complications presented themselves almost immediately—and not always from the outside. For one thing, a good number of Princess's shares were held by pension funds and other institutional investors in the UK that were restricted by law or their own policies from holding stock in non-British companies. A merger with any of the other leading cruise lines would likely force them to sell their stock immediately, a problematic outcome for two reasons. First, it excluded the company's existing shareholders—Ratcliffe's bosses, strictly speaking—from the future benefits of any merger. Most good mergers are predicated on a belief that the combined value of the companies involved will be significantly greater than what the two are worth separately. A stockholder in such a situation has two choices: she can sell out as the stock rises in anticipation of the merger or hold on to her investment in the expectation of participating in the new company's success. If the transaction is a good one, and the investor has time to wait, the second option generally pays off better. If a non-British line were to acquire Princess outright, a majority of the shareholders would be left with no option but to sell immediately—and that in turn had consequences for the new company. Even if Ratcliffe was able to sell Princess at a price high enough to win approval from his British shareholders, their ensuing rush to sell would likely push the stock down to such an extent as to negate the boost from the merger itself. For this problem and others, creative solutions would have to be found.

Secret talks with Star Cruises, the Malaysian company that had controlled NCL since outmaneuvering Carnival in its hostile bid in early 2000, went nowhere. That left three serious options—four, if you included continuing on as an independent company: "a merger of equals" with Royal Caribbean, a takeover by Carnival, or an auction between the two. All things being equal, the last was the most desirable from the standpoint of Ratcliffe's shareholders. However, an auction would require having both Carnival and Royal Caribbean as active participants in the bidding, and that was structurally problematic; as Carnival's far stronger balance sheet left little doubt about the likely outcome of any open bidding contest, Royal Caribbean had little incentive to enter into a fight it was almost sure to lose.

Approaching Carnival directly wasn't a much better option. Sterling and Micky had actually engaged in talks not long before the demerger; they'd ended badly. Knowing Sterling did not want to part with one of P&O's most important assets, Carnival had approached him in the summer of 1999 with a bold proposal: along with a syndicate of investors, it would buy P&O outright. The cruise operation would go to Carnival, and the rest of the venerable firm—"the rump," as the Carnival team called it internally—would go to the other partners or be sold off. Carnival had come in with what P&O regarded as a lowball offer of $7 billion, but Sterling was uninterested in selling, in any event. The confidential meetings, although not terribly productive, had been cordial enough—until their details started showing up in the newspapers. The information was attributed to anonymous sources, but most pegged Carnival for the leak. "That publicity really antagonized the Princess people," remembers one person close to the later Princess deal. "They saw the publicity—I think quite rightly—as an attempt by Carnival to pressure them into negotiation." If that had been Carnival's intention, it was not a success. The talks had fizzled for good; P&O would not even acknowledge that they had taken place. All in all, the experience had hardly laid a solid foundation for P&O Princess, three years later, to risk entrusting its future to Carnival's discretion and largesse.

Though Carnival's $3.3 billion war chest gave it the resources to pay more by far than anyone else on the horizon, Micky's company was still famous for never parting with an unnecessary dollar. Without someone else in the picture to force Micky to participate, it was hard to imagine Ratcliffe cutting a deal that would satisfy his shareholders. "You were never going to get Carnival, with Micky's history and his reputation, to pay full price by approaching Micky and saying we were for sale," remembers one Princess adviser. The industry had been treated to a refresher course in Carnival's tactics not long after the talks with P&O broke down in 1999, when Micky had made a hostile bid for NCL. Star, which would ultimately win the day, had come in very aggressively, and in the end Carnival had teamed up with them to do the takeover as a joint venture rather than see the price of NCL's shares continue to rise. The episode hardly ranked as a success for Micky—Carnival unhappily sold its stake to Star only a few months later—but it served as a reminder of the dangers involved in bringing Carnival into a situation you couldn't control.

Finally, it was unclear whether a Carnival merger was even possible. Although the extent of the industry's consolidation meant there would be antitrust concerns surrounding any deal between the majors, competition issues were especially touchy when it came to Carnival, already so far ahead in terms of market share. Whether authorities in Europe and in the United States would accept a merger that not only reduced the industry to three major players but left fully half of it in the hands of its top company was a long shot at best.

On the other hand, there was much to recommend a deal with Royal Caribbean.

For one thing, a combined Royal Caribbean–Princess entity would vault past Carnival to become the largest cruise company in the world—"Carnival Mark II," as Princess's advisers called it. That kind of size promised to open up synergies and competitive advantages on a scale that the two individual companies in the shadow of an industry leader could only dream of.

That notion alone seemed sufficient to guarantee that Royal Caribbean would bring its best price to the table, even without another party in the mix to bid them up. And if the positives weren't enough to compel a deal that satisfied Ratcliffe, the implied alternative of a Carnival-Princess entity so vast as to consign Royal Caribbean to a distant and permanent second place spoke for itself.

Even leaving Carnival out of the equation, there were compelling reasons for both Royal Caribbean and Princess to consider joining forces. On the financial side, Royal Caribbean's heavily leveraged balance sheet would combine with Princess's comparatively conservative debt load—much of it left behind at P&O in the spin-off—to instantly create a stable yet still aggressively financed company that was all but immune to takeover. Such a combination effectively offered Princess the benefit of all the chances Ratcliffe had never had the opportunity to take.

Of course, consummating a deal with Royal Caribbean wasn't without potential pitfalls. Celebrity's painful integration into Royal Caribbean had become one of the industry's favorite cautionary tales. That episode had unfolded the way it did in large part due to power struggles between Royal Caribbean president Jack Williams and the Celebrity management; it had taken several years for Williams to clean house fully, and the Princess demerger had occurred just as he'd consolidated his control over Celebrity. Ratcliffe—who had no intention of leaving his company at the threshold of its most exciting moment—knew that any deal with Royal Caribbean would mean a showdown with Williams. "It was very obvious that Ratcliffe and Jack weren't going to get along, long-term," remembers one key person on the Princess side. "They just operate their businesses differently. Peter listens to his people and tries to hear all the points of view before making a decision, and he views Jack much more as a hammer-and-tongs kind of guy." And ultimately, of course, there was the question of Richard Fain himself; neither he nor Ratcliffe was accustomed to taking orders.

Although Ratcliffe weighed the political dimensions carefully, he arrived again and again at the same conclusion. "From a personal viewpoint, Carnival was always going to be easier," Ratcliffe remembers thinking. "Royal

Caribbean was more volatile. If Carnival had bought Princess, I always knew Princess would just slot into Carnival much the same way Holland America did. It would have been a very simple bringing together in all the things we'd done—you could easily predict that at the time. A merger with Royal Caribbean wasn't quite as easy to put in place or to implement," he said. But it was doable—and likely at a price Ratcliffe's shareholders could live with. And Princess was in a far stronger position than Celebrity had ever been; a Royal Caribbean deal would be a genuine merger, not a buyout.

The only catch with Royal Caribbean was getting Fain to the table. There was no way Fain would commit himself without measures in place to prevent Carnival from stealing or sabotaging the deal—and flexibility was Ratcliffe's most important asset. Even here, though, Ratcliffe felt he held the advantage. Deal protection measures, commonly known as "poison pills," are commonplace in the United States, where they've evolved in response to the rampant corporate raiding of the 1970s and 1980s. Today, an entire subset of lawyers and investment bankers specializes in developing mechanisms to guard deals and companies from unwanted suitors: clauses allowing shareholders to buy newly issued stock at deep discounts in the event of a hostile takeover attempt, for example, or stratospheric breakup fees designed to deter outside bidders on a transaction. But Princess was a British company, and things are done differently on that side of the Atlantic. In the UK, such measures are seen as counter to the shareholders' right to seek the highest price possible for their investment and are clearly forbidden by the Takeover Panel, Britain's equivalent of the SEC. Even breakup fees are limited to 1 percent of the deal's total value. For Fain to make a deal, he'd have to leave the door open for Carnival, whatever the terms. The question was, would he want the deal badly enough to risk it? Ratcliffe had little to lose by finding out.

It was May of 2001. He picked up his phone to call Miami.

As expected, Fain was skeptical. He could read the dynamics of the situation as well as anyone, and the last thing he wanted was to be used as a stalking horse for Princess to squeeze a higher price out of Carnival. Still, the allure was unquestionable. Royal Caribbean was itself at something of a crossroads. The company had expanded at an incredible rate since Fain took over in 1988; its fleet was now at eighteen ships, neck-and-neck with Princess and Carnival Cruise Lines, if not the combined holdings of Carnival Corporation. In the run-up to the industry's most perilous decade, he had inherited a company with a great brand but a flawed business model and had not only held the line against formidable rivals but had managed to keep the company independent at the same time. The price of autonomy, however, was massive debt: $5.4 billion worth.

Royal Caribbean was no stranger to aggressive financing; after fending off Carnival in 1988, the company had been leveraged to an astonishing 75 percent of its value. Improved performance and an IPO in 1993 had helped to pay that down, but the costs of expansion had kept the company perilously close to the edge of insolvency. A healthy amount of debt can be a good thing for a company, especially a growing one; gains made on borrowed money actually represent more of a profit than those made on equity alone. As the financial markets surged throughout the 1990s, Royal Caribbean's debt was its engine. But many were now openly questioning whether the company hadn't gone too far; the investment houses had recently given Fain's bonds a "junk" rating, which meant that the envelope had been effectively pushed as far as it could go. A merger with Princess would be the ultimate payoff for Royal Caribbean's financial gambles; just as it would allow Ratcliffe the benefit of the risks he'd never been able to take, it would provide Fain with the stability he'd never sat still long enough to achieve. If he could make it happen, he'd have a new company that had ridden its debt through a remarkable wave of expansion and then squared its accounts in one fell swoop just before the risks got out of hand.

The prospect of a Princess merger, furthermore, would have been irresistible even if Royal Caribbean hadn't had a cent in debt. Among the disappointments of the Celebrity merger was the fact that, five years later, Royal remained overwhelmingly a North American–oriented company; the appeal of breaking into Europe alone was still enough to justify a major gamble. But Fain would have to proceed carefully. There was Carnival to worry about, and his own coffers at the time were far from limitless. "I certainly tried to demonstrate a lack of eagerness," Fain remembers of that first telephone call. "I said, 'Well, I'll have to talk to our board and see if it's worth talking about.'" The jockeying for position had already begun.

In fact, the board was concerned—about the Carnival factor, first and foremost. Invoking another surprise attack, Fain himself remarked that he might be "awakening a sleeping giant." But as always he was adept at managing his directors, and the potential benefits of a successful deal spoke for themselves. "It gave us both scale and a European presence—and it gave us a brand," remembers Tom Pritzker, perhaps Royal Caribbean's most influential board member. "We were having a harder time than expected in promoting the Celebrity brand, and perhaps Princess could have helped us fill out the line of brands that we wanted to have." Fain and his team further assured the board that there would be no deal without protective measures, and reiterated his attorneys' strong opinion that a Carnival bid would never make it through the antitrust process. Fain also played on a deep-seated feeling that had permeated the company since 1988: that Royal Caribbean was fundamentally a more honorable company than Carnival, and that the P&O Princess management would recognize and value that distinction. "Great comfort was taken," remembers another director, "from the fact that both Sterling and Ratcliffe were more comfortable dealing with RCCL than with Carnival." The board gave its unanimous approval, and battened down for the coming storm. "We recognized that Carnival surely would come and look, and make very significant efforts in trying to do the deal," Pritzker recalls. "We felt we had maximized the likelihood of it going to us, and we ran that risk."

Fain got back to Ratcliffe in late summer to arrange a time when they could start negotiations. They agreed to meet as soon as possible in Miami for further discussions—at Fain's home rather than at the Royal Caribbean offices, the better to ensure the secrecy they both deemed crucial.

The first time they could both make it was on a Tuesday—September 11, 2001. They settled on a nine A.M. meeting.

Obviously, that session didn't go as intended. As the Princess team was preparing to head over to Fain's that morning, one of them took an urgent call from London. Like the rest of the world, the group spent the next few hours sitting aghast in front of a television; Ratcliffe's New York–based financial advisers—their offices mere blocks from the World Trade Center—frantically worked the phone for news of friends, colleagues and family. Dealmaking, for once, was the furthest thing from their minds.

With little else to do as the day wound on, the group ended up making the trip to Fain's house after lunch, but little real work was done. Much of the afternoon was spent on conference calls with other industry leaders discussing how best to respond to the terrorist attacks. Much later, Micky

Arison would chuckle in disbelief upon learning that Ratcliffe and Fain had both been speaking to him from adjoining rooms in Fain's house.

With commercial air traffic grounded over the next few days, the two negotiating teams had the makings of a merger by the end of the week. It was an odd time to be negotiating a deal. Fain remembers meeting Ratcliffe one of those evenings for dinner at a fashionable downtown restaurant; still mindful of the need for discretion, he'd asked for a quiet table near the back. The two of them turned out to be just about the only diners there.

But it wasn't just the isolation that moved the talks along; the events of September 11 had reinforced Ratcliffe's concerns about P&O Princess's vulnerabilities as a stand-alone company, and they'd lit a fire under Fain. Royal Caribbean was simply not positioned to weather hard times, and it was very much looking like hard times were on the way. The attacks threatened to be devastating for the cruise industry. Everyone was expecting an aftermath of recession, fear of travel and a war. This was the context in which the transaction took shape, and with the markets taking a dimmer view of Royal Caribbean's debt burden than ever, the deal began to look even better for Princess: although Fain would be chairman and CEO of the new entity, with Ratcliffe under him as president and COO, the value propositions had changed considerably. Princess, the smaller company by a significant margin, was actually going to hold a slight majority—50.7 percent—of the merged entity's value.

Yet each side had a sticking point. Fain still needed some form of protection against Carnival before he would even consider going ahead; that hadn't changed. And the dilemma Ratcliffe faced with his British shareholders had if anything grown more acute with the markets in a post–September 11 tailspin: if he pursued a deal that forced his shareholders to sell now, he'd in effect be asking them to lock in their losses.

Remarkably, they found a solution that appeared to solve both dilemmas at once.

Rather than execute a typical merger—a transaction in which one company takes over ownership of the other's stock—they made the unorthodox decision to join Royal Caribbean and Princess together to create what was known as a "dual listed company." According to the arcane arrangement, the two companies would merge while remaining technically independent. Princess stock would still trade in London, Royal Caribbean stock on the Big

Board in New York—but their respective cash flow, management, voting rights of their shareholders and the rest would be bound together by a series of legal mechanisms so that the two functioned as a single entity—each governed by a separate and identical board of directors. It was a radical idea, but not a new one; DLCs have actually existed for nearly a century. The structure was pioneered in 1907 by a pair of oil companies, one British and one Dutch, in order to compete together against John D. Rockefeller's behemoth Standard Oil without losing their national identities—not, in fact, so different a situation from the one Ratcliffe and Fain were facing. The result was Royal Dutch Shell.

DLCs had begun appearing more often during the internationalist 1990s, although not generally as a merger device. Several Israeli technology firms, for example, had used the structure to issue secondary listings of their shares in London after deciding the Tel Aviv Stock Exchange was too small for their needs. But as of autumn 2001 there had never been a DLC merger between an American and a British company; most merger and acquisitions people hadn't even heard of them. Even Fain, the Wharton MBA who prided himself on being one of the most intellectual executives in the industry, was aware of the possibility "only in the vaguest, vaguest of ways."

Once he understood the structure, however, Fain quickly saw how brilliant a solution it was for all concerned. Since Princess would technically remain a British company, Ratcliffe's shareholders could sell or not as they saw fit. More important, from Fain's perspective, a DLC transaction would fall outside the strictly defined jurisdiction of the UK Takeover Panel; because no shares changed hands, it technically wasn't a merger. Legally speaking, he could pile on all the deal protection he wanted and the British authorities couldn't do a thing about it.

If Ratcliffe still harbored any doubts about the feasibility of going directly to Carnival, they'd been put to rest in late September when Carnival's vice chairman Howard Frank—oblivious to what were by now advanced discussions between Ratcliffe and Fain—had called him to discuss the possibility of a deal on the single lowest trading day for Princess stock since the company had been spun off. Frank maintains that it was a coincidence, but for Ratcliffe the timing told the whole story: getting what the company was worth from Carnival without another bidder in the equation was simply not going to happen. He politely rebuffed Frank and returned to the negotiating table with Fain.

By now they were very close. Ratcliffe would get his DLC, and in return he would—reluctantly—give Fain his deal protection. The lawyers had advised both sides that while the DLC loophole afforded considerably more leeway in this regard than the parties would have otherwise enjoyed, the British authorities would still not stand for an unequivocal poison pill. It was simply too . . . American. For the deal to be deliverable—and for the Princess board to sign off on it—they would have to find a way to satisfy both Fain's and Princess's lawyers, which meant constructing "a hurdle, not a barrier," as they spoke of it at the time.

The end result would later become known in countless press releases and angry letters back and forth across the Atlantic as "The Southern European Joint Venture." Although not technically a poison pill, it was nonetheless a powerful deal protection mechanism—a contract that made no commercial sense except as a deterrent to Carnival. Like the DLC itself, it was a complex implementation of an elegantly simple concept. In addition to the merger agreement, the two companies agreed to invest $500 million each in a start-up cruise line for the Mediterranean market, where Carnival had a dominant presence in its Costa subsidiary and Royal Caribbean and Princess were both weak. In fact, the money was more a deposit than anything else; the agreement stipulated that if Carnival gained control of Princess within a specified time frame, the entire joint venture would go to Royal Caribbean—in essence, it was a $500 million kill fee.

Ratcliffe, wanting to keep his options open, had consistently argued against the poison pill, and his team had put off negotiating the point in detail. "He felt that it would reduce the management's credibility," Fain remembers. "And he argued, therefore, that ironically the deal protection would actually make the deal harder to consummate than easier." Although it may have been technically legal, he told Fain again and again, it was clearly skirting the line. And in any case, it was likely to anger P&O Princess stockholders to the point where it might even backfire on them. But Fain knew from experience that Carnival would be coming as soon as the news was out—and that the onslaught would be ferocious. Finally, at a meeting in the London offices of Princess's investment bankers, Fain put his foot down. "It's time to deal with this," he'd said. "If we can't deal with it, we might as well stop talking."

Ratcliffe conceded the point but continued to haggle with Fain over the length of the joint venture's penalty phase. Finally, they agreed that, as long as the venture hadn't reached certain performance benchmarks by January 1, 2003, either party could walk away without incurring any costs. Responsibility for managing the joint venture—and, in effect, for determining whether or not those benchmarks were met—was to be solely in Princess's hands. Ratcliffe also agreed to clauses barring him from entering into discussions with Carnival or anyone else without a firm offer that was both "financially superior" to Royal Caribbean's and "deliverable" from a regulatory standpoint. The deliverability requirement in particular was strong protection; given Carnival's market position, that was a determination that could only be made at the end of a months-long antitrust process in Europe and the United States—long after Princess's shareholders had already voted on the Royal Caribbean deal.

In order for Micky to take the company away from Fain, therefore, he'd either have to absorb the stratospheric costs of the poison pill or somehow offer a binding, one-year option on a price high enough to persuade Princess's shareholders to risk voting down a guaranteed Royal Caribbean merger in favor of a deal that at best faced serious regulatory challenges. Not only that, but he'd have to do it without help from Princess's management and at a time of unprecedented economic uncertainty worldwide.

Still, it was a leap of faith on Fain's part. The expiration date was a little earlier than he would have liked; more important, much of the agreement's strength would depend on Ratcliffe's good-faith efforts to meet those benchmarks. It wasn't bulletproof, but it was the best Fain was going to get. In the end, he gambled on Ratcliffe's intentions. "Once Princess accepted the idea of the deal protection and of the joint venture, I specifically asked whether they were prepared to stand by it and embrace it," he remembers. "And they assured me that they would."

Ratcliffe, however, seems to have been thinking along decidedly different lines—just how different, Fain would discover firsthand during the coming months. Ratcliffe's recollection of these days suggests that he did not share Fain's regard for the strength of the poison pill—that so far as he was concerned, he'd merely postponed the conversation with Carnival's Howard Frank, not precluded it. "My analysis," he remembers, "was, why would I talk to Frank at this time? Because the share price was at an all-time low, I have a potential deal with Royal Caribbean which doesn't close off any future options—so why is it in my interest to talk to him?"

Just over two months had passed since the September 11 meeting at Fain's house, and all that remained now was to get through the legal niceties as quickly and as quietly as possible. In the days leading up to the announcement, the tension had become almost unbearable. A leak would bring Carnival charging in, potentially destroying the $3 billion deal before it had begun. Everything depended on discretion, and with the help of sleeplessness and fatigue, caution began turning into paranoia. The weekend before the merger was to be announced, a member of the deal team tuned in to the Miami Heat game, likely savoring the mental image of Micky's working himself into a courtside competitive frenzy. As the camera panned the spectators, the banker felt his stomach drop: Micky wasn't in his seat. In fact, he was at another basketball game in Hawaii, where his son was managing his college team. But in the conference room in London, the negotiators panicked. "We thought for sure they knew," one of them remembers. "It really caused us, in the final two days, just to go twenty-four hours a day straight to get it done and announced."

Last-minute details kept cropping up, and Sunday evening drew to a close still without a final deal. Then Monday morning, then Monday night. Midnight rolled past with the announcement set for Tuesday morning, and only a number of small loose ends were left to resolve. An exhausted Ratcliffe—keenly aware that a few short hours were all that lay between him and the fight of his life—decided to go home and get some rest. He gave his encouragements and said his good-byes. At the last minute, his thoughts turned back to Fain's poison pill, as they had hundreds of times before. Its disposition would be the key to everything. Before leaving, Ratcliffe pulled his head lawyer aside. "There's only one thing you have to remember," he said. *"This must terminate on the first of January."*

And then he was gone.

From London that Tuesday morning, the news hurtled west across the Atlantic like a hurricane.

At Carnival, the first to get the news was Ken Dubbin, the longtime Royal Caribbean treasurer who'd defected to the Carnival camp in 1999, in large part to help work on the then-promising attempt to buy out P&O. The call came to his house at six a.m., from an investment banker in New York. "It's a done deal," the frustrated voice on the line said. The banker explained the DLC structure—a concept new to everyone at Carnival—and the poison pill, expressed his shock at the turn of events and then signed off, wishing Dubbin good luck in a tone better suited to condolences than to a pep talk. Dubbin immediately called Howard Frank, who listened in disbelief and then got on the phone to Micky, still lingering in Hawaii. By the time Frank got through relaying the details, the adrenaline was coursing through his veins. "We're going," he told his boss excitedly. But Micky, stunned by what he was hearing, was not so sure. His lawyers had already concluded that any deal with Princess would likely face prohibitive antitrust difficulties; it was one of the reasons he hadn't made a play himself. And he'd never even *heard* of a DLC. "Let's think about it," he said. No one knew Micky better than Frank, who could hear the pessimism as clearly as if it had been spoken aloud, but this was one deal on which he wasn't about to step aside. "Okay," he told his boss. "But I'm not going to be able to sleep tonight. I can't. We're going to go for it."

By the time Micky made it back to the Miami offices, his people had been working feverishly for hours to put together a briefing. Bankers on both sides of the Atlantic, visions of huge fees dancing in their heads, had been scrambling to find any lead that might shed light on the situation. An initial picture was emerging, and it didn't look good.

The cost of the poison pill was shaping up to be every bit as prohibitive as Fain had intended. Micky's lieutenants, almost to a person, were in favor of taking an aggressive posture. But then again, they could afford to be. Micky, who owned nearly half of Carnival's equity, had to look at it from a different perspective. "Clearly those decisions were hard because of the family position in the company," he remembers. "Managements that operate under an environment where they either don't own the company or own equity in the company, or own stock options in the company, have a very different view of risk than someone like me, who downside is important to." A worst-case scenario—a bid triggering the poison pill, followed by a major terrorist attack on a cruise ship, for example—could potentially wipe out the better part of the Arison family fortune.

But even that concern was getting several steps ahead: it was far from obvious that P&O Princess could be won by a hostile takeover at all. Micky's last set of talks with Sterling had ended with a direct warning. "Don't go hostile on me," Sterling had said, and Micky had promised that he wouldn't. All the same, Carnival had examined the scenario several times since the demerger and come away with the same conclusion as everyone else: even if Carnival could clear the antitrust hurdle in Europe, which was doubtful, Sterling's stature in the UK business world was going to be too much to overcome. "The parameters of that—especially at the point where we didn't have the information; especially about the poison pill—seemed overwhelming," Micky recalls. "Our bankers were telling us that you're *never* going to do a hostile over a British chairman."

The one thing Carnival had going for it at this point was its own special brand of arrogance: the complete, passionate inability of Micky and his people to believe that any rational party with an option to join forces with Carnival might choose to be part of another organization. "We always felt that we had a better relationship with their management than Royal Caribbean," Micky remembers, "so we always felt—wrongly—that we'd have an inside track at the point that they'd be willing to do something." Frank's take on the situation was blunter. "There's no way," he declared, "that those two cultures can work together."

Ironically, the sentiment was not unlike the sense of moral superiority that had emboldened the Royal Caribbean board. Both sides had failed to grasp just how different this situation was from any they'd faced before. Micky and Fain's deal-making experience had primarily involved companies controlled by either a single owner or a small group of shareholders; in that kind of environment, victory and defeat had often turned on personalities and relationships. But P&O Princess's ownership was radically diffuse and made up of investors who cared about the numbers and nothing else. Ratcliffe's power to influence a vote could only go so far.

As he learned more about the terms of the transaction, however, Micky began to see an opportunity in the poison pill. To the extent that it made acquiring P&O Princess prohibitively expensive, it also meant that he could not possibly be expected to make a firm bid from his position. He was free to shake the trees and see what fell out. Moreover, there was evidence that a Carnival offer might be well received. Ratcliffe's fears about shareholder reaction to the deal protection were proving prescient. Many were offended and alarmed at what they saw as an end run around their rights and responsibilities; some were already threatening to approach the Takeover Panel to intervene. The press was having a field day. The *Financial Times* wrote that "the pill sets an appalling precedent" and complained that P&O Princess was "importing the worst U.S. cowboy bid tactics."

One thing was clear: between the transatlantic DLC structure, the controversial poison pill and the high profile of the industry, the deal would have garnered a certain amount of attention in any environment. But coming as it did at a time when the dot-com bust and September 11 attacks had slowed the rate of mergers to a crawl and left the financial press desperate for a good story, it promised to be one hell of a media circus, and whoever was in the center ring was going to be feeling a lot of pressure. Perhaps that was something Micky could exploit. At the very least, Micky felt, Sterling's failure to attempt a deal with Carnival had released him from his promise not to go hostile.

There was little to be lost, then, by floating a conditional offer. If nothing else, it would help determine the lay of the land.

On December 13 Micky sent a letter to the Princess board outlining a proposition. "We were surprised to see the announcement of the Royal Caribbean proposal," he wrote. "We have decided that, in the circumstances, we should write this letter to the board of P&O Princess to seek to ensure that our proposal receives the attention we believe it deserves."

The letter suggested that Carnival was willing to offer a combination of cash and shares worth 450 pence per Princess share—$4.6 billion, or 44 percent over what the stock had been trading at on the day before Princess and Royal Caribbean announced. Any firm deal, however, would be conditional on clearing antitrust in Europe and the United States, full cooperation from Princess management, and written guarantees that the cost of the poison pill would not exceed $200 million. Micky gave Sterling and Ratcliffe three days to consider the offer before he made it public.

They issued their response right on time: a flat rejection. Carnival's offer, Ratcliffe said, didn't even approach the point at which he'd consider opening talks. Furthermore, the offer was layered in preconditions and didn't even address the possibility or the implications of the DLC structure that was so important to the majority of Princess's shareholders.

Fain was riding in a taxicab when he got the news; jubilant, he called Ratcliffe's pager service and asked to send a text message—"450p? He really is a cheap bastard, isn't he!"—only to be informed that "bastard" was on a list of profanities the service did not permit. Mildly annoyed, he rephrased his message and rode on, picturing the victory ahead.

Three days later, the Princess board announced that it had scheduled an "extraordinary general meeting" on February 14 of the following year to vote on the deal and gave Carnival until January 18 to submit an improved offer for their consideration, if it so desired. The statement was hardly welcoming; it contained the first of what would be many suggestions that Carnival had entered simply as a spoiler and warned P&O Princess shareholders that Micky might be more interested in killing the deal with Royal Caribbean than in pursuing a real transaction. "Carnival's recent unsolicited takeover proposal contains too many preconditions to be recommended to its shareholders," it read. "Carnival is asking shareholders to vote down the Royal Caribbean merger in favor of a takeover proposal that might not be made until October 2002 (or might not ever be made), if Carnival persists with its regulatory preconditions."

Micky fired back immediately. "We are not spoilers," he insisted. "The only spoiling tactics are the poison pills entered into by the P&O Princess board, which have destroyed shareholder value and which have been entered into in the full knowledge of our longstanding interest in P&O Princess."

The war of words had begun. It was late December, and Princess's shareholders were set to vote on the Royal Caribbean transaction in just over six weeks. Micky's fundamental paradox hadn't changed: making a binding offer was simply too risky without Ratcliffe's assistance in determining a fair price, but Ratcliffe had made it clear that he wouldn't even consider a conditional offer from Carnival, much less jeopardize his deal with Fain by helping Micky assemble one. He was a stone wall. And so it seemed that Micky was damned whatever he did: Carnival couldn't make a binding bid in time for the Valentine's Day meeting, and absent such a bid, Princess's shareholders would almost certainly vote for the Royal Caribbean transaction.

Then, in a blinding, staggering glimpse of the obvious, the Carnival team blew the entire transaction wide open. What if Princess's shareholders simply *voted not to vote*? Fain had made his official offer in mid-November; thanks to the deal protection he himself had insisted upon, it would continue to be binding for a year—well past the point where the results of any antitrust proceedings would be known—so long as Princess didn't do anything to activate the poison pill. There was nothing in the agreement to prevent Princess's shareholders from simply adjourning the meeting and waiting until the last minute to make a decision. If Carnival cleared antitrust and the shareholders liked its price, so be it; if not, Royal Caribbean would still be obligated to go through with the deal.

Could it really be that easy? Could both Royal Caribbean and Princess really have overlooked that possibility? As Fain remembers it, the subject had come up during negotiations, but he'd dismissed it. "The issue of adjourning the meeting," he says, "I recall as one we were aware of but did not think it was a significant risk provided that the board and management of P&O Princess fought for our transaction, as opposed to being evenhanded." Fain had put his fate in Ratcliffe's hands. Like the Royal Caribbean board, he'd taken "great comfort" in the strength of their relationship—a relationship that was now about to be put to the test.

Micky fired off another letter, this one outlining the adjournment scenario and reiterating his request for a sit-down, "to better enable us to improve still further our already superior offer to P&O Princess shareholders."

It was met with another flat rejection. "Carnival may be indifferent as to whether it buys your company or retains its position as the leading cruise ship operator in the world by breaking up our combination with Royal Caribbean," Ratcliffe wrote to his shareholders. "In effect, Carnival is asking you to bear all the risk that it is both willing and able to complete its takeover proposal, leaving your company to bear all the immediate costs and lost opportunities of terminating its combination with Royal Caribbean."

The language was as strong as any that had gone back and forth up until this point, yet behind the scenes all was not as it should have been. In the nearly two months that had passed since the announcement of the merger, Ratcliffe had made no serious effort to meet the benchmarks that would cement the joint venture—indeed, to get the new cruise line off the ground at all. Instead, he and his people began issuing "clarifications" about the poison pill, both in formal statements and in comments to the press. "There has been some misunderstanding on certain aspects of the joint venture with Royal Caribbean," Ratcliffe wrote. "We confirm that we may unilaterally terminate the joint venture in 2003 at no cost as long as no change of control of P&O Princess has been completed before the termination date."

For the first time, Fain began to have doubts. As he saw it, his supposed partners had just "laid out a public blueprint" not only for navigating the barriers Fain had erected, but for turning them against him. If indeed the meeting could be adjourned without triggering the poison pill, it would be Royal Caribbean that was trapped. The board, too, began to realize it was in trouble. "We should not have allowed that to happen, given the option of adjourning it for a long time and keeping our commitment alive," board member Tom Pritzker recalls. "We could have structured around it . . . said if you adjourn the meeting or it doesn't come to completion by such-and-such a date, then we have the option to walk. We could have done that, and we didn't do that."

Shifting the focus to the adjournment had been a masterstroke for Carnival: rather than being forced to respond to accusations of spoiling, Micky could now go on the offensive. Suddenly, the man the British papers were calling "Slick Micky" was staking a claim to the moral high ground, attacking Ratcliffe and the Princess board for what he called an "unsupportable and disingenuous" attempt to prevent the auction that was now clearly within their ability to achieve. "We still cannot understand why, if their proposal is so attractive, they needed to protect it with such unprecedented poison pills," he stated. "Carnival and its advisers consider the P&O Princess board's refusal to meet with Carnival as nothing less than a deliberate attempt to prevent its shareholders, the owners of the company, from receiving a further enhanced proposal from Carnival."

Micky sent out his second proposal one day before the January 18 deadline Princess had given—up 12 percent to five hundred pence a share. More important, the letter expressed his willingness to consider a DLC—and even managed to get a dig in at Royal Caribbean as he did it. "We remain open to exploring with you the prospects of offering an alternative structure to your shareholders which retains all of the perceived benefits of the proposed DLC structure with Royal Caribbean," he wrote. "However, having taken legal advice, we are concerned that the DLC structure that you have proposed to your shareholders is defective. . . . Our tax advisers believe that there is a significant risk that the DLC structure will lose its . . . exemption for a significant portion of the combined companies' income."

Hemmed in by the terms of his deal, Fain could do little but try to convince Princess's shareholders that Carnival was indeed in the game solely as a spoiler. "We have seen Carnival's actions and practices in the past," he retorted. "Their actions over the past few weeks certainly appear to follow a pattern we've seen before." But he was not in nearly as strong a position as he might have been. Ratcliffe had repeatedly explained that the controversial poison pill had been Fain's precondition, not his, effectively shifting a good part of the indignation over the tactic to Royal Caribbean while still showing the outward support their agreement required. Furthermore, on Ratcliffe's advice, Fain had left most of the actual shareholder lobbying to P&O Princess. "It didn't make any difference," Fain would later say of the decision. "If Princess wasn't committed to it, it wasn't going to happen—and if they were committed to it, then they were in the best position to do the lobbying."

Ratcliffe, meanwhile, was preparing to leave Fain twisting in the wind. "Carnival came along and said, you can adjourn the meeting; and we chose not to oppose that," he remembers. "We probably could have killed it, but we decided not to. . . . We could have fought it on a number of grounds. Like all facts, you can present them in many ways, and the legal case there was to say, 'You don't really have this right to adjournment.' That's all that we had needed to say, actually."

The attacks proceeded to heat up as Valentine's Day drew closer, and although Ratcliffe continued to promote his deal with Fain, no public statement along those lines was forthcoming. When Princess rejected Carnival's revised offer in late January, Micky was there with a blistering response. "I believe that the board never had any intention of talking to us, regardless of what we offered, and is merely continuing to hide behind their agreement with Royal Caribbean," he thundered. "We have acted in good faith: P&O Princess shareholders will ultimately determine whether their board has acted in their best interests. Since the P&O Princess board will not discuss our superior proposal, we will take it directly to their shareholders."

He turned his attention to Fain as well, landing a series of body blows unprecedented even in the context of their tumultuous history. "Since 1988, when Richard Fain became chairman and chief executive of Royal Caribbean, the performance of Royal Caribbean has been significantly weaker than that of Carnival. Richard Fain would retain these positions under the Royal Caribbean proposal and would be running the enlarged group," Micky said in an open letter to Princess shareholders. "Since Royal Caribbean has historically underperformed, is there any reason why they will improve in the future? We have consistently outperformed Royal Caribbean by a wide margin, whatever our size and whatever the market conditions. It's not size that creates superior operating margins—it's management talent and proven operating practices."

Royal Caribbean took another hit when the UK Takeover Panel, clearly annoyed at the use of the DLC structure to circumvent its jurisdiction, not only took the unusual step of allowing Carnival to delay filing its official offer until the poison pill expired in January of 2003, but also announced that it was referring the Royal Caribbean deal to British antitrust authorities—something no one had expected. One of Royal Caribbean's strongest selling points was that it promised a smooth antitrust clearance as opposed to what would be a bumpy ride at best in any Carnival deal. News of the investigation gave credence to Micky's claim that the two companies were indistinguishable for antitrust purposes—and he made as much of the development as he could. "The P&O Princess board's advice to its shareholders on regulatory issues raises significant questions about its credibility," he wrote. "P&O Princess has claimed that the Royal Caribbean proposal is more deliverable than Carnival's offer on antitrust grounds. P&O Princess's analysis has proven to be wrong and today's decision by the secretary of state makes P&O Princess's determination not to speak to us totally indefensible."

Fain tried to minimize the panel's decision, but there was little he could say. "We have taken regulatory approval for granted," he stated curtly. "This referral in no way detracts from our ability to complete the merger on the agreed timetable."

Although things were moving quickly now behind the scenes, Carnival was still looking very much like the underdog to the outside world. The day after the UK Takeover Panel's ruling, Micky upped his bid to 515 pence per Princess share. It was an unimpressive offer—all Carnival stock this time, and more valuable than its predecessor only insofar as Carnival's share price had risen modestly in the intervening weeks. Less willing now to rely so heavily on Princess from a public relations standpoint, Fain immediately dismissed it himself. "This latest in a series of repackaged preconditional offers from Carnival was only too predictable," he insisted. "They have rearranged the small print but made no real difference to the big picture." The *Financial Times* agreed, speculating that Carnival might be "throwing in the towel" with the new bid. "Two weeks before the meeting," the newspaper opined, "Royal Caribbean still has the edge."

Truth be told, the atmosphere at Carnival—still cut off from Ratcliffe and oblivious to the stresses behind the scenes—was much the same. "The mood at the time on our side was very guarded," Dubbin remembers. "We believed that we were going to get the adjournment, but we were very tentative. We felt Princess and Royal Caribbean were working together in unison; we didn't know that there was any tension in the ranks. We really didn't know about that until it was over." With two weeks left before the EGM, Micky put the odds of success at less than one in ten.

In fact, the tide had already turned. Although Ratcliffe met this last offer with another strong rejection, his statement acknowledged that adjourning the vote would not trigger the poison pill. He further affirmed in a conference call that Princess's lawyers did not believe, as Royal Caribbean had been arguing, that having Carnival in the running was likely to reduce the likelihood of either deal clearing regulators. Fain, appalled, had been in any number of meetings with Ratcliffe's attorneys and heard them give the exact opposite advice. This new statement could only have been the result of what he would later call "lawyer shopping for the opinion they wanted." It was clear that Princess was no longer on his side.

A change of strategy was long overdue. Fain had been trying to stay above Micky's attacks, but the high road wasn't working. "I thought that the hypocrisy was so obvious that there was no need for us to comment on it," he remembers. "And that in fact our reticence to participate in the mudslinging would inure to our benefit. In retrospect, I was wrong." Fain began to go on the offensive; his public statements started showing a new edge. When Princess rejected Carnival's third offer on February 4, he announced that he was "delighted that P&O Princess has reaffirmed the value of our transaction." However, he added, "I would also like to emphasize P&O Princess's analysis that adjournment of next week's EGM could threaten our merger. I have spoken many times before about the disruption caused by this whole process. Further delay, and further disruption, serves the interest of neither set of shareholders."

Carnival, meanwhile, had been losing no opportunity to meet firsthand with Princess investors in London, defending its deal and pouring poison in every ear regarding Royal Caribbean's intentions. Micky argued again and again that Fain was trying to steal their company. And as Fain's talk got tougher, Micky's case got easier. "He made a lot of statements like that that were useful to us," Micky remembers. "Because nobody likes to be threatened. You take that around to their shareholders and say, 'What kind of thing is that? What does he mean by this? He keeps saying that we were the spoiler. Wait a minute—who's the spoiler here? Are we the spoiler? Because we really want to buy P&O. We've always really wanted to buy this company. Maybe *he's* the spoiler.' "

Then, on February 7, Carnival took the remarkable step of raising its bid to 550 pence—$5.34 billion in all. It was the third time it had raised its bid without Royal Caribbean changing the terms of its own offer or anyone else entering the fray—or even a single outwardly encouraging signal from Princess's management. Carnival was indeed in an open auction—bidding against itself. The final offer was more than three times what Princess had been valued at when Frank had called in September, and nearly all of Carnival's conditions had been removed. Pending antitrust approval, the two deals were on equal footing for the first time. Only a day after receiving the proposal—after having considered it "in detail"—Ratcliffe wrote that "the board believes that for the first time the price being offered by Carnival is at a realistic level for those shareholders who want to cash out of both the company and the industry. In contrast, the combination with Royal Caribbean offers significant potential for further value creation." Although Ratcliffe continued to recommend the Royal Caribbean deal—thereby keeping Fain on the hook—Carnival finally saw the encouragement camouflaged in Ratcliffe's rejection.

Soon after, Micky sent off a letter to Ratcliffe in a new, conciliatory tone. "We are pleased that you have acknowledged that our increased offer is at a level that reflects a 'realistic' value for P&O Princess," Micky wrote. "We understand that you may be restricted from speaking to us under the terms of your contractual arrangements with Royal Caribbean. However, if you are able to meet us without breaching these arrangements, we would like to present to you in detail our analysis on the antitrust position and why we believe that our offer faces no greater risk than that faced by the Royal Caribbean proposal."

On the eve of the meeting Fain issued a final declaration to Princess's shareholders. "There is no free option," he wrote. "I want my view to be very clear. If there is no approval of the P&O Princess–Royal Caribbean Cruises Ltd. combination tomorrow, there will, for any number of reasons, be no deals—neither our combination nor the Carnival Corporation take-over. Whilst we have yet to decide what specific actions we would take, it is clear that such an adjournment vote would strike at the heart of our transaction."

It was memorable language, but too little and too late. Unofficial tallies by Princess and Carnival had left both of them certain—though they were still not speaking at the time—that they had the total necessary for adjournment; the Valentine's Day vote would be little more than a showpiece.

But what spectacular theater it made!

The meeting turned out to be an epic in its own right. Five months of brinkmanship had attracted a remarkable amount of attention. Now a new element entered the fray: the retail shareholders of P&O Princess. This was not your average group of internet day traders and grannies with stock tips from the AARP grapevine. Many of the individual shareholders had acquired their stock in Princess following the spin-off as an extension of P&O shares that had been passed down through their families for generations. It was a very, very British group, but for the occasion they shed their customary reserve; one of the nation's cherished institutions had come under attack from the colonial upstarts on the other side of the Atlantic, and they were the last line of defense. Considering that the private shareholders controlled less than 5 percent of the company, they did an impressive job of waving the flag.

To say that the scene at London's stately Royal Lancaster hotel that day was raucous would be rather an understatement. Seeing no benefit in fanning the flames, Fain had declined an invitation to attend, while the Carnival team had each bought a single share of Princess stock to get them through the door. Micky's people knew as well as anyone that they'd be facing a heated atmosphere—they'd actually been advised not to bring their wives—but walking into the big, wood-paneled ballroom, they realized they'd seriously underestimated the level of hostility. "Everybody was booing me," Howard Frank remembers. " 'Get the hell out of here!' They didn't literally throw stuff at me, but I thought they would."

Sterling chaired the meeting, playing the elder statesman to Ratcliffe's maverick deal maker. From where he and the rest of the Princess board sat up on the dais, the room looked more like a Trial of the Century set than a shareholders meeting. In the front row sat Micky, Frank and the rest of Carnival's fifteen-member team. Cascading from the back of the room in an unruly tumult were the individual shareholders, and between the two groups—sitting quietly in their dark suits—were the representatives of the institutional investors who held the company's future in their hands. Overlooking it all were the lawyers, fanned out behind the board members in an anxious swath.

Sterling called the meeting to order, and within minutes one of the institutional investors moved for the adjournment. From there, the proceedings went on for nearly ten surreal hours as the various parties made their cases. One by one, the small shareholders stood up to say their piece. The gadfly swarm took the opportunity to do everything from invoking the memory of Sir Francis Drake to complaining about the advent of the euro. "I want to keep things in England and I want England to be strong," one said, to loud approval from her fellows. Another called Carnival "crude and opportunistic." Through it all, as Sterling struggled to maintain order, Ratcliffe sat and looked on, amused. "All the stereotypes of Britain and America were flashing around, and all the people we were trying to appease—it was just wonderful," he remembers. "In the front three rows, it was packed with the faceless people of capitalism. And this guy from the back stood and he said, 'We've not heard from the faceless people of capitalism. Stand up and speak!' And there was great roars at this."

Finally, Sterling invited Micky to speak—a totally unforeseen move. Micky, being Micky, hadn't wanted to come at all; he'd finally compromised with his bankers to show up to answer questions, but he had nothing formal prepared. But there he was. Microphone stands had been set up throughout the floor, but as he stood up amid the cries of "No! No!" and "Go home!" something in Sterling's body language gave him an unexpected opening. "I was walking up, and I see that he's letting me take the podium," Micky remembers. "I was just astounded. His bankers were mortified. As opposed to letting me stand on the floor and speak from the floor, I was now on his stage, at his podium, speaking. I never imagined that they would let me. Once I saw that they were letting me, I just took it."

The sheer audacity of the gesture sent a momentary hush through the crowd; just moments before, it had seemed on the edge of riot. The butterflies of his introverted youth returning unbidden to his stomach, Micky spoke haltingly at first, hoping to strike a conciliatory tone. "We're brand builders," he told the audience, "not brand destroyers." He had nothing but affection for Britain and its traditions, he explained; his wife and children all held British passports. And if there was any doubt about whether the legacy of P&O Princess would be safe under his umbrella, well, just look at how

Cunard had thrived since Carnival had taken it over. But the hostility of the room was too much for him. This was one of the richest men in the world, after all, long out of practice when it came to rude treatment, and here he'd been sitting for hours listening to his reputation and company run down, sometimes in terms so extreme that Sterling had to jump in to his defense. When one shareholder chimed in that "Carnival's spoiling tactics are working," the irritation finally started showing through. "If we weren't committed, why have we spent the last three weeks going from shareholder to shareholder in your horrendous weather?" he retorted. "I would have sent my lawyers to Washington and thrown eggs at the regulatory hearings. It would have been much cheaper and caused much less wear and tear on my body."

It was time to sit down; Micky was there to play the good cop, and he didn't know how much longer he'd be able to play that role. Before things could go any further, he asked his vice chairman to say a few words. Tall, slim and hard faced under his neatly trimmed head of grey hair, Howard Frank was most definitely not there to play the good cop, and everybody knew it. He stalked toward the stage in his best tough-guy stride.

Princess's lawyers headed him off before he could seize the podium and directed him instead to one of the microphone stands on the floor. From there he delivered the message of a wartime consigliere: "P&O Princess shareholders should not be frightened by threats," he said. "There is no need for you to second-guess the regulators. You should keep both options alive until the regulatory position of both suitors is clarified."

By now it was late afternoon, and the meeting broke for a vote not long after. As officials began the tally, however, what had looked as if it would be the end of a very long day turned into the beginning of a very long night. The high turnout had thrown the voting process into disarray, with investors who'd been expected to vote in blocks casting separate ballots and advance proxy votes being recalled and changed. The meeting was reconvened several times during the following hours. Sterling finally arranged dinner and lodging for visiting shareholders, then at eleven P.M. tapped Princess's CFO to stand in for him as chairman and went home to get some rest. Carnival canceled the reservations it had made for a celebratory dinner.

Back in downtown Miami, another meeting at another hotel was unraveling at the same time. In anticipation of his deal being approved in London, Fain had boldly convened a shareholders meeting of his own. He'd called it for nine A.M.—more than enough time, he thought, for the Princess vote to be concluded six time zones to the east. "Shareholders in crisp suits and dresses milled about patiently," a reporter on the scene wrote, "drinking coffee, sampling fresh fruit and banana cake, and checking in with their offices by cellular phone." As the vote counting was delayed in London, Fain gathered his guests, explained the situation, and asked them to return at one-fifteen P.M. Trying to keep the mood light, he explained the problems with the count and joked that he'd "offered to send over some Florida lawyers if they had any problems with hanging chads or anything." He got the laugh, but then one-fifteen came and went without a resolution. So did four-fifteen, six-fifteen and ten P.M. "Suits and dresses creased," the reporter wrote, "the group dwindled slowly."

The count finally came in at four-thirty A.M. London time. After all the drama and intrigue, Sterling's stand-in blearily announced to a remaining audience of four that the shareholders had voted to adjourn by a margin of more than 1.5 to one.

Back in Miami, the Royal Caribbean board took the news with heavy hearts. Every advantage Fain had negotiated had been eradicated in a single moment; worse, he'd been ensnared in his own defenses. It was a disaster. Royal Caribbean was left facing the one thing Fain had said from the beginning he didn't want—an open auction, with Carnival as the rival bidder. Fain couldn't help feeling that Ratcliffe, who'd pledged to fight for their transaction, had let him down. Placing his trust that way had been a devastating error. "They gamed it," Tom Pritzker recalls. "We should have stopped that. We should not have allowed that to happen."

Ratcliffe, for his part, merely acknowledges that "It was a bitter time."

"He did a deal, at the end of the day, where Carnival could get involved, didn't he?" Ratcliffe would later reflect. "We clearly, unambiguously would benefit from having both people stay in the game, and it would probably have been less clear to Royal Caribbean that that was the case, so relations were not as close in that run-up as you would normally expect." For Ratcliffe, it was all a matter of playing the game. "We were just honoring the agreement," he says. "Under the terms of his contract, he couldn't walk away. He had a contract, as we had a contract, and you had to play that contract out."

Fain knew Carnival had won a major battle in securing the adjournment, but he had to believe that it was only a battle. Certainly, he was anything but ready to surrender. His first line of defense had been devastated, true, but then he hadn't gotten this far in life by taking stupid risks. Behind the poison pill had always been the firm advice that both he and Ratcliffe—and for that matter, Micky—had all gotten from their lawyers that Carnival would have an extremely difficult time getting through the antitrust process. In his heart of hearts, however, Fain hadn't expected to have to test that theory

It was clear from the outset that the regulatory fight would be won or lost in Europe. Back in the U.S., where the Federal Trade Commission was looking at both deals, Royal Caribbean and Carnival were more or less on equal footing. Either merger would create a clear market leader, but the difference between the two—48 percent of the North American market for Carnival-Princess versus 42 percent for Royal Caribbean–Princess—was hardly dramatic, and it was widely assumed that the FTC would either clear both deals when it made its decision in the fall, or neither.

Europe was an altogether different situation. There, Carnival and Princess together would control 32 percent of the total cruise market; a Royal Caribbean and Princess combination would account for barely half of that. In fact, Fain's deal hadn't even come up for review at the European Union level; it had sailed easily past German regulators in January, and an expected approval in June from the UK was its final European hurdle.

Carnival, on the other hand, was going before the EU Competition Commission in Brussels, and the commission had already indicated its skepticism concerning the transaction. Its chairman, Mario Monti, was known to be something of a hawk on antitrust enforcement and little concerned with public opinion. Just the year before, he'd stirred up a transatlantic furor by blocking the merger of industrial giants General Electric and Honeywell after U.S. regulators had approved it—a decision Secretary of the Treasury Paul O'Neill had called "off the wall."

Carnival had filed its paperwork in Brussels in late February, shortly after winning the adjournment. In early April the commission announced that in light of "serious concerns" about the deal, it was initiating an exhaustive investigation. In May the commission sent Carnival and Princess copies of a long list of "objections" to the merger, along with an invitation to respond. For everyone but Fain, the outlook was gloomy; Monti seemed to already have made up his mind. "Everybody's view of Europe was that it was purely political, judged by political things rather than analysis," Ratcliffe remembers. "That's why we thought we were going to lose."

Conceptually, the entire question turned on how the commission chose to frame the European cruise market. At one end of the spectrum was the cartoonishly liberal logic espoused by Carnival and Princess, which suggested that cruising ought to be thought of as part of the broader vacation industry, nothing more. According to this logic, since cruises accounted for less than 1 percent of all the vacations sold in Europe, even a merger that put every cruise ship in the world under a single company's control wouldn't create any competition issues.

Fain's job was to define the market in such a way as to create an opening big enough for Royal Caribbean to pass through without raising antitrust concerns, but too small for Carnival to follow. There were two ways to accomplish this—and between them lay a minefield. If the commission chose to look at cruising as a single, pan-European market, it was clear that a Carnival and Princess combination created problems that a Royal Caribbean merger did not; Carnival dominated southern Europe through Costa, while Princess was an overwhelming presence in the important UK and German markets. Together they would dominate the continent. Royal Caribbean, on the other hand, was a negligible presence in most of Europe. Fain would also win if the commission chose to construe the European industry as being actually composed of several separate, tightly defined markets distinguished by price, national identity or style of service—each with its own antitrust concerns. Since Royal Caribbean's megabrand approach during the 1990s had led it to emphasize large ships appealing to many different passenger categories, it was largely insulated from any competition issues arising from such specific definitions; even the supposedly premium Celebrity brand crossed any number of categories. Carnival and Princess, on the other hand, both operated General Motors–style portfolios of distinct, specifically targeted cruise brands; many were similar to one another, and where there was overlap in specific subsectors there was arguable potential for monopoly.

But the commission could also find that each of the individual countries where Carnival and Princess sold cruises represented a separate market; if they went in that direction, Fain had no chance. In that scenario, Royal Caribbean and Carnival would be on the same footing, at least from an antitrust perspective, and Fain would be back in an open auction he couldn't win. Carnival and Princess were indeed each powerful in Europe—far more so than Royal Caribbean—but their overlap in any given country was considerably less than it at first appeared. Carnival, for example, boasted a remarkable 60 percent share of the Italian market, but Princess's sales there were "virtually nonexistent." Germany and the UK were the only national markets where the two companies had significant overlap, and in both countries Carnival and Royal Caribbean were actually even closer to one another in market share than they were in the United States. If the commission blocked one transaction on those criteria, it would certainly block both, and since neither the German nor British authorities had expressed reservations about the Royal Caribbean deal, there was no reason to think that Monti, if he made his decision on a country-by-country basis, would do otherwise.

Since the Royal Caribbean transaction hadn't come before the European Commission, Fain wasn't entitled, as Carnival and Princess were, to make his arguments directly to Monti. He set out instead to play a game of jurisdictional politics. He was still before the UK Competition Commission; his only chance of influencing Brussels was to persuade the British to evaluate his merger in such a way that it would in turn put pressure on Monti. Royal Caribbean was likely to pass muster whichever of the three possible market definitions was applied to it, but if the British accepted either the pan-European or the highly segmented models, Monti wouldn't be able to clear Carnival without taking the politically uncomfortable step of overturning their decision.

It was an uphill battle. Royal Caribbean was arguing against its own precedent. Back when Fain had still believed Ratcliffe was fighting for their deal, Royal Caribbean and Princess had filed their documents with German authorities jointly. In deference to Princess's greater European experience, Ratcliffe's lawyers had drafted the filings. Later Fain would say that he was shocked to learn that he'd signed off on the same "broader vacation market" argument that Carnival was making. "If this is what we're saying," he told Ratcliffe, "then I've got a real problem with this."

Never mind that Royal Caribbean had actually used the same argument in 1997 when the FTC was examining its acquisition of Celebrity. Carnival was in the game now, and it was time to backtrack. Royal Caribbean in the UK filed its papers separately from Princess, abruptly reversing the position it had taken in Germany. "RCCL accepted that cruising should be identified as distinct from the wider holiday market," the UK report would read.

"Moreover . . . RCCL considered that even the category of all cruises was too broad."

Fain's best hope lay in construing the market as narrowly as possible. He argued that the relevant competition issues lay in a separate submarket of "national brands," which catered specifically to British, or German, or Italian tastes; unlike the national origin theory, in this conception of the market it didn't matter where the passengers came from, but who the ships were designed for. Costa, which marketed itself as "Cruising Italian Style" was a prime example. If Royal Caribbean's reasoning was to be believed, these brands competed in entirely separate arenas from the massive "international" brands like Carnival Cruise Lines, Royal Caribbean and Princess Cruises. Conveniently enough, Royal Caribbean was the only one of the three big lines that didn't have a subsidiary that fell into this category. Costa, which dominated the so-called "Italian" market, was Carnival's. Princess owned several of the leading "German" brands. The two leading "British" brands were P&O Cruises, a Princess subsidiary, and Cunard, which Micky had acquired in 1999. If the commission were in fact to look at the market along these lines, Micky at a minimum would have to sell off one of his holdings in order to clear Brussels—hopefully at a big enough loss to deter him from going ahead.

In a bit of cheek that he hoped would be his coup de grace, Fain incorporated the vaunted poison pill—the paper-only southern European joint venture with Princess, which under Ratcliffe's control had yet to take a single booking—into his indirect attack on Carnival. He argued that the joint venture ought to be considered as if it were already an active competitive presence in the Mediterranean instead of the phantom it was; if Monti were to accept that presumption, he would be looking at a Carnival-Princess merger that created massive competitive overlap in a southern European market where in fact there was only one actual major player. It was tortured logic, but Fain took comfort in the widespread belief that Monti was firmly against the Carnival merger to begin with; all he was doing was making it easier for the commissioner to do what he already intended to.

What followed showed just how completely the alliance between Fain and Ratcliffe had deteriorated. Royal Caribbean and Princess were each continuing to make an energetic case for their merger, but they contradicted one another on point after point in their filings as they did so. While Fain was trying to use the joint venture agreement to demonstrate the anticompetitiveness of a Carnival merger in southern Europe, Ratcliffe was confirming to regulators that it was in fact nothing more than a poison pill—"created and structured to provide RCCL with the deal protection that it required as a condition to their entering into the merger agreement"—and ought not to be taken as a genuine commercial intention.

As expected, the UK authorities cleared Royal Caribbean's transaction in June, but they didn't quite buy Fain's arguments on market segmentation. Rather than endorsing one definition or the other, they left the door open for the EU to define the relevant markets as it wished without risk of political fallout. "We have not been able to come to a single view on these issues," the report stated.

It wasn't the judgment Fain had hoped for, but at least it hadn't validated the opposition's broader vacation market theory. Though it was at best a neutral decision, he tried to spin it as an outright victory. "We have been able to satisfy the UK commission that our merger will not pose any problems from a competition viewpoint," Fain announced. "This is true regardless of market definition—and we note the commission has explicitly concluded that it therefore did not need to rule on the appropriateness of one definition or another." He went on to get a dig in at his rivals. "We welcome the commission's findings that Royal Caribbean and P&O Princess operate in the UK as essentially complementary businesses . . . and that by combining we will in no way reduce the product choice available to consumers. This contrasts starkly with the situation for Carnival and P&O Princess: they are each other's largest and most direct competitors in both the UK and Germany, hence the intense scrutiny now being given to Carnival's hostile bid by the regulators in Brussels."

Micky, of course, was quick to "welcome" the development with his own spin. "We have said all along that both of these deals should be cleared in all jurisdictions," he announced. "From a regulatory perspective they are similarly placed and the UK decision today confirms that our offer for P&O Princess should be cleared by the European Commission. When all regulatory approvals have been obtained, I look forward to taking this deal back to the ultimate decision makers, the P&O Princess shareholders." In fact, he was nowhere near that confident.

It was a horse race now; there was no way to predict what would happen in Brussels, though the odds continued to favor Royal Caribbean.

Soon after the UK decision, a high court in Brussels overturned an earlier

Monti ruling against another tourism industry merger, an acquisition by the British tour operator Airtours, in which, coincidentally, Carnival had been a 25 percent investor. According to the court, the commission had committed "manifest errors" in evaluating that transaction. The wholly unanticipated development instantly transformed the political climate. Monti had already been taking heat for rejecting GE-Honeywell; suddenly, he was looking like an antibusiness zealot. Seizing the moment, Micky fired off another of his now-trademark letters—this time to Monti. Addressing the dignified Euro-crat in harsh language, Micky left no doubt about his intention to litigate if things didn't go his way. "I kind of accused the staff of being very shallow and almost prejudging the deal," Micky remembers. "He took great offense at that and said, 'We haven't made a decision, and I want to hear your point of view.' "

Soon after the ruling, Micky flew to Brussels with his fifteen-person team and spent the evening of July 4 meeting with Monti and his staff. Over the course of about two hours, Carnival attacked Fain's baroque market con-struction from every angle. And they knew just where to strike. "Monti wanted to make sure that he had a good, strong legal case," Frank recalls. "We just pointed out the paradox: how can you say one thing six months ago and another thing today?" By the end of the meeting, Frank remembers, "some of the people on Monti's staff were sure—they couldn't legally support their arguments against us. Their arguments were Royal Caribbean's argu-ment. It became clear to Monti, and then maybe a day or two later they came back with their decision."

Actually, it wasn't quite that soon, as nothing happened publicly until the following week. Despite the fact that Royal Caribbean was technically not a party to the transaction, Fain had requested a meeting of his own when he'd heard Monti was seeing Micky. It was largely a pro forma request, and he hadn't been overly disturbed when Monti turned him down. But then, on July 15, another call came: Monti wanted to see him after all. Fain was in northern England at the time, celebrating the launch of Royal Caribbean's newest ship and in a festive mood. He'd just burst into a rendition of "O Solo Mio" for one reporter's benefit, and even spoke—with equal parts optimism and euphemism—of what he believed to be the impending deal. "Certain parties are throwing tantrums at the moment," he'd said smugly. "But though the invitations have not yet been printed, the romance is still blooming." As soon as the festivities were over, he was in a helicopter on his way to Brussels.

To this day, Fain bristles when he thinks about that session with Monti. "He listened very politely, very carefully," he remembers. "But when we came out of the meeting, in the courtyard was one of our people saying, 'I've just had a call from this reporter. They got a call from the commission indicating that they've changed their mind and that they're now going to approve Carnival.' Literally! I hadn't left the meeting yet."

Fain was beyond incensed. As he saw it, Monti had added insult to injury by bringing him in when his decision had already been made "behind closed doors." He felt toyed with. "No explanations have been given, nor reactions sought, in ways that might have allowed a timely consideration of these parties' views—not least via an oral hearing," he stormed in a press release. "Such procedural shortcuts have sadly diminished the openness and transparency that all parties rely upon in circumstances such as these." Finally the usually judicious Fain was talking like a gunslinger. "We think they made the wrong call," he said, "if they've calculated that an appeal from Royal Caribbean will give them less of a problem: as things stand, our case will be stronger than anything Carnival could have mounted."

Monti, however, didn't budge. "As is normal," a top commission official said, "those who are happy are silent and those that are unhappy are investing a lot of effort in mobilizing the media when they might have invested more effort in making their arguments more convincing." A week after the leak, the commission made the official announcement clearing Carnival's transaction.

There would be no devastating lawsuit, nor any reversal from Brussels. Monti was well within his rights; Fain had played his last card, and lost.

None of the regulators, in the end, had thought much either of Micky's and Ratcliffe's broader vacation market theory or Fain's segmentation scheme. Monti's decision—like the subsequent approval of both deals by the FTC that October—had ultimately turned on the economics of the ships themselves.

Monopolists are dangerous first and foremost because the absence of competition gives them the power to arbitrarily set prices, and the victors had successfully convinced regulators on both sides of the Atlantic that they did not have that power—however the market was construed. It was the same dynamic that had driven the industry's long struggle with discounting over the years. Hotels can turn a profit with an occupancy rate of 75 percent or even lower, but with the enormous fixed costs of building and running a cruise ship and business models that rely heavily on passengers' discretionary spending while on board, cruise lines simply cannot afford to sail with empty cabins. This fact of life puts a downward pressure on ticket pricing too strong for even a company with dramatic market share advantages to overcome. And besides, Royal Caribbean and NCL were still there to keep Carnival honest.

"After either transaction, there still will be two large competitors and a substantial fringe that will compete with the merged entity and could constrain any unilateral attempt by the merged firm to increase price or reduce capacity," the FTC concluded. "All competitors have powerful financial incentives to compete on price, capacity and quality; all have acted on those incentives in the past; and all remaining firms will have unchanged incentives going forward in the wake of either proposed merger." Still, the decision could easily have gone the other way. The deals had passed through only by a vote of three to two and the FTC had made it clear that "absent extraordinary circumstances," it would not look favorably on further consolidation among the majors.

Fain had persisted with the arguments he'd used in the UK, in spite of the fact that he knew differentiating between Royal Caribbean's and Carnival's operations would not be a feasible strategy for success with the FTC. Throughout the final months of the process, Micky had laid into him with accusations that Fain was simply trying to "torpedo" both deals, having decided anything was preferable to a Carnival victory. And in truth, there was little else he could do. His relationship with Princess had almost entirely deteriorated. "We are witnessing two parties to an agreed, friendly merger, taking dramatically different positions with antitrust authorities on points as basic as the definition of the market in which they operate," Micky had gloated just before the FTC decision, still trying to force Ratcliffe to the table. "We are at a loss to understand why P&O Princess would stand idly by and allow Royal Caribbean to seek to sabotage the regulatory process for both transactions."

The answer, of course, was because they could. Royal Caribbean wasn't going anywhere, and neither was Carnival. Ratcliffe wasn't going to be rushed by Micky, or anyone.

He opened talks with Carnival immediately after the FTC's decision—

although so as to avoid triggering the once-fearsome poison pill before a deal was finalized, he continued to publicly recommend the Royal Caribbean merger. It was the first time he and Micky had spoken to each other directly since November 2001. All that remained was for Carnival to agree to the DLC. They worked the issue out in two days of negotiations. "When Micky agreed to that," Ratcliffe remembers, "it was all over, bar the shouting."

On October 25, Ratcliffe finally dropped his public recommendation for the Royal Caribbean deal, and Princess paid out $62.5 million in standard breakup fees. Two quiet months passed as he and Micky waited for the joint venture to expire on New Year's Day, and then Ratcliffe formally recommended Carnival's offer to his shareholders. On April 14, 2003, Carnival's shareholders approved a final offer at their annual meeting in New York, and two days later Princess's did the same.

Nearly forty years after Ted Arison had seemingly lost everything off the shores of Dodge Island, Carnival had a market capitalization of $36 billion. More than a year of paper flying back and forth had passed, and everyone had had enough. The vote, later tallied at 99.7 percent in favor of the merger, was taken by a show of hands.

Just like in the old days.

With Carnival in control of more than 50 percent of the cruise market, the era of mergers and acquisitions had effectively come to an end. The industry wouldn't have to wait long to get a sense of just how dominant its longtime leader had become. Less than a month after the Princess acquisition was finalized, Micky announced that Carnival would be canceling one of the ships it had on order at the Italian yard Fincantieri, and stretching out the delivery schedule on another four.

"We're less than two weeks into the new Carnival–P&O Princess combination and we are already working on optimizing asset utilization to benefit the brands and maximize returns for the group," Micky boasted. "Slowing down the delivery schedule gives us a more rational and efficient timetable to absorb additional capacity. It is also a testament to our excellent relationship with Fincantieri. . . . The level of cooperation they have demonstrated only serves to further strengthen our business partnership."

The shipyard, for its part, had little option but to capitulate to what amounted to a wholesale, unilateral renegotiation of contracts it had signed as much as two years earlier—and to do it with a smile. "Carnival, Holland America and Princess, along with Costa Crociere and Cunard Line, are among our best customers," Fincantieri's CEO said. "We are very pleased to work with Carnival Corporation in adjusting its delivery schedule and look forward to continuing to deliver state-of-the-art vessels that will define the group's brands while providing excellent holidays for its guests."

Fincantieri went on to have a great year, and indeed posted record profits for 2004, but that only served to underscore the point. Where else were they going to go? You couldn't make a living in this business anymore without being on Carnival's good side. Travel agents, too, soon felt the press of the new hegemony as the company's flagship brand cracked down on the unpredictable pricing that had plagued the industry for years. Top-producing agents using their higher commissions to subsidize discounts of their own soon learned of Carnival Cruise Lines' displeasure and understood well that the ire of the entire corporation might not be far behind. Explicit threats were unnecessary: the very notion of a blacklist there was more than anyone could afford to risk.

Royal Caribbean, for its part, emerged from the fight battered but was soon doing better than anyone expected. After a grieving period, the board concluded that a strong second place in this industry was not a bad place to be. After all, there was more than enough to go around—especially now that Carnival was viewing them more as a hedge against monopoly claims than as competition for world-shaking acquisitions. There were simply no more wars to fight. Royal Caribbean's dream of industry dominance may have been quashed, but a rich and undisturbed future seems all but assured.

And so what next, for a money machine like Carnival? "We'll play it smart," Howard Frank says. "I don't think that there's going to be any major deals for us out there going forward. I don't see it. We'll make a small investment here or there where we see it as strategically the right thing to do. But where does the big money go? It'll have to go back to shareholders. You can't get those returns anyplace else."

SOURCE NOTES

Writing this book would have been impossible without the benefit of the efforts of the innumerable journalists, government officials, labor and environmental activists and financial analysts whose coverage of this industry, though disparate and sometimes difficult to find, turns out to be quite comprehensive and in large part performed to the highest standards. An enormous debt remains with those among that number whose work has challenged and reoriented assumptions I've made along the way. Where quotations and facts in the preceding pages came from published sources or otherwise from the work of other journalists, researchers or scholars, I have both listed them below and cited the specific references in my notes according to the page numbers on which they appear. The majority of the quotes and information in this book, however, has come from the hundreds of hours of interviews I've conducted with individuals connected to the cruise industry, including many of the key players at the major lines. A partial list follows below. Thanks goes to the dozens of other cruise executives, vendors, port chaplains, current and former crewmembers, Coast Guard officials and others who also generously gave of their time for this research.

Carnival

Micky Arison, Meshulam Zonis, Bob Dickinson, Howard Frank, Ken Dubbin, Brendan Corrigan, Tim Gallagher, Vikki Freed, Roger Blum, Giora Israel, Everette Phillips, Maurice Zarmati, David Mizer, Peter Leypold, Vitorrio Fabietti, Uzi Zucker

Royal Caribbean/Celebrity

Richard Fain, Ed Stephan, Pete Whelpton, Arne Wilhelmsen, Tom Pritzker, John Chandris, Rod McLeod, Jack Williams, Mike Ronan, Rick Sasso, Harri Kulovaara, Aage

Lindstad, Will Chambers, Adam Goldstein, David Llewellyn, Jack Seabrook, Brian Rice, Rune Flesland, Ole Jan Skogen, Manfred Usprunger

NCL

Knut Kloster, Ron Zeller, Tom Cooney, Duke Hatfield, Mike Ronan, Rod McLeod, Brian Rice, Trygve Hegnar

Princess

Peter Ratcliffe, Lord Geoffrey Sterling, Julie Benson, Stanley MacDonald, Douglas Cramer, Ted Blamey, Wendell Brooks

SOURCES CITED

Periodicals

60 Minutes
AFX European Focus
Bergen Record
British Broadcasting Corporation
Broward Daily Business Review
Business Day
BusinessWeek
Chicago Tribune
Christian Science Monitor
CNN
Consumer Reports
Cruise Industry News
Daily Telegraph
Economist
European Voice
Express
Financial Times
Forbes
Fortune
Gleaner (Jamaica)
Guardian
Hannibal Courier-Post (Hannibal, MO)
Journal of Commerce
Journal of Hospitality Management
Lloyd's List
Los Angeles Times
Marine Money
Miami Daily Business Review

Miami Herald
Miami News
Miami New Times
National Environmental Enforcement Journal
Newsday
Newsweek
Newsweek Budget Travel
New York Times
People
Playboy
Porthole
Sarasota Herald-Tribune
Seatrade Insider
Seatrade Review
South Florida Sun-Sentinel
Times of London
Tour and Travel News
United Press International
Wall Street Journal
Washington Post
World Ports Magazine

Books

Arison, L. (2002). *A Love Story in Mediterranean Israel.* San Diego, Tehabi Books
Brinnin, J. M. (1971). *The Sway of the Grand Saloon: A Social History of the North Atlantic.* New York, Delacorte Press
Burrough, B. and J. Helyar (1990). *Barbarians at the Gate: The Fall of RJR Nabisco.* New York, Harper & Row
Carnival Cruise Lines (1987). *Celebration: The SuperLiner Celebration.* London, Sterling
Chapman, P. K. (1992). *Trouble on Board: The Plight of International Seafarers.* Ithaca, NY, ILR Press
Coons, L. and A. Varias (2003). *Tourist Third Cabin: Steamship Travel in the Interwar Years.* New York, Palgrave Macmillan
Cross, R. G. (1997). *Revenue Management: Hard-Core Tactics for Market Domination.* New York, Broadway Books
Cruise Lines International Association (1996). *The Cruise Industry: An Overview.* New York, Cruise Lines International Association
Cudahy, B. J. (2001). *The Cruise Ship Phenomenon in North America.* Centreville, MD, Cornell Maritime Press
Denton, S. and R. Morris (2001). *The Money and the Power: The Making of Las Vegas and Its Hold on America, 1947–2000.* New York, Alfred A. Knopf
Dickinson, B. and A. Vladimir (1997). *Selling the Sea: An Inside Look at the Cruise Industry.* New York, Wiley
Didion, J. (1998). *Miami.* New York, Vintage Books

Dunn, L. (1965). *Passenger Liners*. London, A. Coles

Gleeson-Adamidis, J. (2000). *If I Were Not Upon the Sea (Under the Captain's Table)*. Athens, Greece, Update Plus

Goddard, D. (1980). *All Fall Down: One Man Against the Waterfront Mob*. New York, Times Books

Grass, G. and K. Winston (2002). *Crabwalk*. Orlando, FL, Harcourt

Israel, G. and L. Miller (1999). *Dictionary of the Cruise Industry*. Colchester, UK, Seatrade Cruise Academy

Klein, R. A. (2002). *Cruise Ship Blues: The Underside of the Cruise Ship Industry*. Gabriola Island, BC, New Society Publishers

Kolltveit, Baard, and J. Maxtone-Graham (1995). *Under Crown and Anchor*. Miami Beach, Onboard Media

Langewiesche, W. (2004). *The Outlaw Sea: A World of Freedom, Chaos, and Crime*. New York, North Point Press

Mancini, M. (2000). *Cruising: A Guide to the Cruise Line Industry*. Albany, NY, Delmar Thomson Learning

Maxtone-Graham, J. (1972). *The Only Way To Cross*. New York, Macmillan

Maxtone-Graham, J. (1992). *Crossing & Cruising: From the Golden Era of Ocean Liners to the Luxury Cruise Ships of Today*. New York, Scribner

Maxtone-Graham, J. (2000). *Cruise Savvy: An Invaluable Primer for First-Time Passengers*. Dobbs Ferry, NY, Sheridan House

Maxtone-Graham, J. (2000). *Liners to the Sun*. Dobbs Ferry, NY, Sheridan House

Muir, H. (1990). *Miami, U.S.A.* Miami, FL, Pickering Press

Pattullo, P. (1996). *Last Resorts: The Cost of Tourism in the Caribbean*. Kingston, Jamaica, Ian Randle

Saunders, J. (1974). *The Love Boats*. New York, Drake Publishers

Schlosser, E. (2002). *Fast Food Nation: The Dark Side of the All-American Meal*. New York, Perennial

Sinclair, U. (2003). *The Jungle*. Tucson, AZ, See Sharp Press

Taylor, F. (1993). *To Hell with Paradise: A History of the Jamaican Tourist Industry*. Pittsburgh, University of Pittsburgh Press

Wallace, D. F. (1997). *A Supposedly Fun Thing I'll Never Do Again: Essays and Arguments*. Boston, Little, Brown

Sources of Financial and Market Analysis

Financial Institutions

Credit Suisse First Boston
Deutsche Bank
Market Scope
Morgan Stanley
Raymond James
Ryan Beck & Co.
Salomon Smith Barney
UBS Warburg

Trade Associations

Cruise Lines International Association
Florida Caribbean Cruise Association
International Council of Cruise Lines

Government, Academic and NGO Reports, Studies

American Antitrust Institute, *Additional American Antitrust Institute Comments on the Proposed Cruise Mergers*, September 3, 2002

European Union Competition Commission, *Case No COMP/M.2706—Carnival Corporation/P&O Princess*, July 2002

Federal Trade Commission, *Royal Caribbean Cruises, Ltd./P&O Princess Cruises plc and Carnival Corporation/P&O Princess Cruises plc*, FTC File No. 021 0041, October 2002

Foer, Albert A., and Robert H. Lande, *The Evolution of United States Antitrust Law: The Past, Present, and (Possible) Future*, American Antitrust Institute, October 20, 1999

Greenpeace, *Playing Hide and Seek: How the Shipping Industry, Protected by Flags of Convenience, Dumps Toxic Waste on Shipbreaking Beaches*, December 2003

Organization of American States. Department of Regional Development and Caribbean Tourism Research and Development Centre (1988). *Caribbean cruise ship study.* Washington, D.C.

Potter, Gary W. and Victor Kappeler. *The Triumph of Conservatism: Ronald Reagan and Organized Crime*, paper presented at the Southern Criminal Justice Association, October 1992.

UK Competition Commission, *P&O Princess Cruises plc and Royal Caribbean Cruises Ltd: A report on the proposed merger*, June 2002

U.S. Congress, General Accounting Office Reports:
- 1993, *Coast Guard: Additional actions needed to improve cruise ship safety*
- 2000, *Marine Pollution: Progress made to reduce marine pollution from cruise ships, but important issues remain*
- 2004, *Maritime Law Exemption: Exemption provides limited competitive advantage, but barriers to further entry under U.S. flag remain*

U.S. Congress. House. Committee on Merchant Marine and Fisheries. Subcommittee on Merchant Marine
- (1986). *Cruise ship industry: hearings before the Subcommittee on Merchant Marine of the Committee on Merchant Marine and Fisheries, House of Representatives, Ninety-ninth Congress, first session, on foreign-flag cruise ship industry, April 10, 1985; U.S.-flag cruise ship industry, May 7, 1985; security of ports and vessels, October 22, 1985.* Washington, D.C.
- (1990). *Cruise ship safety: hearings before the Subcommittee on Merchant Marine of the Committee on Merchant Marine and Fisheries, House of Representatives, One Hundred First Congress, second session, on oversight hearings on safety conditions*

and emergency health care facilities aboard cruise ships operating out of U.S. ports. Washington, D.C.

- (1992). *U.S.-Flag Cruise Ship Competitiveness Act of 1991: hearing before the Sub-committee on Merchant Marine of the Committee on Merchant Marine and Fisheries, House of Representatives, One Hundred Second Congress, first session, on H.R. 3282. October 10, 1991.* Washington, D.C.
- (1994). *Cruise ship health and safety: hearings before the Subcommittee on Merchant Marine and the Subcommittee on Coast Guard and Navigation of the Committee on Merchant Marine and Fisheries, House of Representatives, One Hundred Third Congress, second session. September 28, and October 6, 1994.* Washington, U.S.

U.S. Congress. House Committee on Transportation and Infrastructure. Subcommittee on Coast Guard and Maritime Transportation (2000). *Cruise ship safety: hearing before the Subcommittee on Coast Guard and Maritime Transportation of the Committee on Transportation and Infrastructure, House of Representatives, One Hundred Sixth Congress, first session, October 7, 1999.* Washington, D.C.

War on Want, International Transportation Workers Federation Cruise Ship Campaign, *Sweatships*, 2001

Winerman, Marc, *The Origins of the FTC: Concentration, Cooperation, Control, and Competition*, Antitrust Law Journal, volume 71, 2003

Wood, Robert, *Caribbean Cruise Tourism: Globalization at Sea*, Annals of Tourism Research, 27: 2, 2000

Zhao, Minghua, *Emotional Labour in a Globalized Labour Market: Seafarers on Cruise Ships*, Seafarers International Research Centre, May 2002

Zhao, Minghua, *Women Seafarers on Cruise Ships*, The Sea (Seafarers International Research Centre Newsletter), May/June 2000

CHAPTER ONE: THE PERFECT BUSINESS

Unless otherwise specified, data on *Voyager of the Seas* consumption comes from Royal Caribbean and from the Parmani's Cruise Page Web site at, http://www.fortunecity.com/oasis/tropicana/431/Voyager.html. The calculations on size and weight equivalency (elephants, swimming pools, etc.) are my own, based on generally acknowledged averages.

3 "**ten million Americans,**" Cruise Lines International Association market data

4 "**twenty-five hundred toilets,**" *Lloyd's List*, Nov 4, 1999

4 "**180 years or more,**" Based on *Voyager's* electricity production of 75,000 kw/hr, and the U.S. Department of Energy's estimate of an average consumption of 10,000 kwh per U.S. household.

6 "**on the order of fifteen tons,**" most cruise writers put the average weight gain on a weeklong cruise between five and fifteen pounds. This statistic, though widely credited in the industry, is of course anecdotal.

9 "**two of the one hundred richest people in the world,**" Forbes 400 Richest, 2003

9 "**$7.6 billion in holdings,**" ibid

CHAPTER TWO: O'ER LAND OR SEA OR FOAM

The first parts of this chapter have relied heavily on the work of the maritime historians who've chronicled the age of passenger shipping; three works in particular were especially helpful. *Crossing & Cruising*, by John Maxtone-Graham; *The Sway of the Grand Saloon*, by J. M. Brinnin; and *Tourist Third Cabin*, by Lorraine Coons and Alexander Varias. Helen Muir's history of her city, *Miami, USA*, was both a pleasure to read and an invaluable resource. Frank Leslie Fraser's story was told to me by his son, Lewis, who also provided me with the transcribed remembrances by Captain Carl Brown, who worked for Frank Fraser and later saved the lives of so many when the *Yarmouth Castle* went down. Transportation historian Brian Cudahy included an account of the *Yarmouth Castle* sinking in his *The Cruise Ship Phenomenon in North America*, which was also a very helpful resource here, as were interviews with Ed Stephan and Pete Whelpton of Royal Caribbean, who were running Yarmouth Cruise Lines at the time.

14   "in storms or bad calms," ibid, p. 20

14   "Ten dollar fine on ship captains for each corpse," Brinnin, p. 8

15   "the steady flow of exiles," ibid., p. 8

15   "often as not consumed standing up," Maxtone-Graham, *Crossing & Cruising*, p. 27

16   "look happy," ibid, p. 29

16   "verminous mattresses," Brinnin, *The Sway of the Grand Saloon*, p. 445

16   "riffraff from Southern Europe," Maxtone-Graham, *Crossing & Cruising*, p. 31

16   census data, Lorraine Coons and Alexander Varias, *Tourist Third Cabin* (New York, Palgrave Macmillan, 2003), pp. 12-13

17   "sub-debs, younger members of the smart set," Brinnin, *Sway of the Grand Saloon*, p. 443

17   "the initiate takes pains," ibid, p. 444

17   "It subjects one to the suspicion," ibid, p. 440

17   "the new category of passenger," Coons and Varias, *Tourist Third Cabin*, p. 29

18   "and their inevitable blondes," ibid, p. 59

18   "oh so garglingly good," ibid, p. 47

25   "The only luxury ship," from a collection of vintage postcards posted at www.simplonpc.co.uk

25   "Lovett had built," *Commercial Appeal*, September 15, 1991

25   "converted into Barracks," Helen Muir, *Miami, USA* (Miami, Pickering Press, 1990), p. 210

26   "They fanned out all over the place," ibid, p. 215

26   "Gallons of everything," ibid., p. 236

26   "than the rest of the world put together," ibid, p. 233

27   "wasn't sufficient even to cover debt payments," ibid, p. 162

28   "heat and odors," National Engineers Week Foundation, www.eweek.org

28   "the possibility of lower taxes," Bill Bags, *Miami News*
29   "supermarket-type passenger and baggage processing," *World Ports Magazine*, September 1959
29   "negligible factor in the Gold Coast's travel economy," ibid
30   "Future Port Outdated Already?" *Miami Herald*, July 27, 1963
30   "250,000 people passing through the old seaport," *Miami Herald*, July 12, 1964
30   "scowled for shutterbugs," *Miami Herald*, July 6, 1963
30   "one term of office as sheriff," Muir, *Miami, USA*, p. 222
31   "Rosy Future Predicted," *World Ports* magazine, September 1959
32   "safety procedures and protocols," Brian Cudahy, *The Cruise Ship Phenomenon in North America* (Centreville, MD, Cornell Maritime Press, 2001), p. 11
33   "return to your ship," ibid, p. 11
34   "My baby," *Yarmouth Castle*, www.rmstitanichistory.com/yarmouth/yarmouth.html
35   "State of the Union," Cudahy, *The Cruise Ship Phenomenon in North America*, p. 13

CHAPTER THREE: DODGE CITY

This chapter is based largely on interviews with key players in the early days of NCL, Royal Caribbean and other lines. Also extremely helpful here were Ronald Zeller, Duke Hatfield and Tom Cooney, who represented Knut Kloster as attorney and accountants, respectively, during the breakup with Arison. *Under Crown and Anchor*, an authorized history of Royal Caribbean's first twenty-five years, written by the historians John Maxtone-Graham and Baard Kolltveit, was an indispensable resource in reconstructing RCCL's first steps.

39   "we would have been in the Holocaust," *Miami Herald*, October 2, 1999
39   "kill as many Germans as I could," *In Our Own Hands: The Hidden Story of the Jewish Brigade in World War II*, 1998, Chuck Olin Films
39   "national treasure," *Forbes*, June 21, 1982
51   "and the evangelical fervor to go with it," *New York Times*, December 6, 1970
52   "lovely hills that rise sharply behind the coast," ibid
59   "We shall into cruise," Maxtone-Graham and Baard Kolltveit," *Under Crown and Anchor*," (Miami Beach, Onboard Media, 1995) p. 35
60   "I've seen the champagne," ibid, p. 50
61   "furnished mostly with apple crates," ibid, p. 73
62   "insights into American history and society," ibid, p. 62
63   "Fireworks lit up the sky," ibid, p. 76

CHAPTER FOUR: MARDI GRAS ON THE ROCKS

This chapter was based largely on interviews with the key players at Carnival during the early days. Lin Arison's memoir of her life with her husband, Ted, *A Love Story in Mediter-*

ranean Israel, was a great help in bringing the desperation of the venture during this period to life.

74 "Riklis Driving," *Forbes*, October 8, 2001
74 "loaned him the car and driver," *Washington Post*, May 12, 1981
74 "a Riklis protégé," Sally Denton and R. Morris, *The Money and the Power*, p. 313
74   "Rancid American," *BusinessWeek*, November 29, 1979
74 "flimsy foundation of debt," ibid
74 "detriment of the company," *Los Angeles Times* News Service, in *Bergen Record*, February 28, 1992
74 "Nightmare on Wall Street," *Newsday*, January 21, 1990
75 "stage-door Johnny," *Chigago Tribune*, November 7, 1985
75 "Riklis produced the picture," *People*, February 22, 1982
75 "You should see the breasts," *Miami Herald*, December 4, 1983
75 "ruin my husband's career," *Chicago Tribune*, November 7, 1985
75 "Bo Derek would be nowhere," *People*, February 22, 1982
79 "excellent spick-and-span condition," *Miami Herald*, March 18, 1972
79 "ants pushing a beetle," *Miami Herald*, March 13, 1972
79 "their blue lights flashing," *Miami Herald*, March 12, 1972
81 "I don't see the light at the end of the tunnel," Lin Arison, *A Love Story in Mediterranean Israel*, p. 19

CHAPTER FIVE: LOVE . . . EXCITING AND NEW

The account of *The Love Boat*'s conception and production comes in large part from interviews with its coproducer Douglas Cramer. The shipboard antics are reconstructed from the accounts of a number of longtime cruise ship workers, most of whom preferred to remain unnamed, as well as from Jeraldine Saunders's *Love Boats* and J. Gleeson-Adamidis's *If I Were Not Upon the Sea*.

94 "Nothing is worth the boredom of the deep," *Washington Post*, September 24, 1977
95 "the result would be *Love Boat*," *People*, July 26, 1982
96 "never broken number twenty-five," www.tvtome.com
96 "sturdy young crewmen," Jeraldine Saunders, *Love Boats*, p. 11. Note: actual quote is "crewman."
97 "really took a *vacation*," ibid, p. 13
97 "the warmly," *Chicago Tribune*, February 15, 1985
101 "demanded their money back," Bob Dickinson and Andy Vladimir, *Selling the Seas*, p. 222
102 "and finding a human foot," ibid
103 "sexual prowess," ibid, p. 75
104 "save a favorite hat," *Sarasota Herald-Tribune*, September 21, 1998

105   "abused in a mental hospital," *Los Angeles Times*, March 23, 1989
110   "right smack off the top," Dwight Goddard, *All Fall Down*, p. 188

CHAPTER SIX: RUDE AWAKENINGS

The account of the Honduran strike relies on interviews conducted with several Carnival personnel at the time, both management and crew, as well as with Bill Huggett, the Miami attorney who represented the strikers. The organized crime accounts were invaluably assisted by Bobby Kratish, son of the late indefatigable Mutzie Kratish and Carnival's Miami stevedore to this day, and by Dwight Goddard's excellent *All Fall Down*, which tells the story of the FBI investigation of Miami dockside corruption during the 1970s through the eyes of informant Joe Teitlebaum, a Kratish cousin. Longtime Miami port director Carmen Lunetta was also generous with his time and recollections here, as he was on matters political. Harvey Katz, formerly of Salomon Brothers, was a great help in re-creating the perspective of Wall Street analysts encountering this industry for the first time, as were the files of his and his colleagues' publicly available but difficult to find work that he so meticulously kept for all these years and generously made available to me.

122   "came to $12 million," Maxtone-Graham and Kolltveit, *Under Crown and Anchor*, p. 97
124   "seamless, horizontally aligned whole," ibid, p. 101
125   "more than thirty tons," *Travel Trade*, December 12, 1983
128   "virtually a synonym for organized crime," Gary W. Potter. and Victor Kappeler. *The Triumph of Conservatism*, paper presented at the Southern Criminal Justice Association, October 1992
128   "have been able to put their tax," quoted in ibid
129   "Forget it; it's their territory," *Newsweek*, April 17, 1978
129   "You know how things are," Goddard, *All Fall Down*, p. 32
129   "punch bowl," *Miami Herald*, June 8, 1999
133   "cash, cruise ship tickets and other valuables," Potter and Kappeler, *The Triumph of Conservatism*
134   "trade groups, investment seminars," *New York Times*, March 1, 1981
134   "upwards of $18 million," United Press International, March 11, 1981
136   "subsidize trips to Hawaii," *Forbes*, October 8, 1984
136   "large and visible number of American lawyers," *Washington Post*, December 26, 1982
137   "a legislator with only half the facts," United Press International, March 11, 1981
141   "a fifth again as many people," Cruise Lines International Association historical data
144   "a fine-tuned money machine," Harvey Katz, *Carnival Cruise Lines: Initiating Coverage*, Salomon Brothers financial analysis, 1987
144   "high-cost image," *Economist* Travel and Tourism Analyst, August 1986, p. 48
144   "paid up without question," *Seatrade Review*, April 1985

145 "Carnival's principal market," Katz, "*Carnival Cruise Lines*," 1987
145 "the Arisons' wealth had surpassed," *New York Times*, August 28, 1988
145 "virtually all long-term debt," 1987 *Carnival Cruise Lines Annual Report*

CHAPTER SEVEN: A RUN AT THE COMPETITION

Interviews with Royal Caribbean and Carnival executives formed almost the entire basis for this chapter, although I would never have known which questions to ask had it not been for the excellent account of the merger fight in Maxtone-Graham and Kolltveit's *Under Crown and Anchor*. Thanks, too, to Tom Pritzker for granting a rare interview and to Richard Fain for arranging it.

153 "diverted funds to bribe NYC politicians," *Wall Street Journal*, Sept. 29, 1978
153 "personal legal fees," *Wall Street Journal*, April 7, 1978
153 "to disguise the existence of a Swiss bank account," *Washington Post*, October 25, 1978
153 "aggressive, harum-scarum flair," *Forbes*, August 29, 1983
156 "schmaltz on strings and a white baby grand," *Playboy*, November 1988
157 "parade staircases," Maxtone-Graham and Kolltveit, *Under Crown and Anchor*, p. 138
157 "surging aft on two levels," ibid, pp. 137–138
157 "every ten minutes," ibid, p. 138
157 "ultimate floating amusement park," *Times of London*, February 7, 1988
157 "ruler of the seas," *Chicago Tribune*, January 17, 1988
166 "although the company was thought unlikely," *Financial Times*, September 1, 1988
168 "freeing up every extra dollar," Bryan Burrough and John Helyar, *Barbarians at the Gate*, p. 134
169 "on one thing they all agreed," ibid, p. 5
170 "his first investment capital," *Financial Times*, September 19, 1987

CHAPTER EIGHT: HIDING IN PLAIN SIGHT

Because of the difficulty in getting a firsthand picture of life behind the scenes on a cruise ship, this chapter supplemented the accounts of industry executives and former cruise ship workers with the research of labor unions and scholars, foremost among these War on Want, of the International Transportation Workers Federation, and the Seafarers International Research Centre. Paul Chapman's book *Trouble On Board* was a great help, as were my discussions with him. Ross Klein's *Cruise Ship Blues* is a thought-provoking clearinghouse of information on the industry's more dubious practices, as is his Web site www.cruisejunkie.com. William Langewiesche's remarkable *The Outlaw Sea* was indispensable as a resource for top-notch information in a world that is often difficult to find reliable information about, and I relied on it heavily. Matt McCleery of *Marine Money* magazine was instrumental in helping me remember that among the many scoundrels there are also many decent, honorable operators. The October 29, 1999, *60 Minutes* broadcast "Cruising for Fun and Profit" was also a helpful compilation of information.

181   "So I'm trying," *BusinessWeek*, October 25, 1999
182   "a logic taken to extremes," William Langewiesche, *The Outlaw Sea*, p. 7
183   "old fashioned," ibid
184   "an estimated 17 percent of the government's 2003 revenue," *Business Day*, September 9, 2003
185   "rusting beneath their paint," Langewiesche, *The Outlaw Sea*, p. 33
186   "thousands of sailors were killed in the 1990s alone," ibid, p. 32
186   "No one tried to contact me," ibid, p. 95
186   "It received just over half of them," U.S. Congress General Accounting Office, *Additional actions needed to improve cruise ship safety*, p. 12, March 1993, nos. 93–103
188   "than the day he'd first signed on," *Sweatships*, report by War on Want of the International Transportation Workers Federation, 2001, p. 11
189   "they are subject to discipline," Dickinson and Vladimir, *Selling the Sea*, p. 73
190   "wrong part of the ship," *Sweatships*, p. 12
195   "those who serve them look tired," Zhao, *Emotional Labour in a Globalized Labour Market*, Seafarers International Research Centre, May 2002, p. 11
195   "they are wonderful people," ibid, p. 11
195   "the egalitarian nature and heritage of Americans," Dickinson and Vladimir, *Selling the Sea*, p. 67
197   "even during working hours," War on Want, *Sweatships*, p. 13
197   "the Dutchman is always watching," Klein, *Cruise Ship Blues*, p. 124
198   "employing European servers," *Seatrade Insider*, July 31, 2003
199   "protectionist bent," *Lloyd's List*, May 17, 1993
200   "the mainstream of international commerce," *Lloyd's List*, October 10, 1992
201   "endangering international shipping," *Financial Times*, February 10, 1994
203   "well, you don't pay taxes," *60 Minutes*, October 29, 1999
205   "but you're not carrying your fair share," ibid
205   "to name a few," according to the *Forbes* 2000 list for 2004
206   "The American taxpayer," *60 Minutes*, October 29, 1999
207   "marshal his resources," Arison, *A Love Story in Mediterranean Israel*, p. 149
208   "he bruised so easily," ibid, p.150

CHAPTER NINE: CARNIVAL IS A CARNIVORE

This chapter was compiled almost exclusively from interviews with the people involved in the various transactions.

214   "premature price ejaculation," *Lloyd's List*, April 15, 1991
217   "most ungraceful business shutdowns in history," *Seatrade Review*, March 1996

218   "about thirty thousand passengers," ibid
230   "susceptible to a powerful suitor," *Lloyd's List*, June 19, 1997
233   "beyond dollars and cents," *Tour and Travel News*, July 21, 1997

CHAPTER TEN: INDECENT EXPOSURE

I owe a great debt for this chapter to the reporting of the *New York Times*'s Douglas Frantz, whose groundbreaking series on the industry in 1998 and 1999 was indispensable. Along with candid interviews with executives at the major cruise lines, it allowed a picture that would otherwise have been nearly impossible to assemble.

244   "cushions of their wheelchairs," United Press International, July 11, 1992
245   "escape from the grittier side of life," *New York Times* News Service, September 6, 1998
246   "secrecy as a condition of settling," *New York Times*, November 16, 1998
248   "demanding a kiss good-bye," *Miami New Times*, February 3, 2000
249   "she doesn't need to make a decision right away," ibid
249   "moments ahead of the posse," *New York Times*, November 16, 1998
252   "inside our waters and outside our laws," *New York Times*, December 24, 1999
253   "one hundred tons or larger," statistic from the Australian Shipping Council. The U.S. government starts its reckoning of the world fleet at ships of ten thousand tons or larger, more relevant from an international commerce perspective, but not with regard to the environment. http://www.shippingaustralia.com
255   "investigation continued in Miami," Department of Justice press release #98-429, September 19, 1998
256   "fines had been levied in only two," *New York Times*, January 3, 1999
257   "including hazardous chemicals," Department of Justice press release #99-316, July 21, 1999
258   "in favor of the measure," *New York Times*, November 29, 1999
259   "you've got a credibility problem," *New York Times*, October 7, 1999
259   "the oceans upon which our vessels sail," International Council of Cruise Lines press release http://www.iccl.org/pressroom/press16.cfm
261   "The Good Ship Kaopectate," *Newsday*, August 25, 1988
262   "one infected passenger happened to seek treatment," *Guardian Observer*, July 15, 2001
263   "spreading mayonnaise onto sandwiches," *New York Times*, July 22, 1980
265   "median passenger age of fifty-one," Cruise Lines International Association, 2002 market study
266   "no oversight," CNN/*Consumer Reports*, May 13, 1999
266   "a near-fatal dose," *New York Times*, October 31, 1999
266   "I'm sorry your vacation has been ruined," ibid
267   "don't have the expertise to control a doctor," *Miami Herald*, August 28, 2003
269   "keep Lunetta's political machine humming," *Miami Herald*, April 26, 1999

269   "scoffed with characteristic disdain," *Broward Daily Business Review*, December 2, 1996

270   "perhaps some form of oversight," *Miami Daily Business Review*, May 15, 1997

272   "soliciting political contributions," *Miami Herald*, May 14, 1999

272   "I honestly looked at it as a game," *Miami Herald*, May 7, 1999

273   "this is a wonderful country," *Miami Herald*, October 22, 1999

273   "the final chapter," *Miami Herald*, November 22, 2000

CHAPTER ELEVEN: TROUBLE IN PARADISE

Specific thanks here goes to Polly Pattullo for her *Last Resorts*. It gave eloquent journalistic force to my own long-held gut feeling about the industry's role on the region developed during my years of residence in the British Virgin Islands. The candor of several unnamed senior cruise executives regarding the industry's strategies for managing Caribbean governments was also critical to this reporting.

275   "almost 55 percent of all tourism in the Caribbean islands," Association of Caribbean States, November 2003 report

277   "unemployment rates as high as 20 percent," USAID 2005 Congressional Budget Justification

282   "efforts to boost onboard spending," *Times of London*, June 3, 1993

283   "small operators like us," Polly Pattullo, *Last Resorts*, p. 168

284   "and to his own achievements at home," *Economist*, November 9, 1980

284   "more than 750 people killed in election-related violence," *Economist*, March 15, 1997

284   "reassured jittery business leaders," *Time*, February 20, 1989

285   "a first-class job," *Economist*, March 15, 1997

285   "gobbling up the region's plant, personnel and profits," Pattullo, *Last Resorts*, p. 160

287   "no longer accept mirrors and baubles," ibid, p. 160

287   "we don't want to pollute the environment," *South Florida Sun-Sentinel*, July 1993

289   "we will not be moving," *Journal of Commerce*, July 23, 1993

290   "none of the speakers . . . seemed to have read the script," *Lloyd's List*, March 7, 1994

290   "not everyone accepted these statistics," Pattullo, *Last Resorts*, p. 165

290   "fully 270 percent above," ibid, p. 166

291   "jobs on the docks accounting for the rest," *Tour and Travel News*, April 17, 1995

292   "if we don't work together," *Tour and Travel News*, January 30, 1995

292   "nearly $2 million in such gifts," Florida Caribbean Cruise Association promotional materials

292   "the equivalent of about forty-four cents," a conservative calculation, based on an estimated 50 percent of the ten million Americans who cruised in 2004

293   "They all contribute toward the development," *Journal of Commerce*, December 29, 1997

294 "yet another example of their unwillingness," *Lloyd's List,* April 4, 1998
294 "good tourism industry partners," ibid
294 "in the best interest of Antigua and Barbuda," *Gleaner* (Jamaica), October 15, 2003
294 "stick to our guns," BBC Worldwide Monitoring, September 27, 2003
295 "less than $2 million," *Fortune,* March 29, 1999
295 "without our daily intent to cooperate," BBC Worldwide Monitoring, October 29, 2002

CHAPTER TWELVE: THE PRINCESS'S HAND

Though they were extremely helpful throughout, Richard Fain and Micky Arison were remarkably so during our discussions of the events in this chapter, as was Ken Dubbin, who has had the opportunity to see how things work both at Carnival and at Royal Caribbean, and others at both companies, including Howard Frank and Adam Goldstein. Peter Ratcliffe was also very helpful in our interview. Essential background came from Wendell Brooks of Salomon Smith Barney, one of Princess's investment bankers during the transaction.

298 "bind together the British Empire," *Wall Street Journal,* August 24, 1999
315 "importing the worst U.S. cowboy bid tactics," *Financial Times,* December 22, 2001
320 "Royal Caribbean still has the edge," *Financial Times,* January 31, 2002
324 "approval from her fellows," *Express,* February 15, 2002
324 "crude and opportunistic," ibid
324 "We're brand builders," *Financial Times,* February 15, 2002
325 "there is no need for you to second-guess the regulators," *AFX European Focus,* February 14, 2002
326 "sampling fresh fruit and banana cake," *South Florida Sun-Sentinel,* February 14, 2002
326 "offered to send over some Florida lawyers," ibid
327 "off the wall," *Wall Street Journal,* July 22, 2002
331 "taken as a genuine commercial intention," EU Competition Commission report, p. 54
332 "manifest errors," *Wall Street Journal,* July 22, 2002
332 "O Solo Mio," *Daily Telegraph,* July 27, 2002
332 "the romance is still blooming," *Lloyd's List,* July 18, 2002
333 "our case will be stronger," *Wall Street Journal,* July 22, 2002
333 "those who are happy are silent," *European Voice,* October 31, 2002

INDEX